History and Ethnic Identity Formation in North-East India

About the Editor

Prof. J.V. Hluna graduated with Honours in History from St. Anthon's College, Shillong in 1972, M.A. (History) from Gauhati University in 1974 and Ph.D. from GU in 1986. He is one of the Founder Lecturers of Government Aizawl College, Founder Secretary of Government Hrangbana College, Founder Principal of Government T. Romana College. He joined Pachhunga University College as Lecturer in History in 1977 and attained his Professorship in 2011. He is also the Founder and Acting Head of Department, Department of History and Ethonography, Mizoram University.

Hluna is active social worker and headed Mizo Zirlai Pawl (the largest Mizo Students Organisation) as its President in 1976-78. He is also the Founder President of YMCA in Mizoram and Founder Vice President of Mizo History Association. He had four books in English and four books in Mizo and many other research papers to his credit. His latest and outstanding work in English, co-authored with his daughter, Rini Tochhawng. published by Cambridge Scholars Publishing, 12 Back Chapman Street, Newcastle upon Tyne, NE6 2XX, UK in 2012 is entitled THE MIZO UPRISING.

Dr. Hluna is one of the Founder of People's Conference Party and became MLA in Mizoram Legislative Assembly (1993-98).

History and Ethnic Identity Formation in North-East India

Editor
Prof. J.V. Hluna

CONCEPT PUBLISHING COMPANY PVT. LTD.
NEW DELHI-110059

ISBN-13: 978-81-8069-970-2

First Published 2013

Published and Printed by

Concept
Since 1974

Concept Publishing Company Pvt. Ltd.
A/15-16, Commercial Block, Mohan Garden
New Delhi-110059 (India)
T : 25351460, 25351794, *F* : 091-11-25357109
E: publishing@conceptpub.com, W: www.conceptpub.com
Editorial Office: H-13, Bali Nagar, New Delhi-110 015, India.

Cataloging in Publication Data--Courtesy: D.K. Agencies (P) Ltd. <docinfo@dkagencies.com>

History and ethnic identity formation in North-East India / editor, J.V. Hluna.
p. cm.
Includes bibliographical references and index.
ISBN 9788180699702

1. Lushai (Asian people)—India, Northeastern—Ethnic identity—Congresses. 2. Ethnicity—India, Northeastern—Congresses. 3. Lushai (Asian people)—India, Northeastern—History—Congresses. 4. Lushai (Asian people)—India, Northeastern Politics and government—Congresses. 5. India, Northeastern—Politics and government Congresses. 6. India, Northeastern—Religious life and customs—Congresses. I. Hluna, John V. (John Vânlal), 1947-

DDC 305.8009541 23

Preface

Ethno-culturally the Mizos are strikingly similar to the tribes of south-east Asia while politically they are the sons of India. Tracing this aspect of the Mizo people scholars have presented a number of papers Of late there appears to be an attempt to present a western theory about the origin of the Mizos from Israel This volume thus presents a cross-current of the issues relating to the origin of the Mizos and the editor have *no say* on such views of the authors

Mizo history and culture being uncomprehensive so far the limitations have to be compromised. Our approach to Mizo studies has, therefore, to be multi-disciplinary and comparative and the papers represent scholars of different disciplines The dimensions have been focussed in several papers relating to pre-Christian relation, myths and realities, social changes, historical sources, hill economy and late political impacts on the Mizo people The vastness of the topics speaks for itself and there could be hardly any editing except some minor changes here and there Of course I have reserved the editorial privilege where it is necessary

The Directorate of Higher and Technical Education who is sponsoring the international Seminar is not a professional institution of research and study: Yet it has taken up this challenge with courage and conviction to put the entire dimensions of Mizo studies on an international level. I am afraid and have every reason to believe that these seminar papers might not ever come to light once the Seminar is over. Hence, I have decided to put it in print and took the permission of the Department.

I, therefore, really grateful to Dr. H.L. Malsawma, Director Higher and Technical Education, Government of Mizroam for the issue of official permission vide No F. 14016/1/2012-DTE (HTE), Dated Aizawl, the 6th January, 2012.

Aizawl J.V. HLUNA

Acknowledgements

I, therefore, record my deep appreciation to all those who submitted the papers in time to enable to present in the Seminar. I specially extended my thanks to two of my friends Dr. Sangkima and Dr. Romesh Buragohain who helped me in editing and publishing the papers.

Aizawl
2013

Prof. J.V. Hluna
Editor

Introduction

The Mizo formerly called Lushai/Lusei had perhaps been first contacted by the Pax Britannica in the South tip of Lunglei in the Chittagong of East Bengal axis around 1777. The Honourable Warren Hastings Esq in his letter dated 10th April, 1777 mentioned Kookie men[1] The name Kookie/Kuki and Lushai had been often used synonimously by subsequent writers. The question of identity of Mizo poses a lively academic problems. The Mizo tribe is formed out of a process of synthesis of many sub-tribes in the region over two centuries. The language spoken by the Mizo tribe too was evolved through a process of fusion of dialects of the component sub-tribes. First Mizo contact with civilisation occurred during the 20th century and in course of time the present language had crystallised. The process, however, continues even today which will further bring changes in the language and the system of thought process in years to come.

It is said that the last decade of a century do produce great events for the next century. The phenomenon is termed as 'End of Century Effect'[2] Sure enough also the last decade of the nineteeth century ushered in a new dawn for Mizo. In fact, in the year 1894 two young English missionaries brought novel religion of deep Hebrew and Greek refined thoughts. The *Bible* immediately occupied a high place in the heart of the Mizos. Ever since then the Mizo culture had been almost changed completely by the *Bible* with far reaching effects.

The Mizo language was for the first time reduced into writing by the missionaries using a Hunterian system of orthography[3] The Hunterian orthography was perhaps never adopted elsewhere nor is it traceable anywhere in the world today so far as my knowledge is concerned.

The Mizo language is no doubt a Tibeto-Burman much unlike all other major Indian languages which are but derivatives of Aryan Sanskrit.

language. When the Mizos revolted in 1966, the rest of India quickly interpreted it as due to the alienation of thought under Western influence. It may be noted in passing that the tonal language of Mizo is almost accurately served by the present Romanised script with characteristic sound The real problems might rather be the Mizo problem of seeking large identity out of an age-old tribal Mizo insularity on the one hand and of seeking a proper place in the comity of mainstream Indian nationalism. As Prof. Nirmal Kumar Bose rightly pointed out that the leadership of Indian politics cannot satisfy the Indian masses now by their age old anti-British talk[4] Therefore, the Mizo nationality must be examined as to how modern is modern Mizo intellectuals today. It is only human to have prejudice whether that be an ethnic one or casteist or linguistic in nature the Mizo ethos in this respect is nothing new in the Indian socio-economic scenario.

What a sad age
When it is easier to smash
An Atom than a prejudice
Albert Einstein (1878-1955)

The origin of the Mizo tribe had been a subject baffling solution. In the absence of a written history we cannot trace the origin of Mizo very far with accuracy at all. The folk tales and songs did throw some lights. The mythology of Mizo are similar to many other tales of South-East Asian nations. There are apparently two main theories on their origin. One is that the Mizo came out of a cave called Chhinlung. The last tribe to come out were the Ralte tribe when the lid was closed. This cave might have been located at 12.5 km west of Vlasan in Ximang country in China[5]. Rev. J.H. Lorrain, the pioneer missionary observed that the ancestral home of Mizo would appear to have been somewhere in between South-East Tibet and Western China[6].

Nevertheless, it is never clear whether Chhinlung (Sinlung) was a real cave or a name of an ancestor. Some considered it to be the name of a Chinese ruler from whom they escaped[7]. The supposed route of migration from the cave was through South China, North Thailand, North Burma and into Mizoram. There are many folk tales and songs connected with places and rivers that Mizos passed through in course of their migration and temporary settlements. The RUN and TIAU rivers between Burma and Mizoram figure in every folk song.

Another theory of migration is that the Mizo originated the middle east and then moved through Persia, Afghanistan, Pakistan, Kashmir,

Nepal, the Himalayas, Arunachal Pradesh, North Burma and into Mizoram.[8] The Mizo-Israel people would maintain this as tenable proposition. It is curious to note that the *Hmar* tribe claims to naming the Himalayas based on their folk songs on migratory route by saying 'Hima-loi-ei-ti'[9]. However it must be noted that the Himalayas (hima=snow, alaya=home/abode) is really a Sanskrit word which was in use many millennium earlier than the Hmar language. The claim is untenable and unmaintainable as an authentic one.

A century of exposition of the Mizo to a stronger culture had produced identity crisis. Firstly, the superstition-ridden Mizo culture was denuded by culturally mandatory *Bible* teachings of truth and faith. The root was shaken. Secondly, the Mizo faced problem of adjustment and adaptation to larger Indian setting. He finds the incompatibility of culture cutting across the heart especially in respect of caste system, food habits, social taboos, language and prejudice. You may ask him, "Are you afraid of India or being an Indian?" What do you fear to lose? What can you contribute to make India big? You will get an answer sure but perhaps with skepticism. One Mizo prominent political leader was surely influenced by Bengal during the early struggle for *swaraj* by Mahatma Gandhi, J. Nehru and Subhash Chandra Bose[10]. The Mizo accepted that their destiny is bound with the rest of India, and here a long long way to go still to assert their due place of honour and dignity. That India is progressing steadily during the first half of century of Independence without disintegration itself is a wonder to be admired by the world. The task of social, emotional and economic integration is a challenge and in this the Mizos will continue to be involved.

The Department of Higher and Technical Education of Mizoram was created only in the year 1989. The Department took up the challenge of organising this International Seminar at Aizawl on minority nationalities of North-East India with special reference to Mizos. The scholars and researchers fruitfully interchanged knowledge and ideas through the deliberations.

It is gratifying to have been able to put as many as thirty-papers in print which included six papers from abroad. While some paper are not included and some other papers which are not presented but important for the Mizos History are included in this publication. As the map of India shows, Mizoram is virtually the end of India. One narrow entry corridor allows no easy communications and no exit elsewhere. Mizoram is fenced by international boundaries where 75 per cent of her boundary perimeter is sandwiched between Bangladesh and Myanamar. The very fact that many renowned scholars has indeed flocked to this difficult spot Aizawl, braving hazardous and timewasting journey is deeply appreciated.

The Contents have 43 Chapters and are put in Six groups.

1. Origin and Early Mizo History;
2. Religious History;
3. Political History;
4. Socio-Cultural History;
5. Economics and Development History; and
6. History of North-East other than Mizos.

With the permission of INTACH (Mizoram Chapter), The articles—Mizo and afterlife by C Vanlallawma, Fairy by Lalzuia Colney, Huai by C. Laitanga, Khawhring (Old Mizo belief which no longer exists) by Rev. Dr. C.L. Hminga and The Mizo value (as reflected in oral traditions) by R.L. Thanmawia all translated in English by Rinsanga, I.A.S. (Retd.), Chapter Co-convener and published in its Silver Jubilee Souvenir of 2010 are entered in this book. In the Appendix I the note of Maj. J. Shakespear, the Superintendent of Lushai Hills on the Census Report of 1901, the first census in the Lushai Hills and in the Appendix II the Making of Aijal by Lt. Col. J. Shakespear are also put with some earliest photos of Aizawl.

REFERENCES

1. *Wild Races of South Eastern India*, p. 32, Capt. T.H. Lewin.
2. *Omni*, p. 18, October 1989.
3. *Introduction to Dictionary of the Lushai Language*, J.H.Lorrain.
4. *A Common Perspective of N.E. India*, p. 6, Pannalal Dasgupta.
5. "A Comparative Study of Mizos in India and the Wa Nationality in China"—Ai Rui (unpublished)
6. *The Life and Witness of the Churches in Mizoram*, 1987, p. 13, Rev Dr. C.L. Hminga.
7. *Thlahtu bul Chhuina*, p. 34, Brig Naurliana.
8. *Mizo Thaltu Chhuina*, p. 54, H. Lian Dawla.
9. "A Historical and Political Geography of the Hmar-Mizo", p. 93 M. Phil. thesis by L. Khuma Varte (unpublished).
10. *Ka Zin Kawng* p. 99, Ch.Saprawnga.

Contents

RELIGIOUS HISTORY

SOCIO-CULTURAL HISTORY

ECONOMICS AND DEVELOPMENT HISTORY

HISTORY OF NORTH-EAST OTHER THAN MIZO

List of Contributors

A. Bhushan, Department of Education Punjab University, Chandigarh.

Ai Rui (Dai Name), Cheng Ruiyao (Han Name), The Editorial Department, Yunnan Daily, No. 51, Xinwen Road, Kumming, Yunnan, P.R. China Post Code-650032,

Anuradha Dutta (Dr.) (Ms.), Reader in Political Science, Gauhati University, Guwahati-781014, Assam.

B. Lalthangliana, Lecturer, Hrangbana College, Aizawl, Mizoram (Formerly Lecturer in History, Mandalay University, Burma).

B.B. Goswami, 57, Belvedere Estate, Calcutta-700027.

B.C. Allen, Supdt. of Census Operations, Assam, India.

B.D. Chinara, Pachhunga University College, Aizawl.

B.J. Terwiel, Institute for Volkerkunde and Afrikanistik Ludwig Maximilians, Universitat Munchen.

B.K. Roy Burman, Professor of Jawaharlal Nehru University and Professor of Visva-Bharatgi University and ex-officio Director of the Council of Social Development. New Delhi.

C. Vanlallawma, Lecturer, Hrangbana College, Aizawl, Mizoram.

C.L. Hminga (Rev. Dr.), Serkawn, Lunglei, Mizoram.

Chandralekha Raghuwanshi (Dr.), Programme Officer, M.P. State Higher Education Grants Commission, Bhopal, President, Science, Technology and Environment Forum F-1/49, Hitkarini Nagar, Bhopal. 462016 (M.P.) India.

Dipak Kumar Chaudhuri, Reader in History, Tripura University, Agartala.

H.S. Luaia (Rev. Dr.), Serkawn, Lunglei, Mizoram.

J.J. Roy Burman, Faculty Unit for Social Policy & Social Welfare Administration, Tata Institute of Social Science, Bombay.

J.N. Phukan (Prof.), Department of History, Gauhati University , Guwahati-781014, Assam, India,

J.V. Hluna (Prof.), Department of History, Pachhung University College, Aizawl, Mizoram.

J.V. Hluna (Prof.), Pachhunga University College, Aizawl, Mizoram.

Jean Berlie (Dr.), Centre for Asian Studies, Hongkong University.

Jogamaya K.K. Saikia (Dr.), M.A. (His), M.A. (Socio & Anthro), Ph.D. (Sociology), Department of Humanities, Regional Engineering College, Silchar (Assam) India 788010.

K. Zohra, Department of History, Saiha College, Chhimtuipui District, Mizoram.

K.C. Lalunga IFC (Rtd.), Venghlui, Aizawl, Mizoram.

K.P. Nath (Dr.), NEHU, Mizoram Campus Aizawl, Mizoram 796001.

Kunja Medhi, Gawahati, Assam.

L.B. Thanga, IAS (Rtd.), Luangmual, Aizawl, Mizoram.

L.K. Jha (Prof), Department of Forestry, NEHU, Mizoram Campus, Aizawl 796007.

Lalrimawia, Principal, Government Lunglei College Lunglei, Mizoram.

Lelhmuaka, Headmaster (Rtd.), Mc Donald Hill, Aizawl, Mizoram.

Mahadev Chakravarti (Dr.), Department of History, Tripura University, Agartala.

Myer Samra, Department of Anthropology, University of Sydney, N.S.W. 2006, Austgralia.

Nishipada Deva Choudhury (Dr.), Directorate of Archaeology, Government of Assam, l Guwahi-7810001, India.

P.K. Das, Department of Economics, Government Champhai College, Champhai, Mizoram.

R.L. Thanmawia (Dr.), Department of Mizo, Pachhunga University College, Aizawl, Mizoram.

R.N. Prasad (Prof.), Department of Public Administration, NEHU, Mizoram Campus, Aizawl 796007.

R.P. Tiwari (Dr.), Head, Department of Geology, Pachhunga University College NEHU, Aizawl 796007.

Ranju Bezbaruah, Department of History Gauhati University, Guwahati-781014, Assam, India.

Romesh Buragohain (Dr.), Department of History, Government Lunglei College, Lunglei, Mizoram, India 796701.

S.K. Barpujari (Dr.), Hillside, Silpukhuri, Guwahati, Assam 781003.

Sangkima (Dr.), Government Aizawl College, Aizawl, Mizoram.

Shakespeare (Lt. Col.), Supdt., Lushai Hills District.

Suhas Chatterjee (Dr.), Sibabari Road, Silchar-788002, Assam, India.

T.R. Sareen (Dr.), Director ICHR, 35, Ferozeshah Road, New Delhi.

Virginia M.Di Crfocco (Rtd.), Chulalongkom University, Bangkok.

Zhu Changli (Prof.), Institute for Southeast Asian Studies, Kumming, Yunnan Province, The People's Republic of China.

Zothantluanga Ralte, Department of Sociology, Saiha College, Saiha, Chhimtuipui District, Mizoram

ORIGIN AND EARLY MIZO HISTORY

1

The Early Inhabitants of North-East India

With Special Reference to Mizoram

Nishipada Deva Choudhury

The modern State of Mizoram is situated in the extreme eastern corner of India. It extends between latitude 21° and 25° North, and longitude 92° and 94° East, bounded by Assam and Manipur on the north, Burma in the east and south, Bangladesh and Tripura in the west. It occupied an area of 21,081 sq. km. with the population of 10,91,014 in 2011 and has mostly a hilly terrain, the ranges have an average height of 900 metres and run in north-south direction interspersed by deep gorges in which the rivers flow from the high hills in the north to the Bay of Bengal in the south. The State as a whole has temperate climate. Important rivers are the Tlawng, the Sonai, Tuivawl, the Kolodyne and the Karnaphuli. Here, in the hills and dales, ridges and ravines live the Mizos who fondly call their State, in their Lushai dialect, 'Mizoram'—the land of the hill-men (Mizos).[1]

The North-Eastern India is inhabited by various racial elements. The region received wave after wave of immigrants from south-east Asia and the oceanic world as from India and the west.[2]

The earliest inhabitants of North-Eastern India, referred to as *Mlechhas* and *Asuras* in some early texts, were the Kiratas, Cinas and other primitive tribes.[3] The *Kiratas* or the Mongoloid people were well known to the Vedic Aryans, and they are mentioned in the *Yajur* and *Atharva* Vedas.[4] The *Ramayana* describes them as wearing thick top knots with conical heads, golden in appearance, fair-looking and fierce.[5] The army of Bhagadatta was composed of *Cinas* and *Kirata* soldiers, who were of yellowish complexion, dwelling in the marshy regions and near the sea-shore.[6] The *Visnu Purana*[7] mentions the *Kiratas* as dwelling in marshy land. The *Kalika Purana*[8] describes the earliest inhabitants of this region as *Kiratas* with shaven heads and yellow skins. They were strong, ferocious, ignorant and were addicted to liquor and meat.

According to *Samhitas,* the name *Kirata* was applied to a people living in the mountain caves.[9] The *Kiratas* are designated as 'foresters', 'barbarians', 'mountaineers' in the *Puranas,* who were not other than Mongolians.[10]

The classical writers beginning at least with the first century A.D. seem to refer to some tribes almost in their present habitats. The *Sesatae* of the Periplus and the *Besadae* of Ptolemy were the same hill people of this region allied to the Garos, Nagas Lushai-Kukis or the Mishimis.[11] Gerini identifies the *Tiladai* with the kuki-chins.[12] The Epics and the *Puranas* referred to the 'Cinas'; who are probably no other than Kuki-chins or Lushais.

From the early proto-historic period, this part of India has served as the highway connecting the rest of India with South-East Asia, through which many people of diverse ethnic groups, having different cultural entities and speaking various languages passed. These peoples migrated to this region at different times through different routes.[13]

The possible routes of migration are: The northern passes of Bhutan, Tibet and Nepal; the Assam-Burma routes—one over the Patkai passes in the North East, and the other through Manipur and Cachar in the South-East; the valley of the western side formed by the Brahmaputra-Gangetic plains; and sea-routes by Bay of Bengal *via* Bengal and Burma.[14]

The present day population of this region may be broadly divided into tribal and caste groups. The caste groups or non-tribal groups inhabiting the valley of the Brahmaputra, are Caucasic in origin, having sharp physical features and scopic characters comparable to those of the Caucasic people of parts of northern India.[15] Among them is observed a *plano-occipital brachycephalic type*, known as *Dinaric*. Representatives of the long headed leptornnine of Mediterranean type are also seen among the *Brahmins*, the *Kayasthas*, etc.[16] Of these, the Kalitas are said to be the earliest immigrants, and were the Aryan colonists of this region.[17]

The Aryan speakers migrated to this region mostly from Madhyadesha (Central India) prior to *c.* third century B.C.[18] a A succession of influences, ideas and cultures continued to enter this region down to the mediaeval period.[19]

The tribal groups consisted of the people other than Aryans. They came to this region in different periods in various waves from different directions. G.A. Grierson deals with those tribes from the linguistic point of view.[20]

These tribes are basically from two sub-families: *Austro Asiatic* and *Tibeto-Chinese*.

Austro-Asiatic[21]: *The Austro-Asiatic* sub-family is much more strongly represented in India. There is, first, the great *Mon-Khmer* branch spoken in South-East Asia, of which there are three representatives in Burma in the shape of *Mon-Khmer* and a number of other minor forms of speech belonging to Indo China; and the Nicobarese belong to this branch and seem to form the connecting link between the Munda language and the Mon.[22]

From Indonesia in the south, came the Mon-Khmers, who occupied a large part of further India including North-East India. A Mon-Khmer language is spoken in the *Khasi* and *Jaintia* Hills of Meghalaya.[23]

The *Austro-Asiatic Mon-Khmer* speaking Khasis are said to be the earliest inhabitants of North-East India.[24] The next wave which entered this region, was the Tibeto-Chinese family.[25]

The Tibeto-Chinese family[26]: Tradition and comparative philology agree in pointing to North-Western China between the upper course of the *Yang-tse* and of the *Hoang-ho* as the original home of the *Tibeto-Chinese* race, South-East Asia and North-East India have been populated by successive waves of the Tibeto-Chinese invaders, each advancing in turn down the course of one or more of the principal streams, the *Brahmaputra*, the *Chindwin*, the *Irrawaddy*, the *Salwin*, the *Menam* and the *Mekang*. They drove out their predecessors nearer to the sea-coast or into the mountain fastnesses which overlooked the valleys.[27]

The Tibeto-Chinese family is divided into two sub-families which are the *Tibeto-Burman* and the *Siamese-Chinese*.[28]

Tibeto-Burman: The Tibeto-Burmans appear to have first migrated from their original seat on the upper course of the *Yang-tse* and *Hoang-ho* towards the head-waters of the *Irrawaddy* and the *Chindwin*. Thence, it is believed, some people followed the upper course of the *Brahmaputra* or the *Tsanpo*, north of the Himalayas, and occupied Tibet. Some of these crossed the watershed and occupied the hills on the southern side of the Himalayan range right from Assam in the east, to the Punjab in the west. At the Assam end, they met and mingled with others of the same family who had wandered along the lower *Bhahmaputra* through the Assam valley. At the great bend of the river near the present town of Dhubri, they followed it to the south, and occupied first the Garo-Hills, and then Tippera (Tripura). Some of them appear to have ascended the valley of the Kapih and the neighbouring streams into the hill country of the North Cachar, but the mountainous tract between it and the Garo-Hills, the Khasi and the Jaintia Hills, they failed to occupy, and it still remains the home of the ancient Monkhmer people. Other members of this Tibeto-Burman horde halted at the head of the Assam valley and turned south. They took the possession of the Naga Hills—Some of these probably entered the eastern '_tiaga country directly, but others entered the western Naga country from the south, i.e., Manipur.[29]

Philologists have divided the Tibeto Burman sub-family into two main branches: the Tibeto-Himalaya[30] and the Assam Burmese.[31] There is another branch, which is north Assam Branch.[32] It occupied the hills, north of the Brahmaputra. They are known as the Akas, the Daflas, the Abor-Maris and the Mishimi tribes.

The Assam-Burmese branch is further divided into the following groups: The Bodo, the Naga, the Kaehin, the Kuki-chin, the Burma, the Lodo-moso and the Sakor Lui.[33]

The group of tribes known as Bodo forms the most numerous and important section of the non-Aryan tribes of North-Eastern India. Linguistic evidence shows that at one time they extended over the whole of Assam, west of Manipur and Naga Hills.[34]

Naga group: Linguistically, the group consists of three main sub-groups (a) *western*—which includes—*Angami, Sema, Rengma* and *Kezoma; (b) Central — Ao, Lotha, Tengsa, Thukumi* and *Yachumi; (c) Eastern—Angwanku, Banpara, Chingmegnu, Mutonia, Chang, Assiringia, Mosang, Shangge* and *Namsangia.*[35]

Naga-Bodo and Naga-Kuki Sub-Group: Linguistically, in the former group may be included the *Kacha, Kaberi* and *Khairao;* in the latter, *Maram, Tangkhul; Maring, Phadang, Yiyangkong, Sopvoma* and others, including the *Mikirs.* All these tribes inhabit parts of Cachar and Manipur.[36]

Kuki-Lushai-Meitei Tribes and their Sub-groups[37]: Old *Kuki,* in which are included the *Hrangkhol, Halam, Chaw, Langrong* and others; *Kuki-Chin* which includes the *Meitei*, old *Kuki* and *Chin*; Northern Chin sub-group in which are included the *Thado, Sokte, Ralte, Paite* and others; and lastly the central *Chin* group, which includes the *Lushais* and other allied peoples.

The *Lakhers,* occupying the southern portion of the Lushai (Mizo) hills bordering on Burma, may also be placed in the same family. Most of these tribes are now occupying parts of Manipur, Lushai (Mizo) Hills, Cachar and Mikir Hills. Most of the *Lushai-Kukis* are connected with Burma and Chittagong.[38]

The Siamese-Chinese[39]**:** The next invasion took place in A.D. 1228 by the speakers of the Siamese-Chinese languages. They are represented in India by one group viz. the *Tais.*

Kuki-Chin group[40]**:** The territory inhabited by the *Kuki-Chin* tribes extends from the Naga hills, Cachar and East Sylhet in the north, down to the Sandway district of Burma in the south; from the, Tyitthariver in the east, nearly to the Bay of Bengal on the west. The tribes are also found in the valley of Manipur and in the small settlements in the Cachar plains and Sylhet. Both the names 'Kuki' and 'Chin' given to them by their neighbours, 'Kuki' is an Assamese or Bengali term applied generally to the all hill tribes of this race in their vicinity, while 'Chin' or 'Khyeng' is a Burmese word used to denote those living in the country between Burma and Assam.[41]

Chin Languages[42]**:** The *Chin* forms of speech include something like 40 distinct languages which may be divided into the Northern Chin, the Central Chin, the Old Kuki and the Southern Chin sub-groups. The Old Kuki groups are 16 in number, and most of them are spoken by tribes living in Manipur, Cachar, Sylhet, and Hill Tippera, who migrated to their present settlements at different periods in the last three centuries from their original home in and about Lushai land. Only one tribe, the *Hmar,* remained in its original seat, and their language is at present day much mixed with *Lushai.*

The main migration to the north was indirectly due to the pressure exercised by the Lushais. They pressed the *Thados* from the south, who in their turn pressed the *Old Kukis* northwards into their present homes. The *Thados* now occupied the old home of the *Old Kukis,* but the irresistible progress of the Lushais northwards still continued, and the Thados had to follow those whom they had disposed into almost the same localities; and as their arrival was later, they and their followers became popularly known as *New Kukis,* the earlier immigrants being known as *Old Kukis* which connotes a distinct group of cognate tribes and languages, but the *New Kuki* connotes only one tribe, the *Thados,* out of five closely connected ones, the rest of whom still have in the Lushai and Chin Hills. This whole group of five may be called by the name of Northern Chins. The *Lushais* now occupy the old seat of the *Old Kukis* and subsequently, of the *Thados.* After dispossessing the latter, they still attempted to progress in the north, and it was this which brought them first into hostile contact with the British power.[43]

The central Chin languages are *Shukla* or *Tashon, Lai, Lushai* or *Dulien, Banjogi* and *Pankhu.* These are closely connected with the northern sub-group, but have a still greater affinity with the Old Kuki forms of speech.

As Lai bids fair to become the general means of communication in the Chin Hills, so Lushai has become that of the Lushai Hills. This tract has become the scene of various migrations, new tribes at different times pushing the preceding inhabitants westwards and northwards. The *Lushai,* who are now the prevailing race, seem to have begun to move forwards from south-east in the early part of the nineteeth century. Between 1840 and 1850, they obtained final possession of the North Lushai Hills, having pressed the former possessors, the *Thados,* before them into Cachar. Their name is commonly spelt *Lushai,* but the proper mode, which is employed when speaking of their language is *Lushai.* They usually call themselves *Dulien* and their language is *Dulien Tawng.* The latter has several dialects, of which the best known is *Ngente,* spoken by a non-Lushai tribe in the parts of the south Lushai Hills, in the villages round Demagiri, and in some of the western Howlong villages. Another is *Fanai,* spoken also by a non-Lushai tribe, between the eastern border of south Lushai Hills and the Kolodyne. Standard Lushai is comparatively well known.

Among the tribal population of North-Eastern India, Dr. B.S. Guha[44] has observed three main elements, namely, *Negrito,* Proto-Austroloid and Mongoloid. On the basis of hair form and some aspects of material culture, Guha, Hutton[45] and Mills[46] pointed to the existence of Negrito strain in this region more particularly among some of the *Naga* tribes. But the presence of a *Negrito* racial strain in India has become a disputed subject.[47]

The Mongoloid elements invariably predominate among the tribal populations. The Mongoloid (Tibeto-Burman groups) tribes may conveniently be grouped under several heads like the Bodo, the Naga, the Mizo-Kuki and others.

According to Keane[48] caucasic elements are believed to have been brought to this region through Burma by a section of Mongoloid people, which they received as a result of admixture with the caucasic people.

The Bodos, who occupied a sufficiently large area, suffered much from external pressure of the Ahoms from the east and of the Koch from the west. They were also invaded from the south. They were pressed forward by their co-tribesmen. From this, the Kuki hordes left the Lushai and Chin hills and migrated from south, reaching Manipur, the Cachar plains and particularly the hills of North Cachar, where the population is now mixed, partly Bodo, partly Kuki.

All the Lushai-Kuki clans resemble each other very closely in appearance and the Mongoloid type of countenance prevails. To quote Shakespeare[49]:

> *The Kukis are a short, sturdy race of men with a goodly development of muscle. Their legs are, generally speaking, short in comparison with the length of their bodies; and their arms long. The face is nearly as broad as it is long and is generally round or square, the cheek bones high, broad and prominent, eyes small and almond-shaped, the nose short and flat with wide nostrils. The women appear even more squat than the men; but are strong and lustly.*

The Mizos have recorded history only since the last decade of the nineteenth century when the area inhabited by them, earlier called the Lushai hills, now renamed as Mizoram, was formed into two administrative units under the British rule. From the facts referred to above, it appears that some Mongolian or Tibeto-Burman tribes migrated to the Lushai Hills long back and the process of migration continued till the end of the nineteenth century. Various tribes came from the east pushing the former inhabitants to the hills and the plains in the west and the north. The Lushai, the principal tribe among the present Mizos, came to this territory in the eighteenth century and in the beginning of the nineteenth century. By the middle of this century, they dominated the entire northern portion of these hills forcing the Thados, the then inhabitants of the area, to Cachar.[50]

The Sailos constituted the principal clan among the Lushais and almost all the chiefs belonged to the Sailo clan. With the coming of the Lushais there came an era of dispersal of the tribes like Thado, Biate, Haulawng, Tlang, Hmar, etc. all over Cachar, Tripura and Manipur.

The Neolithic tools found in North-Eastern India are of similar type to those that have been found in South-East Asia and South China. The shouldered hoes, the regular rectilinear variety, is confined to Naga and North Cachar Hills, where it appears to be derived from Burma. The irregular (curvilinear) variety, on the other hand, is restricted to the Brahmaputra valley, Khasi and Garo Hills, where it appears to be the local imitation of the regular variety found in Naga and North Cachar Hills. Both the regular and irregular varieties are common in the whole of South-East Asia as far north as Hongkong. The Hoe-adge is the commonest tool in this region, south-East Asia and Yunnan. Splayed axe is fairly common in Yunnan and other countries of south-east Asia and this presupposes the existence of metal originals. The facetted and the shouldered tools also appear to develop first in metal and these were supposed to be copied in stone. The rounded Butt-axe is also known from Yunnan and Burma.[51]

The Neolithic stone tools of North-East India can be classified into two groups—the first one, including tool types, is almost restricted to the various zones of this region, the second one, including common types wholly foreign, is identical with some of the types of Yunnan and Burma, the shouldered tool being brought to India by the migration of the Austro-Asiatics.[52]

The eastern neolithic culture, distinguished by the occurrence of rounded butt axes and other specialised tools, the latter perhaps involving metalic technique of manufacture, was inspired by the Neolithic and later traditions in China and south-East Asia. Both in technique and form, these tools are different from those of the southern Neolithic cultures. Further, the associated ceramic industries of each culture are basically different from those of others. The two cultures are considered as distinct entities.[53]

Until definite evidences of material cultures of these varied groups, definitely linked up with them, are found in proper archaeological context and their relative chronological sequences are firmly established, we cannot definitely say which of the ethnic groups came to this region and settled down first and which came later, since linguistic Philological evidences give us no proof of the priority of any of these ethnic groups as far as their migrations to this region are concerned.

Mizoram is still untouched by the archaeological explorations and excavations as a result of which, it is difficult to know in their proper perspective the ancient heritage of the people of the State. Even then, the Kukis, Lushais, and Chins, in short, the Mizos, resemble each other closely in appearance which is invariably of the Mongolian type. They migrated to this land waves after waves since early times to the last century from south-east Asia and formed a composite cultural group in the name of 'Mizos' or the children of the Hills and made their own contributions to the cultural mosaic of India.

REFERENCES

1. Suhas Chatterjee, Mizoram *Under the British Rule,* pp. 1-3; Census of India, 1981; Animesh Roy, Mizoram: Dynamics of Change, Intro.
2. P.C. Choudhury, *The History* and *Civilisation of the People of Assam to the Twelfth Century. D.* p. 74; Haimendorf, *The Naked Nagas,* p. 3; Peal, J.A.S.B., LXV, III, pp. 17f.

3. N.D. Choudhury, *Historical Archaeology of Central Assam from the Earliest time* to *Twelfth Century A.D.*, p. 25.
4. S.K. Chatterjee, *The Place of* Assam in *the* History *and* Civilisation *of* India, pp. 15-16.
5. *Kiskindhya Kanda*, XI.
6. *Mahabharata, Udyoga Parva (XVIII); The Sabha Parva (XXIV)-(XXVI) and the Karna Parva.*
7. Book II, III.
8. Ch. 38, 39, 104.
9. Vedic Index of names and subjects, Vol. 1, pp. 157-58.
10. Dalton, *Descriptive Ethnology of Bengal,* p. 103; P.C. Choudhury, *op. cit.*, p. 89.
11. Schoff, The Periplus, pp. 47-48, 261; Taylor, J.A.S.B., 1847, I, pp. 32f.
12. N.D. Choudhury, op. *cit.*, pp. 25-26.
13. *Ibid.*
14. P.C. Choudhary, op. *cit.*, p. 75.
15. B.M. Das, A *Note* on *the Races of Assam*, *Kamarupa*, 1957, pp. 10-13.
16. Dalton, *op. cit.*, pp. 79f,321f,; B.K.Barua, A Cultural History of Assam, pp. 5-10.
17. B.K. Kakati, *The Mother Goddess Kamakhya*, pp. 59-64.
18. N.D. Choudhury, op. *cit.*, p. 27.
19. B.K. Barua, op. *cit.*, pp. 5-10.
20. G.A. Grierson, *Linguistic Survey of India*, Vol. I, Pt. I, pp. 32-38.
21. *Ibid. Vol. I and* III, Pt. I, II and III; S.K. Chatterjee, *Balts and Aryan*, pp. 13, *Kirata Janakriti;* B.K. Kakatl, *An Aspect of Early Assamese Literature*, *pp.* 1-16.
22. G.A. Grierson, *op. cit.*, Vol. I, Pt. I.
23. *Ibid.;* P.G. Choudhury, *op. cit.*,
24. *Ibid.*
25. *Ibid.*, N.D. Choudhury, *op. cit.*
26. *Ibid.*, *Vol. I,* Pt. I, pp. 40-9, Vol. III.
27. *Ibid.*
28. *Ibid.*
29. *Ibid.*, P.C. Choudhury, *op. cit.*; N.D. Choudhury, *op. cit.*
30. *Ibid.*
31. *Ibid.*
32. *Ibid.*
33. *Ibid.*
34. *Ibid.*, P.C. Choudhury, *op. cit*; N.D. Choudhury, *op.cit.*
35. *Ibid.*, P.C. Choudhury, *op. cit*, pp. 85-86.
36. *Ibid.*, P.C. Choudhury, *op. cit.*, pp. 86-87.
37. *Ibid.*
38. *Ibid.*
39. *Ibid.*

40. *Ibid.*
41. *Ibid. Vol. I,* Pt. I, pp. 41-43, pp. 71-72.
42. *Ibid.*
43. *Ibid;* Nirmal Nibedon, *Mizoram, The Dagger Brigade;* Animesh Roy, *Mizoram, Dynamics of Change;* Suhas Chatterjee, *Mizoram Under the British Rule;* Tarun Goswami, Kuki Life and Love; Lt.Col. J. Shakespeare, *The Lushai Kuki Clans;* Bimal Ch. Dev and Dilip Kr. Lahiri, Lushai Customs and Ceremonies.
44. B.S. Guha, Racial Ethnology of India, *Nature,* May 1928, June 1929; C.R.L,1931, I, III; An Outline of the Racial Ethnology of India.
45. P.C. Choudhury, *op. cit.*
46. J.H. Hutton, C.R.I. 1931, I, S pp. 443f; *Caste of India*, pp. 2-3; *J.A.S.B.* XI, p. 17; Intro. to Shaw (Notes on the Thado Khasis, *J.A.S.B.* (N.S.) XXIV, p. 4f.
47. Mills, A Review, 1928. p. 24f; *J.A.R.S.* 1993, pp. 3-6, The Rengma Nagas, pp. 1-6.
48. A.H.Keane, *Man Past and Present,* pp. 186f; Ethnology, pp. 152f, 326.
49. Lt. Col. J. Shakespeare, *The Lushai Kuki Clan,* pp. 1-2.
50. A. Roy, *Mizoram Intro.*
51. J.H. Hutton, Pre-History of Assam, *Man in India,* 1928, pp. 228-32; *J.A.S.B.*, XXII, *Census of India, 1931*, I, I, pp. 357-69; N.D. Choudhury, *op. cit.,* pp. 33-56; A.H. Dani, *Pre History of Eastern India*; T.C. Sarma, Pre-historic Archaeology of Assam.
52. *Ibid.*
53. *Ibid.*

2
Mizo

B. Lalthangliana

Hill people living in the north-west of Burma and north-east of India were used to be known as Kuki to the Bengalis.[1] The earliest use of this name in English is found in 1782.[2] Bengal is found them culturally rather backward, hence the name Kuki which literally means "wild hill people". The Burmese called them "Chin" and we do not yet know why they called them so. Perhaps because they were always found carrying on their backs, bamboo baskets called "Chin" by the Burmese. But this particular Burmese word also means frienship and by a stretch of imagination one could say that once the Burmese and the Chin had lived very closely together. Since there were relations not pertaining strictly to friendliness, I think the explanation "Man with the basket" is most reasonable.

People now living in Mizoram dislike being called Kukis. In fact there are no more Kukis in the true sense of the word. However, Thado and Khuangsai of Manipur are still called Kukis. People who now occupy the Chin State of Burma like the native of Tiddim, Haka, Matupi, etc., call themselves as Zo or Zomi. Several of its variants like 'Yo' in Minbu area, 'Sho' in Pegu, 'Cho' in Mindat, either 'Cho' or 'Kywa' in some parts of Arakan of Burma. are also used. In the Paletwa area of the South Chin State of Burma, the neighbours call them 'Tainkus' Matus called them 'Tlengkaw' and Maras call them 'Tlaikao'.

When the British came to Mizoram in 1871 they found that most of the chiefs belonged to the Sailo sub-clan, which is under the Lushai clan, thus the territories under them came to be known as the 'Lushai Hills.' The meaning of Lushai is also a puzzle. Some suggests that it is a variant of Kuki,[3] which we do not consider as acceptable. *Lu* means head and *sa* or *sat* means to cut off and the combination denotes those who collect human heads.[4] We do not agree with this either. With *Lu* meaning head and *sei* meaning elongated, the name implies a description of people whose head looks elongated because of the hair-knot. This too though a learned explanation carries no weight. There is another difinition. While living in the Kabaw Valley of Burma, each group of people was mentioned by a number and *Lu Se* simply means People Ten.[5] Unfortunately we could not trace the other nine groups. In the absence of any acceptable explanation we can assume that as the people were usually called after the name of their noted or popular chiefs, these people must have been headed once by a man called LUSEIA. The name Luseia is used by the Burmese as well as the British but the people themselves want of be known as MIZO.

The name Mizo is also difficult to explain. With reference to the alpine climate, the people living on the hills could be named *Zomi* or *Mizo*—"people of the cold regions" by their brethren in the hot valleys. Here *Zo* means cold *region* and *Mi* means *men.* But it seemed that no one was left behind when they evaded the Shan onslaught into the Kabaw Valley by going up the Chin Hills. The most suitable explanation seems to be that they are called after the town they built in about 1750 in India, near the Burma border. The name of the town was ZOPUI and the leader was Lallula (? 1730-1807). While living at that town they were often successful in their raids against the enemies and they took pride in calling themselves as the braves of *Zopui*. Here *pui* means big and *Zopui* is `the big town of Zo'. Hence, the term `Mizo' and this name could have appeared only after the town of Zopui was built, i.e., in the middle of the eighteenth century. This is supported by the fact that the name *Zo* is mentioned in the ballad of Lallula's time which is as follows:

> Bearing long sword, men of Zo town,
> Succeeded to cut Mangngul's town like chickens,
> On the bank of Run river.[6]
> Don't think little of Zo town men,
> They could procure Thlanrawn heads a many,
> To hang from the branches of Phanpui[7]
> As the enemy advanced,
> To north and south the people scattered except us the Zo town braves,
> To check the coming enemies in waves.[8]

When Missionaries from England arrived in 1894 to Mizoram, they were honoured by being addressed as "Zosap" or the white man who came to live among the Zo people. In the first Census ever-collected among the people of Mizoram in 1901, there was no one who called himself as Mizo. But in the 1961 Census there were over 200,000 Mizo. Table 2.1 clearly shows that the name Mizo is fairly recent.

Table 2.1: Showing the population growth of various Mizo clan in the first Census (1901) and 1961 Census in Mizoram

Name of Clan	*1901*	*1961*
Hmar	10,411	3,118
Lushai	36,332	—
Mizo	—	213,061
Paihte	2,870	—
Pawih	15,038	4,587
Ralte	13,827	—
Total	**78,478**	**220,766**

The total population in 1961 was three times bigger than that of 1901 and it goes without saying that about 28,000 of Hmar, 109,000 of Lushai, 9,000 of Paihte, 40,000 of Pawi and 41,000 of Ralte declared themselves as Mizo. From as early as 1908, we find that 87 per cent of the population were talking Lushai dialect.[10] In the course of half a century the Lushai who wanted themselves to be called Mizo had grossly outnumbered the others, that only four per cent remained non-Mizo. The Lushai Hills by an Act of Parliament on 1 August, 1954, became the 'Mizo District' and on 21 January, 1972, MIZORAM (Mizo land). The word 'Zo' is now often used as a part of an individual's name and also the Lushai dialect came to be known as Mizo Language.

REFERENCES

1. Lewin, T. 11: *Hill Tracts of the Chittagong and the Dwellers therein,* Calcutta, Bengali Press, 1896, p. 98; See also *Frontier and Overseas Expeditions from India,* Govt. Monotype Press, 1907, p. 235.
2. Rowlins: "Cucis or Mountaineers of *Tipra, "AsiaticResearchers, II,* xii,1792; as quoted in Shaw William: The Thadou Kukis, Govt. of Assam, 1929, p. 11.
3. Shaw, William: *The Thadou. Kukis,* Govt. of Assam, 1929, p. 11.
4. Lwein, Capt. Thomas Herbert: *Progressive Colloquial Exercise in the Lushai Dialect of the 'Dzo' of Kuki Language, with Vocabulary and Popular Tales,* Calcutta, *1974* (Reprint), p. 3.

5. As told by Rev. Tuahhranga of Tahan, Burma on 4 April 1974; he got this definition from an old Burmese when he was with British Missionary, Gordon at Yazago, Burma.
6. Zokhaw val hnamchem kan chawi,
   Mangngul ar ang kan thahna,
   Run kuamah aw e.
7. Ka Zokhua hi dem lo u,
   Thlanrawn thlunglu kan lakna,
   Phanpui zur nguai aw e.
8. Chhimtiang hmartiang,
   Sa ang tlan zo ve,
   Zopuiah hnutiang ka dal nang e.
9. Liangkhaia, Rev.: *Mizo History*, Part II, Aizawl, Zoram Press, 1947, p. 20 and Poonte, B.: *ZoramThlirna,* Aizawl, Loch Press, 1965, p. 20.
10. *The Imperial Gazetteer of India, XVI,* Oxford, His Majesty's Secretary of State of India, 1908, p. 218.

3

The Late Home of Migration of the Mizos

J.N. Phukan

The people now called MIZO occupy a wide belt of territory, mainly hilly, which lies between 21°-24′N and 92°-94′E.[1] besides a fairly large concentration of their population in the State of Mizoram, and in large pockets in Manipur, Assam's North Cachar Hills District and in the State of Tripura, considerable areas in western Myanmar and eastern margins of Bangladesh extending southward in the Arakan Range to about 18°N are inhabited by them. A number of Mizo also live in the Irrawady from about 18° to 20°N.[2]

For long time they have been known to the different peoples and regions by different names but mainly by three well-documented nomenclatures viz., Kuki, Lushai and Chin, all applying to the present day Mizos living in Manipur, Cachar, Tripura, Mizoram and Myanmar. The Kukis are conventionally grouped into Old Kuki and New Kuki, or the early arrivals and the late arrivals, a distinction based upon the sequence of their appearance in their present habitat.

The "Kuki" tribe spelled variously as "Kookie", Kungki", "Cuci" are believed to have been living in North-Eastern India for a long time. References to them come across in the history of Tripura as early as 1512 A.D.[3] Writing in the first decade of the nineteenth century in course of his enquiry of the Ahom kingdom, Francis Hamilton (widely known as Buchanan-Hamilton) says that "Kungkis" (Kukis) were found in Manipur, Cachar and Tripura (the Lushai Hills was then not known) and were thought to be the same with the Nagas.[4] It is generally believed that "Kuki" is a term used by the Bengalis to designated all hill people.[5] It has, however, not been confirmed whether "kuki" was an original word in the Bengali language or was adopted by the Bengalis from some of their neighbours. But the fact is that this term has long been in use in southern

Assam, Manipur, Cachar and Tripura. Had it been a word of the Bengali language, we could expect the Bengalis calling all hill tribes like the Nagas, Garos, Jayantias, etc., by the term `Kuki". The English picked up this term from the neighbourers of the Kukis and applied it to the Lushais and the Chin tribes who possessed common cultural, social and linguistic affinities:

The English administrators adopted the term "Lushai" to refer to the Mizos. It was Mr. Edgar, the Deputy Commissioner of Cachar who first officially used the term "Lushai" instead of Kuki.[6] As for the meaning of *Lushai,* formerly it was thought that this term was derived from the custom of keeping their hair long and fastening it in a knot at the back of the head (lu=head, shai=long, i.e., keeping the head long or long head), or else originated from the custom of head hunting (lu=head, shai=out, i.e., head-cutting). Such interpretations or fanciful explanations, however, ended when Major J. Shakespear, the Superintendent of the Lushai hills and an authority on Lushais, made it clear that "Lushai was our way of spelling the word", but "the proper way to spell the word is Lushei (Lusei)". Following this, it has now been claimed that "Lushai" is derived from "Lusei", the name of the most powerful tribe dominating the Lushai Hills who ruled under the title Sailo at the time of British penetration into the present Mizoram.[7] Some say "Lusei" might have been originated after a person called Luseia, or after the name of a place.[8]

"Chin" as we know, is applied to the Mizos living in Myanmar. But in recent years, the Myanmar Government has also given recognition to "Lushai".[9] The explanation of some authors that this word is applied to the Chin people because they carry bamboo "basket" at their back (chin meaning `bamboo basket') is now being discarded as many other people in Myanmar and other areas in South-East Asia carry bamboo basket at their back, but are not called `Chin'.[10] Following Grierson, it is held that this term is Burmese corruption of the Chinese word "jen" meaning "man" which has been adopted by the Burmese and applied it to denote all hill tribes living in the border region between Assam and Myanmar.[11]

"Kuki", "Chin" and "Lushai" by which names the Mizos as a whole are called, are foreign words to the languages of the Zomis (Mizos).[12] Therefore, following the creation of Mizoram, the word Mizo gained in popularity and wide acceptance, and attempts have now been made to go into its etymology. It is now claimed that "Mizo" has been in use for a long time. Vanchhunga who made an intensive investigation of the Mizo in Myanmar claims that their forefathers used to say as Mizo:

"*keini Mizote* chuan" (we the Mizo)[13]. Some British officials also say that Mizos themselves used the term "Mizo", or its variants "Mezo" or "Mizau" while referring to themselves.[14] Hence, "Mizo" was not an altogether new or unknown word to the Mizos, but was not used by foreigners to designate them. Instead, they widely used the terms like "Kuki", "Chin", "Lushai".

With acceptance and wide use of the term "Mizo", a search is now being made about its meaning. At first it was thought that "Mizo" means (mi=man, zo=cold place) "people from cold place", or "a highlander". But this meaning is now seriously contested on the ground that all other hill people of North-East India would have been called "Mizo" as they all live in highland.[15] According to a Mizo scholar the word "Mizo", variantly "Mi-dzo", or "Mizao" is a combination of the two words "Miao" and "yao", together as "Mizao" is a combination of the two words "Miao" and "yao", together as "Mizo-Tzu" or "Miao-yao" o "Miotzu" by which names the widespread hill tribes inhabiting Yunnan Swechwan, Northern Laos, Northern Vietnam and Thailand are known to the Chinese".[16] He, therefore, thinks that the word "Mizo" is a combination of Mi (man) and zo (man) similar to the Mizo word run in which means (run = house, in = house), i.e., house. Mizo is, therefore, rather like a generic term by which all tribes are covered. B. Lalthangliana while admitting that the name Mizo is hard to explain, says that most likely they are so called after the town Zopui they built in India 20 miles to the west of the Tiau river in about 1765 which means "the big town of the Zo people." By prefixing *Mi* meaning "people" the term "Mizo" came into vogue.[17]

All the names "Kuki", "Chin", "Lushai", or even "Mizo" lead us to nowhere near to the origin of the Mizos and in the absence of conventional source materials like written records or chronicles, coins, inscriptions or other archaelogical evidences, attempts had been made during the colonial period, to reconstruct their early history on the basis of legends, traditions, social institutions, beliefs and customs. In more recent years, further attempts are made by scholars, mostly Mizos, to supplement, confirm or modify earlier findings by resorting to oral tradition, folk lore and folk cultural elements as "survivals" of the past. The process is on, and it is thus tentative to claim any definite theory of their early homeland and their migration.

Their folk songs remind them of a land called Sinlung (variantly Chhinlung) from where their forefathers escaped like *Siel*[18] from the pressure of a more powerful people. The song runs thus:

kan sieng na Sinlung ram hming thang
ka nu ram ka pa ram ngai
chawng zil ang kokir thei chang sien
ka nu ram ka pa ram ngai
(My motherland, famous Sinlung,
Home of my own ancestors
Could it be called back like Chwangzil
Home of my own ancestors)[19]

On the basis of such song, attempts have been made to identify the land of Sinlung. Some think that the Sinlung of the folk song is Tailing or Silung in south-west China.[20] Others think that Sinlung is Sining in Central China.[21] Yet others think Sinlung may be a derivative of Ch' in dynasty (221-207 B.C.) when the Chinese drove out many non-Chinese tribes from their land. Rochunga Pudaite concludes that "it appears historically evident that the Hmars originally came from Central China, following one of these mass migrations, especially those of the late pre-Christian and early Christian centuries".[22] The theory that the Mizos had originally come from Central China has gained currency among Mizo historians and the educated people in particular.[23]

The theory of Central China homeland of Mizo people solely rests on the Hmar traditional folk songs referred to above which makes no mention of China or Chinese people or any other place. It does not speak of crossing high mountains or big rivers on the way. We have, however, not been told whether other Mizo people have similar folk tradition which speak of Sinlung (Chhinglung, a variant) as the home of their ancestors. Since the songs speak nothing about the location of Sinlung, *the ram hming thang* (the land of my ancestors), the search for its identification led to these three theories, not necessarily exclusive of each other.

The process of identification is again rested on the usually accepted theory that many of the Mongoloid peoples of India, Myanmar, Thailand, Laos and Vietnam came down from southern China of the Yang-tze valley and beyond in the north. Although such a theory relating to the Tai migration to Thailand has come under serious attack of some Chinese scholars, Chen Lufan and his school in particular, it still remains the primary basis to explain the movement of Mongoloid people from the north to south and South-East Asia. Hence, the migration of Mizo tribe, like the Burmans, the Tai people, and a host of other people, is explained in terms of this theory. It is in conformity with this theory of southern migration of the Mongoloid peoples from China in particular, some Mizo historians have identified Sinlung, on lexical resemblances of names as the present Tailung or Silung in south-west China, or Sining in Central China, or its equation of Sin with Ch'in dynasty of China.

No doubt, following the movement of the peoples who now occupy the land mass in South-East Asia, it is evident that the Mizos also came from the north, i.e., China. But the claim that Sinlung of the Mizos is a derivative of the word "Ch'in" of the Ch'in dynasty is a mere conjecture without any historical foundation. As stated above, the folk songs or folk traditions of the Mizos make no reference to any other place, river or mountain or people which they came across except the Shans which we will discuss soon. It appears highly unlikely that the Mizos carry only the name of the land from so distant date in their journey through time and space covering several thousand miles and many centuries.

If we were to accept Ptolemy's 'Tiladae' as the 'Kuki' people, as identified by Gerini, the settlement of the Kuki in North-East India would go back to a very long time in the past. As Professor Gongumumei Kabui thinks, "some Kuki tribes migrated to Manipur hills in the pre-historic times along with or after the Meitei advent in the Manipur valley".[24] This hypothesis will take us to the theory that the Kukis, for that matter, the Mizos, at least some of their tribes, had been living in North-East India since the prehistoric time and, therefore, their early home must be sought in the hills of Manipur and the nearby areas rather than in Central China or the Yang-tze valley. This hypothesis needs a very serious study in the light of recent findings of prehistoric and proto-historic settlements in North-East India.

Taking into consideration of the pattern of movement of the tribes of Myanmar and North-East India in historic times, we are more inclined to think that the Mizos came to their present land from south-western China through the corridor of north-western Myanmar *via* the Upper Irrawady valley. And it is for this reason that their folklore, traditional songs and in material culture bear many references to the Shans and the Burmans, who were their neighbours both as friends and foes.

B. Lalthangliana in his *History of the Mizo in Burma,* which has been considered as "the most reliable one" in the field of the Mizo people[25], claims that the Mizo people moved slowly into Myanmar from a place where the borders of Myanmar and Tibet meet in the Seventh century A.D. During the next century, they expelled the Shan Kadus from the Kabaw valley and occupied it where they developed their culture to a certain degree of high standard. There they borrowed the practices of tattooing, the use of elaborate hair pins, brass bangles and brass gongs probably from the Burmans.[26] They also built a town named Khampat which lies on the motor road at a distance of 43 miles from Kale or 32 miles from Tamu towards Kale. However, the present remains of the fortifications at Khampat indicate that it was built in the eighteenth century. It was only in the fourteenth century that the Mizos had to leave the Kabaw valley due to the Shan penetration. During the period of their stay in the Kabaw valley, many Burmese words got into the Mizo language as shown by Lalthangliana.[28]

Pudaite, on the other hand, shows that the first known settlement of the Hmar people was the Shan State where they came into close contact with the Shans as borne out by folk song like the one quoted below.[28]

One of the *Hmar* poets says:

Ka pa lam tlak a tha' n dang,
Sinlung lam tlak aw a tha'n dang;
Shan khuoah thapo in vang,
Tuoichawngin hranlu a tlunna;
Thlomu sieka kemin hril,
Zaing hawngah hranlu bah kan sal

(My father's steps were remarkably good, Sinlung's steps were, indeed, remarkably good; Few are the good men in Shan State, Where Tuoichawng brought the enemy's head; You talked of tips with eagle's paws (meaning war), And we hang the heads high with ropes.

The above poem bears definite indication that Sinlung was somewhere in or near the Shan State where the *Hmar* had to fight with the Shans. It was here that the words of silver and gold were first associated with the vocabulary of the *Hmar* people. One of their chiefs was especially rich and was said to eat only on gold plates. Many of great festivals were connected with their Shan State civilization. The *Khuonglawm* (spring festival), *Lunglak* (autumn festival), and *Sesun* (solemn celebration) are all concerned with Shan. So great was their success that they even praised the Shan youths in songs.

Shan khuo thlangfa pu tling tleng e,
I do thlunglu bakin salh;
Sa sawmfa thlaw ka laimi tha,

(Sons of western Shan State look lovable, But you soundered out only war; With our abundant harvest and men of war, We will make of you a Springtime Festival).

The connections of the Mizos with the Burmese and the Burmese and the Shans in many of their cultural elements and civilisation bring us to the theory that their late home of migration was southern China bordering Myanmar where even today many tribes lead their traditional life.

REFERENCES

1. A.S. Reid: *Chin-Lushai Land,* Reprinted, 1976, p. 4.
2. Frank M. Le Bar *et al.*: *Ethnic Groups of Mainland Southeast* Asia, HARF, 1964, p. 50.
3. G.A. Grierson: *Linguistic* Survey *of India,* Vol. III, Part III reprint, 1967, p. 1.
4. *Account of Assam,* ed. by S.K. Bhuyan, pp. 81-82.
5. G.A. Grierson: *Ibid.*
6. W.B. Oldham: "The Word `Lushai', "*Vocabulary of Lushai Language, ed. by* R.H. Sneyd Hutchinson, Calcutta, 1897, p. 1.
7. Sangkima:"An Etymological Study of the Word 'Mizo' ", Proceedings of the North East India History Association, Seventh Session, 1986, p. 334.
8. *Ibid.*
9. War Office Council Order No. 40/50 of 2 May, 1950 on the status of Lushais as adopted by B. Lalthangliana in *History of Mizo in Burma,* p. 92, Appendix IV.
10. Sangkima: *Ibid.*
11. Bertam S. Carey and H.N. Tuck, *The Chin Hills*, Vol. I, 1976, p. 3.
12. T. Gougin: *The Discovery of Zoland,* 1980, pp. 2-3.
13. *Lusei leh a vela Hnam Dangle,* 1955, p: 1 as quoted by Sangkima, *op. cit.*, p. 334.
14. A.W. Davis: *Gazetteer of the North Lushai Hills,* cited by Grierson, R.B.M Cabe, Foreign Department Proceedings, External, Part A, December 1892, No. 43.
15. Sangkima: *op. cit. p.* 334.
16. *Ibid.*, p. 335.
17. *History of Mizo in Burma*, p. 71.
18. A kind of bovine animal known widely as *mithun* in North-East India.
19. Rochunga Pudaite: *The* Education *of the Hmar people,* 1963, p. 21.
20. Rochunga Pudaite: op. *cit., p.* 22. *Ibid.*, p. 23.
23. Lalrimawia: "Pre-historic and Historic Migration of the Mizos", *Proceedings* of the North-East India History Association, 2nd Session, 1981, p. 25.
24. *History of Manipur, p.* 23.
25. Foreword by Prof. Than Tun, p. viii.
26. *History of Mizo* in *Burma*, pp. 6-10.
27. *Ibid.*, p. 4.
28. *Ibid.*, pp. 6-10.

4
A Comparative Study of the Mizos in India and the Wa Nationality in China

Their Migratory Routes

Ai Rui (Dai Name)

PART ONE

The Wa nationality in China has a long history. In 122 B.C., called the Yuanshou First Year during the reign of Emperor Hanwu in Chinese history, Xinanyi was set up. In 69 A.D., called the Yongping Twelfth Year during the Han Dynasty, Yongchangshire was set up. The historical records in Huayang Kingdom History and Nanzhong History say: "The Yongchangshire., with a territory of 1,500 km. from the east to the west and of 2,300 km. from the north to the south, there were Chuanziong, Danetzhong, Min, Yue and Pu., living in the most southwestly part of the Ningzhou; there lived Min. Pu, Jiuliao Piao, Yue, Luopu and Yuandu peoples." The above mentioned "Pu" and "Luopu" were the ancestors of the Wa, the Bonglong and the Bulang nationalities. "Yue"and Jiuliao" were the ancestors of the Dai nationality, and "Yuandu" were Indians' Since the Tang Dynasty, there have been clear records about the Wa people, who were called "Wangman" during the Tang dynasty, and "Haci", "Hadu", "Hawa", "Kawa" and other names during the Yuan, the Ming and the Qing Dynasties. Since 1949, in accordance with the majority's will they have been called the Wa nationality.

In the Wa society, there has been a popular legend called "Sigang Li" which has two interpretations. According to the one popular in the Wa-inhabited Ximeng Region, "Sigang" means "a rock cave" and "Li" means "coming out". "Sigang Li" means that man came from a rock cave. According to this legend, the god Liji and the god Luan created the Sky, the Earth, the Sun, the Moon and Man who was put in a rock cave. Later small birds pecked a hole in the cave and let man come out. It is said that the cave is located in a mountain near Bagedai (also called Bulade), which is about 12.5 km west of Masan in Ximeng County, China. Up to now, the Awa people in the Ximeng region have regarded it as a holy place where sacrificial rites are often held.

According to the Wa legend in Cangyuan, "Singang Li" means that man came from a gourd which was growing in a rock cave which was located near Bagedai.[1]

In their legends about the origin of human beings the Wa people in Burma and the Lawa people in Thailand also regard Bagedai as the birth place of human beings. This is quite similar to the legend of the Wa people in China.[2] Bagedai is located in the Wa region, Burma, in the middle part of the Awa Mountain Areas and between the Lancang River and the Saerwen River. (The Wa people are distributed mainly over the southern part of the Nu mountains which are generally called the Awa Mountain Area.)

In recent years, in the Cangyuan Autonomous County of the Wa nationality, such relics as stone axes, stone shovels and stone rings of the Neolithic Age have been found and more than 1,000 rock paintings and caves of the Eastern Han Dynasty have been discovered.

The above-mentioned facts have fully proved that at least as early as the Eastern Han Dynasty the ancestors of the Wa nationality were living in the Awa Mountain Areas. At that time, the ancestors of the Wa nationality were distributed in a large area, from the east to the west along the Lancang river and the Saerwen river, from the north in Dehong and Baoshan in Yunnan Province in China to the south in Jingdong in Burma and Jingmai in Thailand. The Awa Mountains were the centre of their distribution.

PART TWO

A comparison of their languages, cultural life, religious beliefs and psychological qualities :

A. The Mizos speak the Lushai language (also called the Duhlien language), which belongs to the Sino-Tibetan Burman language group.[3]

   The Wa language in China belongs to the Wabeng language branch, Men-Cambodian language group of the South-Asian language family. Most words in the SouthAsian language family are based on monosyllabic roots and in some respects such as their measure words expressing the natural units of things they are similar to those in the Sino-Tibetan-Burman language group. The Wa people belong to the Mongoloid race (South-Asian group).

B. The Mizos are living in a patriarchal clan system in which polygamy is quite popular. The policy that the youngest son is entitled to the right of inheritance is being carried out.
The Wa people in China have a patriarchal individual family system. A clan is formed by many families coming from the same ancestry. Each clan has its own family name. Usually monogamy is carried out, but polygamy does also exist. Marriage between members of the same clan is strictly prohibited. Marriage to other relatives is popular. When a woman's husband has died, she usually has to remarry his brother. If the widow is unwilling to remarry her husband's brother, she can remarry another man who has to pay back the "betrothal gifts" given by the late husband upon their marriage. After a son gets married, he will not continue living in his parents' house but he will keep in contact with his parents and brothers. The right of inheritance is up to the father's decision.

C. The Mizos are mainly engaged in agriculture and paddy-growing. They use very primitive methods and tools.[3]

The Wa people in China are mainly engaged in growing crops in non-irrigated land. They apply the method of extensive cultivation which is far from sophisticated. There are two ways of cultivation: One is slash-and-burn cultivation; that is to cut down trees and grass and let them dry in the sun before burning them. After that they will loosen the soil with knives or sharpened wooden sticks without ploughing or hoeing before the sowing. The other method is to "dig or plough a furrow" before the sowing and then let the crops grow themselves. Their tools of production are made of either iron or wood. They are still living in the preliminary stage of the Iron Age.

D. Not long ago, head-hunting was a custom of the Mizos.[4] Before the 1950s, in order to offer a sacrifice to the god of rice and the Wa people in the Ximeng region in China had a head-hunting custom, and this practice often caused fighting with weapons between villages. Every village had one or several antagonistic villages. Because they were eager to take their revenge on their antagonistic village on behalf of their clan, it was difficult for the antagonistic villagers to become reconciled. When a fight with weapons occurred, all the grown-up men would take part in it enthusiastically.

Most of the Wa villages were built on the hillsides. Usually there were 100 families in one village, but occasionally there were up to 500 families in one village. These villages were not formed on blood relationship but on geographical positions. Each village had from at least one to over ten clans and had its clear boundary which separated it from other villages. The distance between two villages was about 10 to 15 km. and each village had its enclosing walls made of timber and thorny undergrowth. Outside the walls there were ditches and the village gate was well built and covered. March, July and August were the head-hunting times, during which the villages were heavily guarded. The villagers would not go far away from their own villages and they went to work in the fields in groups.

Head-hunting, village hatred and fighting with weapons brought great suffering to the Wa people. Under the leadership of the Chinese Communist party and the People's Government, through patient persuasion and education, as well as mediation, the antagonistic villages have become reconciled gradually and the head-hunting custom has disappeared.

E. The Mizos in the past were isolated from the outside world. They carried on a long struggle against the British colonialists who often suffered heavy losses.

In the past, due to their head-hunting custom and the frequent fighting with weapons, the Wa people had very few contacts among themselves, not to mention the contacts with the outside world. However, if there were invasions from other nationalities or from foreign countries, all the villages and tribes would immediately become reconciled and a temporary agreement would be signed in order to fight against foreign invasions. In January 1934, the British invaders took by force the silver mine in the Cangyuan region, Yunnan Province, China. This angered the local Wa people. The heads of Banhong and Banlao called in the Wa people from about ten nearby tribes to gather in Banhong. They killed oxen to show that they formed an alliance, organized three armed forces and swore to drive the invaders out. With the help of other local nationalities, they defeated the invaders and recovered their lost territory.[3]

F. The Mizos believe in a kind of pantheism.

In the past, the Wa people in China usually believed in a kind of pantheism. They thought that everything in nature, including human beings and all other living and non-living things had "spirit". Good fortune, misfortune, safety and danger were all decided by "spirit". Some Wa people believed in Hinayana Buddhism or Christianity.

PART THREE

China began to have business dealings and cultural exchanges with India many years ago. According to the historical records, in about the third century A.D. the people in Yunnan Province, China, and the peoples of Burma, India and Vietnam opened two non-governmental routes by themselves. One was called "Shu-Yuandu Route", with its starting point in the western part of present-day Sichuan Province, through Xichang, Dali and Yongchangshire (in present-day Boashan,, Yunnan Province) and ending in Yuandu (India) Route", with its starting point in Jiaozhi, along the Red River upwards, through Hekou before reaching Kunming. Then, this route turned westwards, through Dali and ended in Yongchangshire.

Yongchang was an important passageway of these two ancient routes to India. In Yongchang, the merchants from Sichuan and Yunnan in China had their business dealings with the merchants from India. The Chinese merchants exchanged cloth and bamboo canes from Sichuan and tea for gold, shells, jades and glazed articles from India. It is quite possible that the above-mentioned "Yuandu People" in *Huayang Kingdom History and Nanzhong History* were the Indians who were doing business in Yongchangshire.

The three historical records, A *History of the Later Han Dynasty, Records of the Later Han Dynasty and Dongguan Records of the Han Dynasty,* say that during the period of the Eastern Han Dynasty, the head of the Shans (the Dais), Yong Youdao, sent envoys three times to Luoyang in China to present treasures. Each time the envoys led an acrobatic troupe and a music band to perform at court, among which there were performances by Indians, such as snake-performing and pole-climbing.

PART FOUR

There were migratory movements in the history of the Wa people. A *Short*

History of the Wa People (1986 edition) says that after the Tang Dynasty (certainly not starting from that time) there were two important migratory movements. One happened during the Nanzhao Period (649-902). 200,000 people in Nancuan were forced to move to Yongchangshire and the people in the Yongchang region (mainly ancestors of the Wa people and some Dai people) were forced to move inland. This resulted in continuously southward migratory movements of the Wa people in Yongchangshire. The other happened in the Yuan and Ming Dynasties (from the thirteenth century to the middle of the seventeenth century). The continuous migratory movements of the Han, the Dai and the Lahu nationalities to the Wa-inhabited areas made the Wa people move southwards or northwards. At that time, the Wa people were still leading a nomadic way of life based on hunting, gathering and crop-growing. Migratory movements were also required for their production and survival.

The historical records have only mentioned the two important migratory movements southwards and northwards without detailed information. That was the time when frequent business dealings were being carried out between China, India and Burma. It is possible that some ancestors of the Dai people and of the Wa people, under the powerful reign of Nanzhao, moved southwards, gathered in the Awa Mountain Areas, through Burma, crossing the Qindum River and then entered India. It is also possible that others moved northwards, crossing the national boundary, passing through Burma, and entered the north-east part of India.

If the above-mentioned hypothesis proves we, I think that their migratory route was the ancient "Shu-Yuandu Route" which fell into two routes leading to India in Yongchangshire. One of the two routes was in the due northern direction from Yongchang to Mizhina in Burma, crossing the Yiluowadi River and the Menggong River before crossing the Qindun River in the west, and led to the Asamu region in the north-east part of India. The other was the south-west route, from Yongchagshire into Shanbang in Burma, along the Yiluowadi River to the seaside, arriving at Jida Port by ship, and also led to the north-east part of India.

If the Mizos have descended from the ancestors of the Wa nationality (the Pu and Luopu peoples) who were forced to migrate during the Nanzhao Period of the Tang Dynasty in China, then it is possible that the present-day Mizos in India and the Wa nationality in China have the same national origin but have become different nationalities.

FOOTNOTES

1. *A Historical Investigation of the Wa Society*, Volume 2, Yunnan Nationality Publishing House.
2. The Border Nationalities in South-east Asia and in the South-west of China, Chap. 13, "Wa/Lawa nationality", Yunnan Nationality Publishing House.
3. See "Lushais" (The Mizos), A Dictionary of the Minority Nationalities.
4. *Ibid.*

5

A Study of the Mizos with reference to their Early Home

Sangkima

Introduction

In the absence of any written records left behind, it is extremely difficult to give an authentic account of the Mizos. The study is mainly based on contemporary documents primarily books written by the British Administrators who wrote their experiences on the Mizos and also other contemporary scholars who deal with the history of the South-East Asia in general and China in particular. These contemporary writings are our main source material. The oral traditions, legends and myths as available also give us some clue. Besides another problem is that the Mizos did not form a homogeneous people with a single culture in the period of our study. They were split up into a very large number of sub-tribes each with a varied customs and dialects. The term 'Mizo' was yet to be coined as generic term. It is only of recent origin. This also creates an immense problem in the study of the Mizos. For this reason, references must be made to other ethnic tribes with whom the Mizos are said to have some close affinities particularly with the major tribes in China. Hence, a comparative study of ethnic tribes may in some way lead us to a certain conclusion in so far as our study is concerned. Therefore, in this chapter an attempt on the early home of the Mizos is made on the following accounts.

Some Accounts

In order to delineate an ancient history of the Mizos a wider scope of study is necessary. From this point of view, a brief survey of their early accounts needs to be examined. For this exercise, as one factor, the ethnology of the Mizos is first to be investigated. Scholars classified the whole human race into three broad races under the terms the Caucosoid, the Negroid and the Mongoloid.[1] Mongoloid is used to designate one of the hypothetical major racial stocks of mankind and is applied widely to all peoples of Asia and other parts of the world whose racial characteristics are found similar with those of the Mongoloid stock. Hence, the Mizos belongs to the Mongoloid race because they are said to have fulfilled all the morphological characteristics of the Mongoloid as summarised by Bowles.[2] All this points to the original habitat of the Mongoloid race. Another peculiar characteristic of the Mongoloid race is birth-mark on the pelvis of every new born child irrespective of male and female. This mark, however, vanishes when he or she becomes two or three years of age. We do not know whether this bears some truth to other Mongoloid races but it is found in to the Mizos.

Ethnic evidence is also to be taken into account as another factor. Scholars have sub-divided Sino-Tibetan family into sub-groups and sub-sub-groups. In these various divisions the Mizos are grouped as Tibeto-Burman family.[3] They speak the Tibeto-Burman language.[4] The home of these peoples is not known but somewhere between Kansu and Burma is believed to be their earliest known home. Hall firmly asserted that the "earliest known home of the Tibeto-Burmese speaking peoples was somewhere between Gobi desert and north-east of Tibet, also possibly Kansu."[5] At the same time, scholars hold different views on the original habitat of the human race and most of them think that man made his first appearance in China: Burkitt said that the later stone age people (Neolithic period) made their movements from China to Central Asia and thence to Europe.[6] It is, therefore, speculated that China is not only the home of the human race but also the home of the tribal peoples who are scattering in the Southern Provinces. Further, China has two major nationalities of China proper who since from time immemorial have been occupying the northern China and have Tartar blood in them and the tribal peoples who constitute the second largest group in China. Latourette writes thus, "The earliest Chinese we know are the northern fringes of a racial and cultural group whose western representatives are the Tibeto-Burman peoples of Tibet, Szechuan, Yunnan and Burma and whose central and southern representatives are the tribes which survives in the hills of Central and South China."[7] They maintain a distinct and separate culture. There are 18 larger minority nationalities. Lolo, Mio, Yao, Lisu, Lashi, Li, etc., are the prominent tribes. They are widely distributed over the mountainous areas of Kwi-chou and Yunnan in the west to Hunnan, Kwangtung and Kwangsi in the Central South of China.[8] The tribal peoples of the South enjoyed an independent life for centuries. But the regions could not remain long isolated. The Chinese expansionism soon reached the region thus consolidating the Imperial power at the centre. Thereupon, China began to interfere into the internal affairs of the tribal peoples. Then, in course of time, the `buffer states' were thus recognised during the Sui and the T'ang dynasties. But they were not incorporated into the Empire until Manchu period.[9]

Thus the regions between Kansu and Burma known as the 'buffer states' form part of Southern China and it occupies in China a significant position in the history of the tribal peoples in general for the provinces of Kwei-chou, Sze-chuan and Yunnan which lie in this region are found to be the homes of various tribal peoples. Kwei-chou was the original home of the Miao-Tzu tribes[10] from which the word 'Mizo' is believed to have derived its origin. The Lao-Shan and Kiu-lung mountains in Sze-chuan province are also said to have been the original home of the Ngai-lao group of Tai, Lolo, Miao and other tribes.[11]

Sze-chwan province regarded as a home of tribal peoples has occupied a unique place in the early history of the Mizos. Traditionally, Mizos claim *Chhinlung* or *Sinlung* to be their original home,[12] and is said be located at Szechwan Province. This is strongly supported by songs and legends that have been handed down to the generations.[13] Yet, it is extremely difficult to ascertain and identify it as a reality or a myth. Whatever might be the case, *Chhinlung* theory has, however, depicted the origin of the Mizos. Mizo tradition claims that once the Mizos came out of a very big 'stone-cave' called *Chhinlung* believed to be located somewhere in China. After coming out of this cave, they left it in haste. According to some, they left *Chhinlung* due to their inability to repulse their enemies or to avoid severe punishments from their cruel and merciless rulers like Cheng, better known as Shih Hwang Ti' (246-210 BC) whose repressive policy forced them to rigorous labour in constructing the Great Wall of China, the length of which is about 2500 miles.[14] According to Gogoi, there were two instances of pressures in 338 B.C. and 224 B.C.[15] In the Great World Atlas,[16] *Chhinlung* (or Xinlong) is shown at Longitude 101°03′and Latitude 31° in the Sze-chwan province. The city is situated on the western side of the Yulung river and on the east of the Yantze Kiang river. According to Chawngkunga, the old forts and defence fortifications which surround the city are still visible. During the Imperial period, it had been the District Headquarters under various Chinese rulers and had been an important port.[17] It is now difficult to line this *Chhinlung* as a place with the prince *Chhinlung* of the Ngai-Lao people who founded the principality in Yunnan in the first Christian era.[18] Prince Chiulung and his followers left their homes and settled in Yunnan due to the Chinese pressures from the North and the North-East.[19] The story coincides with the traditional tale of the Mizos that Prince *Chhinlung* and his follower left their habitat owing to the growing conflicts with his father.[20] Another intriguing question is whether or not the present *Chhinlung* in Szechwan province is named after Prince *Chiulung*. Again, this coincides with Mizo traditional practice that when they were asked to which village they belonged, they used to mention the name of their chief, and not that of the village from where they hailed. Whatever might have been, the fact is that all the places or names like Chiu-lung, Kui-lung, Tsinlung, Sinlong, Xinlong, signifying *Chhinlung* are found in Sze-chwan province alone. This, again, gives us a strong sentimental ground to believe Sze-chwan Province as an early settlements of the Mizos.

Apart from other facts, linguistic affinity also point Yunnan as an original home of the tribals including Mizos because the Logos whose languages "are spoken by scattered populations in Yunnan, Sze-chawan and part of Kweichaw"[21] made Yunnan as their home. A specimen of dialects given below shows linguistic affinity between the Mizos and the Lolos.

English	**Mizo**	**Lolo**
day	ni	ni
pig	vawk (vok)	va
nine	kua (pakua)	kue

Linguists have been trying to classify languages to indicate genetic relationship. Kroeber says, "If a considerable proposition of the words and the grammatical forms of two languages are reasonably similar, similar enough to indicate that the resemblances cannot be due to mere accident, these similar words and forms must go back to a common source, and if this source is not borrowing by one language from another, the two tongues are related by descent from a common ancestor".[22] Grierson puts the Kuki-Chin languages to the Burmese branch of the Tibeto-Burman family.[23] From his classification it seems that the similarity of Tibeto-Burmese speaking peoples cannot be considered as a mere accident. This affirms that the linguistic affinity of the Mizos with that of the Lolos was not a mere accident by descent. From this linguistic evidence it is strongly believed that the Lolos and other tribes had been together somewhere in Southern China or elsewhere.

The traditions of the Karens and the Mizos clearly indicate that the two tribes have a striking similarities which can be considered as a clue to the source of the Mizos. The two have the same tradition in migration. Though it is very difficult to ascertain as to where the Karens have their original home but what is known is that they found their homeland in Yunnan at the beginning of the Christian era.[24] There similarities in traditions, legends and myths are evidently enough to indicate that the two tribes have a common ancestor because for "legends and myths are important elements in the cultural background of a people".

The Karen tradition on migration says that the patriarch who led the people on their way became impatient over his men at one stage and went ahead of them promising to blaze his path that they might follow him through the jungle. After while they followed him only to find that the plantain stalks he had cut off had shot up so high that it seemed impossible to overtake him. As a result, they settled down in the vicinity.[25] The same story is told among the Mizos. According to them, the first batch adzed a tree called *Muk* the cut off which looks so pale very soon. Like the Karens, when the other groups saw the cut they gave up hope of overtaking them. Then they settled down in the wilderness. The Karen people call their mythical founder *Htaw Meh Pa.* The Mizos call him *Thlanrawk Pa.* The Karens call the Creator, Y'wa and the Mizos call *Pathian.* According to Karen people, Y'wa who creates nature is said to have given books to these various children but they were negligent with the book given to them and it is eaten by animals[26] The same story is told among the Mizos but the book given to them is said to have been eaten up by a dog for the same reason. Both the tribes feel themselves to be one of the lost tribes of Israel. Some of the early missionaries also thought that the Karen might be found to be the lost tribes of Israel.[27] This belief is current among the Mizos even today. Many people now have been trying to migrate back to Israel. Recently one Rabi visited Mizoram but the outcome of his visit is not yet known. Many have practised circumcesion rites of the *Old Testament.* In 1960s for the first time there prevailed a wide preaching in what is termed as *Israel ram pem* meaning 'migration to Israel', Collections were also made for this purpose.

A cultural background may also be considered as evidence. *Zawlbuk,* (bachelor's house) formed a part of Mizo culture. It is believed to have its origin in China. Zawlbuk was a nerve-centre of the Mizo society by snapping the Mizo youth into a responsible adult member of the society.[28] Therefore, Zawlbuk became a corner stone of the Mizo society. We do not know its origin, but one thing is certain that it was not a recent introduction to the Mizo society as a part of its culture. Contemporary writings have, however, thrown some light, on the *Zawlbuk*. Its origin may be traced back to China where the Long Houses or Communal Houses were found.[29] According to Loeb and Broek the Long House was brought down from Yunnan to other places in the South-east Asia by the patrilineal Tibeto-Burman peoples and others.[30] The same House was also found among the tribes in the South China area.[31] It is obvious that the Mizos brought it down from China to the present Mizoram. This has indeed a bearing on the origin of the Mizos. The Nagas are also to have the same institution called *'Morung'*[32] Among the tribes of the Chittagong Hills and the *Mawk* of Burmese tribes of the Shan States the same institution was practised.[33] There are some tribes in Arunachal Pradesh who are still having the same institution. But the matrilineal Garo and Khasi lacked it.

An etymological study of the term 'Mizo' may also suggest the origin of the Mizos because the word 'Mizo' variantly 'Mi-dzo' or 'Mi-zao' is believed to be originated from the words 'Miao' and 'Yao' which the Chinese contemptuously and wrongly called as 'Miao-Tzu' or 'Miao-yao' by which name a very widespread hill tribes inhabiting Yunnan, Szechwan, Northern Laos, Northern Vietnam and Thailand are known.[34]

Conclusion

The striking affinity of the Mizos, in languages, mode of living-culture Daos etc., with those of the hill tribes who found Southern part of China as their home, convinces us to believe that they came from the same place of the common ancestor. It may, therefore, be conjectured that while they were in Southern China they came in contact with other hill tribes and as a result there were mutual borrowing of languages and culture. A comparison of words between Lolos and other Tibeto-Burmese speaking peoples with that of the Mizos shows that they are found to be of the same origin. The southward movements of these tribes were the results of the pressures made by the successive Chinese rulers at different intervals. These pressures were continuing until 1661 when the last Ming ruler of Yunnan was captured in the war between China and Burma. As a result of these continued pressures, the Mizos while living somewhere in China along with the Ngai-Lao group of Tai, Lolo, Miao, Yao and others in the Kiu-lung mountains reached Sze-chwan and Kwichwan provinces and in course of time finally they thus arrived in Yunnan Province where they are said to have been settled for a number of years. Therefore, the southern part of China, particularly Sze-chwan, Yunnan, Kwei-chow

Provinces and in wider sense, the entire fringed eastern perimeter of the plateu between Kansu and Burma may be considered as the original home of the Mizos and other tribes of the North-East India as a whole.

REFERENCES

1. Gordon T. Bowles; *The People of Asia,* Weidenfield & Nicholson, London, 1977, p. 12.
2. *Ibid.*, p. 345.
3. Peter Kunstadter (Editor), Southeast Asian Tribes, Minorities and Nations, Vol. I, Princeton University Press, Princeton, New Jersey, 1967, pp. 79-84.
4. A.H. Keane *Man-Past and Present,* Quiggen & Haddon, Cambridge, 1900, p. 193. *Cf.* A.G. McCall; *The Lushai Chrysalis,* Insac & Co. London, 1949, pp. 25-26.
5. D.G.E. Hall; *A History of South-East Asia,* Macmillan Co. Ltd., London, 1955, p. 123.
6. M.C. Burkitt; *Our Early Ancestors,* University Press, Cambridge, 1929, p. 79.
7. Kenneth Scot Latourett; *The Chinese—Their History and Culture,* The Macmillan Company, New York, 1947, p. 33.
8. Chang-tu Hu; *China—Its People, its Society, its Culture,* Hraf Press, New Haven,1960, p. 66.
9. Gordon T. Bowles; *op.cit.*, p. 257.
10. "The Lolos and Other Tribes of Western China" by A. Henry *Journal of the Anthropological Institute of Great Britain and Ireland, Great* Britain Vol. XXXIII, Hanover Square, London, 1903, p. 96.
11. Padmeswar Gogoi; *The Tai and the Tai Kingdoms,* Gauhati University 1968, p. 37 (footnote).
12. Rev. Liangkhaia; *Mizo Chanchin,* Academy of Letters, Aizawl, 1976, p. 1.
13. L. Hranglien Songate; *Hmar Chanchin* (Hmar History) L&R Press, Churachanpur, 1977, p. 11.
14. Kenneth Scott Latourett; *op. cit,* p. 95.
15. Padmeswar Gogoi; *op. cit,* p. 38.
16. Great World Atlas, the *Reader's Digest Association,* London 9.69.
17. C. Chawngkung; 'Speech' delivered on the occasion of Hmar Inkhawmpui at Churachandpur, 25-27 October 1982, p. 3.
18. *Ibid.*
19. *Ibid.*
20. Rev. Liankhaia, *op.cit.*, p. 1.
21. R.A.D. Forest; *The Chinese Language,* Fober and Foberober, Ltd. London, (n.d.), p. 101.

22. A.L. Kroeber; *Anthropology,* Harcourt, Brace & Co., New York, 1948, p. 207.
23. G.A. Grierson; *Linguistic Survey of India,* Vol. III, Part III, Motilal Banarsidas, p. 3, Delhi, 1967 (reprint).
24. H.I. Marshall; *The Karen People of Burma,* University of Columbus, Ohia, 1972, p. 10.
25. *Ibid.*, p. 5.
26. Charles F. Keys; *The Golden Penninsula,* Macmillan Publishing Co.Inc. New York, 1977, p. 52.
27. H.I. Marshall; *op. cit.* p. 10.
28. (Mrs) N. Chatterji; *Zawlbuk as a Social Institution in the Society*, Tribal Institute, Aizawl, 1975, p. 3.
29. Edwin M. Loeb and Jan O.M. Brock; Social Organization and Long House in Southeast Asia "*American Anthropologist,* By I. Aldin Mason (Ed), Vol. 49 (Jan-March) 1947, No. 1, p. 44.
30. *Ibid,* p. 418.
31. Robert F. Spencer and S.A. Barrett; "Notes on a bachelor House in the South China Area", *American Anthropologists"* by I Aldin Mason, Vol. 50,1948, p. 472.
32. G.M. Godden; The Nagas and other Frontier Tribes of North-East India", *Jaigbi,* Vol. XXVII, 1897, p. 47.
33. *Ibid.*
34. *The Society and Social Changes of the Mizos* by Sangkima, Gauhati University, (Unpublished) 1985.

6

A Study of the Ethnic Origin and Customs of the Nationalities in North-Eastern Area in India

A Comparison between them and Some of the Nationalities in Yunnan and Xizang, China and Northern Burma

Zhu Changli

The north-eastern area in India has long been known as an "ethnic groups museum", which is celebrated for its numerous ethnic groups. Various ethnic groups got into these areas one after another in different periods of time, among whom the Negrito people was the earliest. And among them who followed were the Aryans and the Mongolians. It is due to the mixing together with each other over a long period of time that the constitution of the ethnic groups there has developed certain changes.

The north-eastern area in India is a multi-national one as well. Owing to having not carried out national identification, it has not been clear yet that how many nationalities are there. But the number of ethnic appellations known to us are dozens. These nationalities have been living in different historical periods of social development and they have inherited different material culture and different customs and habits. It would further enrich historical science to make a study of these subjects. It should be especially pointed out that the nationalities in this area in India have close relations in every aspect with those in the south-west China and in northern Burma so that it would be conducive to approaching the history of the nationalities in ancient south-western area in China and in ancient northern area in Burma to get a clear understanding of the history of the nationalities in these areas.

The north-eastern area in India is the meeting ground of South Asia and South-East Asia, which culture possesses not only characteristics of

Indian and South-East Asian culture, but also distinguishing features of its own culture. Hence, it would further get a deeper understanding of Indian culture and South-East Asian culture to make a study of the culture of this area.

At present, studies of the history, nationalities and culture of this area both at home and abroad are very few. This chapter is just making a preliminary inquiry into the ethnic origin and customs and habits of the nationalities there.

I. The Same Ethnic Origin

Historically, the north-eastern area in India belonged toAssam Province. After India's independence, the administrative divisions of this area have undergone changes for several times. Now this area is divided into several States named Assam, Nagaland, Mizoram, Manipur, Meghalaya, Arunachal Pradesh and Tripura. The nationalities there are numerous, but according to a division of languages and ethnic groups, there are roughly three categories.

1. The Assamese who has the largest population among nationalities there, are mainly of Aryan origin and simultaneously mixed together with other native tribes belonging to the Mongoloid groups.
2. The Nagas, the Kukis, the Mizos, the Meiteis, the Mikirs and the Garos belong to the Mongolian and the Tibeto-Burman branch of the Sino-Tibetan language family.
3. The Khasis also belong to the South Asian branch of the Austro-Asiatic language family. In this chapter, however, we are going only to deal with people of the second and third categories, the Assamese being outside the range of the study in this chapter.

With regard to the origin of the name of the Naga nationality, there are different versions, which, to this day, no one appears acceptable. With regard to its ethnic appellation, there have been approximately several explanations as follows. One common version, is that the root of the word Naga stems from *nag* which means "Snake" (also means "cobra"), which derives itself from that the Naga people worship the god of snake. But this version cannot justify itself, as the Naga people don't worship the snake, on the contrary, they have snakes as delicacies. The other version holds that the etymology of the word Naga is *nagna* which means "inhabitants in mountainous regions". The point is there are many inhabitants in this mountainous region, why this word is only applicable to the Naga people, it is beyond explanation. Another version believes that the etymology of the word is *nangta* which means "savages". Finally, some people think that the meaning of the word Naga is "the people", the etymology of which *of nog* or *nok* which in the various tribes in the eastern part means "the people".

"Naga" is a name given by others. It is very likely that this name was used by the plains people. The Naga people themselves do not use this appellation, they only use the name of their tribe, for example, the tribe which is generally named Ankami by others call themselves Tanjimia, the Kacha tribe Meichimu, the Sima tribe Simi, and so on.[1]

The origin of the word "Kuki" is not known yet. Some people think that this word was initially written in the Bengali language as "cuci", meaning "mountainous people in Tripura"[2] The Kuki nationality which is now called so is an appellation called by others. The wofd "Kuki" is used in Bengali and in the ancient Assamese language. "Kuki" has a disdainful meaning, which the Kuki people themselves have never used. In Manipur, they are called "Saduo" which has the same meaning as "Kuki". Those who belong to the same nationality are called "Chin" in Burma which means "friends" or "partners".

The word "Mizo means "mountaineers" or "highlanders". "The Mizo nationality "is only used as ethnic appellation for some of those tribes who live in Mizoram, Manipur, Kachar and the Chin mountainous area in Burma who are very similar to each other in language, customs and way of life. The Mizo nationality is also named the Lusai people. "Lusai" is a name of sub-tribe of the Mizo nationality who have long been in a dominant position in the Mizo nationality. Hence, later on, some people name the Mizo nationality as "Lusai" while the Mizo people name themselves Dzo or Zho.

As to the origin of the ethnic appellation of the Meitei nationality, there are several versions as well. One version holds that "Meitei" is a collective noun, originating from (Mi=man) and *Thei* (=separation). The other version thinks that Meitei is a combination of two words, i.e., *Tai* in Siamese and Moy in Kachin language, and holds that the Meitei nationality belongs to Moi which they call themselves, a branch of the *Tai* nationality, namely, the tribal clan which is called Shan in Burmese. But more evidences show that the Meitei nationality does not belong to the Tai nationality, the version, therefore, is difficult to be accepted.[3]

As for the Mikir nationality, "Mikir" is the designation called by the Assamese, they call themselves *Alen,* meaning "man".[4]

The origin of the ethnic appellation of the Garo nationality has long been a point at issue. Someone holds that "Garo" initially stems from the word "*Gala*" which is a name of a branch of an ethnic group called "Garo" and who were the first the European had contacted. Later on, the whole nationality might have been called "Gala". But afterwards, the name was relayed incorrectly from place to place and, as a result, Gala had become Garo ! "Gala" was changed into "Garp". The other version holds that it is related to the immigration of the Zang nationality. It is said that "Garu" was the earliest leader who led the tribe in their immigration had named the tribe after his own name so that afterwards "Garu" had changed into "Garo". But the Garo nationality generally does not use this appellation, they are always calling themselves *Achik,* meaning mountaineers, or *Mande,* meaning warriors, or *Achikmande,* meaning mountainous warriors.[5]

The Khasi nationality is also called *Khaciya,* the meaning of which is not clear. The Khasi people call themselves dwellers in seven shed or in seven dwelling places, about which a legend says that god dispatched six of sixteen tribes to go down to Man's world as rulers.[6]

The ethnic origin of the above-mentioned nationalities is an issue of an endless debate over a long period of time. It is extremely difficult for one to straighten out the ethnic origin of these nationalities, as the historical data concerned are very few. In this chapter, we can just put forward a few superficial views on this issue on an analysis of the materials which we have at present.

We may as well divide the ethnic origin of those nationalities into 3 categories to make things convenient for our observation and study. Those who belong to the first category are Naga, Kuki, Mizo, Meitei and Mikir. The Garo nationality belongs to the second category and the Khasi nationality to third category. All of them have a host of legends circulated to this day among the people and most of these involve their ethnic origin which are for precious materials.

Every tribe of the Naga nationality has various legends concerning their ethnic origin from which we can find out a common ground that the Naga nationality came from the east. An ancient legend is current among the Tankhul Naga People, which states that "there were two brave brothers who led a contingent of troops and came from 'the east of the world' and who were trying to find a suitable place to live. Owing to weariness, they decided to get a place for having a rest. They found a place, but soon they felt very scorching there and found that there were poisonous insects all over the place. They did not like the place and decided to find a better one. They made up their mind to go on another expedition, but they had to divide the troops into two contingents, each of which was to be led by the two brothers respectively. The elder brother named `Nahaga', which means`a very brave boy' in Tankhul tribe's dialect, led his contingent and boldly drove on south-eastward. The expeditionary contingent led by the younger brother, were very tired after the long journey and eager to find a place. Finally settled down on the fertile flat land known now as Manipur valley. Meanwhile, the elder brother led his contingent on. Finally, they settled down in between the Mao tribe and the Ankami tribe. The troops under their command gradually spread out to other places in that area, which are now known as the "Naga mountainous regions."[7]

This legend talked about that the Naga nationality came from "the east of the world" which is very likely the area between Xizang and Yunnan, China. Judging from the place of Mt. Naga, the area between Xizang and Yunnan is to the east of Mt. Naga. Some of the folktales of the Naga nationality "have mentioned *Nchinme* which means China. Hence, it is very likely that they emigrated to Assam from north-east a number of centuries ago during the time of the great Mongolian migration in colonies.[8]

Someone else hold that "the place of origin of the Naga people was north-eastern Xizang and it seems that they were driven to Assam from the south by the Kukis, Lusais, Chins who followed in the wake."[9]

In the above-mentioned legend, it is mentioned that the Naga people did not like the scorching flatlands, which shows that they probably came from a high and cold area which is very likely the Xizang Plateau.

In the legends concerning the origin of other tribes of the Naga nationality, it is said that they had a place of origin in between the settlements of the Mao Tribe and the Malan tribe, namely, the village ten miles south-east of Kohima town. The village is called Makir Village or Meik by foreigners while the Ankami Naga people call it Meikolomili, meaning "place of departure", which is the second peak of Mt. Naga called Capuf. In the legends of the Ankami, Sima, Lota Tankhul, Mao, Manipur Naga people and the Somu Naga, Mao people, they all claim that the Meikir Village and its nearby regions were place of origin of all their own tribes respectively. The Manipur Naga, especially the Tankhul Mao, Malam, Koylo and the Malin people hold that their (including the Meitei people's) ancestral home is the Meikir Village.[10]

Another legend of the Ankami tribe tells that the Kuki, Lusai, Meitei and the Naga people initially belonged to a tribal clan. The ancestor of the present day Ankami people was the eldest brother, the ancestor of the

Lusai-Kuki people was the second eldest brother and the ancestor of the Meitei people was the youngest brother. These three brothers with their family members had once found a place for them to have settled down, but after they stayed for a certain period of time they suddenly separated. The eldest brother took the lead and acted as a guide, the two younger brothers followed closely. As they came across a tract of land all over with bananas. The eldest brother fell many bananas for the purpose of opening a way through the bananas for them to go forward. But at this very moment the two younger brothers were very far from the eldest brother. The two younger brothers were unable to catch up with him when the eldest brother again fell more bananas and went on forward while there were no footprints left all along the way. Thus, the eldest brother went farther and farther. Thereupon, the two younger brothers with their family members chose respectively their individual way to go forward. Then, in the course of time, they were called the Lusai people, the Kuki people and the Meitei people. The eldest brother and his descendants were later called the Tenjim people (but outsiders called them the Ankami people) who settled down at Meiklomia (namely the Meikir Village). But after their settling down there for a number of years, they sensed that the place was narrow and limited so that they began to move in a north-eastward direction and settled down in their present-day habitat Ankami.[11]

There are more similar legends which show that in the course of their movement the Nagas had once lived at the Meikir Village for a certain period of time before they left there and were dispersed over to other places. This also shows to a certain extent that the Naga, Mizo, Kuki, the Meitei and other minority nationality have a connection in their ethnic origin. Hence, in addition to their almost identical languages, there are many similarities in other aspects.

With regard to the ethnic origin of the Meitei people, there is a similar version that they "are considered that they belonged to the Sino-Tibetan language family in north-eastern China, originally living in the area of the upper reaches of the Changjiang (Yangtze) River and the Huanghe River. As they moved to settle down in Upper Burma, they were divided into two sub-language branches. The first is the Tibeto-Burman branch,."[12]

There is a close relation between the Meiteis and the Nagas. It is considered that they were initially a common group formerly had similar habits, rules, customs and beliefs. The Meiteis who later accepted Hinduism, still retain some of their past customs and habits. Formerly, on the occasion of the coronation of the chiefs and queens, they wore the

Naga costumes. The grand hall in which the chief lived was built *ala* Naga style. His attendants followed him with sword and spear in hands in Naga style.[13]

A legend of the Kuki people says that "they initially lived in a place named Sinlung which was in south-eastern China, but later natural calamities forced them to move to the Shan state in north-eastern Assam and to settle down there." An ancient folk song now still sung among the people verifies this legend. This folk song is as follows:

> My Chin land of old,
> My grandfather's land Himalei (the Himalayas),
> My grandfather's way excels,
> Chinlung's (Chin rock) way excels.[14]

This ballad has explained the origin of the Mizo, the Meitei and the Chin as well as that of Kuki nationality. It suggests that ethnic groups like the Kukis, Meiteis and the Chins had for long lived together in the same place where now only the Chins live. The Kukis and the Meiteis might have left that place subsequently.

Thus it can be seen from the above narration that the origin of these nationalities said in the legends are very close.

Historically, the Garo nationality belonged to the Boduo group. This colony included Kachali people including the Kochi, the Meitch, the Garo, the Lalung, the Laba and the Dimasa people. "It was thought that their native place was the intermediate zone between the upper reaches of the Changjiang (Yangtze) River and the Huanghe River in China. In remote antiquity, their nomadic groups moved to and settled down in Assam and northern Bengal and went westward as far as Tipeila.[15]

In the legends of the Garo nationality, they did not trace back to their more remote history, they only mentioned that their initial native place was Xizang. With regard to their route moving from Xizang to Assam, there are different versions. Someone think that they went along the route the other ethnic groups had taken, that is to say, they got into India from north-east of the Himalayas. Someone believe that they got into India from west of the Himalayas. If we take into account the distribution areas of the Bodou groups, then, it is more likely that they got into India from west of the Himalayas. The legends of the Garo people mentioned that when they were out of Xizang, "they got into flatlands by the foot of the Himalayas, then went on moving eastward in search of pasture to the Brahmaputra Valley, and then returned along the original road to the flatlands situated in between the Valley and hills where they live now.

Evidently, they had settled down in the flatlands for a certain period of time before they migrated to the present-day native place of the Garo ethnic groups, the Garo mountain area."[16]

The language of the Garo nationality is very close to the language of the Zang nationality. In his book *The Garos*, Mr. A. Playfair has made a comparison between the Garo language and the Zang language and says that many words and expressions between these two languages are very similar.[17]

The customs of the Garo nationality are also related to those of the Zang nationality, the most evident one is that the Garo people traditionally treasure yaks when there is no such cattle in the areas where the Garo people live. They have to use yak tails whenever they have *Jileiwata* dance. In their words of songs they are always mentioning yak tails. Whenever they are asked that how they know such an animal, they are always telling you in earnest that the custom of making use of yak tails has been handed down from their ancestors. They even tell you that those yak tails which they are using now were brought along by the earliest migrants. They also use yak tails to decorate their sword handles and look upon them as treasures. The Garo people call yak as Meichik or Tanglu, the former of which is quite close to the name Meichu which the Garo people call their native cattle.[18] Why do they respect yak ever so much? Why do they make use of yak tails? And why do they use the name of yak to call their native cattle? If there has been no traditional reason for explaining it, then, it would be very difficult for one to explain it.

As for the origin of the Khasi nationality, owing to there being few data and investigating of it so little, it remains still a question unsettled. The Khasi people hold that they initially came from other place. One version is that they came from the north and had Syhlet as their terminal point of their nomadic activities where they met with the menace of flood in that they got into the now Khasi mountain area. The other version is that they originally got into Assam from Burma *via* Mt. Batky which is one of the routes from Burma to Assam.[19] The second version is more likely, because they had long been loyal to the King of Burma.

There are similar versions among the nationalities who belong to the Tibeto-Burman language branch in northem Burma. The Chin nationality got into Burma in earlier period of time from the north-east.[20] It is said among the Kachin people that their ancestors lived in "Magwaisingyabong", meaning "a smooth mountain top". This area is no other than the high and cold area where Xizang is bounded on the east by Sichuan in China. They moved southward from the north. First of all, they arrived in the high mountain ridges where Burma, Xizang and Assam meet. They later went on moving southward, progressively they got into within the boundaries of Burma.[21]

In the above-mentioned analyses on the ethnic origins, they all mentioned the south-western area in China. Now let us deal with the nationality distributions in ancient south-west China in the light of annals in Chinese historical records which may be conducive to inquiring into the ethnic origin of nationalities in this vast area.

In the Han Dynasty, all the inhabitants in the three regions which then called Qiongdu, Dian and Kunming which included the now area of Kunming and Dali in Yunnan and the now area of Liangshan and Xichang in Sichuan, belonged to the ancient Qiang language branch which later developed into Tibeto-Burman language branch. In his paper "A Brief Account of the Ethnic Groups Society in South-west China from Warring States Period to the Early Days of the Han Dynasty", Professor Fang Guoyu says in "Chapter on Western Qiang Biography in History of the Later Han Dynasty" says "Those whose descendants might be any ethnic group on their own as they liked or might even take yak as their ethnic name were the Qiang nationality in 'Yuexi county, Sichuan". The Yak Qiang nationality was in Shu-Han, a state of Three Kingdoms, whose tribe names were too many to remember." Those were the ancient Qiang people who had migrated to south-west China, dispersed over a vast area, and had many names. Qiongdu, Dian and Kunming all were the dispersed areas of the ancient Qiang people, only their tribe names were too different. Professor Fang adds that "The time when the ancient Qiang People migrated to these three regions was very, very early, it was in the latter part of the Neolithic Age at the latest.[22] It can be seen from the above analysis that in ancient times, the ancient Qiangs were distributed over most parts of Yunnan, from the Kunming area to South-western Yunnan, and then extending to the ancient Ailao tribes regions. According to *Hua Yang Guo Zhi* by Changqu in the Jin Dynasty, "the ancient Ailao kingdom in Yongchang Prefecture was named after Mt. Ailao. The area of which was 3,000 li across from east to west and 4,600 li from north to south where lived the Chuanxiong, the Min, the Yue, the Pu, the Gelo people, and so on and so forth, the chiefs of whom were all called king. Ming emperor set up a prefecture there and appointed Zhengchun, governor of Shu Prefecture. Its governor. Among the inhabitants were the Minpus, the Gelos, the Yues the Pus, Indians."[23]

According to these records, the ancient Ailao Kingdom was really a vast area, for "its area was 3,000 li across from east to west and 4,600 li from north to south", which had present-day Baoshan County as its centre, extending westward to the extensive region to the west of the Irrowaddy River and southward to the area to the south of Fengqing, Licang and Xishuangbanna. The ancient Ailao people was a general designation of numerous tribes. With regard to their ethnic origin, our academic circles hold different views which might be reduced to 3 categories. One is that in the light of the level of the social and cultural development of the Ailao people and their tattoo custom, they should be ancestors of the Dai nationality. The other is that since the Southern Zhao "were originally later generations of the Ailao people" and the Southern Zhao Meng She belonged to the Yi language branch, so, the Ailao people should be a branch of the Yi nationality. Another is that since the distribution regions of the Ailao people were mainly in the distribution are of the Va-Banglong language branch and the Pu people were related to the Puzimans and the Pus, so the Ailao people should belong to the Va-Benglong language branch.[24] Yet these questions remain to be further studied. Besides, someone hold that in the ancient Ailao areas lived "not only the nationalities of the Yi language branch and the Dai language branch, but also the nationalities of the Va-Benglong language branch. The above-mentioned *flua Yang Guo* Zhi also says in explicit terms that `in the ancient Ailao Kingdom in Yongchang prefecture.... lived the Minpur, the Gelos, the Yues,.... the Pus,.... Indians'. Though these nationalities remain to be further studied, yet it is no doubt that what they are referred to are the various nationalities of the above-mentioned three language branches. Therefore, the Ailao people was the general designation of the native nationalities who belonged to the three language branches. As a result, the social development level and customs of the Ailao people were the synthesis of those of the native nationalities who belonged to the three language branches."[25]

The above analysis, I think, has something to recommend it. The distribution conditions of the tribes in this region in the Tang Dynasty might, to some extent, prove this point. From the seventh to tenth centuries, in Yongchang region, the ethnic appellations were numerous and complicated. Among them were Youwang, Wangjuzi, Wangwaiyu, Puzi, Mumianpu, Chikoupu, Xiujiao, Xiumian, Xunzhuan, Mexie, and so on. "Wang" and "Va" which the "Va" nationality call themselves, and `Vo' and `Vu', are all having voiced fricalive sound as consonants, only having vowels making changes. `Wang' and `Va" only vary in sound end. Till now, some of the Va people still call themselves `Wang'. `Wang' is what the nationality call themselves. `Ju' is Yi language while `Zi' is Chinese, therefore, it is very likely that 'Wangjuzi' is the appellation written down by the Han people to show what Southern Zhao called the Wang people. Hence, we may reasonably conclude that Wang and Wangwaiyu;., are the same ethnic group, i.e., the latter Va nationality. 'Puzi' has been generally identified as the Iater Pu people and Puman (i.e., Blang). But according to the records in *Man Shu* by Fanchuo, 'Yueshanpuzi', who lived in the place to the west of the Lancang River, belonged to the Wangjuzi nationality'. The then Puzi must not have been only later Puman, but also a general designation of all the nationalities who belonged to the Va-Benglong language branch. 'The Xiujiao people tattooed them from ankle to calf of the leg' and the Xiumian people., all of them were named after their tattooing custom. Since the Dai people have the custom of tattooing, therefore, the above-mentioned nationalities who had the tattooing custom should be considered as the Dai nationality. 'Xunzhuan' is the ethnic appellation of the Achang nationality or the Jingpo nationality. 'Mexie' is the Naxi nationality."[26]

It can be held that in the ancient Ailao region lived the tribes of the Tibeto-Burman language branch, the Zhuang-Dai language branch and the Meng-Khmer language branch, so that it is only natural that they were moving step by step towards Assam when some areas of Assam might have been probably within the boundaries of the Ailao Kingdom because the then Ailao Kingdom was "3,000 li across from east to west" where even lived Indians.

According to the legends of the Naga nationality, the Kuki nationality, the Garo nationality and so on who belonged to the Tibeto-Burman language branch, their coming from north-west and south-west China just allies with the version that the ancient Qiang people in China were moving south-westward. Thus it proves that their legends are with good grounds. The Garo people also say that their ethnic origin was related to the Zang nationality when our academic circles generally hold that ancestors of the Zang nationality were the ancient Qiang people. It should be said that the ancient Qiang people were ancestors of the Zang nationality, but it does not follow that we should equate the historically recorded ancient Quiang people with a certain modern so-and-so nationality. Because there are differences as well as connections between these two. Let us take the Naga people for instance, owing to their mixing together with the native people for a long period of time, they finally became such a modern nationality. There are comparatively big anthropologically characteristics between the Naga tribes. "Theirs are mainly the yellow race characteristics, but the differences are in hair (They have all the kinds of hair, straight, wavy and curly hair.), height, skin, eyeball colour, and so on, are very conspicuous." Culturally, they have many different points as well. "For example, the Naga people in western part have no tattoo custom, but among the Naga people in central and eastern part, tattooing is very common. The Naga people in western part bury the deceased while those in central and eastern part lay the corpse on a special platform made of bamboo. The Naga people in western part like to erect a monument made of an integral rock, but those in eastern part are not doing so,"[27] and so on and so forth: What has been mentioned here proves that the Naga people have been mixed together with other nationalities' compositions.

In addition, in the vast region across from Assam to Northern Burma and Dian Lake, Erhai Lake in Yunnan, they have excavated stone axes with shoulders or stone axes with handles, all of which are roughly similar in shape[28] and "those stone implements are very close to the cultural system of the ancient Qiang people, especially closer to the Qijia culture the centre of which is south-western Gansu",[29] and proves that the ethnic origin in this area in ancient times might be the same.

The above exposition shows that there is a great similarity between the tribes distribution in Assam and that in ancient Ailao region and the origin of the nationalities of the Tibeto-Burman language branch can be traced back to the ancient Qiang people. As to the nationalities of the Meng-Khmer language branch, they were distributed, in the earliest times, over South-east Asia and south-western Yunnan who must have got into Assam from the ancient Ailao region and northern Burma. It can be seen from various indications that the nationalities in ancient Assam were an important ethnic groups who had exerted a very important influence on other nationalities. The nationalities of the Zhuang-Dai language branch were also distributed, in the earliest times, over South-east Asia and south-western Yunnan, China, while a branch of the Shan nationality, who had got into Assam from northern Burma in the thirteenth century, also exerted a great influence on other nationalities.

II. Similar Customs and Habits

If we contrast the customs and habits of above-mentioned various nationalities with each other, then, it is not difficult for us to find out that there are many similarities between them which can show us from another aspect the relative membership of the same clan between these nationalities. Of course, we should also notice that these nationalities, who have, from ancient times to modern times, distributed over so vast a region and dispersed over so different countries, have progressively lost their original common national traits. And it is only natural that they have been being influenced by other native nationalities, as a result, they have been evolving their individual national traits.

1. Communal House

Many nationalities of the Tibeto-Burman language branch have historically kept this custom. They generally call it *Deka-chang* which means Village Club for young people. The Naga people cal it *Morung,* the Mizo people *Zawlbuks,* the Mikir people *Malo*, the Garo people *Nok-pates.* In the *Deka-Chang,* the young people undergo various training, fostering their moral character. Of course, this is also a place for the young people, male and female, to talk love and pay court to each other

The Communal house of various nationalities is much alike except for slight difference, Let us introduce you to the communal house customs of the Zemi people and the Naga for your reference. "Each village has at least two communal houses: (a) *Hagesaiki,* i.e., 'blockhouse for youngsters', (b) *Lunsaiki,* i.e., 'blockhouse for women'. The collective appellation for the club members is *Kienka.* Every Zemi youth, boys and girls, is a member of *Keinka* from the day of their birth,. Every boy and girl, who grows to seven or eight, has to spend the night in the communal house. If the young people beyond this age still sleep in his parents house, he or she will be considered as a loss of face. A girl works at home in the day time, but has to spend the night in the communal house where she learns, under the guidance of the hostess there, dancing, spinning and weaving, and embroidering. The front of the hostess building is used as communal house. The hostess is their housewife and leader.

"Boys spend all their time in the communal house, only go home for meals or stay at home owing to sickness. No wonder the communal house exerts strong influences on their disposition's taking shape. The leader of the boys club is called Kazepei who is their tutor and commander and whose order they must obey. The boys are engaged in their preparations for the struggle for their living and they learn, under the guidance of Kazepei, grappling, dancing, singing, making baskets and other handicrafts. The communal house for boys is also annexed to the front of the Kazepei's dwelling house.". The boy's making his court to a girl begins in the communal house, which leads eventually to a marriage. A youngster in the communal house for boys goes on the quiet at night to the communal house for girls to lie down by his lover's side whom he is to differentiate if she is his own lover or not, and doing this, may be one way is to scent her smell. Unless the girl's parents strongly oppose it, otherwise, his paying court to her at night will keep going and end in a marriage."[30]

The Kachin nationality of the Tibeto Burman language branch distributed over northern Burma have also the similar communal house customs.[31]

Similarly, the Jingpo, the Lisu, the Naxi nationality, the Hani and the Axi people of the Yi nationality, all of whom belong to the Tibeto-Burman language branch, had communal house custom in the past, especially the communal house of the Axi people was comparatively typical.

In the village where the Axi people live, "they have two communal houses built by collectivity. One is '*Amuliruoyid*', meaning the sleeping place for girls; the other is called '*Chuliruoyid*', meaning the sleeping place for boys. These two communal houses are situated in the centre of the village which has a certain reasonal layout

"According to the customs of the local people, boys and girls, after their thirteen or fourteen, work and live together with their parents in the day time, at night leave their parents and go to the communal house. But the brother and sister are to be separated according to sexual distinction, females go to the communal house for girls, males go to that for boys. The young people, in the communal house, talk about ancient or modern matters, interchange skills of production, and go in for recreational activities. At night, boys go one after another to the communal house for girls of other villages and the communal house for girls of their own village is left for other village youngsters."[32]

According to the Lisu custom, those young people who are beyond twelve, "male or female, have to go to the communal house for night, if they would not go; his or her parents will consider him or her as having no ability. Whenever evening comes, the unmarried young people, boys and girls, go to the communal house for nights."[33]

2. Worship of Stone

The Meiteis, Mizos, the Nagas and others in Assam, believe that all things on earth have a soul each. They worship stones, which they believe, are embodiments of gods and are of supernatural force. The Meitei people enshrine and worship black stones, taking them as goddesses. The Naga people enshrine and worship monotithes. Similar worships are also found sometimes among the Nu people and the Jingpo people in Yunnan. The

Ancient Qiang people worshipped stones as well, especially white stones. It is said that the ancient Qiang people could not win the battle against the Geji people. A god hinted them in a dream to use white stones as weapons and they will win. The Qiang people won the battle as expected. The Qiang people were to repay the god, but no one knew the image of the god, so they used white stone to stand for the god and offered sacrifices to him from generation to generation.[34] The ethnic groups who worship stone take stones as gods who may befall good fortunes or misfortunes on people.

3. Cremation

The Garo nationality, the Mizo nationality and some branches of the Kuki people in the Assam region cremate the deceased. The Mikir people even wrap the unburned bones in a cloth and bury it. This custom is prevalent over the areas, in Yunnan, where the Nu, Lahu, Naxi, Bai; and the Hani people live. This custom must have been related to that of their ancestors, the Qiang people. Tai Ping Yu Lan quoted in Zhuang Zi Yi Pian, saying that "the Qiangs died, they fired the corpse and winnowed the ashes of the dead."[35] The Kachin people in northern Burma are also practising cremation, the difference is that they bury the dead and cremate it when it decays. Some branches of the Chin people have the customs of cremation as well.

4. Drinking Rice Wine

The above-mentioned nationalities all have the habits of drinking rice wine, which has become one of their very important hobbies. They are drinking at ordinary times, but they would drink deep at festivals. As a result, they will consume a lot of grain every year and their skill of making rice wine is also comparatively simple. This custom may have been for ages.

5. They do not drink Milk

The above-mentioned nationalities raise milch cow for meat, they never drink milk.

6. A Younger Brother may Marry an Elder Brother's Widow

The Kuki nationality and the Dimasa Kachali people (the same ethnic origin as the Garo nationality) have this custom. In the Kuki nationality, a younger brother may marry an elder brother's widow, no matter how old she is. But an elder brother cannot marry a younger brother's wife.[36]

The Dimasa Kachali people have the similar custom and a man may marry his wife's sister. The Kachin nationality in northern Burma and the Yi, Bai, Jingpo, Drung, Naxi nationality in Yunnan and the Qiang nationality in Sichuan have the same custom.

The above has shown the contrast between the customs of the nationalities of the Tibeto-Burman language branch in this area. Now let us have a contrast between those of the nationalities of the Meng-Khmer language branch and the Va-Benglong language branch.

Both the Khasi nationality in Assam and the Va nationality in north Burma and Yunnan belong to the Va-Benglong language branch,[37] whose customs are quite similar as well. The glaring one is man's head hunting. Now, except that the Va people in northern Burma keep vestigies of this corrupt customs, the other nationalities have all abolished it. In the past, they all offered man's heads to gods for getting blessings from them. But the legends and practices of the various nationalities were not all the same.

When the British initially occupied Mt. Khasi, they saw the Khasi people dancing around a sacrificial altar with man's heads on it which were their spoils of war. The Khasi people would often offer man's heads to gods, praying for victory in a war. They also worship a god of snake named U Thlen and used man's heads as sacrificial offerings.[38]

There is such a legend in the Va nationality in northern Burma. It says that "two men came out of a cave which belonged to the Pagdai Va people. One was named Dali, the other Yanan. The two were to go to Leileng. During their rest on the way, the. eldest son (or nephew) was grinding his sword when he intended to cut Yaman's hair for the purpose of having a try of the edge of his sword. Unexpectedly, what he cut down was no other than a man's head. Hence, he thought that this showed that gods needed man's heads, as a result, from then on, the custom of cutting man's heads to offer to gods became a common practice. They held that cutting man's heads to offer to gods not only could reduce man's death but also could bring about bumper harvest and economic prosperity."[39]

As to man's head hunting, there are several versions in the Va nationality in Yunnan. One is that in the course of their migration, mankind had met with flood before they cut man's head to offer to gods. The other is that long, long ago, mankind suffered natural and man-made calamities. Men and livestock died in great numbers. Millet could not grow well. The man offered various beasts' heads to ghosts and gods, but no effects appeared. Afterwards, they cut man's head to offer to ghosts to get rid of disasters.[40]

III. Each Other's Influences

Within the scope of our study the Tibeto-Burman language branch; the Meng-Khmer language branch and the Zhuang-Dai language branch have historically exerted influences on each other, among which especially the influence of the Va-Benglong language sub-branches of the Meng-Khmer language branch in earlier period and the influence of the Zhuang-Dai language branch in later period are conspicuous. The influence of the former on others is mainly in customs and habits while the influence of the latter on others is concentrated on formation of society.

A variety of indications show that the nationalities of the Va-Benglong language sub-branches of the Meng Khmer language branch were on both ancient and powerful ones which had exerted important influences on others in this region.

The Man's head hunting practice mostly took place originally among the Va people of the Va-Benglong language sub-branches of the Meng-Khmer language branch. Then, why was there such a similar custom in the Naga nationality, the Garo nationality, the Kuki nationality and the Mizo nationality of the Tibeto-Burman language branch? It is likely that they were influenced by the Va nationality and others.

A legend about "Sigangli" is current among the Va people relating to the origin of mankind. According to the explanation of the Va nationality in Simen, Yunnan, "Sigang" was a stone cave, "Li" meant "to come out", meaning that mankind came out from a stone cave. They say that the first one who came out from the stone cave was the Va nationality, then in turns the Han, Lahu and the Dai nationality. The last one who came out from the stone cave was the San nationality (possibly the Shan). According to the explanation of the Va nationality in Cangyuan, "Sigang" was a bottlegourd, "Li" meant "to come out", meaning that mankind came out from a bottlegourd."[41] Similar, legend is also current in the Naga and Mizo nationalities.

There is a legend circulating in the Mizo nationality, saying that "Their ancestors appeared in Qing Long Cave. According to this legend, long, long ago, a sort of forces of darkness befell on the earth and a disaster followed. In this disaster, all the men were turned into 'various animals and the life of people in the world would come to an end. When people began to appear in Qing Long Cave, they also found that people reappeared on the earth. When this process kept on appearing, some clans emerged. Gods saw that there were many, many people on the earth so that they stopped up the cave with a slab of stone.[42]

Some tribes of the Naga nationality, such as the Fumu tribe, who hold that "they initially came out from Kubaik Cave where they had lived.[43]

The Dae sub-tribe of the Naga nationality in Burma say that their ancestors "originally lived in the earth's crust who bred many kinds of livestock, such as chickens, ducks, pigs, dogs, buffaloes, oxes and "Nao" cattle. Deiman Haman Naga had let an old thin ox bump against and break the earth's crust before the Naga people came on the Surface of the earth. Thereupon Deiman Haman became the ruler of Naga who set up a "Dan Nao" Village which existed to this day in Naga mountain area in India.[44]

The Xunmanla sub-tribe of the Naga nationality living in Burma say that they had come out of bottlegourd. "In ancient times, a flood submerged the land, mankind ancestors suffered a lot. Among the refugees were a young brother and a young sister who found a queer frog being stepped on soon, they could not bear to see it to be done so and they moved the frog to a safe place. Suddenly the frog spoke to them, asking them to climb up "Mengla" tree for the purpose of avoiding the flood disaster. They joyfully climbed up the tree. After the flood receded, they built a small house to live in. Afterwards, a god from heaven hinted them in a dream to get married. Not long the wife was pregnant and gave birth to a bottlegourd. The gourd grew larger and larger. Progressively it could be heard that there were baby's cries in it. The husband cut open the gourd, out came many, many small people with wounds who were ancestors of the Naga people."[45]

There is a custom of a nimbly butchering cattle among the Va people in Yunnan, as important sacrificial religious rites. Whenever they meet with natural and man-made calamities, they perform this to dispel disasters and avoid misfortunes. For example, in a rite of offering man's heads to ghosts, they would often kill nimbly an ox and several buffaloes. The meat is to be snatched to eat by people. The scene of snatching meat is very alarmingly dangers. There is similar custom among the Naga and Garo people when a cremation ceremony for the dead is held. They tie the bull to be killed to a post with fork and kill the bull to be offered when the cremation is finishing soon.

Among the Khasi people, to find a rough monolith as a monument in memory of the deceased is in vogue. In other nationalities, such as the Nagas, the Mikirs and the Mizos, they also use a rock to be a monument, but the scale is not the same as the Khasi people.

The above examples show that the nationalities of the Va-Benglong language subbranches of the Meng-Khmer language branch, especially the Va nationality, have exerted great influences on other nationalities, and also show that they had, in the earliest times, distributed over this area. To this day, the Va nationality is still distributed over Yunnan, China and northern Burma so that it can be thought that they must have been so powerful a nationality, distributing over so vast an area, but, later on, somehow or other, they have become a minority nationality. If not so, then, it would be very difficult for one to explain that how they could exert so important influences on others.

It can be seen from the above analyses that the ethnic origin of the nationalities in this area in ancient times was the same, only later on, it was owing to the different geographical and social environments that different nationalities came into being, but who still retain a certain common traits which provide for us clues for studying their history.

NOTES

1. *Cf. M.* Horma, *The Naga Polity,* 1975, pp. 21-24.
2. *Cf.* "The Tribes of the Brahmaputra Valley", *Journal of the Asiatic Society of Bengal,* 1900, Vol. LXIX.
3. Cf. T.C. Hodson, *The Meiteis,* second edition, 1975, pp. 10-11.
4. S. Barkataki, *Tribes of Assam,* 1969, p. 50.
5. A. Playfair, *The Garos,* second edition, 1975, pp. 7-8.
6. *See* No. 4, p. 34.
7. M. Horam, *The Naga Polity,* 1975, pp. 25-26.
8. *See* No. 4, p. 74.
9. Stephen Faches, *Aboriginal Tribes in India,* 1977, p. 34.
10. *See* No. 1, p. 31.
11. *Ibid., p.* 31.
12. *Folklore* (India), Monthly, in English, January 1982.
13. *See* No. 1, pp. 42-43.
14. *See* No. 4, p. 72.
15. *Ibid.*, pp. 63-64.
16. *See* No. 5, p. 8.
17. *Ibid., pp.* 165-166.
18. *Ibid., pp.* 13-14.
19. *Cf.* P.R.T. Goodon, The Khasis, 1975, second edition, p. 10.
20. *Cf. Burmese Nationalities in Burma Encyclopedia.*
21. *Cf. The Kachin State and the Kachin Nationality in Burma Encyclopedia.*
22. *Collected Paper of Yunnan History Research Institute,* 1982, No. 1, p. 18.
23. *Quoted in Edition of History and Annals of the Nationality Va (draft), edited by the Institute for Nationalities, One volume the Chinese Academy of Sciences,* 1963, pp. 24-25.

24. *Cf. Ibid.*, p. 26.
25. *Ibid.*, p. 27.
26. *See* No. 23, pp. 27-28.
27. *The Naga Tribes in Minority Nationalities in South Asia,* edited by the Orient Institute (U.S.S.R.), 1978, Russian edition.
28. *See* No. 9, pp. 10, 29. *cf.* The Short History and Annals of the Yi Nationality, one volume edition edited by the Institute for Nationalities, the Chinese Academy of Science, 1963, pp. 19-20.
29. Fang Guoyu, 'A Brief Account of the Ethnic Groups Society in south-west China from Warring States Period to Early Days of the Han Dynasty', *Collected Papers of Yunnan Institute of History*, 1982, No. 1, p. 19.
30. See No. 4, pp. 75-76.
31. The Kachin people build a thatched cottage on a conspicuous hillside between villages. These cottages stand alone at the centre of two villages for young people, male and female, to be engaged in social activities and to talk, love and pay court to each other. Those who come of age and are unmarried hardly spend the night at his or her own home. Especially they make it a rigid rule on the basis of traditional customs that those girls who are unmarried have to go to the communal house called 'Molada' in Chin language to spend the night.
32. Yan Ruxian, Song Zhaolin, *The Matriarchy of the Naxi Nationality in Yongring,* Yunnan People's Publishing House, 1983. p. 23.
33. *An Investigation of the Social History of the Lisu Nationality,* Yunnan People's Publishing House, 1981, p. 20.
34. *Annals of Customs of Minority Nationalities in Southwest China,* Yunnan Folk Literature and Art Publishing House, 1981, pp. 283-284.
35. *Ibid.*, p. 282.
36. *Cf.* The Tribes of the Bramaputra Valley, *Journal of the Asiatic Society of Bengal,* 1900, Vol. LXIX.
37. *Cf. A Manual of Population of World Countries (U.S.S.R.),* Chinese translation, p. 482.
38. *Cf.* see No. 19, pp. 97-102.
39. *The Va Region and the Va Nationality in Burma,* p. 43.
40. A summary Report of An Investigation of the Social Economy of the Va Nationality in Simeng, Yunnan, March 1958, p. 78.
41. *Cf.* see No. 23, pp. 10-11.
42. S. Barkataki, *The Tribes of Assam,*1969, p. 82.
43. See No. 1, p. 33.
44. Qiu Wen, A Collection of Folk Songs of the Naga Nationality, *People's Daily (Burma),* 30 July, 1961.
45. *Ibid.*

7

Lungphun

As a Source of Mizo History

Romesh Buragohain

I

The Mizo minority nationality has come to political limelight after Mizoram becoming one of the States of the Union of India. Following a long period of traumatic struggle for independence, the Mizos distinguished themselves as a distinct hill minority people amongst the multitudes of Indian nationalities. Thus they joined the family of Indian nationhood only a few years back. The Mizos, now being intertwined into the wheel of pan-Indian nationalism, has added new colour and dimensions to India's problems and issues of the minority nationalities. But her history and culture, particularly of the pre-British period, still remains to be fully explored. She is still a *terra incognita* as far as her history and culture is concerned. It is in this context, that I have made this very humble attempt to focus on the Lungphun system of the early Mizos as a source material of Mizo history and culture even though it might be very thin and remote for the purpose. This is because of immense historical limitations that we face in the reconstruction of a comprehensive history of Mizoram.

One such limitation is the extremely limited sources. The floklores of Mizoram are yet to be compiled, documented and examined. Other sources, whatever we have, all belong to the post-colonial period, in terms of monographs, stray accounts and some ethnological narratives, left by the colonial rulers of pre-independence days. In the post-indepence period, several research works have been produced but these do not totally sum up to a comprehensive history of Mizoram.

The second limitation is related to the periodization of Mizo history. From pristine stage of the pre-eighth century to the early developed type stage during the pre-seventeenth century and then the march towards modernisation under the impact of Christianity, is a tremendous pace of development within a few years and centuries. The Mizo history within a very short period of time encapsulates the full development from head hunting cultural stage to that of ultra modern video, star T.V. stage of our times. Therefore, it is very difficult to comprehend the entire stages of historical development and as such the usual periodizations into ancient mediaeval and modern does not hold good here and an everlapping is almost unavoidable in which our search has to be made from the scratches and particularly so when we talk of the Lungphun as a source. Further, because of my own limitations in the field, this attempt falls nothing sort of a wild excursion and so do I own the entire responsibility. Therefore, my approach here is quite unconventional. Even then, a semblance of the kind of studies involved, might be established for the purpose with some of the hypotheses as indicated in this chapter.

II

The Mizos as a tribe is fairly widespread in Burma (Myanmar), Bangladesh and in the North-East of India. Although earlier they were commonly known as Lushais, they were also known as Kukis in Bengal, the *Chins* in Burma. The modern term 'Mizo' appears to have been the apparent derivation from the term 'Zomi' of the Chin state of Burma which literally means 'the man of the cold regions' indicating their habitat in hill top colder regions nearer to the clouds. The term 'Mizo' is thus an independent identification of the same group of people living under separate political units. Another popular version of this term 'Mizo' also stands for highlanders.

When and how exactly the Mizo people spread over Burma. Bangladesh and in the North-East regions of India, is still a matter of conjecture in the absence of concrete historical evidence. Be that as it may, it is now a common generalisation that they belong to the Tibeto-Burman races. Some two thousand years back, they might have lived in the T'ao Valley of Kanchu province of the north-west of China and the north-east of Tibet. By the Seventh century, they moved towards upper Burma as nomadic migrants and settled for some time in the Kabaw Valley. From here, their pristine stages began to transform and perhaps they organised themselves into tribal group formations through the practice of tattooing, use of hairpins and other cultural forms. This might have been due to their cultural contacts with the Burmese. But after living for five centuries or so, they had to leave the Kabaw Valley because of the Shan push in Upper Burma region and gradually moved through the difficult terrains in organised groups under particular leaders into India, the present habitat in Mizoram.

They entered India through the eastern side of Mizoram is a historical fact as evidenced by the *lungphuns*. Some of the legends connected with such *lungphuns* are all mythical. Even then, stripping of its mythical aspects, the historical roots of the earliest Mizos might be traced. Further, it might also help in the understanding of the Mizo socio-cultural aspects in its different stages of development. We now present here some of the *lungphuns* and the elements found within these. It may be noted that the *lungphuns* generally mean the erection or planting of the stone monoliths more or less connected with memorial or commemorative purposes. It thus marks the beginning of the stage of rudimentary state organisation of the earliest Mizos in their inchoatcy.

III

1. Lalruanga Lung

There are about five such rocks/stones considerably big for any human being to lift or carry away single handedly. These were found in Suangpuilawn, situated at a distance of about 75 km from Aizawl, in the north-eastern side. Lalruanga, who might have been the chief, is said to have pulled out these stones from the Tuivai river by tying them with a single hair of his person, the marks of which are still to be seen on the stones. It also contains very finely finished holes on it, believed to have been the works of sorcerers. Wherever might be, the river as the source of water, the big stones as the protective means and the heroic feat of the chief might have served as the nucleus to the early organised village settlements of the Mizos.

2. Chhuralung

This is believed to have been erected by the chief, Chhura, to whom the Hmar clan of the Mizos claims their origin. There are no inscriptions on it but some engraving of a human figure holding a spear and the figure of a pig at its bottom are to be seen. The legends connected with this *lungphun* suggest the beginning of the *jhum* cultivation in a large scale and domestication of animals as the first stage of settled family life.

3. Mangkhaialung

Mangkhaialung was the handsome son of the chief of Champhai area, Mangthawnga, belonging to the Ralte tribe of the Mizos. He was arrested and imprisoned by Darkawla, the chief of the Zawngtlang area. But he was killed on his way back home at the Bawlte village. The grief stricken father erected the memorial stone which is known as Mangkhaialung. The rock is considerably big with human figures and mithun heads inscribed on it. A.G. McCall is of the opinion that it is a monolith of the pre-Lushai occupational period. This stone memorial invariably suggests the beginning of the inter-clan conflicts as well as contradictions relating to property and possessions.

4. Lungphunlian

This is a quite a big rock monolith of 10 ft. height, 6 ft. wide and with 2 ft. thickness. This is believed to have been erected by Meitei people because another rock is found nearby with Meitei script on it. It was found in the Tualcheng village. Proper decipheration of the script, may bring new light in Meitei Mizo relations of the time.

5. Lungvando

This is typical rock pillar round in shape and almost of a man's height. This was found in nearby jungles of Biate and Lungdar village situated at a distance of about 80 km from Aizawl. The roundness of the stone is so much of fine finishing that it is believed to be the work of a master-craftsman. It unmistakably points to the Mizo expertise in craftsmanship and artistry.

6. There is one unnamed *lungphun* with script closely resembling to the Shan Burmese alphabet. Unless deciphered, nothing could be said about this.

7. Yet another *lungphun* appears to be more interesting when its inscription is found in Assamese alphabet but with Bengali variation in the language of the inscription. Particularly the letter (R) is in Assamese alphabet. A proper study of this might reveal the history of Mizoram in the fourteenth and fifteenth centuries.

All such *lungphuns* are well preserved in the State Museum of Mizoram. A proper decipheration and study of these *lungphuns* might enfold hitherto unknown facts about the history of the Mizo minority nationality. Hence; epigraphists and historians could undertake this task together.

Glossary

Lung : stone or rock
phun : erection of planting *lian.* big
lianpui : very big
vando : roundness
mithun : a kind of buffalo likeanimal.

Fig. 7.1: Some Lungphuns at the State Museum, Aizawl

Acknowledgements

Dr. J.V. Hluna, Pachhunga University College, Aizawl, Shri R. Rosangluaia, State Museum, Aizawl

Shri T. Nghakliana, fellow of the Mizo literary society, Lunglei Mizoram.

REFERENCES

1. B. Lalthangliana, History of Mizo in Burma, Zawlbuk Agencies, Aizawl, 1977.
2. Major A.G McCall, Lushai Chrysalis, Tribal Research Institute, Aizawl, Reprint, 1977.
3. *Gazetteer of Upper Burma*—Two Volumes.
4. *Lungphunlian.*

8

Documentary Sources on Mizoram

Materials in the National Archives

T.R. Sareen

Historical research is of fundamental importance for all States in India especially those which are rich in history. But unfortunately historical research in India was conducted initially by the British who in their writings quite often ignored the "principles of historiography" and subjected the facts "to a great deal of distortion, misrepresentation and misinterpretation". Adherence to truth, as pointed out by Kareem, "is not a salient feature of Indian history that the British historians have bequeathed to the world". In the interest of truth it behoves us to be cautious while going through their writings and to have reservations regarding the conclusions to which these would lead us.[1]

Till recently, our knowledge about the history of North-East India, especially the hill tribes of erstwhile Assam, was limited and based entirely on the writings of the British. There is no doubt that their studies are quite useful, still it is necessary for us to have a fresh look at the history of the hill tribes of Assam based on the sources available in the different archival repositories.

Mizos are an important hill tribes of the subcontinent. They are racially said to be of Mongoloid origin and they belong to the Tibeto-Burman linguistic group. They live in Mizoram, Tripura, Manipur and Assam[2]. It is generally believed that the Mizos have recorded history only since the nineteenth century when the area inhabited by them earlier called the Lushai hills, now renamed as Mizoram, came under the British rule as an administrative unit.[3]

British officers who came in contact with the Lushai were the pioneers in writing about them for the consumption of the outside world. Their personal likes and dislikes are quite apparent in their writings. Mention may be made of the invaluable work of J. Shakespear, who was Superintendent of Lushai Hills for 14 years and who published his experiences in the work *The Lushai Kuki Clans.* N.E. Perry, Superintendent of the District in 1920s, wrote the book *The Lakshers*—the only comprehensive and reliable book on the Lakher tribe inhabiting the Southern part of Mizoram. Lewin who served as Deputy Commissioner, Chittogong Hill Tracts wrote three books and his *Lushai Primer* became in indispensable handbook for officers and Missionaries in Lushai hills. The last Superintendent of Lushai hills Mr. A.G. McCall published his account under the title *Lushai Cherysalis*, Alexander Machenzie, Secretary to the Government of India in the Home Department compiled his official account entitled *"History of the Relations of the Government with the Hill Tribes of the North-East Frontier of Bengal"* is indispensable work. This is entirely based on original documents.

There is no doubt that the writings by the British officers have been mostly "descriptive in nature covering mainly the existing social systems. The growth of political and administrative systems course, policy and goal—in the backdrop of socio-economic situation—was not specifically studied before. Moreover, the British civil servants were writing from their own point of view with a view to justifying their role in what they did for the tribes.

In the post-independence period, historiography in India has gained much from new source materials and changing historical perspectives. Mizoram along with other States in North-East has attracted the attention of the scholars and a few studies have appeared. Special mention may be made of the work done by Dr. Suhas Chatterjee. His book on *Mizoram under the British Rule* is a detailed account of the British relations with the Lushais. The author has consulted all the available sources and published materials. He has followed it up by another book entitled *Mizoram Encyclopaedia* in three volumes, which is a very comprehensive reference book on Mizoram and will be very useful to the scholars.

Another commendable study which covers even the post-independence period is by Dr. Animesh Ray *Mizoram Dynamics of Change* (Calcutta 1982). Dr. Ray was an I.A.S. officer in Mizoram for a number of years and he has maintained the British tradition of presenting exhaustively the various aspects of Mizo life—political, social and economic based not only on his personal experience, but also on original sources.

Despite these studies, the archival material available in the National Archives of India, Bengal State Archives and Assam State Archives and other places awaits systematic study. One of the greatest handicaps the historian experiences in reconstructing the story of the past is the lack of adequate source material. Though this is not the case with the British rule in India yet the location of the sources is not very well known to the scholars. It has been repeatedly pointed out by historians that the difficulties of the student of modern Indian history consist not so much in the collection of materials as in its exact knowledge. The manuscript materials for the study of modern Indian history preserved in the National Archives of India and other State repositories as well as in England is enormous. In addition to the published and unpublished records, there have accumulated a staggering amount of contemporary literature embodying the swaying passions and prejudices of the men who played various parts in the drama of European enterprise. There are extensive collections, housed in many archives and libraries, of letters received and the copies of letters despatched which it was not unusual for men in high office in those days to keep for themselves. Thus it is impossible for anyone, however, vast his knowledge may be to discuss authoritatively the wide range of manuscript material available at different archival repositories in India and abroad.

In their classic compendium of research practice, Langlois and Seignobos remark that "Documents are the traces which have been left by the thoughts and actions of men of former time", and it is only through these traces, they argue, that we can know the past. "For there is no substitute for documents: no documents, no history". This contention is rooted in the nineteenth century revolution in historical writing initiated by Ranke, and it became the corner-stone of professional academic history. Written documents discovered in libraries and archives were regarded by Ranke as superior to observational and archaeological evidence and to reminiscences and oral traditions.[4]

The rationale for preferring documentary evidence to all other sources of evidence about the past is, in part, a sheer matter of survival. For the distant past it is generally the case that interviewing and observation are impossible, and that documents have survived in great numbers. The expansion of the State and the growth of the economy in the modern period have generated massive quantities of written material which give us detailed contemporary views of past events. These documentary survivals are regarded as especially valuable because they "are not deliberately designed for the benefit of the historians" and so can be seen as the objective residue of the past; they provide the historian with the unwitting testimony of the people in the past.[5] These remarks are applicable to such archives as are normally created in the day-to-day transactions by organs of the State in the course of their activities. But in the case of archives that were the result of the activities of an alien power bias can be assumed to be always present; and allowance must as constantly be made for it.

The main repositories housing archival sources for the study of Mizos include (1) The National Archives of India, (2) The State Record Offices at Bengal and Assam, (3) The India Office Library and Records; (4) The British Museum (now British Library); (5) The Public Record Office, London; (6) The National Library of Scotland. I will confine myself to the archival materials available in the National Archives of India since my knowledge about the other repositories is quite limited.

Under the British, the present Mizoram was known as Lushai country or Kuki Hills which was ruled by independent chiefs. As such the records were created pertaining to Lushais from 1860 onwards and under Kukis before that date. The regular reference to Lushai hills in the records began to appear in the early years of the nineteenth century with the extension of British influence in North-East especially after the Blackwood expedition of 1844 which was undertaken to punish the Kukis for their raids. Blackwood expedition was followed by Lister's expedition in 1849 culminating in what is termed as Lushai expedition which was undertaken in 1871-72. Though the Lushais did not come directly under the British till the end of the nineteenth century, yet the various expeditions which were undertaken to subdue them generated a lot of documentary material. This documentary material is recorded mostly in the proceedings of the Foreign Department.

The records of the Foreign Department are indispensable for the study of the Mizos and are recorded under three heads: Foreign, Political and later on External. These consist of the Proceedings, Consultations, copies of letters despatched and copies of letters received from England. Prior to 1860 are indexed under the head Kookies and deal mainly with the question of raids but also contain information about the other tribes and to the genealogical antecedent of Kooki chiefs.

In order to stop the raids, the Government of India sanctioned a number of military expeditions from time to time. The records of these expeditions available in the Foreign Department throw light not only on the military aspect but also to the explorations in the Lushai country. The army was assisted by the civilians who undertook the survey of the hills and its people thereby commenting on the socio-economic conditions of the Lushais.

Besides this the reports provide a detailed account of Lushai customs, manners and their institutions. They also throw light on the status of the leading Lushai chiefs their relations with one another and with the rulers of Manipur and Tipperah (now Tripura). The reports of Captain Edgar and Captain Lewin are invaluable for the study of the Lushais. Edgar, in his report thoroughly analysed in detail the history, topography, Lushai customs, flora and fauna of the undiscovered country. His report, in short, "is a mine of information hitherto unknown to the outside world and no serious student of Mizo history can proceed an inch without this report"[6] His views moulded to a great extent the policy of the Government of India towards the tribes. He believed that "by a just and prudent course of action we could bind the Kookies to us by ties so strong and lasting that the tribe, instead of being a source of difficulties and danger to us, used become our strongest frontier defence".[7] It will be worthwhile to correct the impression the frontier tribes were "of a low civilisation" and savage in their habits.

The records of the Foreign Department before 1884 are classified under different heads, i.e., Political, General, Military, Finance, etc., and recorded under 'A' and 'B' Category. After 1884, the records are marked under the head External, Frontier and General, etc. This classification continued till 1921 when the files were recorded under a single file system.

Besides the reports of Edgar and Lewin referred to above, another report covering the period from 1873-1889 gives a comprehensive view of the Lushais, their relations with each other, with the British and especially about the institution of "The Bazars" which were especially introduced by after the expedition of 1871-72. These were mainly the trade markets. Through these trade markets the British kept a close watch on Lushais and their country. According to this report.

> "Apart from their being a valuable means of communication, their presence, undoubtedly influences the chiefs in maintaining friendly relations with us. They not only supply a regular revenue to the chiefs, but they enable the Lushais in general to acquire most of their wants at very little cost and trouble, viz., that of collecting wax, tea seed, and rubber in the jungle, and of cutting bamboos and other forest produce. Perhaps the most remarkable feature in all our dealings with these tribes is the dread of the chiefs lest the Bazars should be closed, their willingness to send guards for the protection of the traders and their readiness to make reparation to traders."

Since the Lushais were still independent of the British control, the Bazars were the best means of information on the Lushais. The report mentions that "the traders at the Bazar have always proved one of our principal sources of news in Lushai land, and information regarding internal movements of the tribes is generally first received through them".

"Since the Bazars are, under favourable circumstances, kept up all the year round, we could rest assured that as long as they were open, any important information would always be conveyed in due course to the authorities. Apart from the bazars, our means of communication with the Lushais is decidedly inadequate".[8]

Though it is claimed by the British, that they did not interfere in the internal affairs of the Lushais, but it will be interesting to study, how gradually, they moved towards the policy of annexation of these territories. A few studies have been undertaken on the political relations of the Lushais with the British but no monograph has been prepared on the economic and social condition of the tribes. Besides the records of the Bazars, the reports on the famines which ravaged the tribes during 1881-82, are full of information on their economic condition: This could be supplemented with the report of the Settlement which was undertaken after the Lushais came under British jurisdiction in 1895. The yearly administrative reports and the census data can further help in writing the economic history of the Lushais.

Besides the economic condition, it will be interesting to study, how gradually the British started having a control of the Lushai especially after the famines. The Chin Lushai Expedition 1889-90 led to the occupation of the Lushai Hills by the British. For the first time the independent chiefs realised that "they were no longer the master of their land".

From the Chin Hills expedition to the annexation of the Lushais, it is an interesting story, which is fully told in the records of the Foreign Department.

On September 6, 1895, the South Lushai Hills were formally annexed to the British India and included within its territory under the administration of the Lieutenant Governor of Bengal. Under the same proclamation of the Governor-General North Lusai Hills was formed a separate district under the Commissioner of Hills and Surma Valley (Assam) with the headquarters at Aizawl. Both the units were, however, amalgamated into one unit known as Lushai Hill District in April 1898 and were placed under the control of the Lieutenant Governor of Assam. These were governed by an officer known as the Superintendent of the Lushai Hills District.

Besides the records of the Foreign Department, the constitutional changes which were introduced in the area by a declaring them as "Backward tract" in 1891 and as "Excluded Areas" by the Act of 1935, can be studied from the records of the Home Department and the Reforms office. It will be interesting of study the British motives in declaring them as "Excluded Area" which as Chatterjee writes kept them away from the "main stream of Indian life". Perhaps one significant result of keeping the Lushais away from the main stream of Indian life was that these tribes became very loyal and subservient to the British. This became apparent during the Second World War, when the Lushais whole-heartedly cooperated with the British in opposing the Japanese and the Indian National Army. The anti-Japanese and anti-I.N.A. propaganda of the Government was responsible to a great extent for the hostile attitude of the hill tribes to the Indian National Army. The story as to how the I.N.A. and Japanese forces met with resistance from the various tribes on the North-East Frontier is yet to be reconstructed.[9] The records of this period available in the National Archives of India and Ministry of Defence, historical section are still not open for consultation. The exact role which the Tribes of North-East Frontier played in halting the I.N.A.'s march on the Delhi will become clear only after the records are made available to the scholars.

It is just possible that for their help during the war, the British dangled before them the bait of making the area into a "Crown colony" after the War when India was being promised freedom. There are hints about this in the correspondence published in the *Transfer of Power volumes*, but our knowledge about it is still incomplete. I hope some scholar should get access to the material available at different places and write the complete story.

Besides the regular series of records under the Foreign Department the references to the Lushais are found in other stray series also. For example a little known series under the head "Foreign Department Notes" which were compiled by the British officers from time to time during the nineteenth century contain detailed information about Lushais, for example, there is a note on the Lushais and Kookis prepared before the expedition of 1871-72. (No.C 153). Another note (No. C 153A) gives information about the Pedigree of Looshai Chiefs. Major J.V. Gugne's precis on Eastern Frontier Defence contain more information on the boundaries then available anywhere else (*c*.154/275). A detailed account of the raids by the Lushais justifying the British Penetration of the Area is found in Note No. C210. Besides the above, the collection contain report of Major Edgar on his tour of the Lushai country (*c.*155), details about Chittongong Hill Districts (*c.* 210), etc.

Another collection under the head Foreign Miscellaneous have four volumes (241-244) which contain correspondence on the North-East Frontier prepared before the expedition undertaken by Major Blackwook. Similarly the Proceedings of the Military Department and Survey Department are equally important for the study of land-routes, construction of roads, system of communication etc. The National Archives of India has also now acquired the microfilm copies of the private papers of the various Viceroys and Secretary of States from 1860 to 1947. These papers are likely to be useful for studying the history of Mizoram. The above is by no means an exhaustive account of the Archival sources, but only in indication that a detailed study of the British rule of the Lushais is very necessary in order to understand many of the current problems which the State is facing. The proper study of the past is very essential to understand the present. It is believed that the policy of deliberate segregation followed by the British resulted in the isolation of the Mizos from the National life as well as in the economic backwardness of the Mizo people. Hence, "today's problems in Mizoram are the logical outcome of the administrative policies followed by the British in these hills".[9] Due to this, it is necessary that a comprehensive account of the past two hundred years of Mizos may be prepared based on the sources available at different places.

NOTES

1. C.K. Kareem, *Kerala under Hyder Ali and Tipu Sultan* (Cochin 1973), p. 1.
2. Dr. Suhas Chatterjee, *Mizoram under the British Rule* (New Delhi 1985), p. 1, Fereword.
3. Dr. Animesh Ray, *Mizoram-Dynamics of Change* (Calcutta 1982), p. 2.
4. Langois and Scignobas, *Introduction to the Study of History* (London 1908), p. 17.
5. John Scott, *A Matter of Record* (London 1990), p. 11.
6. Suhas Chatterjee, *Mizoram Encyclopaedia,* (Delhi, 1990), Vol. II, p. 260.
7. See Report of Edgar in Alexander Mackenzie, *History of the Relations of the Government with the Hill Tribes of the North East Frontier of Bengal* (Calcutta 1884), p. 415-47.
   This book contains many other valuable documents on the Lushais.
8. R.G. Woodthrope, *The Lushai Fxpedition along with a Compilation on The Lushais 1873-1889.* (Shillong 1889), p. 17-25.
9. Dr. Animesh Ray, *op. cit*: p. ix-x.

9

Minority Nationalities of North-East India—The Mizos

Suhas Chatterjee

The Mizos are a very interesting community in the north-east India. They live in Mizoram, Jampui Hills in Tripura, Lakkhimpur in Cachar and North Cachar in Assam, and Jiribum in Manipur. They also live in Tiddim district and other parts of Chin Hills in Burma and also in the Chittagong Hill Tracts in Bangladesh. In short, they are concentrated in Burma, India and Bangladesh. Majority of them, however, live in India. Originally, a migratory tribe, the Mizos entered into India from Burma, when, we cannot ascertain exactly. As there had been so many class and sub-class there were inter-tribal rivalries and no political unity amongst them. Their political status, before the advent of the English, was somewhat independent nominally under titular sovereign.

They lived under a gerantocracy where the Chiefs were the immediate rulers. The chief (the bigger one) had his council of advisors and in the villages (the smaller ones) the subordinate chiefs had their village councils. The chief provided protection to his *quom* and in return received unquestionable obedience from his subjects. They lived a community life where *Zawlbuk* (the bachelors dormitory) had a significant role to play. In the absence of a strong religious organization or any powerful social or cultural institutions, the relationship between the powerful chiefs and his subordinates had been like that of a marginally lose confederation. They often clashed *inter se* leading to serious breach of peace.

The British administrators had to come heavily upon those disturbers of peace. This intervention became all the more necessary to stop the Mizo raids into the British territories. However, the British policy initially had been conciliation and when it did not work well, the Lushai country was annexed in 1890 after the Chin Lushai Expedition 1889-90. However, the Proclamation of the Governor General was made in 1895. At first there had been South Lushai Hills, North Lushai Hills and Chin Hills as the separate administrative units. The Chin Hills Regulation compiled by Bertram Carrey was the code for the administration. The Superintendent with their *Durbars* ruled the Lushai Hills district. In the villages there were several village councils. The Lushai Hills district was a non-revenue earning district and the Government of Assam delinked its administration from the "mainstream. The Government of India Act 1935 made Lushai Hills an "Excluded Area". The Inner Line Regulation and excluded area status made the Lushais to live in splendid isolation.

The World War II made the Mizos conscious about their nationality. The Japanese forces had been advancing menacingly and after the fall of Burma, the position of Lushai Hills became critical. Japan had her grand design and chalked out the Imphal campaign. The Japanese captured the Burma Road, and the war patrol party made incursions in the Lushai Hills from Burma. A.G. McCall, the Superintendent, evolved the *Total Defence Scheme* which demanded the total allegience of the Mizos to the *Durbar* and to the Lushai community. This pledge of the *Total Defence Scheme* made the Lushais conscious of their separate identities as a nation just at that time came the declaration of the President Roosevelt (22 February, 1942) on the right of self determination of the nations. The educated Mizos were inspired by the said declaration which was incorporated into the Atlantic Charter. The Kulikawn Resolution of the Lushai Association (1946) had been the direct outcome of the Atlantic Charter. The resolution is a milestone in the history of Mizoram. The Mizo Union, new political party was born as an offshoot of that resolution.

The new political party was steeped into the political tradition of India and one of the platforms of the all embracing Indian National Congress. The composition of Mizo Union, however, was elitist. A section of the party members disliked its elitist outlook and they formed United Mizo Freedom Organization (UMFO). That party's founder was an expatriate from Burma and UMFO was a pro-Burmese party. The clash between the M.U. and U.M.F.O. was the characteristic of the political development of the Mizos of the period preceding Indian Independence 1947. Meanwhile the *Saprawnga* episode in the Chiefs' Council caused flutter in the whole of Assam. McDonald, the Superintendent was re-called by the Governor and G.N. Bardoloi began to take special interest in the Lushai Hills. The incident inflamed the passions of the Mizos in the Mizo Hills and the rage was transformed into anti British national sentiment. The Mizo Union became very popular as it was in the forefront to channelise the Mizo national sentiment into a concrete political force.

L.L. Peter, the successor of McDonald, following the traditional British policy of Divide and Rule managed UMFO to fight the Mizo Union. The historic resolution of the *Durbar* (14 August, 1947) on the eve of Independence reversed the process of Indianization of Mizo Sub-nationalism. Peter acted in a manner reminiscent of the King of Kashmir and the Nizam of Haiderabad. This resolution, rather, in its spirit haunted the minds of the Mizos for long forty years. The radical Mizo National Front philosophy of *Sovereign Mizoram* was the direct outcome of Peter's political thought.

The Nehru Charter ensuring the tribal identities and the movement of the Khasi leaders especially the All Party Hill Leaders Conference acted as incentives to the Mizo leaders to demand autonomy. Recommendations of Pataskar Committee for the all-round development of the Mizo Hills district as a special case to remedy the defects of our past masters acted as a catalyst in the process of socio-economic changes in Mizoram. The reports of Tarlok Singh Committee and Asoka Mehta Committee aimed at reconstructing the Mizo economy on modern lines. Todays economy is political economy and economy is the basis of political system. A nation marches with the rapid growth of economy. The free flow of fund washed away many superstitions, inhibitions, and narrowness of the gerantocracy. The free flow of currency notes was not necessarily an unmixed evil in the socioeconomic development of the Mizos. It provided the necessary infrastructure of political growth.

The extension of "sixth schedule" of the constitution to Mizo Hills and sending of representatives to Assam Assembly and Indian Parliament roused the political consciousness of the Mizos as they got the opportunity to have the political experience in the broad national perspective. Notwithstanding the changes the new system brought, the political apparatus of the Mizos were monopolized by the elitist section of the society. To a section of people the abolition of chiefship failed to produce the desired result as the fruits of the liberation were gobbled up by the new political masters depriving the poor. Pu Laldenga, an ex-army man and an out and out commoner was the symbol of the radical thought.

The M.N.F. rebellion 1966, sent shockwaves to the nerves of the North Block in New Delhi. The *Operation Security* and other counter insurgency measures were adopted to fight the militarism of the MNF. But militarism was only a part of political extremism of that radical outfit. No wonder Laldenga mustered assistance from the enemies of India who wanted to wage a proxy war within India indulging insurgency in North-East India. Mrs. Indira Gandhi, the Indian Prime Minister, viewed the Mizo insurgency as a political problem having its roots in the wounded regional sentiments and age old economic neglect of the deprived Mizos. She was magnanimous and never lost sight of the real issues associated with the main grievances of the Mizos. True, the prolonged insurgency brought inhuman miseries to the people and stopped the wheel of economic progress of the Mizos, yet she never lost her patience and gave patient hearing to the demands of the MNF Supremo.

Granting of Union Territory status to Mizoram and sudden rise of financial allocation from 2.62 crores to 8.88 crores in 1971 brought a sea-change in the political outlook of the Mizos. Union Territory status satisfied the political aspiration of the Mizos but the infighting among the political leaders especially among the legislators invited repeated impositions of President's Rule, thereby pointing out the glaring weakness of the Mizo political system to adjust properly with the norms of western democracy. An opinion became current that the Mizos were yet to qualify for democratic functioning and hence return to rule by bureaucracy would suit them. However, the Government brushed aside those ideas and allowed the law of the land to take its own course.

Mrs. Gandhi's appeal to the MNF to surrender their arms and come to a political settlement through negotiation within the framework of the Constitution had cut the ice and forced the MNF functionaries to start dialogue with the Government. The granting of general amnesty had already blunted the MNF edge. The *returnees* were properly rehabilitated and even accepted in the ruling Congress party to share power. All these weakened the foundation of narrow chauvinism of the radical Mizos paving the path of gradual assimilation of the Mizo *quom* into the main stream of Indian national life. The military dictatorship in neighbouring Myanmar and theocracy in Bangladesh added miseries to the Mizos living there. The Mizos of Mizoram compared their lot with the Mizos of Burma and Bangladesh and reached the conclusion that they were fortunate to cast their lot with India. The position of today is substantially different from what it had been forty years ago.

The idea of *Sovereign Mizoram* with the implications of alluring greater Mizoram was a political impossibility frought with logical sterility and hence an impracticable proposition bordering the phraseology of political sibboleth. The conscious Mizos rejected that philosophy. That is the reason why they do not support the Burmese Mizos' claim of merger of Chin Hills with India. A modern Mizo, after the Mizo Peace Accord

1986, is content with his Indian citizenship like a Bengalee or a Punjabi and never thinks deeply into the internal affairs of Bangladesh or Pakistan. At the same time a modern Mizo is all the more proud of his Mizo identity and his tribal status which Constitution of India ensures them.

NOTES

A. Mackenzie, *North East Frontier of Bengal,* p. 366.
A. Ray, *Mizoram: Dynamics of Change,* pp. 97-98.
B.J.P. August 1872. No. 548.
S. Chaterjee, *Mizoram Encyclopaedia*, Vol. III.
Ibid., Vol. I, pp. 80-84; 135-141.

10

Ethnicity and Statehood in Mizoram

Anuradha Dutta

The story of British annexation of the Lushai Hills (later to be known as Mizoram) abounds with a series of raids and counter-raids culminating in the loss of Lushai independence and annexation of the Lushai land to the British dominions. The British took notice of the Lushais after the annexation of Cachar. The Lushais used to come to the plains to sell their forest products, especially rubber and cane, and to raid. The raids had several causes: gradual extension of tea gardens into areas inhabited by Lushais, raids for food and also heads, native daring and the spirit of adventure on the part of the tribesmen, the practice among the Lushai chiefs of those days of subordinating other weaker chiefs by raiding the latters' villages causing their migration to the plains forming British dominions, etc. The Lushais came to the notice of the British in the plains of Cachar around the year 1840 while the first raid occurred in 1849 attracting a punitive expedition. Till about 1868, there was no raid worth the name. But when troubles occurred, a punitive expedition was answered by further raids. Beginning with 1870 and for about twenty years there were raids and counter-raids. Beyond the raids, there were the separate risings of the Western Lushais and Eastern Lushais in the early 1890's. Attempted imposition of revenue and introduction of forced labour in the form of demands for 'coolies' were the prime causes of the Lushai revolts. The revolts were suppressed by the British and by 1895, the North-Lushai Hills district was placed under the jurisdiction of the Commissioner of Assam while the South Lushai Hills was left under the administration of the Lt. Governor of Bengal. On 27 January, 1898, the Government of British India decided to constitute the whole of the Lushai country into one unit under the administration of Assam and this was given effect to on 1 April, 1898. A single officer styled as the Superintendent of Lushai

Hills, with headquarters at Aizawl, was placed in charge of the district while the internal management of the villages was left with the respective chiefs.[1]

David Scott, Agent to the Governor-General for the whole of the eastern frontier, took the initiative in distributing copies of the Assamese version of the *New Testament*. He was particularly interested in the spread of Christianity among the hill tribes. The operation of the principle of *divide et impera* (divide and rule) in the hills and plains of Assam was sedulously pursued by the British, although it was the Inner Line Regulation of 1873 which formally separated the hills from the plains.[2] The alien rulers successfully instilled it in the minds of the tribes of the Lushai hills or Mizoram that their land had never formed a part of India. Under the Government of India Act 1935, Mizoram came to be administered as an 'Excluded Area' under the charge of an omnipotent Superintendent, aided as he was by a number of 'puppet chiefs' while the people had no representation either in the Central or Provincial legislature.[3]

When Britain's transfer of power to Indian hands was on the anvil; the political future of the Lushai hills came to be debated both at official and non-official levels. Conscious sections in Mizo society were very unhappy with the wholly unrepresentative character of the British administration and, hence, the emerging Mizo elite took the first steps towards fulfilling their urges and aspirations through the establishment of a political formation, the Mizo Union, on 9 April, 1946. The Mizo Union had for its aims the removal of the autocratic chiefs and their replacement by popularly elected representatives. The organisation increased its popularity with amazing rapidity and expressed itself in favour of remaining within India. On this issue, however, defections took place with the result that the breakaway group formed a rival organisation under the name and style of United Mizo Freedom Organisation seeking union with Burma.[4]

The Constituent Assembly's North-East Frontier Tribal and Excluded Areas Sub-Committee recommended the conferment of an autonomous status on the Lushai hills under the Sixth Schedule to the Constitution. The Constitution provided for the constitution of District Councils and Regional Councils. Thus, the tribal areas specified in Parts 'A' and 'B' of the table appended to paragraph 20 were declared to be tribal areas within the State of Assam. Part 'A' included the United Khasi-Jaintia Hills District; the Garo Hills District, the Mizo District, the North Cachar Hills, and the Mikir Hills. Thus, Mizoram came to have a District Council.

As against the Constituent Assembly's scheme of things, there were schemes and even machinations galore regarding the future status of the Lushai land. The United Mizo Freedom Organisation championed the cause of union with Burma. Certain ideas were floated about union with Pakistan, or an independent State, or even a Crown colony under the British. Further, a novel scheme was put forward by the so-called People's Representatives' at the instance of A.R. Macdonald, the British Superintendent of Lushai Hills.[5] The scheme envisaged complete autonomy in internal administration; while the Government of India would have control over arms, defence and foreign affairs. The Indian Government was to give a regular fixed amount of grant for development and administration until economic self-sufficiency was achieved.[6] The Mizo Union mattered in Mizoram at that time and it rejected the scheme in its entirety. However, consensus was reached at a meeting held on 14 August, 1947 among representatives including the Mizo Union, tribal Chiefs and 'other outstanding leaders'—the 'accredited leaders of Lushai political parties'—that Mizoram would join the Indian Union on condition that Mizos would have a right to 'opt out of Indian Union after ten years if they wish to do so'.[7] The United Mizo Freedom Organisation was implacably opposed to any formula at all which suggested even a temporary union with India. Thus, even while the Mizo Union hailed the freedom of India on 15 August, 1947, the rival organisation used violence to break up the procession taken out on that day at Aizawl by the Mizo Union. The United Mizo Freedom Organisation, however, could not make any headway; starting as a breakaway organisation; it was later on converted into the Eastern India Tribal Union which also began to fizzle out due to clashes at the leadership level.[8]

The Mizo Union became the ruling party when the Mizo District Council was inaugurated on 25 April, 1952. For more than seventeen years the Mizo Union continued to occupy that position. The district was renamed as Mizo Hills. The anachronistic Chieftainship was abolished with payment of compensation.

Inadequate relief measures by the Government of Assam to combat the large-scale *Mautam* famine in Mizoram in 1959-60 brought about a sea-change in the political situation. Insurgency caught the soul of the Mizo people, as it were. Conferment of the status of a Union Territory on Mizoram on 21 January, 1972 proved to be a halfway house only and the road to Statehood as outlined in the Memorandum of Settlement (Mizoram Accord) of 30.6.86 was beset with much somersaults and twists and turns centring round the basic question of identity crisis of a people aroused;

aroused by ethnic politics and all that it means in a new wave of as sertiveness embracing different ethnic groups. It is appropriate at this stage to allude to the phenomenon of ethnic politics in the entire north-eastern region with particular reference to Mizoram.

II

Assertion of the separate tribal identity basically led to the creation of the separate entities with the break-up of the old composite State of Assam. But even after the creation of separate administrative units, differences among different ethnic groups surfaced leading to socio-political movements centring round what has commonly came to be known as the identity crisis. At times smaller communities tend to associate or merge forming thereby bigger entities to facilitate movements with political demands. Ethnicity, regionalism or sub-nationalism in the region raised complex issues practically in every area of the region including Mizoram backed by movements at times championing secessionist demands or demands for complete autonomy. All this have led to the development of what can be termed *ethnic politics*.[9]

Fredrick Barth defined ethnicity as 'the social organization of cultural difference'.[10] India remains a multi-ethnic, multi-lingual and multi-cultural country with a number of major and minor nationalities, micro nationalities and the tribal people. It goes without saying that societies could be multi-ethnic and multiracial without, however, major cultural divisions.[11] At times a territorial minority could demand and have territorial autonomy or even independent statehood; but, options left to a dispersed minority are severely limited. Thus, if the situation so warrants, dispersed minorities could resort to techniques of pressure including violence.[12] A study of some ethnic movements in India's North-East serves to show a good deal of perceived or actual deprivations motivating ethnic activism. As a scholar puts it, although no specific attribute is invariably associated with all ethnic categories, there must be some distinctive cultural feature that evidently separates one group of people from another, no matter whether that feature or features be language, territory, religion, dress, etc., or any of them,[13] or, nationality characteristics.[14]

As for ethnicity, Barth conceptualised it as a largely subjective process of status identification. Therefore, it followed that ethnic groups are formed to the extent that actors use ethnic identities to categorize themselves and others for purposes of interaction. Evidence from India's north-east suggests that inter-ethnic contact and interaction even while starting with co-operation could take the form of conflict, as in Mizoram, when any ethnic group singly or in combination becomes assertive to the point of demanding a separate identity to give expression to their ideas of modernisation. Thus, ethnicity could both be an objective and subjective phenomenon. As observed by a competent scholar, ethnic populations are one type of structural phenomenon and ethnic groups are quite another, and each type may differently influence the system of inter-ethnic relations that might obtain among individuals.[15]

Virtually all the numerous ethnic communities in India's North-East including the vocal 'dominant group' and 'subordinate group' in each of the units at one time or another in the recent past have become political actors with a view to fulfil their urges and aspirations. The forms of action ranged from peaceful protests, for instance, as in Assam and Meghalaya, and armed struggle, as in Nagaland, Tripura and Mizoram. As a scholar rightly observes, the hill districts of Assam administered separately from the plains since the British days emerged into separate hill States precisely because of their compactness and elite articulation.[16] And this articulation assumed a strident form in Mizoram following the *Mautam* (famine) of 1959-60. It seems appropriate at this stage to make some analysis of the ethnic structure of the Mizo population of different ethnic groups before dealing with the armed revolt began in the zero hour of 28 February and 1 March, 1966 under the leadership of the Mizo National Front (MNF) on the issue of Mizo identity and eventual conferment of Statehood on the Union Territory of Mizoram.

In Mizoram, fifteen ethnic groups or populations have been traced so far: Lusei, Paite, Hualngo, Tlau, Thadou, Ralte, Hmar, Mara (Lakher), Pawi, Bawm, Pang, Chakma, Riang, Biate and Magh; excepting for the last four groups, the other eleven population groups are together called the Chin Hill tribes.[17] Studies have shown that at different times and even now some sections of the *Maras, Pawis, Paite, Hmar* and *Chakma* assert their distinct identity. It has been established that the Maras and thePawis have their distinct identity and history.[18] The different groups received added importance during the course of the agitation for a separate homeland for the Mizos.

According to one scholar, the word Mizo is a blanket term 'having a political undertone' and that the word Mizo refers to all those who choose to apply this term for them; a Hmar living in a village in the interior of Mizoram would call himself a Mizo, although a Hmar villager living near or in Manipur would call himself a Hmar.[19] Mizoram's commonly accepted etymological significance has been that it is the land or country of highlanders. But according to another interpretation, the meaning of 'Mizo' is not merely a highlander, the word 'zo' was perhaps derived from 'zhou', the name of a clan in ancient China; the same source interprets that 'zo' could also possibly have been derived from the word 'yau' (pronounced as 'zou') which means tiger, i.e., brave or great in the Burmese language; the reference is to the 'Zo' kingdom in Upper Burma in eleventh or twelfth century A.D., and hence, the source believes that the Mizos are the descendants of the Zo dynasty.[20]

The findings of the above two sources would serve to show that the Mizo population included, in the main, the Lusais and some of the subjects of Sailo chiefs, at least in the initial stage. However, as pointed out by another scholar, attempts at bringing all the Chin Hill tribes under the generic name Mizo were made following the *Mautam* (famine) of 1959-60.[21] The agitation motivated people belonging to different ethnic groups to accept the Mizo identity. The feeling of oneness generated by tragic famine conditions brought about a transformation in the course of the agitation: an overwhelming majority of the population in Mizoram identified themselves as Mizo. A scholar having extensive experience in field studies concluded that it was justified to say that "the people of Mizoram are Mizo".[22] The recognition of Mizo identity energised the anti-famine and political movements, and sizeable sections of the people of Mizoram found in the MNF a leader, a flag and a cause.

III

The MNF owed its origins to a non-political cultural society, the Mizo Cultural Society, through the instrumentality of Laldenga. The Cultural Society, organised a procession peacefully to protest against ineffective relief measures when the famine overtook Mizoram. The occasion was the visit of Capt. Williamson Sangma, the then Assam Minister in charge of Tribal Areas Department in 1960. Government servants also participated in the procession. The Assam Government took it as an affront and barred Government servants from membership of the Cultural Society. Laldenga, who served as a clerk in the Mizo District Council office of the time, resigned from service and was promptly appointed Secretary of the Mizo Cultural Society. The Cultural Society was, however, ill-equipped in handling severe famine conditions whereupon the Mizo National Famine Front was formed in the same year with R. Dengthuama (later to become a Congressman) as President and Laldenga as Secretary. The anti-famine and thus anti-Government movement was getting rapidly politicised with the result that the Mizo National Famine Front was ultimately converted into a political association under the name and style of Mizo National Front on 28 October, 1961 with Laldenga as Chairman and Vanlawma as Secretary. In the years that followed, the Mizo Union became ineffective and the MNF made rapid strides organisationally and politically to the point of challenging the authority of the Government of India.[23]

In view of its radical demands, the MNF grew into an extremist organisation. It stood for 'a sovereign independent State of Mizoram'. The Mizos were visualised as a distinct nation. In his Memorandum to the Prime Minister of India, Laldenga said:

> "The Mizos from time immemorial lived in complete independence without foreign interference. Their territory had never been conquered or subjugated by the neighbouring States. the Mizos. (were) subsequently brought under the British political control in December 1895 (?) when a little more than half of the country was arbitrarily carved out and named Lushai hills and the rest of their land was parcelled out of their hands to the adjoining people for the sole purpose of administrative convenience. The Mizos stood a separate nation, even before the advent of the British government. In nutshell, they are a distinct nation, created, moulded and nurtured by God and nature".[24]

It may be noted in this connection that the Mizos have many things in common and among them area common religion in the form of Christianity, similar customary laws, etc. Now a near common political assertiveness pointed to a radically new direction.

Laldenga's MNF made elaborate preparations for an armed insurrection: these included collection of huge funds, recruitment and training of volunteers with arms and ammunition from neighbouring East Pakistan, organisation of training bases in that country; and, there was massive anti-India propaganda offensive. After insurgent attacks of Aizawl and Lungleh on 28th February - 1st March, 1966, a parallel government was set up with an army of its own. The MNF naturally went underground when on 2 March the Government of Assam declared Mizoram a 'Disturbed Area'. Laldenga and his associates made their way to East Pakistan whence acts of reprisal were carried on all those who were considered to be anti-Mizo. The army in their turn could not distinguish between rebels and innocent persons with the result that largescale operations in Mizoram led to untold sufferings for the common people. This further alienated them from the constituted authority.[25]

The Mizo unrest had many twists and turns. The fall of the East Pakistan regime and the emergence of Bangladesh deprived the MNF of the facilities of their rebel operations from that country. Following this 1971 debacle of the rebel organisation, a number of MNF leaders and their followers, especially from the intelligentsia, surrendered to the Government. It was in this background that Mizoram was constituted as a Union Territory on 21 January, 1972. In the elections that followed, the Congress won 6 seats out of 30 seats while the Mizo Union made headway in the electoral front. In February 1974, increasing mutual cooperation led to the merger of the Mizo Union with the Congress. They proposed talks between the Government of India and the MNF and at their instance in November 1974, the Mizoram Peace Advisory Body was set up with the concurrence of political parties, church leaders, social organisations and eminent public figures.[26]

After the liberation of Bangladesh, Laldenga shifted his headquarters to Karachi, sought foreign support for his cause, while the MNF shifted their base of operations to the Arakan jungles. But following the Shillong Accord in 1975 between the Government of India and sections of the Naga underground leaders, and even before it, a number of followers deserted Laldenga's camp. By December 1975, more than two hundred MNF personnel surrendered to the Government. A disappointed Laldenga had to agree to an Accord with the Government of India on 1 July, 1976 acknowledging Mizoram's status as an integral part of India. Further, they agreed to abjure violence and suspend all activities besides handing over their arms and ammunition to the Government. Peace appeared to return to Mizoram and 7 July, 1976 was observed as a Thanksgiving Day in Mizoram with special thanks giving services in all the churches and institutions.[27]

Under the 1976 Accord, Laldenga agreed to discuss the issues raised by the MNF within the framework of the Constitution of India and surrender arms within three months. But Laldenga did not go ahead and three months passed away. In the Mizoram Assembly elections in 1978, Brigadier Sailo's People's Conference Party won the elections. There seemed to be little prospects for the MNF to come to a position of power in Mizoram and it was principally this circumstance which led Laldenga to rejoin the Arakan-based MNF. Violence returned to Mizoram and it had its toll, ever since June 1979, in several casualties, both civil and military.

Laldenga, however, made another somersault. He again expressed his desire for a negotiated settlement around 1980. His new demand centred round the creation of a *Greater Mizoram* with adjoining areas of Assam, Tripura and Manipur and the establishment of an interim government with himself as its head even when a duly constituted legislature was functioning.[28] This time the MNF appeared to act with greater sincerity for a negotiated settlement. Insurgency did not bring any laurels and nearly two decades of armed confrontation brought only miseries to the people.

The initiative for renewed talks with the MNF was taken by the late Prime Minister, Shrimati Indira Gandhi. After a series of talks with Laldenga representing the MNF, the Memorandum of Settlement (Mizoram Accord) was signed on 30 June, 1986 between the MNF and the Government of India. The Accord noted that the settlement was reached on the acceptance by Shri Laldenga on behalf of the MNF of the two conditions, namely, cessation of violence by the MNF and holding of talks within the framework of the Constitution of India.

Clause 4.1. of the Settlement stated the agreement of the Government to initiate measures "to confer Statehood on the Union Territory of Mizoram" with a view to "satisfying the desires and aspirations of the people of Mizoram". The Government promised to secure the amendment of the Constitution and other laws for the conferment of Statehood. It was agreed that the amendments would provide for among other things, the following:

4.3 (i) The territory of Mizoram shall consist of the territory specified in sec. 6 of the North Eastern (Reorganisation) Act 1971.

(ii) Notwithstanding anything contained in the Constitution, no Act of Parliament in respect of,

(a) religious or social practices of the Mizos,

(b) Mizo customary law or procedure,

(c) administration of Civil and Criminal justice involving decisions according to Mizo customary law,

(d) Ownership and transfer of land shall apply to the State of Mizoram unless the Legislative Assembly of Mizoram by a resolution so decides:

Provided that nothing in this clause shall apply to any Central Act in force in Mizoram immediately before the appointed day.

Laldenga did raise the demand for the unification of Mizo inhabited areas of other States to form one administrative unit. But apart from merely referring to Article 3 of the Constitution of India, no commitment was made. It was agreed that if it so wished, Mizoram could have a High Court of its own and that it could have a separate University in the State in accordance with the prescribed procedure. The Government agreed to payment of ex gratia amount to heirs/dependents of persons who were killed during disturbances in 1966 and thereafter and also to payments of compensation relating to damage to crops, buildings destroyed/damaged during operations in Mizoram. It also agreed to the payment of rental charges of lands and buildings occupied by the Security Forces.

It was an historic Accord in that the 1966 insurgency had come to an end and Mizoram became a State of the Indian Union.

IV

Mizo identity found constitutional recognition with the formation of the State of Mizoram. The official language of Mizoram is Duhlian, stated to be another name for the Lusai language which is blended with others.[29] Cl. 12 (i) of the Mizoram Accord stated: "the provisions of Part XVII of the Constitution will apply and the State will be at liberty to adopt any one or more of the languages in use in the State as the language to be used for all or any of the official purposes of the State".

Mizoram has achieved a high percentage of literacy: under the 1991 Census, it is 81.23 per cent as against the national literacy rate of 52.11 per cent. The high percentage embraces the economically advanced major ethnic groups. Constitutional rights for instruction at primary stage through mother tongue under Art. 350A of the Constitution are duly recognised for minority ethnic groups like *Maras* and the *Chakmas*. Other minor ethnic groups like *Pang* and *Bawm* appear to feel that there is scope for greater encouragement in developing their languages. Under the Mizo identity umbrella during the period of the agitation there was no scope for inter-ethnic disaffection to the point of fighting for ethnic identity. But in the post-Accord period, certain ethnic groups are asserting themselves in a situation of almost worldwide assertion by ethnic groups. The MNF ceased to be an insurgent group after the Mizoram Accord, although press reports indicate resentment among MNF ranks over non-fulfilment of certain provisions of the Accord relating to rehabilitation. A new insurgency has surfaced in Mizoram, that of the Hmar People's Convention (HPC) which has been waging a militant struggle for a homeland for the *Hmars* in North Mizoram.[30] Ethnic assertion by non-dominant ethnic groups is a part of the current ethnic scene in many parts of the country and other countries as well. Decentralisation of powers combined with balanced economic development might provide a way out of the *impasse*.

REFERENCES

1. Far facts stated, vide Sir Edward Gait, A History of Assam (LBS Publications, Gauhati, 1981, second edition, reprint), pp. 318-19; H.K. Barpujari, Problem of Hill Tribes: Northeast Forntier: Inner Line to the McMohan Line, Vol. III (Spectrum Publications, Gauhati, 1981), pp. 84-110; 'Proceedings of Northeast-India History Association, Sixth Session, Agartala', 1985 (To be cited as PROC henceforth), Paper by Lalrimawia entitled LUSHAI RISINGS 1890-95, pp. 255-260.
2. Vide Journal of the University of Gauhati, Vol. IX, No. I: Arts 1958, Paper by Debo Prasad Barooah entitled *The Rebellion of 1857 and Its Impact on Assam*, p. 17; for Inner Line, Gait, *op. cit.*, pp. 335-36; Barpujari, *op. cit.*, pp. 10, 117-18.
3. *Cf.* Barpujari; *op. cit.*, p. 339.
4. Vide North East Session All India Congress Committee Jawahar Nagar Gauhati Souvenir (20-22 November, 1976), to be cited henceforth as Souvenir, entry by Sri Hrangaia entitled Emergence of New Political Scene in Mizoram and Role of Congress, p. 37; also, PROC. Paper by J.V. Hluna entitled Mizo Problems Leading to Insurgency, p. 443.
5. Vide Proc, p. 443.
6. S.K. Chaube, *Hill Politics in North East India*, Calcutta, 1973, p. 71.
7. Vide PROC. pp. 443-44.
8. SOUVENIR, pp. 37-8.
9. Vide author's paper, Movements for Ethnic Assertion in India's North-East, presented at the XV World Congress of the International Political Science Association, 21-25 July, 1991 at Buenos Aires.
10. Cited in Regina E. Holloman, Sergei A. Arutimunov, Perspectives on Ethnicity (Mouton Publishers, The Hague, 1978), p. 3.
11. *Cf.* Joe R. Feagin, Racial and Ethnic Relations (Prentice Hall, Inc., New Jersey, 1978), p. 1.
12. Ivo D. Duchacek, Comparative Federalism: The Territorial Dimension of Politics (Holt, Rinehart and Winston, Inc. New York, 1970), pp. 97-99. *Cf.* Paul R. Brass, Ethnicity and Nationalism: Theory and Comparison (Sage Publications, New Delhi, 1991), pp. 1820.
13. Brass, *op. cit.*, p. 18.
14. *Cf.* Feagin, *op. cit.*, p. 9. Also, Leo A. Despres, 'Toward a Theory of Ethnic Phenomena' in work edited by Despres, Ethnicity and Resource

Competition in Plural Societies (Mouton Publishers, The Hague, 1975), p. 188.
15. Vide Despress, *op. cit.*, p. 196.
16. Vide entry by S.K. Chaube, entitled Tribal Societies and the Problem of Nation-Buiiding in Nationality, Ethnicity and Cultural Identity in North-East India (Ed. B. Pakem) (Omsons Publications, New Delhi, 1990), p. 19. The book to be cited henceforth as *Nationality*.
17. Vide Nationality paper by S.K. Bhattacharyya entitled *Population Heterogeneity and Ethnic Identity in Mizoram*, pp. 302-303.
18. *Cf. Ibid.* p. 305; also, S. Chatterjee, *Mizoram Encyclopaedia*, Jaico Publishing House, 1990; 4th edn., p. 3.
19. B.B. Goswami, *The Mizo Unrest—A Study of Politicisation of Culture* Alekh Publishers, Jaipur, 1979, pp. 20-22. 20. The source is Vanlawma, cited in *Nationality*, p. 300.
21. S.K. Bhattacharyya, vide *Nationality*, p. 300.
22. *Ibid.*, p. 301.
23. Facts from Souvenir, p. 38.
24. Quoted in Barpujari, *op. cit.*, p. 340. For details, Vide Nirmal Nidedon, *Mizoram: The Dagger Brigade*, New Delhi, 1980.
25. For facts, Barpujari, *ibid.;* Nibedon, *ibid.*
26. Vide Souvenir, p. 39.
27. *Ibid.* Barpujari, *op. cit.*; pp. 343-44.
28. *India Today* (New Delhi), 16-31, August 1980; editorial in *The Assam Tribune* (Gauhati), 21 April 1981.
29. Vide *Nationality*, p. 306.
30. *The Telegraph* (Calcutta), 17 January, 1992.

11

Mizoram's Freedom Fighters: Kalkhama and Lianphunga

S.K. Barpujari

Ruled by their valiant chiefs, the Mizos better known to outsiders as Lushais, were a very warlike and adventurous people. As "jumer of forests", they were a roving people who lived mostly on agriculture. Hunting also occupied an important position in the life and economy of the Mizos. Prior to the establishment of British rule over them, they used to raid their neighbourhood for wealth as well as people to make them slaves. Exclusive in spirit and independent in disposition, the Mizos were passionately attached to their land and forest which had never failed them at any time of their history. They could never tolerate encroachment on their land and forest by any outsider on any pretext, however justifiable that might be to the encroacher.

Since the British annexation of Cachar (1832) and more so from the fifties of the last century with the extension of the plantation, opening of vast tracts of forest lands and prohibition of elephant-catching by the hillmen while granting the same right to Military Authorities and "Sahibs", or other parties brought the freedom loving Mizos into open conflict with the British imperialists.[1] Although in the beginning, a policy of conciliation was followed by the British Government to deal with the Mizo raiders, repeated raids by these hillmen compelled it to adopt a "Forward Policy" which resulted in the successful Lushai Expedition of 1871-72. This had brought in its train extension of British influence into the hills inhabited by the Mizos. After annexation of Upper Burma (1885), the British Government saw no reason why the Lushai Hills, the only terrain between India and Burma should not be brought under its control to complete the process of colonisation of the North-East.[2] Therefore, the annexation of Lushai land or Mizoram in 1890 was the culmination of the aggressive policy adopted by the British which made them the virtual master of the Mizos. But this position was gained not without a challenge from the Mizos led by their powerful chiefs despite their internal feuds and lack of solidarity.

The Mizos were fortunate in the past to have a number of chiefs and chieftainess[3] who fought with all their courage and determination to drive out the hated foreigners who had come to rob them of their independence. The names of such fighters for Mizo's freedom and independence are legion, but it will be worthwhile to recall the names of two such heroes who sacrificed their lives a century ago under tragic circumstances in a British jail for the cause of their motherland. They were Kalkhama and Lianphunga, the most powerful of the several sons of the Sailo Chief Suakpuilala who also played a conspicuous part in the Anglo-Lushai conflict till the time of his death.

Kalkhama was the eldest of the sons of Suakpuilala. Ever since 1872, both the father and the son stood as sentinels in the southern frontier of Cachar by maintaining the ascendency of the western section of the Lushais as against their counterparts the eastern and the Haulong (Howlongs). It was an open fact that with the help of Suakpuilala the District Officer of Cachar not only opened the Lushai Hills for imperial interests but broke the supremacy of the Lushai community. Things, however, took a different turn in 1880 after the death of Suakpuilala; the old feuds between the western and eastern Lushai were not only renewed, but quarrel among the several sons of the late chief reappeared with greater vigour.[4]

Now the leadership of the western Lushais devolved on Kalkhama he was able to maintain the supremacy of his tribe despite the opposition of his rivals. But his relationship with the British deteriorated as soon as he refused the offer of friendship by the officials of Cachar.[5] It may be stated that unlike his father Kalkhama had little or no love for the British and the latter considered him and his cousin Thangula as "blood thirsty and violent" in disposition. Even during the life time of his father, the British found him a hard nut to crack due to his "obstinacy and misconduct". Lianphunga, younger brother of Kalkhama was a chief of considerable "force of character" had great influence over his brothers. All the chiefs between the Sonai and the Dhaleswari obeyed Kalkhama and Lianphunga.[6]

During 1888 and 1889 several occurrences took place in quick succession. The most serious of which was the murderous attack in March 1888 on a survey party under Lieutenant Stewart who was killed along with two English corporals by men of a Shindu chief Howsatta about twelve miles north-east of Rangamati. A month later a raid was led by the Lushais on the Pakuma Rani' s village within British territory, killing the Rani with twenty one of her men and carrying off thirteen persons.[7] However, the most daring one was undertaken by Lianphunga assisted by Zahrawka (Zarok), both sons of Suakpuilala on the Chengri valley in January 1889. It was reported that a party of 600 Kukies descended on the valley and in course of three days, the raiders attacked and burnt 24 villages, killed 100 men and carried off 91 as prisoners.[8]

Although the Government of Bengal believed that the raid on Pakuma Rani's village was committed by Kalkhama and his son Rai Bahadur Haricharan Sharma, the Extra Assistant Commissioner, after thorough enquiry absolved Kalkham from the alleged guilt. Sharma attributed the same to the sons of the deceased chief Vutaia.[9] In December 1888, a punitive expedition was despatched to the hills to avenge the murder of Stewart and punish the guilty chief associated with the raids in the Chittagong frontier. The plan was subsequently changed and a bigger force was sent not only to punish the tribes, but to subject them, to explore and open out the little known tract between Chittagong and Burma and establish posts for the protection of the frontier. This was the famous Chin-Lushai Expedition of 1889-90.[10]

The expedition was somewhat successful so far as the submission of several chiefs and rescue of captives were concerned, but the cunning Lianphunga evaded capture by General Tregear and Daly, commandant Surma Valley Military Police although he was under the "clutches" of the latter. However, the expedition attained its primary success in the occupation of the Lushai Hills and in the establishment of a number of posts at strategic points such as Aijal, Changsil, Fort Tregear, etc., which were connected by road and telegraphic communications.[11] On April 1,1890 Captain Browne took charge as Political Officer of the North Lushai Hills, with his headquarters at Aijal, which meant the occupation of the Lushai country. But many of the chiefs were yet to be brought under submission; they were opposed to Browne's demand for house-tax and supply of forced labour for road construction.[12]

Kalkhama who had lost his former position after the destruction of the old village of Lianphunga and creation of the forts of Aijal and Changsil was still at large. After capturing Lianphunga, Browne proposed to punish him and Zahrawka for their complicity in the Chengri valley raid which had been confirmed by the admission of Lianphunga himself in his deposition before Daly on February 9 and Browne on June 13, 1890 respectively.[13] Browne announced in an assembly of chiefs at Aijal that the two chiefs would "no longer be recognised as chiefs or allowed to build a new village". However, if they themselves would "promise good behaviour" and "furnish sureties in support of their intentions", the order would be for four years, and that at the end of that period a fresh order would be issued, the nature of which would depend on the way they had behaved in the meantime. But about the complicity of Kalkhama and other sons of Suakpuilala, Browne had not heard anything from the Lushais whom he had met.[14]

Already the discontent among the hillmen were brewing against the imposition of revenue (house-tax) and demand for forced labour."The announcement of the punishment of Lianphunga and Zahrawka (Zarok) added fuel to the fire. The western chiefs led by Kalkhama organised men to rise against the British. Browne was not aware of the preparations for an uprising in the Lushai village due to interruption of communications as a result of heavy rains. On September 9, he was ambushed on his way to Changsil with his escort of four men by the followers of Thanruma, another powerful Lushai chief. Browne was severely wounded and three of his men were killed. Browne just after 15 minutes of his arrival at Changsil succumbed to his injuries. Simultaneously Kalkhama men attacked and besieged Changsil and Aijal. It was gathered that the whole countryside of North Lushai Hills was in revolt. Two detachments were despatched to relieve Aijal and Changsil, but Lieutenant Swinton of the detachment was killed along with several of his men wounded.[15]

After Browne's death McCabe, Deputy Commissioner of Lakhimpur was appointed Political Officer to succeed him. Accompanied by Captain Williamson, the new political Officer arrived at Changsil to undertake operations against the offending chiefs. In course of three months, all offending villages were destroyed or burnt and their chiefs including Kalkhama surrendered. The villages under these chiefs were fined in guns and were required to supply labour without payment.[16] The chiefs Kalkhama, Lianphunga and Thangula who had been involved in the uprising were detained in Silchar jail pending the final orders of the government. While suggesting their deportation for a "definite number of years", McCabe in his letter addressed to the Chief Commissioner of Assam stated:

> Khalkhama was the spirit in the recent rising, and I consider his deportation will have a good effect on the Lushai chiefs generally. Lianphunga has a bad record and the punishment inflicted on him last year does not seem to have proved an effective deterrant. He openly disregarded the orders of the Government, rebuilt his villages.

> During the present outbreak he has undoubtedly been our most subtle though not prominent opponent and his presence in these hills would always prove a source of danger to us. Thangula Raja is Khalkhama step-brother and his right hand man in the attacks on Aijal and Changsil the deportation of Khalkhama, Lengphunga will prove a salutary effect and facilitate the administration of the Lushai tribes.[17]

The Government of India concurred in the opinion of Mr. J.W. Quinton, Chief Commissioner of Assam; Kalkhama, Lianphunga and Thangula were accordingly ordered to be detained for ten years under Regulation III of 1818. They were deported to Hazaribagh (Bihar) for detention in the jail of that district. It came to light from the telegraphic communication of the Chief Secretary, Government of Bengal to the Secretary to the Government of India in the Foreign Department of September 12 and 15, 1891, that Kalkhama and Lianphunga committed suicide in the Hazaribagh Jail.[18] The Deputy Commissioner of Hazaribagh who conducted an enquiry into the matter stated that the two chiefs hanged themselves in the jail latrine with ropes prepared by them from pieces of cloth torn from their dhoties. These ropes were made by degrees whenever they went to the latrine and kept these concealed among several clothes they used to wear.[19] It was ascertained from the Inspector General of Jails that the chiefs never complained of any ill treatment in the jail or about the diet given to them. They were also given tobacco and alcohol and never created any suspicion of "meditated attempts at escape or suicide".[20]

The Government of Bengal also informed the Government of India that the "unfortunate occurrence"—suicide of Kalkhama and Lianphunga was not due to "want of supervision or to any fault of the jail authorities". In the opinion of the Government, the incident "caused little or no interest among their late subjects". This view of the British Government cannot be accepted in totality because even after the punishment given to the chiefs, many of the Lushai chiefs could not reconcile to their loss of independence and sovereign rights. In fact, a period of resistance had begun in the Lushai Hills which did not end till 1895. Tribute or Taxation and increased labour imposed upon the chiefs were at the root of the "armed conflict" during 1890-95.[21]

At the time of the passing away of the two valiant fighters, they were in their forties. Languishing in a British jail far from their hills for whose freedom and independence they had fought and suffered preferred to sacrifice their lives by their own hands. They perceived very clearly that even at the end of their ten years' of deportation if they were freed and allowed to return they might not be able to enjoy the power and position of chiefs amongst their people as they previously did. The tragedy is that though they have sacrificed their all, their souls could not rest in peace as their hills have been robbed of independence by the foreigners whom they despised. But the names of Kalkhama and Lianphunga will always remain in the pages of history in the list of the forgotten heroes in the country's fight for freedom against foreign rule.

REFERENCES

1. Lalrimawia; "Economy of the Mizos", *Studies in the History of North East India,* Shillong, 1986, pp. 166-7.
2. S. Chatterjee, *Mizoram Under British Rule,* 1985, pp. 99-100.
3. Benaitomgi (Vanhnuaithangi), Darbile (Darbilhi), Repuiliani (Ropuiliani) are a few among them
4. S. Chatterjee, *op. cit.*, pp. 90-96.
5. *Ibid.*
6. Assam Sectt. Record Foreign (A) Nov. 1890, No. 14, Browne to Chief Commissioner, Assam, 4 August, 1890.
7. B.C. Chakravarty, *British Relations with the Hill Tribes of Assam 1964*, 1964, pp. 75-76.
8. *Ibid.*
9. S. Chatterjee, *op. cit.*, p. 100.
10. R.N. Reid, *History of the Frontier Areas Bordering on Assam,* pp. 7-9.
11. S. Chatterjee, *op. cit.*, pp. 104-106.
12. H.K. Barpujari, *Problem of the Hill Tribes NE. Frontier,* Vol. III, p. 96. SN.6.
13. Foreign Political proceedings (External) Oct. 1890, No. 138. *Extract from the Diary of W.W. Daly* (Jan. 9 to Feb. 11, 1890)
14. *Ibid.*
15. S. Chatterjee, *op. cit.*, p. 107.
16. Assam Sectt. Record, Foreign (A) Dec. 1892 No. 86, McCabe to Chief Commissioner, Assam, Jan. 19, 1891.
17. Quoted in Reid, *op. cit.*, p. 19.
18. Assam Sectt. Record Foreign (A) May 1892, No. 140, Chief Secretary, Bengal Govt. to Secretary, Govt. of India Foreign Deptt. Sept 24, 1891.
19. *Ibid.*
20. *Ibid.*
21. R.N. Reid, *The Lushai Hills.*
    (Reprint edition, Aizawl 1978), p. 29.
    Sangkima: "Relations Between the English and Lushai Chiefs etc." in: *Proceeding* Volume Shillong Session (1989), N.E. India History Association, p. 439 ff.

12

The Heritage We Received from Our Forefathers

K.C. Lalvunga, IFS (Rtd.)

Ever since Mizoram was annexed to the then British Indian Empire in 1890, it has been a part and parcel of the empire which has later became the Republic of India. We are proud to be a part of the great republic, and we are equally proud, if not more of our separate identity yet loyal to the republic whose free citizenship we accept. What is the separate identity which we prize so high? They are the language we speak, Tibeto-Burman in origin, our racial affinity to the Mongoloid stock, our legends that tell us of the simple life our forefathers lived and the values believed in, our history which was orally passed down to the generations (for there was no script before 1894 when the missionaries introduced phonetic alphabet from the existing roman script). Our feeling of belonging to a unique community, right or wrong, and above all, our new found faith, Christianity, which gives us all the elements of civilization and the cause which gives us something to live by. We believe that during the long course of history we have been providentially formed as a spearate ethnic tribe, speaking separate language, living in a different way as a separate regional entity and believing in one common faith which gave us directly an international outlook in life.

The status of Mizo as a part of Indian nationality has lately been defined that Mizos have been separated from the main body of India by the British or Christian missionaries for their colonial perpetuation. Indeed British adopted rigid rules called Chin Hills Regulation and Inner Line Regulation to protect us from being assimilated by the bigger community of India. This new theory is completely wrong. The fact is that the Mizos have become Indians only after the annexation of Mizoram to the Indian empire. While we appreciate the broad mindedness of these people who give our status a new definition, for their patriotic outlook for the Pan-Indian national unity, we need not take the wrong premises as a base for historical interpretation to suit our ideas. We do agree even with the idea of emotional integration of India, and need not be persuaded to change the course of history. History is history, we cannot rewrite it to suit our political views. I will repeat that Mizos have been in existence as a tribe since we left our south Chinese home in the dim past. We are, therefore, a separate regional ethnic people trying to maintain our regional identity within the Union of India. On the other hand, there have been lately some sort of attempts to show ourselves as a remnant of an old civilization, trying to give exact dates or century as to the time when, for example, we migrated from Tibet to South China, or we took part in building the great wall of China or that we marched along the victorious army of Genghis Khan and the like (these are all to me far-fetched and unproved ideas). While we must have some distant affinity with those people such statements are nothing but wild imaginations.

Major McCall, ICS, Superintendent of Lushai Hills (as Mizoram was then called) must have been one of these people who advanced such theory. He was of the opinion that the Mizos, because of the high standard of their social ethics, must have been the component part of the civilized nation sometime in the dim past; a high tribute to the Mizo way of life! True, our social values and our way of practising them closely follow what people called Confucianism. This shows our ethnic proximity to the Chinese. But I do not think that we need necessarily be a part of some more civilized people only because we have maintained a high standard of social ethics. If we look clearly the topographical condition where the Mizos found themselves, I believe that they had to maintain that kind of social ethics if they like to survive the ordeal of jungles and its peril. Let me explain how this is the case in Mizo life, and it is in fact, the main theme of this article.

As far as we know from the verbal history, the Hnamte clan did not have a chief. That was a serious lack in the old Mizo life for a chief was important to keep enemies away. As any group of people could suddenly turn hostile in those days and plunder the village, it was good to have a strong chief or leader to protect life and property. They were, therefore, induced to invite Zahmūaka of Tlangkhua to become their chief. Tlangkhua was one of the principal villages of the Lusei clan. That incident in history approximate to the end of the sixteenth century or to the beginning of the seventeenth century. This is not, however, to suggest that Hnamte were the first Mizo clan to have chief. In fact, it is said that the Mizo did not have a separate royal house, rather every clan had their own chief. We are talking about how one of the Mizo tribes Hnamte had their own chief. It is said that Zahmuaka turned down the invitation first, but accepted it later because of the insistence of his wife. The contract between Zahmuaka and the Hnamte clan rather looks like a page from the social contract theory of Rousseau, a French philosopher. According to the agreement, chieftainship was offered to Zahmuaka on condition that he ruled his village like his own household. Should any member of the Hnamte clan became destitude for any reason, and seek shelter under his roof, Zahmuaka should not enslave him but receive him like his free villager, and allow him to pay ransom for his freedom at better time. Another important provision in the agreement was that all the villagers pay him paddy tax, was added to which meat tax, honey dues, fish dues, free labour to construct the chief's house as time went on, and thereby making the burden of the people heavier and heavier till about three centuries later when the grievances of the people exploded into an open rebellion against chiefs. This happened some two or three decades before Mizoram was annexed to the *Indian Empire.* Resistance to the chief's authority was not, therefore, new to the Mizos. Chieftainship was finally abolished in 1954 after the District Council was established according to the Sixth Schedule of the Constitution of India.

Zahmuaka had six sons, and seventh died at childhood. Each one of them was the progenitor of a royal house but sooner or later, their downfall followed either for their misrule or for their incapacity to maintain their sovereignty. At last the descendants of Sailo, one of the great grandsons of Zahmuaka survived the ordeal and became the founding father of the ruling family of almost the whole of Mizoram for three centuries.

The social, economic and political condition of the land was semi-primitive, semi-civilised. There was no communications with the outside world. Travellers, traders and raiders followed the edge of mountain ranges, river or streams and the like. No hospital, no school, nothing of that kind. One may call it a primitive society, in fact that term comes closest to the reality. Houses were small and were made of bamboos and sungrasses. Utensils were made of clay for the art of pottery was very elementary. Cotton was grown and coarse clothes were made for various needs. Dying stuff were made from indigo and only black and white colour could be made. Other coloured stuff for special dress like *Puanchei, Puandum, Thangchhuah Puan, Tawlhloh Puan, etc.*, are imported from India and Burma. They are quite comparable to the hand woven clothes of Laotian, Vietnamese and other oriental peoples. Domestic animals were chickens, pigs, goats and *mithun.* Dogs and cats were domesticated, of course. *Jhuming* was the way of cultivation. Rice, maize and millets were the staple foods. So also were the yam, sweet potatoes and few kinds of vegetables including pumpkins and coarse beans. Village blacksmiths, criers, and the priests were important people of the village, of course, under the chief and his elders. Chief selected his elders from all clans so as to ensure that justice is done and made it appear that it is done. Weapons consisted of bows and arrows and spears up to the end of the eighteenth century, flint locked gun was introduced only by the turn of that century. These weapons and the special Mizo knives *(dao)* and axes were the only weapons of battles and raids. Drinks was mainly rice beer of some varieties including the fermented one called *Rakzu.* There was no caste system, but a little elementary class system was there because of the seeds being sown, by the chiefs! Under the Sailo chiefs, Hnamte, for that matter all the Lusei clans justified their rule by successfully leading the Mizo tribes to curve out permanent abode which we now call Mizoram; and by ensuring the survival of our culture, language, and cohesion of the tribe a future nation was born. In order to achieve this end the Sailo chief and his villagers had three distinctive tasks to perform. First and foremost was the defence of the village; second, was production of sufficient food for the whole village; and thirdly, maintenance of law and order in the village which consisted of four to six thousand souls in the thick of the jungles.

In defence matter, the chief was the supreme commander of the village youngmen who marched according to his direction. In order to give full protection to the villagers, all the able bodied man had to be mobilised and given some training of that sort. For this purpose youngmen had to be put together under one roof to readily repulse attacks by enemies or wild beast which may try to feed on domestic animals like pigs, goat or *mithun, etc.*, or against marauders from the neighbouring villages or from across the Chin Hills, for no other raiders of significance could come from any other parts of the world.

Village youngmen above the age of fifteen up to thirty or more were required to sleep in the *Zawlbuk* which also served as village club where all men including the old ones normally met for their pastime. Morning or evening, anybody who did not have any chores to attend just came to the *Zawlbuk* and discussed all kinds of subjects under the sun. In fact, it was in the *Zawlbuk* where children mainly learnt useful lessons of history, biography, stories of adventure and romance or anything that came for discussions. Boys played various games of competition including the one as to who dared to place the live faggot farthest in the dark jungles, and by playing such kind of games village boys learnt to brave all physical and mental dangers around. Village weapons like flintlocked guns, spears and shields or *daos* were kept in the *Zawlbuk*. Vigilant party was made among the village youngmen to guard against surprise attack by night or even in daytime when all able bodied men were out in the fields.

Boys below the age of fifteen were required to collect firewoods in the forest at daytime and leaders of the young bóys were appointed mainly to oversee that all boys collected according to his allotment. These firewoods were burnt at night to give light and warmth all night at *Zawlbuk*. When a boy came of age and was about to assume more responsible position, he would show his public hairs to prove his age. This little crude ceremony was the joy of all boys young and old, and they insisted that it be held!

It is said that *Zawlbuk* was built mainly for the purpose of village defence. In the absence of *Zawlbuk* the whole village could be wiped out in one night. Heart rendering incidents of surprises are replete in the annals of Mizo history, like the one of *khawnglung* or the ransacking or *mangchini-nu* village; where enemy dodged the vigilant party and surprised *Zawlbuk* and killed almost all the inmates and transported the survivors to far off villages in Chin hills and other places.

Normally Lusei tribes are best in the frontal attack, but the Chin tribes were terrible at surprises and guerrilla warfare because they could suffer hunger and solitude for days and days and then would appear suddenly before their victims, normally, in the absence of their men folks. It is not a fair fight, but surprisingly they seem to know the facts and realities of the war! As a result, they could always strike terror deep into the heart of their opponent. Even when we were young, that is just before the second world war, long after the Pax britanica was declared, mothers still threatened their naughty children to stop crying lest Chins would capture them !

In the Mizo village all men are acquainted with each other, and the village elders keep careful account of the heroic performance of each and every youngman, and they know who is brave and diligent. During the festival or sacrificial day of the chief or a well-to-do man of the village, the bravemen of the village was honoured with the symbolic offer of rice beer in a shapely horn of *mithun* or wild buffalo called the braveman's cup. Until and unless the braveman of the village sip the zu, no other in the village could drink his zu (rice beer). That was the highest honour a man could receive and in order to receive that honour many youngmen lost their lives. This public reward fostered healthy competition among youngmen and the result was safety and freedom for the village.

Among the qualities that the Mizos had fostered in their life was the spirit of *Tlawmngaihna* which eludes exact literal translation. The nearest translation in English may be *an ideal of life in which a man could not be outdone in doing good to others.* When a man is *Tlawmngai,* one cannot defeat him in doing good to others, and that self-sacrifice sometimes demands life itself. It is comparable to the spirit of HMS BERKENHEAD which sunk off the coast of Africa sometime in the beginning of the nineteenth century. It is said that during the first world war, some two thousand Lusai labourers were sent down to France, and that was only a quarter of a century after the annexation of Mizoram, and the spirit of *Tlawmngaihna* was still the guiding light for Mizo youngmen. Many times the Mizo boys refused to retreat from work even after the clock struck the retiring hour if they had not yet finished their days work. It is a shame to leave the work half done irrespective of the situation. They, therefore, carried with them their sylvan tradition even in France much to the chagrin of their European counterparts.

The next important task of the chief was to see that his villagers are self sufficient in food, failing which the alternative was famine and pestilence, for there was no central government and there was no FCI to supply food! Each and every family had to feed not only itself, but must have some provision for future too. True, if anybody could not carry on their *jhuming* for some reason and became destitute, the chief cut the portion of well-to-do's paddy and give it to the needy at nominal price. The chief was something like the village father who had to see that everybody works and everybody eats well. Sometimes when somebody could not work in the field for sickness or for any incapacity, the whole village helped him and finished the job. But, any self respecting man tries his best to avoid such a situation ignoring even sickness unless it is so serious as to render him to bed. Owing to the spirit of *Tlawmngaihna,* people try to avoid bothering neighbours. By imposing such an iron discipline upon themselves, ihe Mizos cultivated the high standard of diligence and self-respect. Experience told them that it was the only way to face the hardship of their surrounding habitat.

The third important function of the chief and village elders was to see that peace and order were maintained within the village. The Mizos are not litigant as a rule but in big villages whose inhabitants exceed five to six thousands, there could be many civil and criminal cases. Suffice it to say that all the cases have to be settled amicably, and in doing that, they evolved a clear and elaborated customary laws which were later codified by N.E. Parry, ICS, Superintendent of the Lushai Hills (1924-28). By doing so the Mizos developed a deep sense of respect for law, a strong sense of unity and family feeling. Even today, there is hardly any tribe or community in India who are as compact and brotherly as the Mizos. Pu Lallhlamuang Kcivom in his book *Zoram Khawvel* rightly observed that the Mizos of the Mizoram State has an island mentality, that they look as other parts of the world as something beyond their own abode, and thereby built quite an inaccessible wall around them. If that is so, Mizos are yet to come out of their cocoon !

Apart from that the chief and his elders had many other things to decide: things like selection of land for *jhuming* and catching fishes in dry season when villages go to the river which they normally poison with the bark of the tree or by making *Ngawi* by the whole village. *Ngawi* is a large bamboo trap fastened to the trunk of the tree which is placed as a bulwark of dam across the river. The *Ngawi* or bamboo trap is so big that the whole village had to build it. That is why the chief came into the picture. Villagers are divided into groups so that one group goes one after another to the *Ngawi* to collect fishes so that the whole villages have equal share.

An ominous decision that the chief had to make was when going out to raids in the neighbouring communities. This adventure gave the Mizo the name of Head Hunters about which enough have been said. Probably the communities around us have more thing to say about these stories. From 1826 to 1889, Mizos made *tens and tens* of raids to the plains curving out tributary villages and towns within the British Indian territories from which they collected taxes. In one of these raids, they killed a British tea planter, James Winchester and captured his little daughter Mary Winchester in 1871. The British sent three-prong expeditions into Mizoram, one from the south, another from the north and the third from the east. Mizoram was, therefore, finally annexed and we lost our sovereign right to rule ourselves.

When the British annexed Mizoram to their colonial empire, they being commercial people knew at once that maintenancc of law and order in a country like Mizoram would be a burden to their colonial exchequer. They, therefore, allowed the ruling chiefs of Mizoram to continue their rule, of course, under the supervision of the District Commissioner called Superintendent. That was the cheapest administration they could devise. But the chiefs were first of all reduced to the level of vassalage. The District Commissioner was firmly in control and not the chiefs.

We must, however, appreciate that the British administration was the first civilized administration the Mizos had ever experienced. There is no doubt about the peace and prosperity the new administration had brought in. New songs and dances came out in praise of the new life the people enjoyed. In the mean time missionaries arrived and the whole populace embraced Christianity within fifty years of their arrival. As we look back now, we are able to discern more clearly the changes the colonial rule had brought about. It is easy to blame the colonialism, and it cannot be said a good system for all conditions, but we must remember that colonialism had brought with it a civilizing factor and Mizos are the true beneficieries.

The Mizos are now under the influence of a new way of life. They could not remain as they had been. The first blessing was the absence of enemies or raiders against whom the Mizos had always to be vigilant. Peace and prosperity prevailed and the restless souls who raided or were raided settled down and adopted a peaceful life. But it has been rightly observed that every good system has a seed of its own destruction. As peace and prosperity come to the land under the foreigners' leadership, all the old values evolved under the leadership of old Mizo administration have been washed down the drain. As the material gains are snowballing, moral degenerations have set in. The village youngmen do not find it necessary to sleep in the *Zawlbuk*, and with the collapse of *Zawlbuk* the spartan discipline binding the Mizo boys also gradually collapsed, and the braveman's cup no longer attracted them. His usefulness in the society is now down to the extent the braveman's cup has lost its attractiveness. Diligence, honesty respect for the elders and above all the spirit of *Tlawmngaihna* have departed from the Mizo lives. Schools and churches could hardly take the place of Zawlbuk.

Education, health care, communications, trade and commerce and governmental services have done tremendous works for material prosperity. But the new elites could not take the place of the feudal chiefs because of the colonial master who did not hold moral responsibility for the society. In the absence of right leadership the high sense of Mizo morality has decayed and the whole society seems to be the victims of moral corruption brought in by the change of time. The traditional chiefs who failed to imbibe the spirit of the new age brought in by education, etc., could not lead the people in their new venture and Mizo society became leaderless at a time when good leadership was most needed.

In course of time, independence came not so much by our demand as by providence. We have, therefore, been overtaken by the events and by the new republic. Our cultural aspirations have clashed in some way with that of the new nation especially their anti-Christian missionary attitude as an example. We are, therefore, not sure, where we stand. Our old society have gone, we are confronted with new situations. This is not to be confused with the 20 years of insurrection which was brought to an end by the memorandum of understanding with the Government of India, but culturally we are not very much in agreement with the anti-west and the pro-communist stand taken by the Government of India. This ideological clash is evident whenever there is some international clash between different ideologies, e.g., in every Israel-Arab clash, Mizos are fundamentally with Israel, or in the Falkland war, absolutely with the British side, or in the Gulf war, totally with America. If it is a simple a tribal deviation, time will heal. But if it is something deeper, we have to make some new adjustment without sacrificing our faith, our culture, our language and dialects, history and our land, all of which we inherited from our forefathers. There is no point in going in for insurrection as some of us had done, but we have to settle the fundamental differences amicably and democratically. This is the watchword of modern day which we have to follow because unity is always paying if it is done between equals. Thanks to the collapse of communist hegemony, much of our anxiety is over.

I have taken international conflicts—as an instance, that is, only an indication of our differences with the rest of India but our real problems lie nearer home, in our adjustments with the bigger communities.

Since we have attained the statehood, we are crossing a new frontier for the third time since we were annexed to the *empire.* All that we need to make our new life more rewarding is to revive our old values and add our new found faith of the former and, therefore, give fresh blood to our Mizo regional entity.

Bibliography

I have taken references from the following bibliography mentioned hereunder. I have written the manuscript from my knowledge which I gained from reading the books mentioned below as well as from verbal communications from my father, my aunt and friends. Following are the list of books.

NOTES

A. Thanglura, *Mihrâng Leh Sahrâng.*
B. Lalthangliana, *History of Mizo in Burma.*
Chaltuakhuma, *History of Mizoram.*
Col. Shakesper, *Lushai Kuki Clan.*
J.M. Lloyd, *The History of Mizo Church.*
Lalthlamang Keivom. *Zoram Khawvel.*
Major McCall, *Lushai Chysalis.*
N.E. Parry, *Monograph on Lushai customs and ceremony.*
Pastor Liankhaia, *History of Lushai.*
Reginald A. Lorrain, 5 *years in unknown jungles.*
Rev. Liangkhaia, Mizo awm dân hlui.
V.L. Siama, *History of Mizo.*
Vumson, *Zo History.*

13
The Mizos in Mizoram

Lalhmuaka

How the Name is Derived

Now one can say when and how the name of Mizo was derived; it can be said of it only by reckoning. Below is given two informations

> 'Chhak tiang Mizo pa, phelraw chawi a,
> Sa tinreng kap e".

It means 'Mizo men of the east killed various animals with bamboo spears. A match-lock gun was first obtained when the Pawi riders attacked the Ralte people when they were in the Lentlang range long before they came down to the present Mizoram. Secondly, Surg. Leut. Col. A.S. Reid says in his book Chin Lushai Land (Published in 1893). "I believe the Lushais call themselves "Zao". "Zao" may mean Zofa.

Who are They

The Principal tribes are Ralte, Hmar, Mara, Pawi, Paite, Lusei, Vaiphei, Thahdo, etc. The Mizo race is the result of a fusion, so is the language in which Pawi words remained embedded mainly in old verses. So, in these respects the name Mizo is similar to the American or the British.

What are the Unifying Factors

The factors are as follows:

(i) Time. For many many years they lived together in one region.
(ii) The rule of mainly the Sailo and Pawi Chiefs. Under this rule

they had broadly common performance of religion, of administration of justice (i.e., customary laws and uses), and a language which is understood by all. Secondly, the iron rule of the British Government. Third, the last but not the least, Christianity: the Church. Upto the end of the Second World War, Mizoram can be said of having One church.

Why did They Leave Their Old Home?

The answer is as follows:

(i) Their old home on the LENTLANG range had become unproductive due to long cultivation.
(ii) Internal conflicts. Fighting among themselves was almost daily occurrence.
(iii) External pressures. Raiders or invaders from the north and south.

As mentioned in the above, when a big festival was being held when the Pawi riders suddenly attacked them; and in the ensuing fighting a match-lock gun was taken from them.

How and When They Moved Down

In their old home, each of these tribes or clans had a chief of their own, except the Hmar tribe and Pachuau clan. The approximate time can be ascertained by a book. The Lushai Kuki by Leut. Col. J. Shakespear, in which it mentioned that the first batch of the fleeing people reached Cachar in 1780 (pp. 185) when the Mizos drove them out. Secondly, in the Chin-Lushai Land, in page seventh we read, "The first record of the raids of these savages dates form 1777 when the chief of Chittagong. applied for a detachment of sepoys to protect the inhabitants against the incursions of the Kukis".

(i) The Hmar clan of the Mizos came first and settled mainly on the first range of mountains to the west of the Tiau river, the boundary line. They remained here for, probably, more than 200 years when the main bulk of them moved towards the north in Cachar and Manipur.
(ii) The Palian and the Zadeng chiefs were the next comers. The bypassed the Hmar clans and went down right upto the western boundary. They were, some years after, subdued by the Sailo chiefs.

(iii) Chuaungo, Chuauhang and Hauhnar clans came and bypassed the Hmar people and settled round Saitual, about 60 km due east from Aizawl.

(iv) Many other clans came. The last is the Sailo Chiefs. From this time to 952 when the Chiefships was abolished, there were 12 generations.

(v) Thangluah chiefs also bypassed the Hmar clan, entering into Mizoram in the south region. When they were in the border area of the west, they were to fight with a few Sailo chiefs. Being weaker they had to move towards the south. The greatest chief was the friend of Lt. Col. Tom Herbert Lewin. From Chin-Lushai Land, we have the following extract—"At Burkal (now in Bangladesh) the funeral was joined by Rutton Puya (Rothangpuia), the Kuki (Lushai) chief, of whom we have heard so much ~~and who we have heard so much~~ and who since 1860 has been our more or less faithfully". Rothangpuia first raided this region, was defeated and submitted to the British Government in 1860. In January 23, 1871, Mary Winchester about 5 years and the daughter of the Manager of Winchester Tea Estate was captured by Lushai (Mizo) raider; she was rescued by the above-mentioned general on the 21st January, 1872. Here they were on their way to Sailam where the white girl was kept.

When the British Government came to possess the land in 1889-90, Colonel Skinner inspected the selected site of Aizawl, the 15th of February 1890; it was first strongly recommended by Mr. Daly, the Political Office of Cachar. Soon the construction of the fortification started. On the 17th March, Colonel Skinner started out for Cachar by the Tlawng river.

The first-two missionaries Rev. J.H. Lorrain and Rev. F.W. Savidge came by the country-boat in the Tlawng river from Silchar and got out from the boat and reached Aizawl on the 11th January, 1894, and settled on the spot which is now the playground of Higher Secondary School. On either side there was a small village. The two missionaries had no arms for self-defence, neither had they armed attendants as government officers. So they first regarded them 'Vagabond Sahibs', as such they failed to get labourers. The administrative officer came to know it and gave out orders that "No one can buy salt without a slip which the missionary will give". Their opinion of them soon changed. Some years later Rev. Lorrain wrote thus,—"From the first the people treated as their friend. We were unarmed and we trusted the Lushais entirely and never was found them false to us".

Crossing of the Red Sea or a big river, in which a column of smoke during the day, and a fire at night were mentioned to be roaming about.

> "When we are preparing for the big festival,
> We had to cross the Red Sea,
> Our enemies were coming after us with chariots,
> The Sea swallowed them all
> As if they were meat
> We are led by the cloud during the day
> And by fire at night.
> Take those birds for the food and
> Drink water coming out from the rock".

14. In many of the chants used in various sacrifice and in other sacred matters, the name of Manasia or Manase is often pronounced. We khow that Joseph had two sons by his Egyptian wife, viz., Ephraim and Manasseh.

Mizos belong to the Manasseh Tribe—one of the Lost Ten Tribes of Israel.

(1) At family offerings the chant is "The children of Manase offer Thee animal's blood, O God of High".

(2) Anyone coming sick from the paddy field is believed to have been stuck by the evil one living in the spring near the field, and offering is given on the spot. The chant is:
"If tied, untie him,
If manacled, unlock him,
We are taking Manase home,"

(3) At the sacrifice for healing epilepsy, the priest chants:
"Release him, we are above your power,
We are children of Manase".

(4) When selecting a paddy field site, if they found anything suspected to be 'taboo', they shout, saying, 'Go away, go away, we are bringing Manasia here".

(5) When a new settlement is made, clearing the jungle for that purpose is done, the first sappling felled is accompanied by a chant:
"You are obstructing our grandfather Manasia".

(6) When offering a sacrifice for sin, the priest chants:
"God of heaven and of the earth, we, sons of Manasia, who are on earth, are offering you the heart and liver of the animal for forgiveness of our sins".

(7) The traditional handed down orally to posterity says, 'Whenever you pray to God, the name of forefather Manasia must be pronounced.

Thus, the fact that the Mizos claimed to be the children of Manasseh, the chosen of God, is significant and noteworthy.

Be the Hatefutsoth, the Museum of the Jewish Diaspora in Tel Aviv, Israel invited me to attend the opening of the exhibition entitled, '*Beyond the Sambatyon: The Myth of the Lost Ten Tribes*' on 15th August, 1991. And I have participated the exhibition as one of the Manasseh Tribes.

RELIGIOUS HISTORY

14
Pre-Christian Religion of the Mizos

J.V. Hluna

Introduction

Most writers described the Mizo religion as animism. McCall observed that, before the occupation of their land by the British the Lushais were wholly animists.[1] They believed that life was subjected to a number of evil spirits which could only be appeased by sacrifices. They believed that every big tree, hill, big stone, etc., were inhabited by various spirits and that they were responsible for their illness, death, droughts, storms, bad crops or accidents which befell on them.[2] Thus, they lived in terrible fear, always afraid to anger the evil spirits which might harm them. As a consequence Lewis in his book *The Lushai Hills,* said Lushai religious energies are all centred on propitiating the evil spirit, and the sorcerer's magic is in demand to determine what animal should be sacrificed to appease the genius which sends the calamity and sickness.[3] They offered sacrifices very frequently to the evil spirits which abandoned both in the jungle and in the rivers to avert their anger.[4] However, it must be understood that the Mizos did not worship these evil spirits or demons. They only wanted to propitiate them as they were believed to be the causes of their illness and injuries.

Existence of God

The Mizos had a vague idea of God. They believed in the existence of one supreme God whom they called *Pathian,* a god of all humanity and goodness and thought that he lived beyond the sky as such he was recognised as *Chung Pathian* (God above us). They did not believe that he had much to do within their daily life. Sacrifices were not made to obtain peace with God or redemption as in some religions.[5] The term *Khuanu* (mother of nature) was also used to mean or as a synonym with *Pathian* particularly in song and poetry. It was regarded as the guardian and keeper of a village. As Lewis observed that sacrifice was made only twice in a year to the good spirit before and at harvest.[6] To the Mizo mind Christ's resurrection appeals with force, for in that he grasps the truth of the son of the Good Spirit triumphing over all the powers of evil.

Good and Evil Spirits

Besides they also recognised the presence of other Supernatural beings and were respected with specific names like *Vanchungnula* (maiden of heaven), *Khuavang, Lasi* and *Ramhuai* (demons or evil spirits). There were again various forms of *Ramhuai* such as *Tau, Chawm, Khawhring, Phung, Hmuithla.* The *Lasis* were not considered as demons or divinities. The *Lasi* seemed to be only concerned with wild animals, over whom they were believed to have complete control.[7] Many hunters were believed to be possessed by *Lasi* known as *Lasizawl.* The *Lasizawl* received a sign from the *Lasi* and consequently they became successful hunters. The *Lasis* were found to be numerous in number and were inhabiting the jungle. The Mizos believed that the *Lasis* were beautiful maidens and they could fall in love with hunter and bless him for his success. They were believed to be the agent of God.

Priests and Religious Sacrifices

There were *Puithiam* (Village Priests) who were responsible to perform traditional ceremonies and rituals. Each clan had a priest and the method of performance varies among them. The *Puithiam* occupied an important place in the Mizo society. No religious ceremony or rituals could be performed without him. There were two types of *Puithiam* whose function was different from each other. Saiaithanga observed that the *Sadawt* performed traditional religious ceremony and he was responsible to invoke the blessings from God for the people whereas the *Bawlpu* performed the rituals to propitiate the evil spirits to cure their sickness.[8]

A series of religious rituals performed by the *Sadawt, Fano Dawi* was one of the most important ceremonies. This sacrifice was performed by killing a black cock beside the rice bin (*Buhzem*) of the chief to ensure good crops and to prevent to many mosquitoes: It generally takes place in June. *Hnuaite* and *Hnuaipui* sacrifices were also performed for the enrichment of the soil and the surrounding of the house. *Sedawichhun* was another part of religious performance. A *mithun,* two piglets and boar were killed for the purpose. *Sekhuang* sacrifice was performed along with Se*dawichhun* with a bullgayal and a boar, other baby pigs were also necessary. *Mithi rawplam* ceremony was a time of feast and dance in honour of the dead and their ancestors. After a man has performed *Mithi rawplam* or *Sekhuang,* he could wear *diartial* (a striped turban) and could have windows in their house. Ordinary man without such performance could not have it.

Feasts performed by the Mizos

Khuangchawi, ceremony was the next step. It was performed after the repetition of *Sedawinchhun* ceremony, according to the customary practices. It was the biggest and most important ceremony. A man who performed such ceremony was known as *Thangchhuah*[9]. This was called *In lama Thangchhuah.* The *Khuangchawi* feast lasted for five days with series of specific feasts for the ceremony.

There was another type of *Thangchhuah* called *Ram lama Thangchhuah.* A man had to kill a number of certain prescribed wild animals like *Savawm* (bear) *Sakhi* (barking deer), *sele* (wild gayal), *sazuk* (samber deer), *sanghal* (wild pig), *Rulngan* (a large poisonous snake) and *Muvanlai* (hawk).[10] It may have taken almost one's entire life to complete the whole series. Therefore, many people could not afford to do it. However, *Thangchhuah* was the most coveted goal which every Mizo longed to perform and thereby their whole endeavours throughout life centred trying to achieve this goal. Those who could perform *Khuangchawi* or *Thangchhuah* were esteemed very high. They not only received social recognition in every sphere but also they had the right to live a perfect and happy life in the next world (Pialral).[11] So a man who performed such ceremony was entitled to wear a special dress designed known as *Thangchhuah Puan**. ThangchhuahPa* (man) was entitled to sit next to the chief at feast and he could use *Diartial* and could have

* Thangchhuah—This title was given to a man who has distinguished himself by giving a public feast. The possession of the title was regarded as the passport to tha Pialral.

** *Thangchhuah Puan*—The cloth worm by *Thangchhuah* to make to his distinction. His wife also entitled to wear this cloth. It was a black-stripped design.

windows and *bahzar*† at his house. The common people could not have them. Thus it is not surprising that the Mizo activities were centred, trying to achieve such performance for social and religious matters.

Zaudawh, the highest feast which a Mizo could achieve, could be performed after three *khuangchawi* feasts. There were only few who could perform it. It required at least 14 gayals and 13 pigs.[12] Besides this, according to Liangkhaia, *zu* (rice beer) of about 1000 *ngan* (pots) were required. A *Zaudawh* man could then build a kind of belvedere outside house with windows on all sides. Women could use it for weaving purposes and children use it for games. Only who could attain *Zaudawh* could have built such building. A man who completed these whole series was called *Zawhzawzo* and they were very rare indeed.

Life after Death

The Mizos had certain beliefs about the soul. They also believed in life after death. The generally accepted theory was the presence of *Mithi Khua* (dead men's village) and *Pialral* (paradise) somewhere beyond the world. This belief was instrumental in moulding the cultural norms and values. *Pialral* was meant only for *Thangchhuah* whereas *Mithi Khua* was for the spirits of the ordinary men where they would continue to work and toil. When a man died his spirit would go to *Mithi Khua* through the lake *Rihdil.*[13] Crossing *Rihdil* they came to a hill known as *Ilringlang tlang,* where the land of the living could be seen. Here they were sad and full of sentiments as they look back and viewed the world of men which they have left behind. But a particular flower grown there called *Hawilopar* (flower of no turning back) made them forget all their desires and longings as they plucked and put in on their hair. Moreover, there was mythical spring called *Lunglohtui.* By drinking the water of this spring they completely forgot the past and they were in haste for their destiny. On the gate of *Mithi Khua Pu Pawla* (a giant) with a huge pellet bow met them. If a man had not performed any ceremony and had not killed man and animals *Pu Pawla* shot him severely which had a painful effect for many years. But *Pu Pawla* did not dare to shoot *Thangchhuah* man at all. He did not shoot even infants dead at birth *(hlamzuih).* He may not shoot a young man who has enjoyed three virgins nor at one who has enjoyed

† *Bahzar*—An enclosed Varandah with a raised floor at the back of a Mizo house.

seven different women, even if they were not virgins, but women, whoever they may be, he always shoot at.[14]

Here at Pu Pawla house roads to *Mithi Khua* and *Pialral* were divided.[15] In *Pialral* food and drinks are to be obtained without labour, which to the Mizo appears the height of bliss whereas in *Mithi Khua,* life will be troublesome and difficult, everything being worse than in this world.

Sacrifice to Evil Spirits

The Mizos were very evil spirit minded. They made various sacrifices to these evil spirits or demons to propitiate them. Of the many sacrifices *Khal,* was one of the most popular ones. It was a sacrifice to the spirits which were supposed to be the cause of one's ill-health and misfortunes.[16] There were different kinds of *Khal* depending on certain animal used for the sacrifice. Those were, *Arkhal, Vawkte Khal, Kel Khal, Vanchung Khal, Khal Chuang* and *Lasi Khal.* While performing such a sacrifice, according to Challiana, the family members of the offerer could not speak to strangers for three days.

Daibawl was another sacrifice offered outside the village for a sick person. A red-cock and hen were used for the purpose. The sacrifice itself, excepting the parts placed on the altar and left there was often cooked at the spot and part of it were eaten by the priest and his assistant. Besides, there were different sacrifices connected with hunting, killing and agriculture and for various sickness. The Mizos were always conscious of the presence of evil spirit around them. They believed that every movement was closely watched by unseen spirits. Therefore, they were often careful not to incur the displeasure of the spirits which may harm them. Even before taking meal in the jungle, a small portion of food would be kept aside for the spirit saying *"Khuatlai"* (let the spirits be satisfied). Thus it appeared that they were always in constant fear of the evil spirits. They were more concerned with them to please them.

REFERENCES

1. A.G., McCall, *Lushai Chrysalis,* 1949, p. 67.
2. V.L. Siama, *Mizo History,* 1975, p. 25.
3. Grace R. Lewis. *The Lushai Hills*, Baptist Missionary Society, London, 1907, p. 29.

4. Maj A.G McCall, *op. cit.*, p. 68. Also E.L.Mendus, *The Diary of a Jungle Missionary*, Liverpool, 1956, p. 37.
5. Rev. J.M. Lloyd, *On Every Hill,* Liverpool 1955, p. 19.
6. Grace R. Lewis, *op. cit.*, p. 29.
7. Lt. Col. J. Shakespear, *The Lushai Kuki Clans,* Reprinted 1975, p. 68.
8. Rev. Saiaithanga, *Mizo Sakhua* (Mizo Religion), Maranatha Printing Press, Aizawl, p. 9-10.
9. N.E. Parry, *A Monograph on Lushai Custom and Ceremonies* (Reprint 1976). Tribal Research Institute, p. 91.
10. Pastor Challiana, *Pi Pu Nun,* 1982, p. 55.
11. *Ibid.*
12. Rev. Liangkhaia, Mizo Sakhua article contributed in the book entitled "*Mizo Zia Rang*" by Mizo Academy of Letters, 1975, p. 11.
13. Rihdil—A lake to the east of Mizoram. Supposed to be passed through by the departed spirit on their way to *Mitthi Khua*
14. Lt. Col. J. Shakespear, *op. cit.*, p. 62.
15. J.M. Lloyd, *op. cit.,* p. 21.
16. Rev. Saiaithanga, *op. cit.*, p. 33.

15
Mizos and After Life

C. Vanlallawma

It is quite a difficult task to collect supporting documents and materials relating to our subject. In Philosophy the subject would be termed as "Doctrine of Immortality of the Soul", and this perhaps is the most important branch in the study of the history of man. In layman's term it may be put as "a belief that the soul cannot die". Every society believes that the soul lives on even after the earthly body has perished. But there may be variations in this belief which may be categorised under four heads: (1) That the soul of a man is preserved in the lives of his descendants (posterity); (2) That the soul, on liberation from its earthly prison (body) assumes another form; (3) Soul is immortal and so it does not perish along with the earthly body; and (4) At the death of the body, the soul is fully under the rule and control of the creator.

There are yet certain less individualistic beliefs in the immortality of the soul. If a person had performed certain deeds which are worthy of remembrance and praise by the future generation then such a person has immortalized his soul. He has achieved "social immortality". Certain others believe that their souls are preserved in the lives of their descendants and, therefore, to them, having offsprings would mean a prolongation or extension of their lives. Such persons may be said to believe in "biological immortality".

Hindus are less individualistic in their belief. They believe in "pantheistic/impersonal immortality". That is they believe that all individual souls would merge into one divine soul.[1]

Root of Mizo Belief

Mizo belief in the immortality of the soul is amply evidenced by the folklores and legends much before their history is reduced to writing. Somewhere around the year 1935 one 'Sadawt'(a clan priest) by name, Hangpuia said: "Our knowledge about the immortality of the soul has been evident even from the story of Tlingi and Ngama."[2] Religious philosophers claimed that the root of beliefs is experience. The fact is that all religions, customs, cultures, knowledge and laws have their origin in experience. According to Hangpuia, the story of Tlingi and Ngama from which observance of Mimkut (the oldest of Mizo festivals) started may also be the source of the Mizo belief in the immortality of soul. A close examination of the story reveals that Tlingi and Ngama were lovers since their youth and their love for one another increased more and more after their marriage. Shortly after their marriage Tlingi died tragically and Ngama in his sorrow cried himself to dead inconsolably and gained entry down into the deadmen' village. On meeting his beloved he found to his dismay that she had lost a lot of weight and had become lean and thin. He asked her why and she replied "I have become thin and also sad because of scarcity of food here". She beseeched him to go back and to bring her some of the harvested crops from their field. On waking up Ngama did exactly as his wife had told him by putting food near the water pots inside their house and beckoned her to take it.[3]

One day later on, in the beautiful autumn sunset Ngama was again in his nostalgic mood and paining for his departed wife he cried himself to dead again. This time, as he entered the deadmens' village he found that his wife had regained her weight and she looked happy; and she readily disclosed to him she had fed on the food that he had brought for her. Henceforth, Ngama made it a point to keep aside a certain amount of his harvest for his dead wife. This practice soon gained popularity and the Mizo would put aside some amount of their harvest for the sake of alleviating the misery of the departed ones. It can, therefore, be said that this apparently simple story is the root of belief and practice in the olden Mizo society.

Rihdil (Rih Lake)

In Mizo culture the importance of Rihdil is mainly because of the belief that the spirit of the dead passes through this lake on its way from this life to the next one. The source of this belief has its origin in a dream. There is a story that long ago, when the Mizos had just migrated to this land, there were lot of games in and around Rihdil. Game hunters used to have a good time there. Once such a group of hunters set up their camp by the side of the lake. At the dead of night one of the hunters heard a sound of someone passing nearby. It was the sound of his wife's voice that he heard. Since there was no village nearby, he could not make sense of it all so he went back to sleep. After some time he was again awakened up by the same sound and it seemed to be closer than before and the voice audibly said "Oh no! I had completely forgotten to tell my children about the meat I had kept over the fireplace in an earthen pot. With their father still out hunting, I am afraid they would have to eat without meat". On hearing this the hunter became very restless. When he returned home he found that his wife had indeed died during his absence. He looked over the fireplace and sure enough there was some meat inside an earthen pot exactly as mentioned by the voice that he had heard.[4] It is because of this dream that Rihdil has been considered to be the passage way of the spirits soon after their release from the physical body.

Belief in *Mitthi Khua* (Deadmens' Village) and *Pialral* (Beyond river Pial)

Perhaps because of the reasons highlighted earlier, the belief that the souls of the dead would gather at some place became so prevalent. The quality of life at such a place was considered to be inferior to the earthly life. Among the Mizo the names given to some edible crops and animals attributed to that of dead men are much inferior to the real ones For instance, what is named as "Mitthi Savawm" (Dead mens' Bear) is only a hairy caterpillar. Deadmens' village is not even considered to be up above but much below the real world. Rev. Challiana said, "We believe that the dead reside somewhere below us and all the dead would go down there. They would still retain their same bodies and go about their business as in this life".[5] When Ngama met the spirit of his wife, it was mentioned in Mizo "*a zu hmu a*" meaning "he went down and met her" and this is quite consistent with the belief that the dead gather somewhere below us. But this slightly contradicts Lalmama who said "The Mizos believe that the souls of the dead gather at a place (*Mitthi khua*, which would literally mean the land of the dead). That would not mean anything beneath us but somewhere in the air that surrounds us.[6] It would, therefore, be very difficult to know exactly where the souls would gather, either below us or around us. Nevertheless this should not be allowed to distract us since in matters like this, even developed religious beliefs do not have a more consistent interpretation.

In the year 1893, Rev. G.O. Newport presented a paper "Mission Work among the Lushais" in the Missionary Conference at Bangalore. What he wrote about was: "Two places or conditions are held to exist after death. One of these is called *Piel ral* and corresponds to our heaven. The other is called *Mithi khua*, but it seems doubtful whether this is simply a place of ordinary existence for those who are not good enough for heaven, or whether it corresponds to our hell. A big river 'Piel' flows between these two places, and no one can pass over it from one place to the other. Mighty hunters and great warriors go to *Piel ral*, where they live at ease and have no trouble of any kind. They hunt and enjoy themselves. No woman can go over there, but small children of both sexes who died before they left their mother's breast could enter in and reside there".[7] This is perhaps the oldest written documenf on this subject.

According to him, Pialral is a place which is superior either by degree or by quality from *Mitthi khua*. Anyway it is a place reserved only for those who are considered to be powerful or wealthy enough in society during their life time. It also means that it is a place where only those who had achieved excellence in special spheres, at home and in hunting or in warfare are permitted entry into. Their existence there would be far more pleasant and enjoyable than those at *Mitthi khua*, as they would not be expected to labour anymore. Its location according to Pastor Challiana is not very far from *Mitthi khua*.[8] As to why it is called *Pialral* it is sufficiently clear from the earlier assertion (The other side of river Pial).

Pathway for the Dead

When someone dies his soul proceeds towards *Mitthi khua*. During this part of the journey such souls are filled with much sorrow and nostalgia and they miss their previous life (earth). After some time they would arrive at "Hringlang Tlang" (a hill from where the soul can clearly view the living world), where their nostalgia would be aggravated to the extent of shedding tears.

Beyond that, beautiful mystical flowers called *Hawilopar* (flowers which take away the desire to look back at what had been left behind) grows. They would gather the beautiful flowers and henceforth being enthralled by the beauty of the flowers they would lose all desires of turning back. Then they will come to a fountain called "Lunglohtui". Anyone who drinks from it would not only lose all desires for earthly existence but their yearnings for this life would automatically disappear. Their yearnings would now only be focussed on the land ahead—*Mitthi khua*.

They would now proceed undisturbed towards *Mitthi khua*. On reaching it they would be greeted by a massive individual called Pawla, holding his pellet-bow in his hands. His pellets are as big as eggs. He would interrogate the new comers. If he is not satisfied by their answers as to their eligibility for entry (that is, possessing the highest recognised social accreditation achievable only by well-to-do persons or outstanding hunters who can bring home specified number of games of prescribed varieties) Pawla would volley shots of massive pellets from his bow. The effect of a hit from his bow is said to result in painful injury lasting for three years. The socially accredited persons and renown hunters were alone eligible to pass unharmed. For instance, the renown hunter would ceremoniously pass through by riding on the deer he had killed, while putting on a multicoloured turban with two tails of drongo sticking out of it. Twining the horns of the deer would be a king cobra that he had also killed. An eagle that he had captured in his lifetime would fly above his head. In his front and back there would be an entourage of wild animals that he had killed to achieve the coveted accredition. Those approaching Pawla with such grandeur would be allowed to pass through without being questioned.

Babies are also permitted to pass. The reasons are that when Pawla would aim his bow at them the babies would challenge saying "Would you dare to shoot us? If only you had let us grow up till our maturity, who could not tell what great and gifted individuals we would turn out to be? It is your fault for taking us before we could prove our worth".[9]

The non-privileged ones would definitely be shot by Pawla and so out of sheer fright they would hesitate to approach him to the extent of hiding here and there but would be mercilessly dragged out of their hiding places by Pawla's wife,—Sanu so that they could be shot at by her husband. If there are no souls to shoot at on any given day Sanu would enthusiastically run around and snatch the lives out of unfortunate ones and bring them to be shot at by her husband. She would perform her duty with so much zest and gusto that her daily chores like weaving would always be left with very little progress. This is the reason that when someone dies suddenly and unexpectedly there is a saying that Sanu has taken him/her.[10]

REFERENCES

1. W.S. Sahakian and M.L. Sahakian, *Ideas of the Great Philosophers*, Barns and Noble, 1966, p. 108ff.
2. J.F. Laldailova, *Thu Ngaihnawm Bu*, 1978.

3. Thanga, Mizo Kut Chi Thumte, *Thu leh Hla (Fur Chhuak)*, 1965, p. 8-11 and Rev. Zathanga, *Mizo Kut Chhuahna Thu*, Robawm, 1946, January and May Issue
4. Lalmama, *Mizo Titi*, 1963, p. 4.
5. Challiana, *Pi Pu Nun*, 1978, p. 41.
6. Lalmama, *Mizo Titi*, 1963, p. 7.
7. Rev. G.O. Newport, *Mission Work among the Lushais*, Harvest Field, 1894 February
8. Challiana, Pi Pi Nun, p. 43.
9. Lalmama, Mizo Titi, p. 9, 10.
10. K. Zawla, *Mizo Pi Pute leh An Thlahte Chanchin*, 1989, p. 43, 44.

16

Fairy

Lalzuia Colney

In the Mizo belief, there are various spirits or supernatural beings which, at certain times of their choosing can assume the form and likeness of real human beings. Those spirits are called *huai* (demon), *phung* (spook), *thlahrang* (haunting spirit), *khawhring* (evil eye), *tualsumsu* (possessed person), *zunhindawt* (wraith), *hmuithla* (Apparition), *chawm* (a kind of demon), *ramhuai* (a devil) and *lasi* (fairy) in accordance with their different characters and manifestations. All these spirits except *lasi*, are considered to be malevolent and to encounter them is horrifying experience. *Lasi* are generally seen in dreams and is taken as a big fortune. All the wild animals are under the control of *lasi* and any hunter who is posessed by a *lasi* will be very successful in hunting.

Lurh tlang (Lurh mountain) and Tan tlang (Tan mountain) in the eastern side of Mizoram are the main habitat of *lasi* and is called capital of *lasi*. The king of *lasi* is Lalchungnunga and his wife is Tantinchhingi. This couple are the supreme commander of *lasi* and they have a handsome son called Thangchina. Just like human beings *lasi* also used to call each other by name and as such their names are known to us through their calling. The other identified *lasi* are Partinchhingi, Lamritlingi, Thliahlala, Tlukpuiliana and Dartinlala. Those names are to be found in the old song as this—

> Lurhpuia mi, Tan ami tuan in rel emaw,
> Tuan kan rel lo ve Lalchungnungan laimi man e,
> Serh kan kham reng e.
> Lamritlingi te, Dartinlal lan rawh,
> Thliahlalan dawn rawh e.

Though *lasi* were usually seen in dreams, there are certain people who had encountered them in real life. *Lasi* would observe the daily activities of human beings with great interest and they were fascinated to watch a hunter in the forest and in the process the female *lasi* would pick and choose men of their liking. Married men or bachelors would be very happy if they saw *lasi* in their dreams and sometimes *lasi* damsels would try to entice men to marry them with a promise that they would be able to shoot any wild animal of their liking. Such intimacy could go very deep in dreams, however, no man is known to have married a *lasi* in real life. Such of those men who had romantic link with *lasi* in dreams are known as 'possessed by *lasi*' and they would be very successful in hunting. Not to be outdone, old and aged *lasi* ladies were known to woo men with the same result.

Possession by *lasi* could come to an end at certain times and in such cases the concerned person would have to perform certain rituals and sacrifices called *Lasi Khal* and if the sacrificial offerings are responded by *lasi* the old relationship could be restored and the man would become possessed by *lasi* once again.

It is believed that the first generation between *lasi* and human beings originated from one Lianlunga who married a girl called Rohniangi of Zawngte Village which was situated in the east of Tiau river. Lianlunga with his friend Rokhawliana migrated to the west of Tiau river and both of them belonged to Hualngo clan. Lianlunga had two sons—Lianchia and Thalunga and also a daughter called Chawngtinleri who had grown up to be a very beautiful damsel. This couple did not live long and Chawngtinleri was under the care of her brother, Lianchia.

Thangchina, the son of Lalchungnunga, the king of *lasi* was deeply attracted to Chawngtinleri and Lalchungnunga, the king also liked Chawngtinleri to be his daughter-in-law and to look after the wild animals with care. He then sent emissaries to ask for the hand of Chawngtinleri for his son, but Lianchia being conscious of the beauty of his sister did not give a positive response to the offer of marriage. But the Lasi king was very determined to win the hand of Chawngtinleri at all costs and was ready to give anything for the bride to the extent of parting with even his most valued animal *Nghalphusen* (a special species of wild boar).

Once more the *lasi* then sent emissaries to Lianchia, who on that particular evening was in a drunken mood and readily agreed to the proposal offered. The emissaries went back home with full satisfaction. When the morning came Lianchia on coming to his senses wanted to cancel his commitment of the previous night. But by then, it was too late because while Chawngtinleri was pounding rice in the morning, the *lasi* party had come and taken her away. All that he could hear was the scream of Chawngtinleri saying 'My brother Liana, save me' and the sound of the falling pestle with which she had pounded rice in the morning. Lianchia was crestfallen and then set out to search for his sister and wandered about endlessly at Tan tlang in his search. Even the *lasi* did not fully endorse the matrimonial alliance made with the human female and they declared a rest day in which no normal activities would not be carried out and sang a lamentation for the human girl as follows—

Those at Rih and Lurh mountains,
Will you do your normal chores?
We ourselves will toil not
For Lalchungnunga's elopement we approve not
We will have a rest day instead.

One day Chawngtinleri, without making herself visible, spoke to her brother saying "Big brother, do not trouble yourself searching for me for I am in this situation due to your own decision." Lianchia also did not have much to say and he had no other alternative but to reconcile himself as such. So this was the first marriage between human beings and *lasi*.

Thereafter, the *lasi* as promised gave Nghalphusen to Lianchia for him to bag during his hunting at Saikhum. The *Lasi*, however, told him not to smile when Nghalphusen appeared before him. When Nghalphusen did actually come out before Lianchia, he found, to his surprise that the boar turned out to be absolutely fine and splendid game and out of sheer happiness he could not help smiling, whereupon the Nghalphusen grunted and sped away. The *lasi* were bent upon letting Lianchia shoot Nghalphusen and they let the animal to appear before him three times, but each time Lianchia could not resist smiling ultimately leading to his failure to bag the prize game. Sometimes later on, the Nghalphusen moved to Tawi mountain and this, Hualtungamtawna, another famous hunter and his friend had come to know of and they made great attempt to hunt down the splendid animal and the attempt resulted in the accidental death of Hualtungamtawna caused by this wild animal. It is said till today traces of Nghalphusen could still be seen at Tawi Mountain clearly.

Chawngtinleri then had a baby-son but would not let her brother see the face of the baby. But once in her absence, her folks chanced to see face of the baby and to their horror they found that the head of the baby was that of goat. This incident had greatly annoyed the *lasi* so much so that they made the eyes of Chawngtinleri slanting in a vertical way. Then Chawngtinleri lost her human form and actually became one of the members of *lasi* family.

Chawngtinleri used to weave cloths, the length of her loin loom spread from Lurh mountain to Tan mountain and she used Sialsir (a kind of hawk) to carry the warp yarn to and fro over the great chasm for her weaving. In course of time, the family moved from Lurh and Tan area to Theiriat of south. Chawngtinleri and her brother Lianchia still missed for each other very much and she told him that she would wave white cloth when her family reached Theiriat. And when they did reach Theiriat, Chawngtinleri true to her words, wove a white cloth which was seen by her brother from a long distance. The place where she wove the white cloth has become known as 'Chawngtinleri Puan thin tlang' (the hillock where Chawngtinleri waves her cloth) even to this day.

Many traces of Chawngtinleri can still be seen in and around Tan and Lurh areas and one cave is known as 'Chawngtinleri Puk' (Chawngtinleri's Cave) and below this is a good flat land called 'Chawngtinleri hmun hlui' (Chawngtinleri's old site) where Buizova (the legendary male singer of the Mizo) and others performed *chai* (one of Mizo community dances) with great enthusiasm and in high spirit to such an extent that even the *lasi* around this place could not sit still and all became excited. The event came to be known as 'Chawngtui Chapchar Kut hmang' in Mizo history.

There were some other persons who were 'possessed by Lasi' and one such man was Rokhawliana who was a good friend of Lianlunga, the father of Chawngtinleri. Though Lianlunga himself was not possessed by Lasi but his wife, Rohniangi was and this was the reason why Lianlunga was very successful in hunting.

Once Rokhawliana and his friends went hunting in Tan mountain and in the course of their hunting they reached a certain place where they found a young *lasi* girl weaving cloth. The girl happened to be very beautiful and they became enamoured with her beauty and sat around her. After some time they asked her to tell her name but she refused to tell, however, due to their repeated requests she said that she was the elder sister of Thangi. When the day drew to a close, she persuaded them to leave her promising them that they would shoot certain wild animals on their way home. Accordingly, one of them shot a big deer and the other a *kawlfung* (a bison). In spite of her fervent pleas, Rokhawliana alone would not leave her. The *lasi* at last rolled up her loom and suddenly disappeared among the rocks and Rokhawliana was at his wit's end. As it was already dark, he wanted to request the *lasi* to guide him home and made his request like this—

> The sun has already set for a hunter like me,
> I beseech the fair lady to take me home,
> And I will relate all this to my mother at home.

Then as he was about to leave and the *lasi* suddenly reappeared and they were together up to the wee-hour of the night till the girl gave him a small ball of a size of cherry plum and told him to toss the ball in front of him and it will show him the way home. In the morning, when Rokhawliana looked again at the ball he found a single red bead and then he became a '*lasi* possessed' and he successfully shot many wild animals.

Once Rokhawliana was performing *se chhun* (one of the important festivals that only a rich man could perform) and he also invited *lasi* who had obliged him by coming to the festival. Rokhawliana told his mother, "Mother, give those children food", at which the they became greatly annoyed particularly at being termed as 'children' and all ran away. Rokhawliana immediately pursued and searched for them in Lurh and Tan mountain till he found them, but could not take them back to his *sechhun*.

Hranghleia of Chawngtlai was another case of *lasi* possessed who died at 88 years of age in 1942. Those *lasi* who possessed him warned him not to clap his hands at community singings ever failing which his death would be near. When he became 80, once of his friends were successful in their hunting trip and they chanted *hlado* (successful hunting song) at the entrance of their village and he became so nostalgic that he climbed at the top of *leikapui* (a raised platform adjoining a house) and responded their *hlado* this way—

> I'm so nostalgic recollecting my old days of hunting,
> Now I became old as a dying flower,
> With no strength to go a hunting.

That night they celebrated the head of the kill as custom demands at Ralkhama's house with drinks and they soon became highly spirited singing and dancing. Tears streamed down the cheeks of Hranghleia as he looked back his hey-days of yore. He could no longer refrain himself and clapped his hands once but suddenly remembered what the *lasi* had told him whereupon he could only groaned uttering "Oh my good Lord"! But it was too late and he died on April 10, 1942. The wild animals shot by him inscribed in his memorial stone are—Elephant: 2, Bison: 15, Tiger: 3 and others: 300.

This small presentation encapsulates how the old Mizo experienced the existence of *lasi* and *lasi zawl* (*lasi* possessed). Their main habitats were Lurh mountain and Tan mountain situated in the border of Mizoram and Myanmar in the east, Lurh is 6,350 feet high while Tan is 6,320 feet high.

17
Huai

C. Laitanga

The word, *huai* means evil spirit that haunts certain places, or object or thing; it manifests to man in different forms, manners and can disappear instantly. J.H. Lorrain in his *Dictionary of Lushai Language* defines *huai* as evil spirit, a demon, a devil. Lt. Col. J Shakepear in his book. *The Lushai Kuki Clans* mentioned that, the Lushai believes the hills, streams and trees are inhabited by various demons. These are known as *huai*, those inhabiting water being called *Tuihuai* and those residing on land known as *Ramhuai*. To clarify his definition he mentioned some accounts of the doings of *huai* which were narrated to him by Suakhnuna. Of these accounts one is as follows, "A woman of Lalbuta's village went out of her house at night for purpose of nature. Her name was Mangami and she was pregnant. The *huai* of the Tuitlin precipice caught her, and forced out the premature child and then carried her off down the rocks. The young men of the village went to search for her and found her naked in the jungle at the foot of the precipice where the *Ramhuai* had left her. She knew nothing about it when she recovered her senses". Also he mentioned, "There is a lake called Dil, between the southern border of the Lushai Hills and the Aracan Hill tracts which was credited with being abode of many *Tui huais*. No hill man would go within sight of the water, and when I first went there I had great difficulty in getting men to accompany me. The story is that, some foreigners visited the place once and one of them climbed on a tree overhanging the water, hence he dropped his knife into the lake and sent one of his men to fetch it. The diver returned without the knife, but with tales of wonderful beings beneath the water. The foreigner fired his gun into the lake, whereupon number of *Tuihuai* emerged and chased the whole party of intruders catching and carrying off all except their leader who made good his escape".

I am not in contention with Shakespear or J.H. Lorrain in regard to the definition of *huai.* My long experience in the field of Mizo culture and numerous contact with the well informed elderly persons convinced me that, *Ramhuai* is a generic name of evil spirits which consists of specific spirits like *huai, phung, chawmnu, inthumkar, khawhring, hmuithla, thlahrang,* etc. So Huai(s) are not supposed to move about frequently but stay in their respective abode as in the case of Dilhuai mentioned above by J. Shakespear. The Executive Committee and Publication Sub-Committee of Mizoram Upa Pawl (Mizoram Senior Citizens' Association), having more than 50,000 members all over Mizoram are also of the opinion that *Ramhuai* is the common name of evil spirits.

Ḥuai is, therefore, a sub-group of *Ramhuai* which are numerous in Mizoram. We may discuss one by one as follows:

1. *Sih Huai*: There are numerous small springs which generally rise in muddy soil in Mizoram called Sih, the spot remains damp and moist all through the year and the water is generally warm and often brackish which is liked by wild animals and are, therefore, frequented by them. Mizo of the past believed that there was at least one family of *Sih-huai* in every Sih. Sometimes the family members of *Sih-huai* would laugh so happily that even human beings often could hear it. There is a poetical expression, "*Sih Nau Ang Nui*", which means laughing like the children of *Sih-huai.* In some of the bigger springs, many *huais* lived together under their Chief named, *Chham,* who was said to be very lazy and would sleep underneath all the time. The chief was fed by other members, he even pass out his excreta in sleep which is, reddish in colour. When the excreta came out to surface it could be seen by naked eyes and was called *Chham ek,* that means the excreta of *Chham.* Since *Sih-huais* were attributed to causing illness and sufferings, nobody would like to have such spring within their jhumland or paddy field. *Sih huai,* in fact would not welcome any human intruders within their jurisdiction. While in the course of selecting jhumland, if *sih* could not be avoided totally, then in such cases, one had to perform *Sih Siam* sacrifice in order to appease the *huai.*

2 To perform *Sih Siam* sacrifice the following ingredients were needed:

A Set of Gongs,
Red cock—one,
Hen—one,
Bungpui—Banyan tree made of bamboo,
Mithun-5, made of clay,

A couple of fishes—made of clay,
Theirual 5—small bamboo tubes each of 4 inches in length,
Priest and his assistant.

On the day of sacrifice the plot owner, the priest and his assistant with all the ingredients required for the purpose went to the jhumland. The assistant with the hen stayed at *jhum* hut and the owner and the priest went to the spot with red rooster and other materials. Reaching the spot the priest would go down to the *Sih* and chanted incantation as follows:

> Are you your parent's children?—(he himself answers) No.
> Call them, "*Manmasia* has come,"
> Do they come home?—(he answers) Yes, what do you want?
> Nothing, but I ask health and long life,
> For Lala's family (the owner of the plot)
> Oh Great one, here I bring five mithuns to your home (He would perform the act of driving mithuns).
> Here I planted a big banyan tree—(he says) You may do it. Oh. Pathian above, May I put banyan tree here? -
> You may do it. Here I offer my mithuns, my fishes, my *rawcheh* And my set of gongs.

Then he would cut the throat of the cock and allowed its blood to drop over all the materials except the banyan tree. The priest would then recite his incantation—*Turung turh, turung, turung turh*, and would dance while singing. Then he offers *saserh* which includes tip of the wing, beak, leg and tail of the cock. After that the priest and the owner would go back to the *jhum* hut and cut the hen also. Then they would cook and eat the meat in the *jhum* after which they would go home. The *Sih huai* may not then be troublesome to the owner of jhumland. Mizo believed in a number of *Sih huai* and their names are suffixed after the names of the animals that frequented the *sih*.

***Zawng Sih Huai*:** *Zawng* means monkey and *Zawng sih huai* is *huai* living in *Zawng sih* which is frequented by monkeys. *Zawng sih huai* were most ferocious and dangerous to man.

***Sakhi Sih Huai*:** It means *huai* of a spring frequented by barking deers. This particular *huai* was also said to have been very dangerous.

***Sazuk Sih Huai*:** Spirits of springs frequented by sambar deers and were said to be kind and calm.

A tale is told as follows—"Once a man stayed overnight in his *jhum* hut for some days. One night a *Sih huai* made a '*kuk*' (a Mizo equivalent of 'Halloo') and the man responded with the same cry. The *huai* came nearer and nearer to the man, at last it opened the door and entered the hut in the form of human figure. The *huai* invited the man to come for a drink of beer. Without question, the man lit his bamboo torch and followed the *huai* not knowing that it was a *huai*. They went on a flat and smooth footpath for a while till they reached a good Mizo thatched house, which appears to be a house of well to do family; entering the house, the man just tucked his smoking pipe on the front of a bamboo wall. Then he joined the drinking party happily. Later, the man went back to his *jhum* hut and slept as usual. In the morning he happened to realize that, he forgot his smoking pipe in the house where they had drunk beer the previous night. He then traced back the path he had followed and could find out his way with the help of ashes left along the path, though the path had been very smooth that night, in reality it was very rugged, passing through cliffs and precipices. At last he reached the place and found that his smoking pipe was tucked at the edge of a crab's hole. Such was the relation between man and *Sih-huai* in the past and it was the belief of Mizo that holes in springs were doors of the houses of such spirits.

Tlang Huai: Mizo attributed that, all the major hills and mountains in Mizoram had their respective *huais*. The precipices, the cliffs and the shelves or ledges on the face of precipices were their good dwelling places. *Tlang huai* lived in groups and their system of administration was something akin to the system of Mizo village. The head of a group was known as Chief whose authority was unquestioned by other members. With a view to extend their domain, the chiefs would fight wars among themselves. For instance, the chief of *Chhawrpial huai* was in dispute with *Reiek huai* and wanted to punish him. But he knew that, he was not strong enough to do it, so he made an alliance with the *huai* of Tlawng River. The battle commenced and *Tlawng huai* tried to destroy Reiek Mountain by strong force of current from the south. However, the moutain was too firm and strong for him and failed in his attempt, as a result of which it had to make abrupt detour just to the south of Reiek Mountain which is now called, 'Tlawng nuar' (abrupt change in the direction of river flow).

A tale of battle between *Inbuk huai* and combined host of Khawpuitan and Reiek Huai is reproduced here from my memory. A certain person reproduced the eye witness account in a local newspaper, a copy of which I had kept for future reference but I have misplaced the same and could not trace it out. Inbuk is a big mountain with peculiar shape in the Len range in Chin Hills of Myanmar and its *Huai* being conscious of his mighty prowess was very boastful in behaviour. *Khawpuitan huai* (near Chawngtlai village) could not tolerate the arrogance of *Inbuk huai* and planned to launch a surprise attack. To ensure complete success, *Khawpuitan huai* sought the alliance of *Reiek huai*. Then a big host of army in the form of *Sialsir* (a kind of swift flying hawk) moved to invade *Inbuk huai*. However, *Inbuk huai* had intelligence report of the impending danger and prepared to ambush the combined army on their way and amassed as many number of fighting force as he could collect and moved out to meet their enemy in the form of *Sialsir*. The two hosts of Army met just above Haimual Village a few miles to the north of Rih Lake. They fought a very fierce battle in the air. There was continuous thunderous sound in the air. The people of Haimual village could not do any work but watched that magnificent battle. In the course of fighting, a great number of *Sialsir* birds dropped down dead and the battle lasted for many hours which ended ultimately in a draw. It was said that large number of dead *Sialsir* were lying on the ground when the battle was over.

The huai often wage war among themselves and at the same time would enter into matrimonial alliances with one another. In doing so, they adopt the system of distribution of subsidiary marriage prices to near relatives as was prevalent in the Mizo society. For instance a *huai* girl of eastern belt married to a *huai* boy of western belt would give morning mist, as *Pu Sum* (subsidiary portion of girl's marriage price payable to maternal uncle to *huai* of Hmawngva stream), chief of *Pukpui huai* received Tualthu, as Palal, (subsidiary portion of girl's marriage price payable to male relative) and chief of Saza mountain received Mungek as *Niar*, (subsidiary portion of girl's marriage price payable to maternal aunt).

Phawngpui Mountain had a son who fell in love with the daughter of the chief of Chiria Mountain in Chin Hills, Myanmar. So Sangau sent a mediator to Thunbawng chief of Chiria, after some negotiations both the parties came to an agreement for the marriage. According to their agreed terms, Chief Sangau had to pay a couple of gibbons *sans* its future off springs and chief Thunbawng had to give one pine tree as dowry. It is said that the gibbons had no issue till their death and the pine tree of Phawngpui had no offshoot and stood solitary till recently. By now the Forest Department planted a number of pine trees and made a very good pine forest.

Dil Huai **(Huai of lake):** To Mizo, big lakes and deep pools in rivers were the dwelling places of *huai*. One story of *Dil huai* described by J. Shakespear in his book *Lushai Kuki Clans* has been mentioned earlier.

We may now discuss stories of few *Dil huai* to clarify the nature of such *huai*. Rih lake, the largest lake ever known to Mizo had its own *huai* who were not harmful to man in normal situation. The lake was so large that nobody could swim across except one Darkawlchhuna. One day while Darkawlchhuna was swimming across the lake he felt so proud of his ability and shouted out loudly, " Here I am swimming across Rih lake and I will never get drowned", whereupon the *huai* got annoyed and attacked him in the form of snake with ferocious fins and killed him.

In the Mat river there is a deep pool named, 'Vanzema-Li' and the story of this deep pool is commonly told as, "Once there was a community fishing in this particular deep pool, a young man named, Vanzema, a very good swimmer dived deep into the water. At the bottom of the pool he found a dry cave with an old man splitting bamboo for making baskets. The old man told him never to come again as otherwise he would surely die. Coming to the surface, Vanzema told his friends what he saw at the bottom of the pool but nobody believed him. Vanzema vehemently asserted adding that if he were to dive again he would surely die. Still his friends refused to believe him and demanded at least a piece of bamboo brought from the bottom of the pool would make them accept his story. Vanzema refused to be called a liar and just to prove his story he decided to dive again on condition that, they should tie his leg with long rope and hold it. And as soon as he tugged the rope they should pull him up. So Vanzema dived again and after a while the rope was tugged and immediately they pulled up and Vanzema came out headless. Since then the pool was called Vanzema-Li (Vanzema's pool). It may be assumed that *huai* of water were harmful only when they were provoked.

***Lungpui Huai* (Huai of rock):** Big rocks particularly of unusual shape were believed to be inhabited by *huai*, who could be harmful to man but helpful if one pleases them. Phunhnawma a great hunter was said to have offered sacrifices to the *huai* of rock mount in North Vanlaiphai area. As a result he became a close friend to them and they offered him wild animals for his game. According to the traditional practice followed by Mizo, if a man could kill a prescribed number and varieties of wild animals he would attain an honoured status in the society called Thangchhuah. In fact Thangchhuah was the highest social title a Mizo could attain in life; he was respected in the society and entitled paradise after death.

When I worked as Research Investigator in 1976, I had a chance to visit Thingsen Village, five kilometres south of Saiha, a District headquarters not far from the village, there was a very tall standing rock which they believed to be home of many *huai* and no one dare to have jhumland nearby. One particular Christian man cut the forest and brought this spot under his jhumland. I met and interviewed this man who had told me that one day a *huai* came to him in the form of an Assam Rifle personnel in civil dress who assaulted and tortured him severely. He fell unconscious and was carried home by his fellow villagers and recovered after weeks. NGO of the village helped me to visit the rock and showed me what they believed to be living room, chicken basket, nesting basket for fowls, etc. of *huai* on the rock. To me this was simply a natural formation of rock.

In Huai (Huai of building): There are talks of *huai* of buildings in Miz oram. Their presence is usually confirmed by unusual and unnatural sounds heard in the building from time to time. There are hardly any tales about this haunting spirit. One was narrated by C. Rokhuma Mission Vengthlang, Aizawl—a Padmashree awardee. He said once Huliana and Nghakliana along with another friend, all of them residents of Mission Vengthlang locality, went to Sairang to do the work of repair of the Inspection Bungalow there. On reaching Sairang, they stayed in one of the rooms of the Inspection Bungalow. At mid-night they heard unusual sound in the building to which they did not pay much attention. One evening before it was fully dark, Hulliana went to the verandah of the Bungalow and there he saw a long figure covered with white cloth lying in one corner of the verandah. He was slightly frightened and called his friend to give him a piece of cut timber which he threw over the body of the figure and a drum like sound was produced. Thereupon, the figure slowly got up and entered into the room. Three of them immediately followed the figure but no sign of it was further seen. The next day, they told their story to the people of Sairang who replied, "There are *huai* in that Bungalow". The three men, however, did continue to stay in the Bangalow till they completed their work. The nature of *huai* of buildings is apparently not harmful but very disturbing for the inmates.

Thing Huai (*Huai* of Tree): Big trees especially, banyan trees are also believed to be inhabited by *huai*. There is another kind of tree called, "*Thing lu bul*" which is also taken to be the abode of *huai* and could cause illness or even death so people would never like to touch it or fell it. While selecting land for jhuming they would avoid such of those areas having *Thing lu bul*. The *huai* of tree were dangerous and harmful to men. One, R. Darhlira, Electric Veng, Aizawl described *huai* of banyan tree in his book entitled, *Khawkil Bung huai*, that gives us clear idea about *Thing huai*. I wish to reproduce few lines of this book as written records of the story of *huai* is very rare. 'Khawkil was once a respectable village with more than 300 households. It was a village of a famous Sailo Chief Lalburha but the village is no longer in existence now and its location is somewhere in the area of the present Darlung village. There was a big Banyan in the outskirt of Khawkil village which was the abode of *huai*. As mentioned by Darhlira, one evening when young men of the village as usual, were courting one girl, suddenly there was an unusual atmosphere prevailing in the village in that animals like pigs, goats and mithuns moved around in panic. Then the *huai* of banyan caught a hen which cried out continuously and very loudly. Young men rushed out to catch the hen but the sound moved up to the top of the banyan tree and sometimes to the ground. So it was very difficult to locate the exact place where the hen was. The chase to retrieve the hen ended in failure. Similar terrifying incidents were often told in the olden Mizo society

On another occasion in Khawkil, children playing outdoor in the evening heard a cry of a boy in the nearby jungle. The adults did not pay any attention. But in the late night, it was found that a boy of about 9 years old was missing and the whole village was in red alert. All the able male members of the village rushed out in search of the boy. They could hear the voice of the boy but could not locate the exact place. The village people searched hard for many days but failed. After a week or so the dead body of the boy was found in the deep jungle. Everybody believed that the boy was taken by the *huai* of Khawkil banyan tree.

Huai are, therefore, evil spirits inhabiting certain object or place who had social life more or less as that of real people. They could appear to men in any form and disappear as and when they like. We have come across the wars and battles, peace and intermarriage among the *huai*. Some were in family with children while most of them did not seem to care for family. Their existence cannot be denied but no one could fully understand them.

18
Khawhring
(Old Mizo belief which no longer exists)

C.L. Hminga

In the Zotawng Dictionary compiled and published by R.K. Ngurchhawna and his brothers, *khawhring* is defined as a kind of evil spirit, which according to the old belief of the Mizo, could enter into human being and wild boar. It could capture or wrestle with a person. When a person suddenly has a stomach pain and says, "I am so and so, I want this and that", the person whom he or she named is regarded to be possessed by *khawhring* spirit1. Rev J.H. Lorrain, in his *Dictionary of the Lushai Language* stated *khawhring* to be the same as 'evil eye' in English. He always mentioned 'evil eye' and *khawhring* spirit as synonymous. But the definition of 'evil eye' in the Oxford Dictionary and Chamber's Dictionary did not suggest the presence of evil spirit in the 'evil eye'. Unless there is implicit meaning in the 'evil eye' I do not think there is justification in saying *khawhring* is the same as evil eye.

Writing in 1912, Lt. Col. J. Shakespear, one of the pioneer British administrators in the erstwhile Lushai Hills District regarded the existence of *khawhring* to be a widespread belief among the Mizo tribes. He actually had written extensively about *khawhring* from which I shall make some quotations. The following quotation will show his impression of *khawhring*:

> "The belief in *khawhring* is universal and from the following translation it will be seen that the unfortunate women who were accused of being possessed by such a spirit have good reason to be grateful that the control of the country has passed into our hands. The belief is that *khawhring* lives in certain women whence it issues forth from time to time and takes possession of another woman, who falling into a trance, speaks with the original

hostess of the *khawhring.* A missionary described to me a weird scene of excitement which he once saw, the object being to exorcise a *khawhring* which has possessed a girl. Amid a turmoil of shouting, drum beating, and firing of guns the spirit was ordered to quit its temporary abode and return whence it came".

The origin of *khawhring* described by a Mizo for Shakespear translated in English is interesting and I am quoting here:

"Wild boars have *khawhring*, once a man shot a wild boar while out hunting. On his return home they cooked the flesh. Some of the fat got on the hand of his sister, who rubbed her hand, and the wild boar's *khawhring* passed into her. On the next day, without any provocation, she entered another girl. She took entire possession of her. People said to her, "Where are you going to?" She replied, "It is the wild boar my brother shot." "Well, what do you want?" they said. "If you will give me eggs I shall go away," she replied. They gave her eggs and she went. Presently all those who borrowed the *hnam* (a plaited cane band for carrying loads) of the girl with the *khawhring* also got possessed. If one with a *khawhring* has a daughter the child is always possessed; so no one wants to marry a person with a *khawhring*. Even now, we being to some extent Lusheis, we do not like to let a person possessed by a *khawhring* enter our houses, and if such a one sits on the bed of a true Lushei, she will certainly be fined a *metna* (mithun or gail). Those possessed of *khawhring* are disgusting people, and before the foreigners came they were always killed".

I believe the missionary mentioned by Col. Shakespear was one of the pioneer missionaries of the Mizos, Rev. J.H. Lorrain whose *Lushai English Dictionary* contains considerable information about *khawhring* which he thought more or less the same as 'evil eye' in English, and to know his understanding of *khawhring* let me quote from his dictionary;

1. *Khawhring nei (neih) v*; to have the 'evil eye' or to have a *khawhring* spirit; to be possessed of the 'evil eye' or *khawhring* spirit. n. one having the 'evil eye'.
2. *Khawhring tai, v.* to exorcise the 'evil eye' or *khawhring* spirit. This is carried out as follows: The exorcist takes a little cold water in a gourd ladle and after sundry incantation adds to it a pinch of soot or dirt of any kind from each of the three stones

which support the pot over the family fire, and also three live ambers from the fire itself. The water is given to the affected person to drink".

Fortunately, I discussed this subject with Rev. Dr. H.S. Luaia who claims to be 99 years old and to have personal knowledge of *khawhring*, He told me that his late father, Suakkunga was an exorcist of *khawhring* and he had seen many times how his father performed his duty. It was just the same as what Lorrain has stated in the dictionary. Dr. Luaia told me also that there were three women in their village who were branded as *khawhring nei*.

Conditions of a person seized by *khawhring* spirit is stated by Lorrain in his dictionary as follows:

1. One who has been seized by the *khawhring* spirit of another through whom it speaks and demands certain things and sometimes proclaim whose *khawhring* it is. The seizure is generally accompanied by colic like pains. The belief that such pains are caused by the *khawhring* spirit of another is open to grave abuse, anyone having a grudge against another being thus able to accuse that one of being her tormentor and thus giving that person the unenviable reputation of having *khawhring* or 'evil eye'.
2. The seizure by a *khawhring* spirit, as above, or the pain caused thereby. adj. seized by a *khawhring* spirit or 'evil eye'. The verb is expressed thus: A *khawhring* spirit has seized me. A *khawhring* spirit has seized him."

Col. Shakespear mentioned a ceremony practiced by the Mizos to ward off *khawhring* spirit which is called '*khawhring thiar*'. "Three days after the birth of a child a small chicken and seven small packets of rice and vegetables are suspended under the edge of a front verandah. This is called *arte hring ban* or *khawhring tir*. The object is to satisfy the *khawhring* (see Chapter V para 12) and prevent it entering the child" Lorrain also said that *khawhring thiar* is to ward off the 'evil eye' or *khawhring* spirit by performing the ceremony which averts the baneful influence of the 'evil eye' or *khawhring* spirit."

Though Col Shakespear said that *khawhring* is universal among the Mizo tribes (including the sub-tribes) he also stated that *khawhring* is unknown among the Lakher or Mara clan who maintain that there are no wizard or witches among them. This statement was repudiated by

Dr. Chawngkhuma Chawngthu, a lecturer at Saiha Government College who told me that the belief in *khawhring* very much exists in Maraland and people still fear *khawhring* even these days. I am inclined to believe that Shakespear is justified in saying that belief in *khawhring* is universal among the Mizo tribes because I came to know that the Mizo sub-tribes who live in Tripura also believe it. About twenty years ago I visited Gongarai, a Mawlsawm village in Tripura. I was told that there was a married woman who was supposed to have Khawhring, She and her husband were expelled from the village and they were living at that time in an isolated jungle. I did not see the person but Rev H.S. Luaia claimed to have seen her.

Having spent my boyhood at Chawnhu village, near Lawngtlai in Pawih area I know that there was this belief among the people. My late father who was a circuit pastor had more than thirty village churches in his care. Once he told me that he had to deal sometimes with *khawhring* problems. I remember what he told me of one case. His host at Thingfal village, a church leader there told him that his younger brother married again after his first wife died and that wife under the influence of *khawhring* used to ask for a gun. Apparently the woman coveted a gun for her son. His host asked my father for an advice. My father advised him to tell his brother to give her a good thrashing if she asked again. His advice was taken and the problem was solved.

As indicated by Col. Shakespear's remark that such unfortunate women who were accused of being possessed by *khawhring* spirit have good reason to be grateful that the control of the country has passed into the hands of the British administrators, the menace of *khawhring* has ceased to trouble the Mizo society. The fact that Major A.G. McCall, Superintendent of Lushai Hills in the 1940s did not mention *khawhring* in his book *Lushai Chrysalis* published in 1949 is a proof that the British administration has successfully done away with what Lorrain said, the baneful influence of *khawhring* spirit. The present young Mizo generation may not have even heard the name *khawhring*, not to speak of knowing what it is.

19

Mizo Value, Beliefs and Practices vis-à-vis Christianity

K.P. Nath

The Mizo Value

A Mizo youth cherished to be brave as this was mostly desired of him by the elders in the society. This was obvious for a hunting and warring people which the Mizos were. They had to occasionally fight to protect their village against external aggression from a neighbouring village. Internecine feuds were frequent and the young men of a village were needed to remain alert to fight as and when such situations arose. The village society was cohesive and would often meet in community feasts that took place after any animal sacrifice performed a villager or after a successful community hunting. In hunting physical prowess and bravery in facing fierceful animals in the jungles were required to be possessed by the youth. For all such reasons bravery in a young man was highly valued by the elders in the society. The Mizos had evinced their appreciation for bravery in a number of ways. The number of enemy heads taken by a villager during a raid in a neighbouring village increased his esteem in his own village. Such enemy heads were displayed over an implanted bamboo pole at the entrance of the village. Also, the heads of fierceful animals killed were displayed on the walls of the hunter's verandah to show the number of animals he had hunted. The Chief also honoured a hunter if he had killed a specified number of wild animals by bestowing on him the title *Thangchhuah* and offering him seat next to him on any social occasion. Whenever a male child was born in a village, the elders would come to see him and would bless him to be brave so as to be able to kill an elephant. These eloquently speak how bravery as a trait in a young man was valued in the Mizo society. A girl was, however, required to be only beautiful and adept in household work, because that would increase her value as a bride. When a girl child was born in a village, the elders would come to see her and bless her to be very beautiful so as to be able to fetch a mithun as her bride-price.

Next to bravery, a decent and courteous behaviour with others was what was considered of value for everyone—young and old, men and women, Acts of decency and courtesy were considered to form norms of good conduct and as such were valued in the society. Showing reverence to elders was one among the many acts of decency which the children were required to learn. Girls were especially taught to be courteous even with their suitors whom they actually might not like.

Every Mizo was expected to abide by *tlawmngaihna*, a code of conduct characterised by 'selflessness', 'other mindedness' or 'service before self'. A Mizo would sing': *Aw tlawmngaihna hlu* (O *tlawmngaihna* precious). This indicates how *tlawmngaihna* was endearing to every Mizo heart. If any villager was sick and was unable to slash and burn the jungle for Jhuming, his neighbours would readily come forward lending helping hands to do the work for him. If a villager was short of rice, those having plenty would readily share the same with him. If a villager was found carrying heavy loads, others would eagerly offer to carry the same for him. These are only a few examples of the many ways how *tlawmngaihna* was expressed by a Mizo to keep his fellow men happy, contented and comfortable, sympathy, compassion, fellow-feeling were the traits very fondly cherished by a Mizo in his heart. This made the difficult life on the hills very pleasant and worth living. It is because of this that signs of contentment were writ large on the face of every Mizo, young or old.

The Mizo Beliefs

The Mizos in the early days lived with many beliefs. Belief in the existence of evil spirits was one of the them. The Mizos believed that the evil spirits lived in the hollow of big trees, large pools of water and caves, cliffs and precipices of mountains. Human eyes were not able to see them. But they created hazards to human life. Disease, distress and death were caused by these evil spirits. To avert such danger one was required to propitiate these spirits through adequate animal sacrifice. Out of this belief priesthood developed in the Mizo society. In every villages there were priests assisting the distressed people in offering the sacrifice. A feast would follow with the animal so sacrificed.

The Mizos also believed in the existence of life after death and also in the existence of two afterworlds: *Mithikhua* (dead men's village) and 'pialral' (paradise meant for the distinguished persons). Ordinary men after death would go to *mithikhua* where they would have to work hard as on earth for a living. But to *pialral* only the chosen few who had earned fame on earth by being conferred *Thangchhuah* by their Chiefs would go. Their life in *pialral* was pleasant as they were not to do any work there.

The Mizos believed that the spirit of a person after his death, *thlarau* as they called it, continued to live with his family for three months during which he was offered bed to sleep at night and food to take during meals. A sitting space at the dining table with dish or food before it was left vacant when other members of the family used to take meals with the belief that the spirit of the departed member joined them at meal times. This food was afterwards thrown away. This practice continued for three months after the death of any member in a family.

After the expiry of three months the spirit was believed to leave the house for place called *Hruaikawn* which was approachable from all directions, where he would join other spirits waiting for him for a long sojourn under the guidance of a leader spirit.

On their way they would cross first a vast lake called *Rihdil* and then a vast heath called *Rihmual*. Then they would ascend to a hillock called 'Hringlang tlang' on top of which they would take rest for a while. As they gazed around from the hill top, the distant villages in the valley surrounding the hill would come upon their view. They would recognize their homes and the mourning members of their family. Pangs of separation would be too difficult for them to bear and they would feel restless to return to their homes and family. But the leader spirit would not allow that under any circumstances. He would pluck 'Hawilopar', a kind of flower growing on the hill and put them on the head of the spirits. This would greatly subside their desire to return.

After taking rest there for a while, they would start moving again and descend the hill from the other side. Soon they would come across a stream called 'Lunglohtui'. They would sit by its side, wash their face, wipe their tears, quench their thirst with its water and feel refreshed.

From there they would proceed towards another hill called 'Zinghmun tlang' (a hill now considered to be about 20 km east of present Falam village) where recorders lived, who would hand over to each spirit details of his activities during his life time, activities that would either qualify or disqualify any individual spirit for entering *pialral*. Those not qualified to enter *pialral* would enter *mithikhua*.

From 'Zinghmun tlang' the spirits would enter the yard of Saitu Pawla, the ever vigilant catapult shooter. As from this yard the paths to *mithikhua* and *pialral* got bifurcated, nobody could avoid this place. Pawla would know if a spirit in his or her lifetime had or had not courted with his or her opposite sex and would shoot with his catapult at one who had not done so. As Pawla abhorred virginity, he expressed his indignation towards any spirit which avoided sex during his or her life-time by shooting with his catapult.

From Saitu Pawla's yard one path led some spirits to *mithikhua* where they would live ever after doing all the painful labour for a living as they did when they were alive on earth. Those ordained to enter *pialral* would take the other path and would be bestowed there with all the choicest food and cherished pleasures.

Mizos Social and Religious Practices

Apart from occasional animal sacrifice to the supposed evil spirits, the Mizos also observed festivals in between agricultural seasons. These festivals were more social than religious in their character.

Chapchar Kut

Chapchar kut was observed sometime towards the end of February or the beginning of March after the jungles were slashed and left to dry for *juhming* The burning of dry leaves, branches and twigs was undertaken only after the festival was over. Before the day fixed for the festival, the villagers would go out for community hunting in the jungle and fishing in the river to collect sufficient meat and fish for the community feast in which the whole village would take part. *Lalmual* or the wide space front of the Chief's house was used for the purpose. Every arrangement for the community feast was made there. Each household was also expected to brew rice-beer and bring the same to pour into a big earthen pot for those gathered to seep intermittantly. All would join and partake of the feast in great gaity and enthusiasm. After the feast was over mass singing and dancing with the beating of drum and gong would take place. All kinds of dances would be performed by the village youths and maidens in which the elderly and old people would also join. *Chai Hla* or the Mizo traditional songs would be sung in merriment. New songs would also be composed and sung. People would sing and dance non-stop for the whole night till it was dawn; otherwise the festival would not be allowed to continue for the next day. The duration of the festival depended upon the supply of rice-beer. Generally it was continued for two to three days, sometimes even more. The festival would come to a close with the drying up of the pot of rice-beer and along with this the enthusiasm of the singers, dancers and drummers.

Mim Kut

Mim kut was observed generally in the later part of August or early part of September when the first vegetables, particularly *vaimim* or the maize from the *jhum* would be harvested. It was a ceremony of remembrance of and thanks givings to the dead members of each family, especially to those who died during the year. On the day of the festival, a raised platform made of bamboo near the kitchen would be cleaned and cooked food with fresh vegetables and maize would be served on the platform for the soul of the dead ones to come and partake of the food so offered. In the evening all the villagers would assemble in the house of one who had recently died and would sing *khawhar hla* or the mourning songs. This was a ceremony meant for the dead and, therefore, had certain religious significance apart from the social.

Pawl Kut

Pawl kut was observed in the month of December after the harvesting of paddy from the *jhum* was over. *Pawl* literally means 'hay'. The festival was so named as it was associated with hay. After harvesting in the field was over, children in the village would collect stems or grain out of hay that had been left unnoticed in the field. They would also go from door to door asking villagers to part with a little of their grain. Before the day fixed for the festival rice beer would be brewed out of the collected grain and would be brought in a pot on the place where the villagers would assemble to celebrate the festival. All would seep rice-beer from the pot and sing and dance till late in the evening. Even children would be permitted to drink rice-beer on the occasion. In every household people would kill animal and enjoy and good and hearty meal with new rice obtained from the *jhum*. Even in a very poor family also, at least a chicken would be killed to celebrate the festival.

On all festival occasions young and old alike would wear new clothes. They would visit each other's house and share meals. Community feasts would also form a part of all festivals.

Advent of Christianity and its Impact on the Mizos

Christian missionaries started coming to the Mizos from the last decade of the nineteenth century. They established schools and hospitals and won the heart of the people. With initial barriers broken the Mizos began to accept Christianity. Within the period of less than half a century all of them became Christians.

The Mizos had always valued fellow-feeling, brotherhood, compassion and sympathy. As Christianity also preaches the same, the religion did not bring any major change in their value pattern. But Christianity has brought a sea change in the traditional socio-religious practices of the Mizos. Of the three festivals, while *Chapchar kut is* still observed as the festival of gaity and merriment and mass singing and dancing, the two other festivals, *Mim kut* and *Pawl kut,* are no longer observed. Drinking of rice-beer on festive occasions as was practised before is no longer in vogue as Christianity prohibits such drinking. *Chapchar kut,* however, is not observed in village as used to before, but in the State and District headquarters under the aegis of the Government as a Mizo national festival with the objective of preserving the old culture from dying.

Now *Chapchar kut* is not the principal festival of the Mizos as it used to be earlier. Its place has been taken by Christmas which is observed with great fervour and enthusiasm. Christmas songs in churches are sung in chorus by well dressed youths and maidens which form an important part in the observance of the festival. On Christmas day each house is decorated as also the church premises. Mass prayers are offered in the churches. This is followed by community feasts which may last for a day or two after the Christmas day. Dramas based on any episode on Jesus Christ are also staged in various places. With festoons, music, carnivals and busy shopping the whole atmosphere turns joyous. Good Friday is also observed as another important festival with solemn prayers in the church.

Christianity has also almost totally shaken most of their old beliefs, particularly the beliefs about the evil spirits. People threw away all sacrificial pots after being convinced that Jesus had conquered evil spirits and that there was no danger from them if one had accepted the Christ.

Christianity has also brought to them an altogether new concept of sin, of hell, of fear of damnation in eternal hell-fire for sinners and of the idea that once one was a Christian, there was no fear from hell, as Jesus takes away all sins. This belief that had been instilled in people gave them impetus to accept Christianity. Many other beliefs on which the religion is based were instilled in them through the psychological process of indoctrination. Indoctrination is a slow but sure process of implanting into uncritical mind certain unfounded beliefs so as to achieve a desired end. The sole objective of indoctrination is to close the mind to reason and to instil steadfast faith so as to establish someone in power or authority as the church, the Pope or the hierarchy of priests. Indoctrination is never undertaken for the well-being of the individual mind. The individual is sacrificed for the interest of the system. One line of thought is put so forcefully, so authoritatively, so repeatedly, so uncompromisingly that the victim of indoctrination does not find scope to think and decide for himself. Ultimately he loses all habits of independent thinking and accepts what is communicated unquestionably. He weeps, screams and swaggers in religious congregations indicating that his indoctrination is complete. This happens with people following any organised religious faith.

What is, therefore, needed for Mizoram is higher education of the highest order. It is only then all doctrines and dogmas from people's mind will disappear as mist before the sun.

20

Christianity and the Lushais of Tripura

A Peep at the History

Mahadev Chakravarti

It becomes evident from some documents that with the beginning of the twentieth century, a good number of Lushai families came down to Princely Tripura and first settled in the east of the then Dharmanagar Subdivision. Ultimately the Lushais moved towards the Jampui and Sakhan Hills to find their homes on the high altitude in the heart of the deep and dense forests so far infested by wild and ferocious animals.[1] In a letter to the Government of Tripura, L. Huapliana Sailo records the story how his father Dokhuma, the son of famous Suakpuilala, came and conferred upon the title of Raja by the Maharaja of Tripura. Similarly, K.T. Chawma Sailo, another Chief of the Jampui Hills, in his representation recounted the story of his forefathers' adventures in Tripura. To quote K.T. Chawma Sailo:

> "My humble self is a son of Late Hrangvunga Sailo of Jampui Hills, who and his forefathers ruled for more than 300 years over the Lushai Hills people of the part of Kirat Country, i.e., within Assam and Tripura. My beloved late father before his death settled in the soil of Tripura for the last 50 years and ruled over the Lushai people of Tripura as a Lushai Raja."[2]

At the beginning of the twentieth century, the Lushai Chief was practically the leader both in secular and religious affairs of his people and he was "Ceasar and Pope both rolled into one". Due to the lack of communications, the control of the Tripura Durbar over the Jampui and Sakhan Hills was practically non-existent. Even as late as 1948 the Dewan of Tripura wrote:

> "This Eastern-most hills area of Tripura State, in which the Lushai tribes reside, is, for all practical purposes, inaccessible from Agartala and more so during the rains."[3]

Thus the inaccessibility of the region, the distance from the capital, the entire ecological setting, the power and position of the Chief and the overall type of social structure are the important factors to be looked into. The Christian Missionaries braved all the eventualities to pass through "high forest and bamboo jungle, with entanglements of thorny scrub, canes, creepers, and nettle, through which it is impossible to force a passage without much cutting and clearing, excepting along the regular used tracks of wild elephants."[4]

How the Christian Missionaries through medical aid and other welfare activities won the heart of the disadvantaged would become evident from a part of the 'Welcome Address' to the Dewan of Tripura Durbar by Thanglura on behalf of the Lushais, Kukis and Riangs at the time of Dewan's visit to Fatikray (in the plains near Kumarghat in the North Tripura District) in 1931 A.D.:

> "In these days there are some Christians among us. Mr. Roberts and his men, whom we must not forget to thank, sent us some compounders and medicines and in future we hope by all these means to rise up and increase in number"[5]

At that time the headman of a village was the focus of special attention as he was the key-man. In a quarterly bulletin (October, 1931), issued by the North East India General Mission with headquarters in the U.S.A. and Great Britain, Pastor N. Luaia, Field Superintendent, in a note on 'Work in Tripura State' recorded the following:

> "I do praise our Lord Jesus because he is leading us victoriously in our work in Tripura State. One whole village that had gone back has now joined us again after expressing their deep repentance.
> From April I could only engage myself in visiting, the churches. The first village I visited was Vanghmun. Here I got three new converts. They were the Headman of the village, his wife and his son. He had two sons, the elder of which was a Christian. The Headman was always against Christianity. He even prohibited his wife to become a Christian.
> In course of time there arose a great quarrel in the family. His second son, who was not a believer, became insane.
> The father was moved to tears and found that he, himself, was a great sinner in the sight of God.
> He was the headman of the village, but he called the elders of the Christians and announced publicly his acceptance of Jesus as his personal Saviour, and, at the same, time, his wife and his

distressed son came and yielded themselves to him who loved them with an everlasting love.
I sent out word to all the surrounding churches to pray for these new converts. This is only one instance of the joy in our work. Every church I visited was very happy in the Lord. I received two new converts at Phuldungsei whose ages were about sixty years. I also baptized one old man.
We held Communion Services of the Lord's Supper at two of the churches."[6]

From the above accounts of pastor N. Luaia we get some idea about the missionary activities as early as 1931 in Vanghmun and Phuldungsei villages of the Jampui Hill of Tripura. In 1931, the total Lushai population in Tripura was 2,175 only (see Table 20.1).

Table 20.1: Total Number of Christians among the Lushais of Tripura

District	*Total No. of Lushais*			*No. of Christians*		
1. West Tripura						
1971 Census	*Person*	*Male*	*Female*	*Persons*	*Male*	*Female*
R	19	14	5	19	14	5
U	95	44	51	94	43	51
Total	114		Total	113		
1981 Census						
R	49	31	18	44	27	17
U	70	40	30	67	38	29
Total	119	Total		111		
2. North Tripura						
1971 Census						
R	3510	1716	1794	3509	1716	1793
U	15	5	10	15	5	10
Total	3525		Total	3524		
1981 Census						
R	3546	1826	1720	3535	1822	1713
U	10	5	5	1	1	0
Total	3556		Total	3536		
3. South Tripura						
1971 Census						
R	33	21	12	22	19	3
U	0	0	0	0	0	0
Total	33	Total		22		
1981 Census						
R	59	34	25	58	34	24
U	0	0	0	0	0	0
Total	59	Total		58		

It will be evident from Table 20.2 that the major religions of Tripura are Hindu and Muslim. The position of the Buddhists is third and that of the Christians is fourth in the Censuses. The total number of Christians in Tripura, according to 1981 Census, 24,872 constituting 1.21 per cent of the total population of the State (Table 20.2). But among the Lushais of Tripura, almost all of them have today embraced Christianity. Table 20.2 gives the district-wise population break-up and the number of Christians among the Lushais of Tripura. Table. 20.1A shows that out of 3,734 Lushai people the number of Christians were 3,705, according to 1981 Census.

Table 20.1A: Total of Lustais in Tripura.

		1971	1981
A.	Total No. of Lushais in Tripura	1971	1981
	1. West Tripura	114	119
	2. North Tripura	3525	2556
	3. South Tripura	33	59
	Total	3672	3734
B.	Total No. of Christians among the Lushais of Tripura	1971	1981
	1. West Tripura	113	111
	2. North Tripura	3524	3536
	3. South Tripura	22	58
	Total	3659	3705

Table 20.2: Lushai Population of Tripura since 1931 as per CRI

Year	*Total Population*	*Tribal Population*	*Lushai Population*
1931	382,450	192,249	2,175
1941	513,010	256,991	1,991
1951	639,029	237,953	1,947
1961	1,142,005	360,070	2,988
1971	1,556,342	450,544	3,672
1981	2,053,058	583,920	3,734
1991	2,744,827	....	....

Regarding the beginning of Christian missionary activities in Tripura, the present author has dealt with the subject in detail in a separate chapter.[7] In 1922, Birendrakishore Manikya of Tripura informed Sir William Marris, the then Governor of Assam that Raja Dokhuma and Sardar Hrangvunga, who were originally residents of the Lushai Hills District, came to settle on the Jampui Hill at the beginning of the century with all their followers, most of whom were Christians.[8] In the words of Birendrakishore Manikya:

Table 20.3: Census of 1981 showing Distribution of Population of Tripura by Religion

Religion	*Pop.*	*% to Total Population*	*Decadal Growth (1971-1981) in %*
Buddistis	54,806	2.67	+29.61
Christians	24,827	1.21	+58.28
Hindus	1834218	89.34	+31.61
Jains	297	0.02	-20.08
Muslims	138,529	6.75	+33.25
Sikhs	285	0.01	-10.38
Others religious persuasion	27	N	N
Religion not Stated	24	N	N
Total	2,053,058	100	

N = Negligible

Source: Census of India 1981, Series 21 (Tripura), Part I of 1985, p. 3; Some Basic Statistics of Tripura 1985, Directorate of Statistics, Government of Tripura, Agartala, p. 9.

Christian agencies are at work on the Jampui and Sakhan Hills where the Lushais have settled, under the direction of Missionary body in Calcutta. As a Hindu, their activities may not be pleasing to me personally, but, as representing a civilized Government claiming allegiance of people professing different faiths, I cannot object to Christian activities within reasonable limits.[9]

In 1931, the Dawn of Tripura, in a letter to Dr. G.G. Crozier, the Field Secretary, North East India General Mission, pointed out that the first batch of Christian cultivators numbering about forty migrated into Tripura in 1912 A.D. with the Lushai Chief Hrangvunga who ultimately settled in Tripura with a following of one thousand.[10] We have some idea about the exact number of Christians in 1917 A.D. from a letter of Rev. F.G. Sandy addressed to Rev. W.R. Roberts, the Field Director of the North East India General Mission.[11]

According to Rev. F.G. Sandy, the number of Christians among the Lushais in Princely Tripura in March 1917 were the following:

Jampui No. 1	100
Jampui No. 2	180
Jampui No. 3	50
Sakhan Hill	50
Total	380

It is interesting to note that although in 1917 A.D. the number of Christians was only 380, in the 1931 Census, out of a total of 2,175 Lushais in Tripura, 2,102 returned themselves as Christians and only 73 Lushais as non-Christians.

Table 20.4 shows that amongst the nineteen classified tribes of Tripura, the increasing trend of conversion to Christianity is particularly noticeable among the Tripuris. "Since 1972," according to Cunville,[12] "the Jamatias and Rupinis were also turning to Christ in small groups." The total number of Christians among the tribal people of Tripura are not yet available, the number of Christians has considerably increased since 1981, as evident from different non-official surveys and reports.

The story of the activities of the Christian Missionaries is more or less same everywhere. The Missionaries braved all the eventualities to go to the deep forests, to scale the hills, to build the churches in the interior, and through medical aid and other welfare activities won the heart of the disadvantaged. It becomes clear from Table 20.1 and 20.4 how Christianity is making inroads amongst some tribes of Tripura. Looking particularly at the Lushai of Tripura, it is commonly believed that those who have embraced Christianity are highly advanced because the Missionaries usually equip their followers to grasp and pick the fruits of modern development in every sphere of society. From membership of closed society, the Lushais of Tripura today, mostly because of the influence of Church, are exposed to forces of modern development.

If we cast a glance at Table 20.5 it would be found that 68 per cent of Lushais in Tripura are literate, according to 1981 Census, whereas the percentage is only 23 if all the Scheduled Tribes are taken into account. Christianity has introduced a new kind of social control and social values. The present author has shown elsewhere[13] how as a consequence of the constant protest movements launched by the Christian youths the institution of chieftainship was given good-bye from the social life of the Lushais of Tripura.

Table 20.4: Number of Christians among the Scheduled Tribes of Tripura

SL. No	Scheduled Tribes	1961 Total No.	Census Christian	1971 Total No.	Census Christian	1981 Total No.	Census Christian
1.	Bhil	69	1	169	1	838	3
2.	Bhutia	7	–	3	–	22	–
3.	Chaimal	50	–	–	–	18	1
4.	Chakma	22,386	5	28,662	202	34,797	17
5.	Garo	5,484	1,698	5,559	2,315	7,298	3,943
6.	Halam	16,298	253	19,076	520	28,970	3017
7.	Jamatia	24,359	–	34,192	1	44,501	501
8.	Khasia	349	216	491	269	457	357
9.	Kuki (Including many Su b –Tribes)	5,531	2,345	7,775	2,783	5,502	4,442
10.	Lepcha	7	–	14	6	106	9
11.	Lushai	2,988	2,950	3,672	3,659	3,734	3,705
12.	Mog	10,524	6	13,273	3	18,230	3
13.	Munda, Kaur	4,409	73	5,347	189	7,993	130
14.	Noatia	16,010	5	10,297	2	7,182	83
15.	Orang	2,875	24	3,428	9	5,217	38
16.	Riang	56,597	1,705	64,722	2,668	84,004	4,974
17.	Santal	1,562	2	2,222	6	2,726	23
18.	Tripuri	189,799	54	250,545	6	330,872	1056
19.	Uchai	766	254	1,061	544	1,306	750
20.	Unclassified	–	–	36	–	147	–
Total No. of Scheduled Tribes in Tripura:		360,070	9,591	450,544	13,183	583,920	23,052

Source:
(i) Census of India 1961, Vol. XXVI, Tripura, Part III & VA, pp. 321-22.
(ii) Census of India 1971, Series 20, Tripura, Part IIC VA, pp. 132-33.
(iii) Census of India 1981, Series 21, Tripura, Part IX, pp. 671-77.

Table 20.5: Educational Levels of the Lushais compared to other Tribes in Tripura

Name of Total (T) The Urban (U) Tribe Rural (R)		*Population*			*Illiterate*			*Literate & Educated*			
		Person	*Male*	*Female*	*Persons*	*Male*	*Female*	*Persons*	*Male*	*Female*	*% of literac*
All Scheduled Tribes											
	T	450,544	230,544	220,000	382,840	176,130	206,710	67,704	54,414	13,290	15.02
1971 Census	U	5,485	2,954	2,531	1,584	564	1,020	3,901	2,390	1,511	71.12
	R	445,059	227,590	217,469	381,256	175,566	205,690	52,024	52,024	11,779	14.33
	T	3,672	1,800	1,872	1,275	531	744	1,269	1,269	1,128	65.27
1971 Census	U	110	49	61	39	15	24	34	34	37	64.54
	R	3,562	1,751	1,811	1,236	516	720	1,235	1,235	1,091	65.3
All Scheduled Tribes											
	T	583,920	297,612	286,308							
1981 Census	U	7,668	4,141	3,527	1,625	645	980	6,043	3,496	2,547	78.80
	R	576,252	293,471	282,781	447,582	197,380	250,202	128,670	96,091	32,579	22.32
Lushai	T	3,734	1,936	1,798	1,193	547	646	2,541	1,389	1,152	68.05
1981 Census	U	81	46	35	17	6	11	64	40	24	79.01
	R	3,653	1,890	1,763	1,176	541	635	2,477	1,349	1,128	67.80

Source : Census of India 1971, Series 20 (Tripura), Part IIC (i), p. 18.

Census of India 1981, Series 21 (Tripura), pp. 628–33, 652–55.

REFERENCES

1. A study on the Lushais of Jampui Hills in Tripural Directorate of Research, Government of Tripura, Agartala,1988, Appendix No. 7, pp. 30-31.
2. *Ibid.*, p. 30.
3. Letter of the Dewan of "Tripura to the Adviser to the Governor of Assam, for Excluded Areas and States, No.1074/H/CA-20, dated 22 July, 1948, Agartala; (Secretariat Archive, Agartala, B1/S11).
4. Foreign and Political Department Report 1874 on Eastern Boundary of Hill Tippera, (Indian Reprint), Government Research Institute, Government of Mizoram, Aizawl, 1980, para 18.
5. Welcome Address to the Dewan of Tripura by Dr. Thanglura at Fatikroy, North Tripura, on 19.3.1931; (see Appendix No. 5 in *A Study on the Lushais of Jampui Hills in Tripura, op. cit.*)
6. Quarterly Bulletin issued by the North East India General Mission (Founded 1910), *Work in 'Tripura State* by Pastor N. Luaia, Field Superintendent, October 1931.
7. Mahadev Chakravarti, (i) "The Beginnings of Christian Missionary Activities in Tripura" (mimeo.), Academic Session, 53rd Session of the Indian Historical Records Commission held at Guwahati in February 1990; (ii) "Growth of Christianity in Tripura and Some Tribal Movements in Tripura Since Independence" (mimeo.), Seminar on "Social Movements in Tripura Since Independence" held on 10 February 1990 at Tripura University, Agartala; (iii) "The New Zealand Baptist Mission and the Beginnings of Christian Missionary Activities in Tripura" in the Proceedings of North East India History Association, Tenth Session, Shillong, 1989.
8. Letter of Birendrakishore Manikya addressed to Sir William Marris, Governor of Assam, dated Agartala, 25 July, 1922.
9. *Loc. cit.*
10. Letter of the Dewan of Tripura to the Field Secretary, NEIGM, No. 570, dated 17.2.1931, (Secretariat Archive, Agartala, B2/S20).
11. Letter from Rev. F.G. Sandy to Rev. W.R. Roberts, Field Director, NEIGM, 1918, (Sectt. Arch. B2/S20).
12. Rieweh R. Cunville, "The Tripuris of Tripura" in E. Roger, Hed Lund (ed.), Church Growth in the Third World, Bombay, 1977, p. 261.
13. Mahadev Chakravarti's papers in A Study on the Lushais of Iampui Hills in Tripura; *op. cit.*; "Tribal Chief and his People—A Case Study" in S.B. Saha (ed.), *Tribes of Tripura: A Historical Survey*, Agartala, 1986.

21

Changes in Tribal Societies in Tripura

The Lushai Reform Movement (1946-1950)

Dipak Kumar Chaudhuri

Prior to its merger with the Indian Union in 1949, Tripura had been a Native State, with its territories clearly divided into two distinct parts: the Hills, and the Plains. In the hills, the Maharaja of Tripura ruled as an independent King; but in the plains, he was a mere zamindar under the British. The zamindari portion of the State was, however, an integral portion of the kingdom, and, as such, not saleable even in case of default of Government revenue.

This topographical and political division of the State was also reflected in the nature of composition of the population of the State. While the population of the zamindari,—which formed the British District of Tipperah under the jurisdiction of the Bengal Government,—was dominated by the Bengalis, the population of the hill portion,—which was variously known as the "Independent Tipperah", the "Hill Tipperah", and later, the "Tripura State", —was predominantly tribal.[1] Census figures indicate the existence of as many as seventeen different tribes in Tripura.

In their social behaviour, the different tribal societies were naturally guided by their own customary laws. The traditional social hierarchy of all these societies in Tripura, as elsewhere, was characterised by Chiefs at the top of the social ladder, with special powers and privileges. But as their powers and privileges were not defined, and the customary laws, in most cases, not codified, the Chiefs were often guilty of excesses and abuses of power. The Royal House of Tripura, which belonged to the numerically most dominant Tripura tribe, had always found it convenient to maintain this traditional system of chieftainship with all its social autonomy. The system worked well, of course with occasional disturbances, like the king-vassal relations of medieval societies.

Of all the tribal societies in Tripura, it was the Lushai community, which enjoyed the maximum degree of autonomy, and, as such, the Lushai Chiefs had been far more powerful *vis-à-vis* other tribal Chiefs. The Lushais were settled in the Jampui and Sakhan ranges, in the north-eastern region of Tripura. There were four Lushai Chiefs: two in the Jampui range, recognised by the Tripura Durbar as Rajas, and two in the Sakhan range, not recognised as Rajas, but having the same powers and privileges. Around 1946-47, however, the Lushai people of this region started a movement with a view to put an end to the powers and privileges of the Chiefs, and thereby, free themselves from the traditional feudal bondage.

This essay is based on original archival sources, mostly in manuscript forms, and so far little used. It tries to trace the origin and nature of the movement, and the reaction of the Tripura Durbar, which gradually changed with the changed circumstances, paving the way for the ultimate demise of chieftainship.

Origin and Nature of the Movement

In order to trace the origin and understand the nature of the movement, it is necessary to look at the peculiar position of the Lushais in Tripura. In 1911, a severe *mautam* (famine) hit the Lushai hills (the present day Mizoram). Faced with the dire prospect of starvation and death, a group of Lushais, nearly a thousand in number, migrated into the State of Tripura, under their Chief, Hrangvunga. They settled in the Jampui range, which was mostly uninhabited during that time. Then, at the request of Hrangvunga, another Lushai Chief, Dokhuma, came in along with his men. Two other Lushai Chiefs settled in the Sakhan range. The Tripura Durbar recognised Hrangvunga and Dokhuma as Rajas.[2] It was settled that as token of allegiance, the two Rajas would pay a yearly visit to the State capital, Agartala, and pay *Ghar Chukti Kar* (household tax), collected from all the families living under them. A rent of Rs. 3 per *kani* land was also fixed as land revenue,[3] though it was never put into practice.

Thus ever since 1921, when the first batch of Lushais had migrated into the State, the Lushai Chiefs found themselves in an enviable position as there was virtually no control over them from the Durbar because of the geographical location of the region. In a letter dated 8 September, 1948, the Dewan of Tripura admitted the peculiar position of the Lushais in Tripura.

> "Due to inaccessibility of the area from the State capital, the Lushai Chiefs had been allowed a considerable number of

> autonomy by the Tripura Government for a long time past. Except for a loose allegiance to the Ruler and a formal *Ghar Chukti Tax* (house tax) levied on the households, the State has never derived any land revenue from the area. Even the collection of *Ghar Chukti Tax* realised through Lushai Chiefs, and not directly has always been merely a token collection.
>
> ...The Government has no Forest Customs and Police Station in the Lushai area. As such no forest revenue accrues. Nearest Police Station Fatikroy is 15 miles away from Lushai area. However, *Brindiyas* (traditional couriers of the Ruler) were sent out inviting the Lushai Chiefs to appear before His Highness as a mark of their continued allegiance.[4]

Thus the Lushai Chiefs were left to themselves bound by no law of the State. As their powers and privileges were not defined, they exacted all sorts of dues from the Lushai people which gave rise to serious discontent. One such thing was the *Fathang*, i.e., four tins (approximately one maund) of paddy per family collected by the Lushai Chiefs from their respective jurisdiction. The families which got special privileges from the Chiefs regarding selection of plots for *jhuming* and the like had to give *Fathang* to the extent of six tins of paddy. Secondly, there was the system of *Sachhiah* which was a payment made by the subject to the Chief; by this system the Lushais were made to pay to the chief the front leg of any animal killed and the defaulter was required to pay a fine of Rs. 40. Thirdly, there existed the custom of *Zalen* and of *Ramhual* by which some men could obtain the best plot of *jhum* lands by paying five maunds of extra paddy to the Chief. Fourthly, there was the custom of *Papelhman*, which was a fine of Rs. 40 realised by the Chief from a subject who had received favour from the Chief previously but now attempted to leave the Chief. Fourthly, there was the custom of *Zarzotawp*, i.e., confiscation by the Chief of properties belonging to a migrating subject. Finally, the Chiefs received free and forced labour whenever required from the subjects.

To these privileges of the Chiefs were added their special powers. Each Lushai Chief had his own independent court from which there could be no appeal though in other parts of Hill Tripura *Pahari Adalat* or Hill Courts were established by the Government of Tripura. The Lushai region thus became a state within the State. And whenever there was any sign of resistance by the Lushai people, the Durbar came forward to protect the chief. In 1944, for example, the Durbar solemnly announced:

> ". . . . it be declared to all concerned that the people of the Lushai tribe inhabiting in the State must continue to live under the customary authority and control of the Chiefs recognised by His Highness and at present under the Chiefship of either Hony. Second Lt. Rajkumar L. Huapliana Sailo or Hony. Lt. Rajkumar K.T. Chawma Sailo, as the case may be and all people of the Lushai tribe must obey the Lushai Chief and render allegiance to the Chief according to the custom and practice prevailing among them as approved by His Highness, even if they go in for land cultivation or gardening or any other business or profession."[5]

But neither the Royal Proclamation upholding the causes of the Chiefs nor the insularity of the region could prevent the tensions that had been generating between the forces of change and the forces of continuity from coming into the surface during the period following the Second World War. Among the forces of change, the most important was the influence of Christian missionaries. The Lushais were the first among the tribes of Tripura to embrace Christianity and come under the influence of Christian missionaries. While the Christian doctrine of equality kindled new hopes and aspirations among the people, the missionaries worked for the spread of education among them. And this resulted in the growth of a new generation Lushais who began to question the very rationale of the powers and privileges of the Chiefs in the absence of any corresponding duties on their part. Side by side, a new economic structure was gradually emerging among the Lushais. Under the guidance of the missionaries, they began shifting from the traditional *jhum* cultivation to settled farming and gardening. The old production relations, institutionalised in the chieftainship, which arose out of the *jhum* cultivation of a communal nature, needed a revision. Thus a conflict between the forces of change and the forces of continuity was brewing. There was also a surge for democratic institutions all over India during this period. Demands for civil rights and equality and for the introduction of democratic elements in the socio-political structure were rapidly gaining strength. While the Indian National Congress began preparations for a democratic India, the All India People's Conference undertook to oversee the people's movements in Native States. But, as Sumit Sarkar points out, the All India People's Conference all along remained "essentially an occasional gathering of middle class politicians, concerned with questions of civil rights and responsible government, and seldom raising specific peasant or tribal issues."[6] This resulted in the emergence of separate tribal movements, with specific tribal issues, which were essentially different from all India issues. One example of this type of tribal movement was the Union of the Lushai people, living in the Lushai Hills, known as the Mizo Union founded in 1946. One of its aim was to do away with the powers and privileges of the Chiefs. It gave a great fillip to the Tripura Lushais. In fact, it was the Mizo Union which invited the Tripura Lushais to join them in order to make it an all Lushai movement against the Chiefs.

The Tripura Lushais had, as yet, no organisation of their own. As such, under the leadership of Ch. P. Thanga and Lalchhuanga, they formed a Union and immediately joined the Mizo Union in 1946, and submitted Rs. 200 as affiliation fee.[7] But soon the Tripura Lushais found that they had "nothing in common with the British Lushais either socially or politically."[8] Hence, on February 22, 1947, they formed a separate Union of their own and named it 'Tripura Lushai Union'[9]

The object of the Union, declared Ch. P. Thanga, the Chairman, in his letter to the Dewan of Tripura, dated October 18, 1984, was:

> "To introduce with full approval of the State certain improvements which should apply only to our community.
>
> 1. We seek, first of all, that the powers, privileges, and duties of the Chiefs be defined so that all may be aware of them.
> 2. We request that a central court be formed to judge all cases of disputes of a serious nature. At present there is no control over ruling authority in Jampui, the Chiefs are above the law. The members of the Central Court may be elected by the village panchayats.
> 3. We further pray that under Central Court there should be village panchayats, freely elected by the village dwellers.
> 4. We seek information of the following specific points :
>   (a) Is it lawful on the part of the Chief to seize belongings of his migrating subjects?
>   (b) Is it an obligation on the part of a subject to give *Zarzotawp* or *Paelhman* to the Chief in paddy of any amount when he migrates?
>   (c) Does abolition of some oppressive customs mean curbing the power of the Chief?"[10]

The above letter indicates two important characteristics of the Lushai movement in Tripura. To start with, it was not an anti-State or anti-Maharaja movement like other previous tribal movements in Tripura.

Rather, it was an appeal to the State authority, the Maharaja, to define the powers, privileges and duties of the Chiefs, who, due to the lack of control because of the peculiar geographical position of the region, made their own laws. And since, there was no State-court other than the courts of the Chiefs, there was no scope of appeal against the misdeeds of the Chiefs. Secondly, the method adopted by the Union was a constitutional one. They wanted to change their existing social conditions with approval of the State. And for that, an official recognition of the Union became an urgent necessity.

This urgency can be seen in another letter of the Chairman of the Union, dated 31 October, 1947, addressed to the Dewan:

> "As we felt the urgent need of recognition by the State, we conditionally joined the Tripur Sangha.[11] Under the Tripur Sangha we formed a separate Union of our Union with separate Constitution, we are told by Tripur Sangha that our Tripura Lushai Union was recognised by the State through it. (But) Coming to know that we are not benefited by our joining the Tripur Sangha, we felt the need of having an official recognition of our Union."[12]

The Constitution of the Union mentioned above, throws light on the nature of the Lushai movement. The Constitution specified in detail the aims and objectives of the Union: to check the unlawful activities of the Chiefs and to do away with certain oppressive customs which had so long prevented the economic progress of the Lushais. To effect such a social transformation, a breakthrough in the traditional power structure was necessary, and that was provided by the introduction of democratic elements in the Lushai society. Thus, the Constitution declared:

> For the sake of convenience every Lushai village is regarded as forming one unit which has its own office bearers to see that members of the Union follow the rules and regulations as laid down by the Assembly and also execute orders. All these Units are grouped into three Blocks—Jampui Block, Sakhan Block, and Pamchera Block. Each block has its own office bearers. All the office bearers of the Unit or Block are to be elected by secret ballots.
>
> The Assembly has two Committees—The Working Committee and the Executive Committee. Members of the Working Committee are office bearers of the Units, Blocks and the Assembly. In case of emergency it has the powers to exercise

> the functions of the Assembly. The Executive Committee consists often members, six of which are Assembly office bearers and the other four elected by the Assembly. The duration of the term of the office bearers is three years.[13]

Thus the Constitution sought to democratise the traditional social hierarchy of the tribe. In order to maintain the autonomy of the Lushais and for the interpretation of their customary laws, the Constitution also provided for an independent judiciary. This was vitally important as there were four independent courts under four Lushai Chiefs in Tripura, from which there could be no appeal. As a result. "When cases arise between subjects, one Chief with those of another, the one party has to go to his Chief and the other to the other Chief."[14] Consequently, cases remained untried. Hence, it was necessary to have "one ruling court—The Central Court."[15]

The Constitution also specified the scope and policy of the union:

> This Union is confined within our Lushai community only and it will always be loyal to the State Government. Our policy is to change and modify our bad and oppressive customs gradually."[16]

From an analysis of the Constitution, certain distinctive features of the movement can easily be identified. First, it was a movement of a particular community with specific issues involving that community alone. That was why the Lushai Union separated itself from the Tripura Sangha and the Mizo Union, which has been more political in nature. The separation from the Mizo Union was all the more important because it explains the different nature of two movements launched by the Lushais of the same region in spite of their having similar socio-cultural background, though distinct political identity. While the Tripura Lushai Union was essentially a social reform movement, the Mizo Union was more than a social movement. It had distinct political aims and one of them being the unification of all Lushais into a greater Mizoram. The Tripura Lushais became apprenhensive of losing their own separate identity. To emphasize this difference in the nature of the two movements, the Lushais of Tripura refused to adopt the term 'Mizo', and deliberately took the term 'Tripura Lushai Union." Secondly, the Union adopted a moderate policy of agitation by means of democratic institutions. It is, indeed, plausible, that the Lushais of Tripura had been aware of the Reang unrest (1942-43) in Tripura which turned violent, and the consequences thereof. This awareness probably made them adopt a policy of prayer and petition to the Maharaja's Government for the recognition of their Union and approval of their activities.

Reaction of the Tripura Durbar

The Tripura Durbar was totally unaware of the happenings in the Jampui hills due to the inaccessibility of the area and the resultant lack of communication. Quite apart from this the State Government was beset with all sorts of pre- and post-partition problems because of its proximity to the newly-created state of East Pakistan. It was only in 1948 that the Durbar became aware of the Lushai problem when conflicting reports began to pour in. The police sources from Kailasahar sent a report, dated 8 June, 1948, informing the Government that "the Lushais of Jampui hills have formed a Union amongst themselves. They donated Rs. 200 in aid of the Mizo Union of Aijal hills in anticipation of getting recognition of their Union by Mizo Union."[17]

But reports of more serious nature were forthcoming. A letter from Shillong, dated 9 June, 1948, signed by one John F. Manliana (Lushai), informed that "Some Lushais serving in the Pakistan Armed Forces had been sent out by the Government in disguise to Tripura State and Lushai hills, particularly in those areas where Pakistan and Indian boundaries met, in order to secretly send in Lushai and other hill tribes (who use Lushai dialect) to Pakistan for recruitment in the Pakistan Armed Forces. That those secretly sent persons are also instigating the Lushai and other Hill Tribes of Tripura State and Lushai Hills to demand for a separate State of their own, with the plea that neither the Tripura State nor the Indian Dominion Government, are taking or will take proper steps to improve their conditions."[18]

Similar warning came from the Office of the Adviser to the Governor of Assam for Excluded Areas and States: "We have been receiving reports recently about growing activity in the hills of the Tripura State. You are perhaps aware that there has been a similar ferment in Manipur, where some of the hill tribes have been moving for secession from the State to join either Mizoram or Naga Hill District. advise you to keep a very careful watch." In August 1948, the Office of the Adviser again informed the Tripura Government that "Our latest information is that one Chawma, Chief of Sabual, who was an Honorary Lieutenant in the last War, has formed a party styled as the "Hill Tribal Union" and has also pursuaded some of his fellow to follow him. The objective is said to be to form a separate State in Tripura. It is also reported that many unlicensed guns are in the possession of the peoples of the area."[19]

Meanwhile, to counter the activities of the Tripura Lushai Union, the Lushai Chiefs of the Jampui-Sakhan region had organised themselves and formed a union of their own, known as the "Tripura Mizo Chiefs' Council" (1948).[20] In a letter to the Maharani dated 25 September, 1948, the Council complained about the activities of the Union, accusing that it was not only secessionist in nature, but with communist leanings, which, unless checked, might be shortly turn out to become a Communist Party, and that without approval of the Durbar, it was trying to legislate new customary laws and practices completely defying the authority of Chiefs.[21]

Thus the initial reaction of the Government of Tripura, formed on the basis of such unfavourable reports, was one of alarm and hostility. In a strongly worded letter to the Secretary, Tripura Lushai Union, dated 4 October, 1948, the Dewan, A.B. Chatterjee, warned that:

> ...by assuming recognition of the Union without the Previous approval of the Government, you are, in point of fact and law, disregarding the lawful authority of this Government, A copy of the proclamation issued by your Union about elections etc. and the stipulation therein that the village Council Members of your Union will exercise judicial functions amount to a challange to the authority of the State and also the direction that judicial functions now performed by the Chiefs, with the approval of this Government, may be violated with impunity. I have requested Rev. Jones to make you understand the implications of such unlawful activities and would request you to cease them forthwith. This Government, while encouraging progressing measures will not allow any unwarranted assumption of authority. It must be clearly understood that all power in this State must be derived from the Ruler."[22]

But the Government soon became convinced after proper enquiry through police sources[23] that the Lushai movement was neither secessionist nor communist in nature. The Government also realised that in the changed political climate of the country, it would be difficult and unwise to check a people's movement against a system which had become an anachronism in a democratic India. Hence, it was felt the necessity to consider a plan of reform of the system, which became, in fact, an imperative, in order to wean away the Lushais from the Communist movement that had been gaining momentum in some other parts of Tripura. This changed attitude of the Government of Tripura was reflected in a note which A.B. Chattterjee had left:

I am leaving this note for my successor. I have interviewed both the two Chiefs recognised by the Late Maharaja and the Government of Tripura and the Vice Chairman and the Treasurer of the Lushai Union of Tripura State. It is rather a hopeful feature that the Union which is a progressive body does not want to have any connection with the Mizo Union of Lushai Hills area of Assam, Due to activities of Missionaries over a very long period the Lushais are more advanced educationally and otherwise than any other hill tribes in Tripura State. In fact nearly 90 per cent of them are literate and have been taught English. As such it would be difficult to keep these educated Lushais under the bondage of the two Chiefs. I have explained to the Vice Chairman and Treasurer of the Union that the process of democratisation will have to be naturally gradual and slow. They have appreciated this and I believe will react favourably to some liberalising measures introduced by the State. I am inclined to believe that the Lushais of this State are more with the Union than with the two Chiefs. The two Chiefs naturally want to retain all their privileges and power and, and if they are deprived at once and altogether, they may, by virtue of their long standing superior social and economic status, create trouble. My idea is to introduce some measures of reform which will withdraw the more flagrantly dictatorial power and privileges of the two Chiefs and distribute the power among a body of men on a loosely elective basis."[24]

The successor to A.B. Chatterjee was B.K. Acharjya. He was, however, undecided about the course of action to be taken in this regard and at the same time, he was suffering from Communist phobia. This psychological factor was reflected in his letter to N.K. Rustomji, the adviser to the Governor of Assam, dated 19 June, 1949:

> "I have not yet made up my mind whether this demand of replacing appointed Chiefs by elected Chiefs should be conceded. (There is) always a possibility that election may bring into power an individual who has communistic leanings, or contacts with Communists of Burma. (I) want advice."[25]

B.K. Acharjya, however, recommended the posting of a Magistrate, a Police outpost and a platoon of the lst Tripura Rifles in the area.

Rustomji, in his reply, clearly outlined the policy of the Government of India with regard to the Lushai Hills and made it clear that the Government of Tripura should conform to this policy. Thus he wrote:

> "The move of the Lushais in Tripura is probably an offshoot of the general move in the Lushai Hills District, the main object of which is to do away with the system of Chiefs. There is evidence that this movement has communist inspiration and probably communist support as well.
> There is no doubt, however, that there are cases in which Chiefs are abusing their powers.
> What we are trying to do is to remove some of the more glaring abuses of the present system, and for this purpose, the Superintendent has recently summoned some of the leading Chiefs of the District. The best course would be to warn the Chiefs, as we have done, that the State will not uphold them in any abuse of their power, and that it will be in their interest to take the people more in their confidence."[26]

So long, however, the Lushai Union was maintaining a low profile as it had not yet received an official recognition from the State Government. On 9 September, 1949, came a turning point in the history of Tripura; on that day, the Tripura Merger Agreement was signed. And on 15 October, the administration of the State was taken over by a Chief Commissioner. With this ended the monarchical rule in Tripura. The Lushai Union immediately took advantage of this change of Government from monarchy to democracy. An assembly of the Union was held at Vanghmun which elected a Committee of 20 members to discuss matters relating to the traditional customs of the Lushais.[27] This Committee held its first meeting on October 25, 1949, at Tlaksih, and passed a number of resolutions severely curtailing the power and privileges of the Chiefs.

To start with, the Committee took upon itself the title of "The Social Customs Reforming Committee". It was to be a permanent body and its members were to be re-elected after every five years. It was empowered to introduce better and progressive customs among the Lushais of Tripura. It demanded the abolition of the custom of privileged classes and declared all Lushais to be equal in the eye of customary laws. As a corollary of this demand, the Committee recommended the abolition of (1) the custom of "free and forced labour" and the custom of *sachhiah* as these had been symbols of slavery; (2) the customs of *zalen* and *ramhual;* (3) the custom of *papelhman;* and (4) the custom of *zarzotawp.* A separate resolution was passed declaring that the properties, including houses and gardens, of a migrating Lushai were not to be confiscated by the Chiefs. The custom of *fatang,* however, was maintained for the time being; it was resolved that each Lushai family would subscribe two full *kerosene tins* of paddy to the Chief annually or rupee one in cash. And finally, the Committee recorded its absolute loyalty to the existing Government of Tripura.[28]

All the resolutions of the Social Customs Reforming Committee were then sent to the Chief Commissioner for his approval. The observation of the Chief Commissioner, R.R. Roy, in this regard was a definite reversal of the policy followed so far. In a historic letter, dated 24 November, 1949, addressed to the Chairman, Tripura Lushai Union, the Chief 20 & 30 Commissioner declared:[29 & 30]

> "Regarding the proposed abolition of certain customary payments made to your Chiefs, and certain privileges and powers now exercised by your Chiefs, I would inform you that such practices are not being upheld at present by any laws of the land and that it is open to the Lushai people themselves to alter and abolish such customs by general opinion. As it is against the policy of this Government to interfere unnecessarily in the manners and customs of tribal people, you yourselves will have to devise means by which old customs which you now consider to be undesirable should be abolished. The only thing that I would advise you to bear in mind in this connection is that such changes should be brought about by lawful means and the weight of public opinion and not by resort to any acts which affect public peace and tranquillity or contravene the existing laws of the land."

Thus at last, the Tripura Lushai Union received the blessings of the Government to go ahead. The new Government of Tripura made it clear that it would not uphold the causes of the Chiefs. Thus the movement which started from below seemed to take the nature of a movement from above. By 1951, even the custom of *fathang* was stopped by the Reforming Committee. Police reports, of course, indicated that the Chiefs were collecting *fathang* from some "meek Reang people who lived under them."[31] Gradually Chiefs themselves became indifferent to this system as they had neither the power nor the patronage of the Government to enforce it.

In 1954, the Assam Lushai Hills District (Acquisition of Chiefs, Rights) Act was passed which abolished the system of Chieftainship; the rights and. interests of 259 Mizo Chiefs and 50 Pawi-Lakher Chiefs were vested in the Government. In Tripura, however, no such law was passed as the number of Lushai Chiefs was very small and as they could not put any pressure. The system of Chieftainship in Tripura simply withered away in the 1950s under public pressure.

REFERENCES

1. The tribal people had always been the numerical majority in Hill Tripura. The demographic change of the State took place only after the partition of India, when refugees from the neighbouring East Pakistan began to pour in. The 1951 Census for the first time showed that the tribal people had lost their numerical majority.
2. Information regarding the Lushai Chiefs can be found in the Revenue Department file, TSA No. 1333JFI/CA dated 24.7.48 :
   A. *Area of the Lushai Villages*
      1. Villages under Chief Huapliana Sailo, S/o Late Raja Dokhuma: 32 sq. miles (Jampui Range)
      2. Villages under Chief Mitien Chwma Sailo, S/o Late Raja Hrangohunga: 16 sq. miles (Jampui Range).

   B. There were two other persons, Lal Dinga and Thang Luaia in the Sakhan Range who held some villages under them, but were not recognised by the Durbar.
   The area under each was 12 sq. miles. They were considered as village Headmen.

   C. The total area of the Lushai region was 72 sq. miles.
3. *Ibid.*
4. Letter from A.B. Chatterjee, the Dewan, to N.K. Rustomji, the Adviser to the Government of Assam for Excluded Areas and States, dated 8 September 1948, D.O. No. 1501/H/CA-06) (B-1, SI-17, TSA).
5. Vide A.M. Dutta (Ed.) A *Study on the Lushais of Jampui Hills in Tripura* (Agartala, Directorate of Research, Government of Tripura, 1987), p. 29.
6. Sumit Sarkar, *Modern India 1985-1947* (India, Macmillan, 1983), p. 360.
7. Letter from the Chairman, Tripura Lushai Union, to the Dewan, dated 31 October, 1948 (B-1, S1-17, FN-CA-66, TSA).
8. *Ibid.*
9. Report of C.I. of Police, Kailasahar, dated 8 June, 1948 (B-1, S1-17 TSA).
10. Letter from the Chairman, Tripura Lushai Union, to the Dewan, dated 18 October, 1948 (B-1, S1-17, TSA).
11. *Op. cit.*, p. 2.
12. *Ibid.*
13. The Constitution of the Tripura Lushai Union can be found in the file of Dewan's Office (B-1, S1-17, FN-CA-66, TSA).
14. *Ibid.*
15. *Ibid.*
16. *Ibid.*
17. Police report from Kailasahar, dated 30 August, 1948 (B-1, S1-17, TSA).
18. Letter from John F. Manliana (Lushai) to The Maharani Regent, dated Shillong, 9 June, 1948 (B-1, S1-17, TSA).

19. Letter from N.K. Rustomji to the Dewan, D.O. No. 445/C, dated Shillong 3 August, 1948 (B-1, S1-17, TSA).
20. Letter from N.K. Rustomji to the Dewan, D.O. No. 874/C, dated Shillong, 20 August, 1948 (B-1, S1-17, TSA).
21. Letter from the Chairman and Secretary, Tripura Mizo Chiefs' Council, to the Regent Maharani, dated 26 September, 1984.
22. *Ibid.*
23. Letter from A.B. Chatterjee, the Dewan, to the Secretary, Tripura Lushai Union, dated 4 October, 1948, No. 1749/H/CA-66.
24. I.B. Report, Agartala, dated 30 August, 1948; Report from Hari Das Benerjee, S.I., I.B. and C.ID. Office, Agartala, dated 15 June, 1949.
25. A.B. Chatterjee's Note, dated 24 October, 1948.
26. Letter from B.K. Acharjya, the Dewan, to N.K. Rustomji, No. 551/H-66, dated 19 June, 1949.
27. Letter from N.K. Rustomji to B.K. Acharjya, D.O. No. 23/44/C-1038, dated 28 June, 1949.
28. Letter from the Chairman, Tripura Lushai Union, to the Chief Commissioner, Tripura, dated 12 November, 1949.
29. Letter from R.K. Roy, the Chief Commissioner, to the Chairman, Tripura Lushai Union, No. 1526/CA/66, dated 24 November, 1949.
30. Report of D.O., Kailasahar, to the Secretary, Revenue Department, No. 3274/24-2, dated 26 October, 1951.
31. *Ibid.*

Abbreviations Used

TSA	Tripura Secretariat Archives, Agartala.
B	Bundle. SI. Serial No.

22

Religious Transformation in Mizoram

An Overview

J.J. Roy Burman

Taking cue from Tylor, one of the founders of evolutionary school in anthropology, Lowie defined that 'Religion is a verily universal feature of human culture, not because all societies foster a belief in spirits, but because all recognize in some form or other awe-inspiring, extraordinary manifestations of reality'.

D.N. Majumdar, the proponant of the Man, Area, Resource, Co-operation, "gave a cultural definition to religion. According to him, religion is the human response to apprehension of something of power, which is supernatural or supersensory. It is the expression of the manner, and type of adjustment effected by a people with their conception of the supernatural. Religion had been regarded as a product of civilization, until Tylor gave convincing proof that primitive societies have their own versions of religious activity, not very different from that of the civilized societies. According to Durkheim, religion is `a unified system of beliefs and practices related called a Church all those who adhere to them (1912)". Clifford Greetz, formulated a more comprehensive definition of religion. A religion is a system of symbols which acts to establish powerful, pervasive and long lasting moods and motivations in men by formulating conceptions of a general order of existence and clothing these conceptions with such an aura of factuality that the moods and motivations seem uniquely realistic.

Louis Schneider views that definitions of religion vary. "It seems that there is no end to the formulation of definitions of religion. But different definitions are not always necessarily incompatible. Sometimes, at any rate, ostensible divergences turn out to be the effects of looking at different aspects of the same thing. The different approaches to the study of religion basically emanate from the `evolutionism' in anthropology.

Both the Historical particularists and the followers of "grand concept of evolution" believed in that the complex, heterogeneous present has arisen, more or less gradually, out of a simpler, more uniform past. The relics of the past are still to be found scattered.

While to Tylor animism was the earliest form of religion. According to Frazer, the mental progress involved was magic to religion to science. For Durkheim evolutionary advance considered in the emergence of specific analytic, profane ideas about "cause" or "category" or "relationship" from diffuse global sacred images. These collective representations, as he called them, of the social order and its moral force included such as '*mana*', '*totem*' and 'god'. Though Durkheim overcame the stigma of studying the origin of religion, his studies were not completely devoid of the evolutionary framework. All the scholars mentioned hitherto knowingly inadvertently become subject of portraying a general schema of a "folk and universal" religion. A folk religion, as the name suggests is bound to a particular people, folk or tribe, just as the particular people, folk or tribe is bound to the particular religion, who says either says the other. Universal religions are detached from a folk base. They address themselves to individual men anywhere and everywhere. They speak to man as a being who universally has a problem in relating himself to his cosmos and whose particular tribal affiliation is in principle totally accidental or irrelevant. According to his schema, Christianity is a universal religion, while Hinduism is a national folk religion and not a world religion.

Apart from the concepts presented by various scholars, the main dialogue on religion veers around the views propagated by Max Weber and Karl Marx. Weber sought to refute the historicist school by emphasizing that studies of culture and history cannot avoid the use of typological concepts, and that the most important task is, therefore, to attempt to make these concepts explicit. A strategic element in Weber's confrontation of the Marxists, the utilitarians, and the historicist school was his insistence on a 'value-free' social science. His major contribution in the realms of religion stems from his famous essay, the *Protestant Ethic and the Spirit of Capitalism* (1904-05). He avers mainly two factors in it: (i) that in many parts of the world great material achievements had resulted from the work of monastic orders dedicated to a life of the spirit; and (ii) the ascetic Protestant sects were noted for their economic success, especially in the early phase of modern capitalism.

The Marxists aver that Marxism is a science. And such a science had been held to be incompatible with religious belief on two grounds. The first, and more straight forward only is that Marxism contains a material metaphysic. As stated by Engels, "if the unity of the world consists in its materiality", then all statements, including religious ones, are ultimately reducible to statements about the movement of matter. Secondly, religion can be dismissed not in a metaphysical, but in functional terms—religion is an instrument of class rule, and ideological but work of the dominant class. This view too assumes that religious assertions must always be a cloak for something else, obviously so in the case of conservative religions, but equally so in the case of radical religious movements (Anabaptists, Cargo cults) which must be cloaks for political demands. The traditional Marxist metaphor from heavy engineering—that of base and superstructure—tends to put religion on the tip top of the superstructure.

The issues on religion which has been thus put forward can be succinctly summarised as the following: (a) Evolution of religion from elementary forms to complex forms—folk—Universal religion continuum; (b) Functional utility of religion to reinforce the moral binding forces of the society; (c) Religion as one of the basic factors of social change; and (d) Political and material factors—as historically perceived as the basis of religious and other social changes. To be precise, none of these dimensions deal with the aspect of religious conversion.

An examination is being made here in the light of the theoretical postulates presented earlier to what has exactly happened to the religion of the Mizos in Mizoram. The Mizos are the conglomeration of ethnic entities, who basically inhabit the central and north districts of Mizoram. There are also certain groups living in some areas of Manipur, Assam and Tripura bordering with Mizoram. The Mizos comprise of a number of subtribes or clans. The main groups among them are the Lusais, Raltes and Hmars. A number of other groups apart from these who identify themselves as Mizos are known as Awzia.

The Mizos used to originally believe in a religion of their own, which is often termed as animism—though it is often resented by the Mizos themselves. The British conquered Mizoram in 1891 and put it under 'Excluded Area Zone'. The British did very little developmental works and their main concern was maintenance of law and order. The mission aries pioneered into the area in 1894. Within almost 50 years of their efforts, the missionaries succeeded in coverting more than 90 per cent of the Mizos into Christianity.

Impact of Christianity

Christianity is supposed to have caused a tremendous impact on the life of the Mizos. The impact of Christianity can be studied from the perspectives of social, cultural, economic and political life of the people.

(i) Christianity and Social Change

One of the most striking features of the impact of Christianity on the social life in the introduction of modern, western education, which, in turn is supposed to have had a profound effect on the life style and consumption pattern.

The literacy level provides an instant indicator to the impact of Christianity. In 1981, while Arunachal Pradesh had 4.28 per cent Christians, the percentage of literacy was only 20.79 in thc Statc. In contrast Mizoram with over 88 per cent Christian tribals had 59.88 per cent literacy.

Hluna states, "Thus one important role played by the Missionaries or the church was the introduction of education. The Missionaries did not only preach Christianity but they also introduced the system of learning and reading. This was apparently for the effective teaching of the faith and it formed to be more useful and effective than any other thing. There never was any history in the development of a nation so rapid and so fast as the Mizos in their development of education.

This Missionaries were also aided by the government, as many of the government schools were amalgamated with the Missionary schools. The art of reading and writing was a completely new and fascinating experience to the people. Moreover, each new converts' ambition was to be able to read the Bible and the hymn books prepared by the Missionaries. Sunday was devoted to learning the scripts when adult learnt to read and write!

In spite of promotion of general education in the State, the Missionaries paid little attention to the growth of higher education and impart technical skills.

It also needs to be pointed out that in its endeavours to promote education in the region, the Missionaries needed out the system of "Bachelor's dormitory" or *Zawlbuks* which provided the base for imparting useful technical knowledge turned to the local requirements. The Young Mizo Association, the youth clubs were strongly favoured by the Missionaries for a replacement.

Apart from education, health is another field in which the Missionaries are thought to have brought about significant departure from the past traditions. The Synod Hospital at Durtlang is still supposed to be one of the best hospitals in Mizoram. Apart from running hospitals, the Missionaries can also be credited for carrying out extensive medical care in the interior areas.

In spite of the good work done by the Missionaries in the field of health care, it seems that their efforts were made more as a strategy to gain access to the region. Lal Dena observes, "The rationale for missionary's involvement in medical work was not merely a humanitarian motivation—a desire to help needy people. Nineteenth and twentieth century missionaries who established hospitals and schools saw these institutions as aids in saving souls for Christianity. The experience and force of circumstances made missionaries realize more and more that saving the souls must be accompained by the saving of bodies. Medical work was also one of the most effective means of destroying the traditional world-view and belief system which was essentially supernaturalistic'. Thus, one of the intentions of the Missionaries to introduce modern healthcare could also have been to displace faith healing prescribed by age-old traditions. All the more, it may be such that the western medical system did not permeate the roots as it generally presumed. Its main influence transcended to the general value system of the tribals towards life and the eccelesiaticals.

(ii) Impact of Christianity on the Cultural Life

The impact of Christianity among the Mizos is usually considered to be most distinctly manifest in the cultural sphere. Spread of western dress and pop music along with the changes in the culinary practices are often ascribed to the intervention of Missionaries. Apart from these, many other facets of cultural life and thought to have undergone significant due to the impact of Christianity.

One of the most significant cultural practices which is supposed to have disappeared from the State, is the system of Head Hunting. The number of human heads slaughtered by the Mizo youth was supposed to mark his status and determined his eligibility for marriage. The interventional of the Missionaries have brought a stop to this system to a great extent. Many other cultural elements are also believed to have withered away with the intrusion of the Christian Mission. A.C. Roy (1982) observes that, under the old Lushai (Mizo) customs if a mother died at child birth, the child was also buried along with the mother. Cow or goat milk was a taboo among the Lushais. Hence, it was difficult to keep a motherless infant. The custom continued till the missionaries started homes for the motherless babies. Customs regarding the death and burial home also changed. Earlier the dead babies were buried near the house. Chief's bodies were kept for months in large hollowed-out logs before burial. Now all the burials take place in a burial ground under Christian rites.

There are, however, diverse perceptions about the impact of Christianity on the cultural life among the Mizos. Many are of the view that changes induced by the new religion are only at the surface level. On the one hand, they suggest that by helping the tribals to interpret some of their traditions in more universalistic terms in a selective manner by providing church services in tribal languages, many missionaries, if not the church institutions as such have played important roles in reinforcing the tribal identity. This point of view is not without some basis. But at the same time, one has to take note of the empirical evidences of a different order.

A.C. Roy observes interestingly, "the spread of Christianity was also due to some waves of revivalism which paradoxically converted more people in a wave than could be done by sustained proselytization. In the revivalist movements, a large number of people would profess their powers of oracle. There would be great mass dancing with drum beats, hysterical singing of hymns and sometimes also bouts of *zu* (liquor) durinking. The movements made Christianity more adaptable to the people with their age-old ground of the new religion and with the old animism, drawing more people to the new faith".

The author himself observes that one of the main cultural factors of acceptance of Christianity, apart from the political exigencies is the allowance to perpetuate the basic elements of the traditional social structure by foreign missionaries. They did not attempt at changing the traditional unilinear segmentary systems like lineage, clan phratry. The basic function of the segmentary system is to regulate the use of natural resources, with which the kin groups are associated at different levels. In fact, even in the church management, kinship and clan affiliations continue to play an important role, particularly while electing the members of the managing committees. (A lot of these have now perished since regrouping of villages). The Mizo churches also respect the traditional age differentiation and status differentiation to a large extent. Sitting arrangement in the churches during the service is usually made according to age/sex/marital status/birth status differentiations. Apart from these, certain cultural elements associated with death, birth or marriage rituals are still observed by the Mizos. All these ceremonies are based on the age-old philosophy of altruism or *Tlawmngaihna*, a concept close to the core of Mizo identity. The young Mizo Association, a modern version of the traditional *zawlbuk* or Bachelor's dormitory, which is to be found in every village of Mizo predominated areas of Mizoram, is very much organised on religious lines.

There are a number of other pre-Christian cultural elements still surviving among the Mizos. Predominantly, among them are, the sowing festival or harvesting festival. the *kuts* without their old rituals; the system of *in-lawm*, exchange labour the marriagable partners of opposite sex; the *nũla-rim*-wooing session between young boys and girls in the evenings; *Mizawn inchuh* the ritual carrying of dead bodies and mock fights between neighbouring villages; *Hnatlang*—community social work, etc.

Lal Dena observes, 'Ironically, the people also saw Christian ideas of Supreme God as referring to the Supreme Being of their animistic religion. In fact, the Christian God and the Supreme Being of their traditional religion were addressed by the same name *Pathian.* There was, thus, an indigenous concept the Supreme Being which was continuous in its essential with the Christian concept'.

The role played by the Church in the dynamics of ethnic processes has been quite significant though it does not appear to have been very consistent. At one level supra tribal level, while Christianity is felt to have strengthened the ethnic identity, at the local level different church denominations seem to have assisted in retaining their ethnic identities. It has been observed that while in Aizawl district, where the Raltes are predominant in number, the Presbyterian church rules the roost, while in Lunglei district where the Lusais are preponderant, the Baptist church has its sway. Inter-denominational marriages almost always result in both the bride and groom adopting a new Church.

(iii) Impact of Christianity on the Economic Life

Clifford Manshardt observes, "When Christianity came to India, offering to her outcaste peoples' hope and deliverance, a great number responded. The desire for righteousness was not always separated from the desire for food or economic advancement. The missionary treatment of these outcaste converts has not always been wise. Oppressed by the great poverty of the people, it has been easy for the Missionaries to hand out money". Though the method adopted by the Missionaries as observed by Manshardt could be true in some parts of the country, empirical evidences do not hold good in the north-eastern region. Though there is no stark poverty in Mizoram, as compared to the rest of the country, the technology involved with the economy did not appear to have made any significant departure from the past, even after the advent of Christianity. Majority of the people in the rural areas yet thrive on shifting cultivation, hunting and gathering. Settled cultivation which has emerged in a low key of late, cannot be said to owe much to the effort of the evangelists. Even the growth of the tertiary sector in the recent times is due to the policy of the government, rather than the Church.

The Church can, however, be credited to, for having developed certain institutions which help the poor and destitutes. Hluna observes, 'Many Christians have the habit of giving offerings or tither to the Church. Thus every year the money accounts from these offerings alone may be about millions of rupees or so. Women are also engaged in raising fund. One of the regular practices for such is that women put aside a handful of rice before cooking it every morning and every evening. At every two weeks the ladies collect the amount of rice and they sell it to the needy people at a low rate. From this too, the church is collecting a large amount of money. Besides, in many villages, one or two sticks of firewood are set aside by each family or by the female members and the money thus raised from this are used for the mission work. There are instances where church-*jhum* was made for growing rice, cotton, etc. Women also made some clothes, bags, etc., turn by turn and the money incurred through these activities were meant for the church. Sometimes, in recent times the church occasionally arrange fêtes to raise fund for buying Hospital beds, mattresses, X-ray machine, etc.

It is thus apparent that the Mizo churches rather than depending on foreign donations are themselves mobilising resources for evangelical work. Their effort has not been so much as to develop high-tech economic development, but equitable distribution of resources. It may surprise many, that the Mizo churches are even funding to carry out evangelical work not only in other north-eastern States but also in some parts of central India and also in a few South-East Asian countries.

(iv) Impact of Christianity on the Political Life

Politics and religion do not appear to have been exclusive of each other in Mizoram, more significantly since the inception of the British rule. The pre-British religion was mainly oriented to either aiding some of the tribals to maintain a buffer rules between neighbouring kingdoms and prohibited trade through the region or facilitating trade through their respective domains without formation of economic classes. Some of the scholars like B.K. Roy Burman ascribe systems of regulated head-hunting and potlatches to be some of the religio-cultural traits which were functional in maintaining the bridge-buffer roles in an egalitarian setting. The rapid improvement in the trade along the sea routes and changes in the political equations at the regional and continental level are supposed to have rendered the traditional religions obsolete, and this facilitated the intrusion of colonialism along with Christianity.

Lal Dena observes, "In the nineteenth century Christian missions and colonialism seemed to follow upon each other in Africa and Asia. It is for that reason that in the eyes of many African and Asian peoples, colonialism was seen to assume both the role of a 'politician' and a 'priest' and Christian missions appeared to be a part and expression of western colonial expression. Some of them even go to the extent of characterising missions as merely the hunting dog of western imperialism".

Lal Dena, however, also observes that relationship between the Cross and the Flag was not as smooth as is usually assumed. While the Church had really some pious interests, the colonial interest was motivated by commercial interests. Therefore, the inter-connection between them was more in the nature of highly temporary process which was solely determined by the principle of expediency.

In the post-independence period, the role of the church, according to many in India, has been very dubious and suspect. But, a closer scrutiny of the church activities indicate that their role has varied according to the needs of the time and space. While sometimes it has sides with insurgency and underground movements of the people, sometimes it has also tried to bring about reconciliation between the conflicting forces. It appears to the present author that the positive and creative role played by the church in revitalising the democratic process at the grass-root level and also in the regional and national politics, pales out its negative features. Hluna has quite distinctly indicated the positive role played by the church during the turbulent period in Mizoram. In spite of being alleged to be siding with the insurgents, the Presbyterian church in particular tried to mitigate between the underground army and the security forces. In fact, at times it even invited the wrath of the insurgents. The Baptist Assembly of Serkawn too followed the suit of the Presbyterian church when they openly charged the MNF responsible for the sufferings of the innocent Mizo people. On 8th September, 1966, both the Baptist and Presbyterian church together urged the Mizos to shun away from violent methods to safeguard their religious rights. In the subsequent years, a Christian Peace Committee tried to bring political settlement of Mizoram within the framework of Constitution of India.

Christianity and Democratic Functions

It has been observed though the Catholic Church had entered into North

East earlier than the Protestant denominations, the latter made a more pervasive entry into the region. This appears mainly due to the fact that Protestant denominations function more democratically and allow a free hand to the local people to manage their own churches. The Catholic churches in contrast are mainly dependent on the Parish priests and the Cathecist. Only very recently they have decided to introduce the Parish Calichist—represented by the local people to run the churches. The outcome of the same is, however, yet to be felt.

Christianity and the Nation-State Formation

The very desire of the Mizos to uphold their traditional democratic political system may be considered to be one of the most important factors for rapid proselytization into Christianity. When the traditional system was in jeopardy by the intrusion of the political system of a nation-state with a coercive machinery to back it up, and the fear of their cultures being swamped by the predominant Hindu and Muslim cultures of their neighbourhood, along with their resources being usurped by the state and private interests, intuitively as a reflex the Mizos sought for a religion which provided a better politico-economic leverage. Such interests were thus over-riding factor for rapid accept of Christianity rather than to exotic cultural elements borrowed western technology, material incentives or spiritualism. The observation made here is vindicated by what B. Mishra states, "In retrospect, it would appear that the real growth of Christianity in North-East India to a large extent is due to the converts finding Missionaries instead of Missionaries soliciting them". The church has thus played an intermediary role in the transition from the amorphous tribal political system to the formation of a modem national-state and not so much as an agent of social change. The church has on the one hand prevented the local tribes from disintegrating and helped in maintaining the ethnic identities, on the other it has also assisted in the penetration of a state machinery albeit with significant reforms.

To summarise, the impact of Christianity on different facets of tribal life has been enormous. But, on the whole, it appears that the trends of change depend on a mix of both exogenous and endogenous factors. The changes based on diffusion theory which are usually assumed do not seem to explain all the aspects of change which have been noticed among the Mizos.

Theoretically, the entire process of Christianisation and social change may be fundamentally examined through the Marxian and Weberian axioms. The study presented here basically indicates that, anxiety to safeguard the material resources by the Mizos by strongly asserting their right to self-determination and sustaining the democratic principles along with identity management processes have been the main features of Christianity. It is also apparent that Christianity, rather than being an exclusive agent of social change, has itself been subjected to modifications and has also acted as a catalyst to reinforce the tribal *status quo* in the regional context. Thus, no current theory of religion in vogue seems to be applicable to explain the factors of conversion and impact of Christianity in Mizoram. However, on the whole historicity, of the political and economic forces seem to have played the crucial role.

NOTES

Dena Lal, 1988: *Christian Missions and Colonialism*, Vandrame Institute, Shillong, 1988.

Hluna, J.V.: *Church and Political Upheaval in Mizoram*, Mizo History Association, Aizawl.

International Encyclopaedia of Social Science, Volume 13 and 16.

Manshardt, C.: *Christianity in a Changing India*, Y.M.C.A. Publishing House, Calcutta.

Roy Burman, J.J., 1988: "Christianity and Development among the Hills Tribes of NorthEast India" In *Journal of Indian Anthropological Society*.

23

Judaism in Manipur and Mizoram By-Product of Christian Mission

Myer Samra

Christian missionaries began their operations in the territory of present-day Mizoram and the tribal areas of Manipur in 1894, just three years after the Chin-Lushai Expedition and the Anglo-Manipur War, through which the British gained effective control of these territories. While the number of missionaries stationed in this region was always small, they were amazingly successful in their work. By 1951, there were 177,575 Christians in Mizoram as recorded in the Census of India, and 98,394 in Manipur. (Quarishi 1987:22)

Christianity has continued to make gains since Indian independence, even after foreign missionaries were excluded. Thus by 1981, there were 400,000 Christians in Mizoram, accounting for 83 per cent of the population, and 420,000 in Manipur, or 30 per cent of the population of that State. These converts come predominantly from the tribal communities.[1] Tribals make up 95 per cent of the population of Mizoram; in Manipur the Kuki, Naga and other tribal groups constitute 32 per cent of the population (Thanzauva, 1989: 2), so we see that in a period of under one hundred years, the tribal populations of these two States have overwhelmingly adopted Christianity.

Generally, the missionaries are recalled with affection. Their readiness to operate in difficult conditions and their dedication to their calling are beyond question. Nor is there any doubting the value of the work they performed, bringing with them elementary education, literacy and western medicine. However, as Khuanga (1989: 97) records, in the process of Christianisation and "in the name of development and civilisation much of the valuable tribal traditions have been destroyed".

As westerners who shared with the colonial administration notions of their cultural superiority, the missionaries and the native assistants they recruited played a major role in the undermining tribal traditions, some of which could have been retained without compromising essential Christian values. Protestant missionaries condemned the brewing and consumption of *zu* (rich beer); animal sacrifices; tribal dances and music. The *zawlbuk*, the seperate quarters where bachelors lived together for village defence and learnt traditional social values, was opposed as a breeding-ground for immorality. Christian sexual mores were enforced, and tribal dress was discouraged. Conflict arose between the Christian converts and those who sought to live by the old ways, while village headmen and chiefs lost their authority to the missionaries.

Quarishi (1987: 38) observes that "the repudiation of tribal myths and beliefs without their replacement by new ones", left "the tribal mind in a total vacuum". This disorientation is starkly illustrated by von Furer-Haimendorf, recalling the concern of an elderly Naga villager, that the Christians "say all of us who worship our gods will go to hell. I had a wife who was so good. She died sometime ago. Has she been put to fire?" [quoted in Quarishi (1987:39)].

Lal Dena (1988:110) records that the first native Christians became a new elite who "began to look with disgust at their traditional values through the glasses of their new masters. They acted and even preached that their ancestors were 'savages', 'head-hunters' so as to make their fellow tribesmen ashamed of their past". Despising their traditional ethos, they imitated the culture of the Europeans.

The spread of Christianity has spawned the development of new religious cults which Goswami (1980) has designated "by-products of Christianity". Many of these display a sentimental attachment to the community's pre-Christian traditions.[2] Groups which identify the ancestors of the Chin, Kuki and Mizo tribes (hereafter referred to collectively as Chikim[3]) with the lost tribes of Israel fall within this category. While they retain the biblical world view learned through the missionaries, these groups manage to restore some dignity to their ancestors. Rather than viewing their forebears as "head-hunting savages", such groups find that their ancestors displayed many admirable qualities and values similar to those taught by the missionaries.[4]

When the idea of their Israelite origins first arose among the Chikim is not clear, though it is apparent that some tribals found parallels with their traditional practices when they first heard about the Israelites from the missionaries. At times, the missionaries themselves may have suggested these similarities.[5] A significant link in this development was the custom of animal sacrifice, evoking the sacrifices prescribed in the *Bible*.

Thus, Zaithanchhungi, a popular writer from Mizoram, recalls an occasion when a Mizo Salvation Army Brigadier remarked to her that "the way of worshipping God by our Ancestors (was) the same (as) the Jews".[6] Questioning this statement, she learns that Rev. Thangkunga used to tell of an encounter between one of the early missionaries and a *Bawlpu*, a traditional Mizo, sacrificial priest. Observed the missionary:

> You look like the descendants of the Jews. But your faces are not like the Jews, you look a bit different. But you have the same way of doing things. The Jews, Israel, are chosen by God. God has given them His words, the *Ten Commandments*. Every nation can join them as we white people do. You are nearer to them than we white people (are).

Remarking on the animal sacrifice which the *Bawlpu* was performing, a ritual which involved pouring out the blood of the sacrificial animal, the missionary opined:

> Your way of living, custom, culture are like it is said in the *Bible*. In the *Bible* it's written—do this, do not do it. These (commandments) are already taught by your ancestors. There are no other people like you (anywhere in the world). But you are different from Israel because you don't know your God. Now you need not worship with the help of the blood of the animal. Jesus Christ died in Calvary for you.[7]

While this account suggests that some level of identification with the Israelites of the *Bible* may have been encouraged by the missionaries from the time of first contact, there has gradually been a shift in perception; from "looking like the descendants of the Jews" in the eyes of some missionaries, an appreciable number of Chikim have now come to assert that they indeed are descendants of Israelites. An intermediate position is traceable in a recollection that from around 1925, a Mizo named Chaltuahkhuma, from reading the Holy *Bible*, noted many, parallels with Mizo traditions are suggested that "the Mizos might be the lost tribe of Israel".[8]

The popularity of revivalistic Christianity in the region has helped to spread the notion of Israelite origins. The Christianity that the missionaries initially presented to the Chikim was a puritanical Calvinistic

Protestantism, marked by orderliness and sobriety. Subsequently, Chikim were introduced by Welsh evangelists to the more spirited revivalist tradition, with its emphasis upon the Holy Spirit, prophecy, and speaking in tongues. This version of Christianity was eagerly taken up by many of the naturally ebullient Chikim who on becoming Christians had previously been obliged to repress their high spirits.

Reivalism or Pentecostalism, a legitimate Christian tradition which was attractive to the Chikim, led to a dramatic increase in conversions, beyond the wildest imagination of the missionaries (Dena, 1988:102). Yet despite its success in spreading Christianity, Revivalism also had undesired consequences, for the missionaries and for the colonial administration.[9] Consequently in 1935, the Welsh Presbyterian Church in Mizoram forbade all revivalist manifestations, including "listening to voices, prophecy (and) speaking unknown tongues" (Goswami 1908: 43).

This ban, however, was impossible to enforce. Having unleashed the power of Christian spiritualist practices to the Chikim, the missionaries simply could not coax the genie back into the bottle. Revivalism has remained a potent force in religious practice. It has led to the composition of many new Christian songs and the development of a synthetic religious musical tradition, combining western and tribal elements. It has, furthermore, been responsible for increased Christian enthusiasm, and more generous offerings to the Church (Lalbiaktluanga, 1989:64).

The impact of Revival, however, has been still more dramatic. By giving legitimacy to the concept of possession by the Holy Spirit, it permitted new interpretations of the *Bible* and supernatural truths—in a manner apparently revealed by the Holy Spirit, even where these interpretations contradict the orthodox teaching of the missionaries. As McCall (1949:223) comments:

> This revivalist movement was fairly widespread, and the Missions were trying faithfully to keep it within the bounds of decency. But what they never bargained for was that, not having outlawed at the outset an unindigenous and clearly unhealthy manifestation of wild Lushai within a Christian framework, the day would surely come when their own Lushai Church leaders and colleagues would deny to their European preceptors their right to give a final ruling on what the *Bible* did or did not sanction.[10]

In the light of this background, we note Lalbiaktluanga (1989:66) records that a revivalist named Saichhunga from the village Hlimen had made the claim that the Mizos were "the lost tribals of Israel. In 1951, the statement of Saichhunga was confirmed as true by Chala of Buallawn village". This history is substantiated by those who have accepted the claims. In the words of one disciple:

> In the year 1936, the word of the spirit of our Lord came to Pu Kapa and Pu Saichhuma, telling them that we are Israel. Also in 1946, the same message was received by Pu Chala of Buallawn village. Henceforth from every part and every corner of Mizoram we cried longing for our homeland, Israel . . . . and search(ed) every possible way for contacting . . . . Israel.[11]

From this account it is clear that the connection with the Israelites had not been realised until "the word of the Lord came to our prophets since 1936", even though this revelation explains a history that would stretch back over two and a half thousand years.[12]

Chaltuakhuma's views did not lead him to think about Judaism or to conclude that it was appropriate to attempt to follow the Jewish religion. As with the parallels drawn by the missionaries, Chaltuakhuma's musings lead to a strengthening of Christianity, by suggesting a connection with the people from which Jesus, the Christian Messiah had sprung. However, when we reach the visions of Pu Chala (also referred to as Mela Chala), we find new implications in the connection. Pu Chala's followers believed that the Chikim had an obligation to return to their ancient homeland, the land of Israel, and accordingly from this time groups have sought permission to settle in Israel, permission not granted by the Israeli authorities, who have remained unconvinced by the Chikim's claims.[13]

Even the desire to "return" to Israel has its foundation in Christian teaching, notably the eschatological vision of the *New Testament* book of Revelations, with the war of Armageddon at the end of days. Only if they settle in Israel, the faithful believe, will they escape the general destruction. Early during the period of insurrection which has come to be known as the Mizo Unrest (1966-1986), as Goswami (1979: 193) has noted, such millenarian ideas gained many adherents and the Mizo Israel sect initially supported the rebels who they thought, "were fighting for the religious cause", although the followers of the sect were subsequently disillusioned (Goswami, 1980:46)

After the conclusion of the Mizo Unrest and the admission of Mizoram as a separate State in the Union of India, belief in the Israelite origin of the Chikim has continued to find favour, and new sects with this belief have sprung up. While the early "Mizo Israelites", products of a

Revivalist Christianity, were pre-occupied with messianic concerns which led them to seek emigration to Israel—as the one place on earth which would survive the impending cataclysm—Chikim groups which nowadays profess their Israelite roots have added to the range of doctrines to which they subscribe.

These groups share many views in common, although at the same time they diverge from one another on particular points which come to be seen as crucial markers of group identity. Such divergences are expected given that the Chikim Israelites have relied on direct revelation to guide their progress. Where different prophets have provided inspiration, their particular visions have shaped the beliefs and practices of their followers, sometimes in quite unusual ways. *As Time* magazine (Johnson 1987) reported when Mizoram achieved statehood:

> Jewish sects are believed to be offshoots of Christian fundamentalist groups but new sects continue to spring up in the hills of Mizoram. One is called Enoka Thlah (descendants of Enoch), whose members claim that God has been speaking to them through a teenage boy since 1985 when the youth relayed God's message that Mizos were really a lost tribe of Israel. More recently the messages have ordered them to celebrate the Sabbath on Saturday and to stop eating pork. A couple of weeks ago, the youth told the cult members to obtain and sacrifice a white horse and a black horse. The members obeyed. Growing crowds of new believers are overflowing the group's little prayer hall.

Similarities, on the other hand, stem from the fact that revivalist groups share a common tradition of applying the *Bible* to make sense of their situation, increased familiarity with the beliefs and practices of Jews in the rest of the world, and the imitation by one group of practices adopted by another.

One sees such an evolution in the identification of the putative Israelite tribal origin of the Chikim. When Mela Chala declared that the Chikim were Israelites, he did not indicate to which of the Ten Lost Tribes of Israel they belonged. By 1972, however, one group was already asserting "The Tribal Jews of Manipur are originally descended from one of the ten lost tribes of Israel whose name was called Manasseh, son of Joseph and father of Machir" (Benjamin and Stephen 1972:2). Other groups have since adopted the same view.[14]

Such an identification arose by deduction rather than prophecy. As Zaithanchhungi (1990:20) explains, "In many of the chants used in various sacrifice(s) and in other sacred matter(s) the name of Manasia or Manase in used". This name has come to be equated with that of Manasseh in the *Bible*. Let us select one example from Zaithanchhungi showing how these names were used:

> At Kawngpui Sial (a pre-Christian sacrifice for success in hunting), the priest followed by his party chants, "Those above and those below, go away, flee, we the children of Manasia are coming" (1990:30).[15]

Having divined a connection with one of the Israelite tribes, some groups have adopted a new name, Bene Menasheh, the "Children of Manasseh" in Hebrew. As Well (1991b:18) observes, "The significance of the new identity is far-reaching for it. dovetails elements in traditional religion (and not in Christianity) with a significant force in the Jewish religion", namely the fate of the Lost Tribes and the hope that some day they would once again be reunited with the Jewish people.

Today, many groups accept the Chikim/Manasseh identity and are attempting to follow "Judaism" in some form (Samra, 1991). This may be conventional Orthodox Judaism, or so-called "Messianic Judaism", a cult which couples the observance of precepts from the *Old Testament* such as circumcision, observance of Saturday as the Sabbath, dietary restrictions and the Jewish festivals, with the Christians's faith in Jesus (or Yahshua as these groups prefer to call him) as the Messiah.

There is an ironical aspect in these developments. Of all the elements of their traditional culture, animal sacrifice was the one practice which initially led to the identification of the Chikim with the Israelites in the *Bible*. We have observed that sacrifices have been revived, where the prophet so directs, among the group calling itself *Enoka Thlah*. However, in modern Judaism animal sacrifices are no longer performed, so that those who try to follow Judaism now find they must discard the very ritual which had sparked their affiliation to the Jews in the first instance!

In this chapter we have seen how Judaism has arisen in Manipur and Mizoram, essentially as an unintended "by-product" of Christian missionary endeavours. While conventional Christianity taught the Chikim that they were the heirs of "head-hunters" and "savages", that assessment of their past is now being revised, even by the followers of conventional Christianity.

For those who have been influenced by Revivalism, the revision has been easier to achieve. Direct revelation could be utilised to disclose that they were in fact the descendants of Israelites, while the sacrifices executed by their forebears could indicate adherence to an ancient form of Judaism. Connection with the Israelites, the "heroes" of the *Bible* and the people to whom Jesus himself belonged, provides psychological comfort, a basis for finding a new sense of dignity in one's past, and the opportunity to work for a better future. The potency of these concepts is underscored by the number of groups which have adopted them.

Goswami (1980:45) predicted that the "by-products" of Christianisation would be ephemeral. Certainly, the speed with which new groups have come and gone bears out this forecast. I look forward to following these groups into the future to see whether these ideas ultimately recede into oblivion, or whether they will continue to display a positive, creative potential.

REFERENCES

1. Throughout India, Christian missionaries have had greater success among depressed castes and tribal communities than among Muslims and caste Hindus, for "Once the fourteenth century missionary realised that the high castes could not be converted easily, he diverted his attention to the marginalised groups who were more open to receive his message" (Fernandes, 1981:22). In Manipur, the missionaries were permitted to evangelise the tribal communities, but not the dominant, Hinduised Meiteis (Dena, 1988:34).
2. Banks (1961) discusses the *Pau Cin Hau*, a movement of religious innovation from the Northern Chin (Tiddim) area around the turn of the century, displaying elements of syncretism between traditional religion and Christianity.
3. In using the term *Chikim* to designate the constellation of tribes variously referred to as Chins, Kukis and Mizos, I am following the practice of S. Kipgen (1990) and a number of other writers from Manipur. Thangjom (1990:19) indicates that he coined the term in 1971.
4. Such a reassessment of their pre-Christian traditions is also being made by conventional Christian theologians. See Lianzauala's (1989) theological interpretation of the traditional ethic of *Tlawmgaihna* (working for the good of the community rather than for one's self-interest), and Thanzauva's (1989) characterisation of the *zawlbuk.*
5. Missionaries elsewhere have directly identified tribal communities with the ancient Israelites. Dr. Francis Mason, an American Baptist working among the Karen in Burma from 1814, maintained that this tribe was *"of* the seed of Israel"; that their indigenous form of worship and belief in "an eternal god called *Y-wa"* were similar to those of the ancient Israelites (Weil, 1991a: 85). In the 1920s the Scottish missionary, Thomas Torrance

gave a similar assessment of the Chiang-Min in Szechuan, China (Weil, 1991a: 94).

6. Letter to Rabbi Eliahu Avichail dated 6 December, 1983.
7. Zaithanchhungi is attracted to the idea that there is a great deal in common between the ancestors of the Israelites and the Mizos. In 1990 she published a book highlighting the similarities and drawing the inference that the Mizos "may claim to be the lost tribe of Israel" (1990: vii).
8. Letter from Zaithanchhungi to Rabbi Avichail dated 24 August, 1984.
9. See McCall (1949: 219 to 225) for an account *of* the "Kelkang incident" and other cases indicating the damage reeked by Revivalism in Mizoram.
10. The term "Mizo" is now used where "Lushai" would appear in colonial accounts. Goswami (1979: 20 to 24) elucidates the political significance of this change in designation. The new name was chosen by the Mizos themselves, not imposed upon them.
11. Letter dated 3 February, 1984, from Levy Benjamin, General Secretary of MPSNEIM (Manasseh People Shinlung-Israel North East India, Mizoram) to the Chief Rabbinet (read Rabbinical) Council, Israel.
    Whereas Lalbiaktluanga speaks of one "Saichhunga", Benjamin calls this man "Saichhuma". Laibiaktluanga tells us that Chala of Buallawn "confirmed" Saichhunga's statement in 1951; Benjamin offers 1946 as the appropriate year.
12. The biblical northern Kingdom *of* Israel was conquered by Assyrians in 721 BCE. Its inhabitants were taken into exile and vanished from history. The fate of these people, the Lost Tribes of Israel, has inspired many legends and much wild conjecture.
13. Under Israel's Law of Return, every Jew, and anyone who can show one or more Jewish grandparents, is entitled to claim Israeli citizenship. Hussain (1991) records that "18 Mizo boys and girls and a few Manipuris have migrated to Israel". One should be clear, however, that this has occurred after their formal conversion to Judaism, not through acceptance of their Israelite claims.
14. In a letter of *News from Israel,* a magazine published by the Israeli Consulate in Bombay, Dr. H. Thangruma (29 July, 1980) seeks guidance on the tribal origin of his people. The majority of the Mizos, himself included, "feel ourselves to be the genuine descendants of Manasseh". However, a minority claim "We, the Mizos are the descendants of Ephraim". At the time of his writing, Dr. Thangruma relates, this "argument on genealogies" had been raging for two years.
15. Some writers, particularly those from Manipur, use the word *Manmasi* in place of *Manasia/Manase.* Thus Sawngtinlam (n.d.) offers a number of instances when this word was used, one of them being when about to dig a grave. A libation is poured into the ground and the priest chants "Make way, O stones and trees, for the children and *Manmasi* has gone to claim

their own possession" (n.d.:28). The possibility that *Manmasi* also depicts a version of *Manasseh* seems somewhat more remote

NOTES

A.G. McCall,1949 (reprinted 1977). *Lushai Chrysalis*. Calcutta: Firma KLM, on behalf of Tribal Research Institute, Govt. of Mizoram, Aizawl.

B.B. Goswami, 1979. *The Mizo Unrest— A Study of Politicisation of Culture*. Jaipur: Aalekh Publishers.

—— 1980. By-Product of Christianity on the Hill Tribesmen of North-East India. *Review of Ethnology*. Vol 7/1-9: 42-46.

E.P. Banks, 1961. Pau Cin hau: A Case of Religious Innovation among the Northern Chin. [Paper read at American Anthropological Association annual meeting in Philadelphia. Mimeographed copy held at Fisher Library, University of Sydney].

F.A. Quarishi, 1987. Christianity in the North Eastern Hills of South Asia: *Social Impact and Political Implications*. Dhaka, Bangladesh: University Press.

H. Thangjom, 1990. Towards Constructive Destruction. In *Kut Festival Souvenir*. L. Haokip (ed). Imphal, Manipur: State Level Kut Committee, pp. 19-21.

K. Thanzauva, 1989. Theology *of* Zawlbuk. In *Towards A Tribal Theology: The Mizo Perspective*. K. Thanzauva (ed.). Mizoram: Mizo Theological Conference, with the help of Eastem Theological College, Jorhat, Assam. pp. 99-108.

L. Dena, 1988. Christian Missions and Colonialism: A study of missionary movement in Northeast India with particular reference to Manipur and Lushai Hills 1894-1947. Shillong: Vendrame Institute.

M. Johnson, 1987. Statehood for a Strange Land (Mizoram's new leader pledges to preserve its uniqueness). Reported by Ross H. Munro/Aizawl. *Time*. 2 March 1987, p. 21.

M. Samra, 1991. The Tribe of Manasseh: 'Judaism' in the Hills of Manipur and Mizoram. *Man in India*, 71 (1): 183-202.

P.L. Lianzuala, 1989. Toward a Theoloy of Mizo *Tlawmngaihna*. In *Towards A Tribal Theology: The Mizo Perspective*. K. Thanzauva (ed.). Mizoram: Mizo Theological Conference, with the help of Eastern Theological College, Jorhat, Assam pp. 54-62.

Rev. Khuanga, 1989. The Role of Christianity in the Socio-Economic Praxis of Mizoram. In *Towards a Tribal Theology: The Mizo Perspective*. K. Thanzauva (ed.). Mizoram: Mizo Theological Conference, with the help of Eastern Theological College, Jorhat, Assam. pp. 90-98.

Rev. Lalbiaktluanga,1989. Theological Trends in Mizoram. In *Towards a Tribal Theology: The Mizo Perspective*. K. Thanzauva (ed.). Mizoram: Mizo Theological Conference, with the help of Eastern Theological College, Jorhat, Assam. pp. 63-71.

S. Kipgen, 1990. Secretarial view of Kut. In Kut Festival Souvenir, L. Haokip (ed). Imphal, Manipur: State Level Kut Committee. pp. 1-3.

S. Weil, 1991 a. *Beyond the Sambatyon: The Myth of The Ten Lost Tribes*. Tel Aviv: Beth hatefutsoth, Museum of the, Jewish Diaspora.

—— 1991b. Conversion among the "Children of Menasseh". [Unpublished paper, School of Education, the Hebrew University].

Sawngtinlam. (n.d.). *The Tukbemsom Tribe, Kangkopki, Manipur*: H. Seilal Press.

V.L. Benjamin, and Y. Stephen. 1972. *Mongoloid Israels of Manipur State*. Bualzang: Manipur Jewish Organisation.

W. Fernandes, 1981. *Caste and Conversion Movements in India*. New Delhi: Indian Social Institute.

W. Hussain, 1991. Migrating to the promised land. *The Telegraph*, Calcutta. Sunday, 24 November, 1991, p. 11.

Zaithanchhungi, 1990. *Israel-Mizo Identity. Aizawl*, Mizoram: St. Joseph's Press. Aizawl.

POLITICAL HISTORY

24

Traditional Political Institution of Chieftainship in Mizoram

Powers, Functions, Position and Privileges

R.N. Prasad

The chieftainship originated in the physical and intellectual power of any person who used to command a large number of people and to repel any attack by other chiefs and enemies. In other words, one, who had the ability to organise a force, became a chief. Such a person became the guardian and defender of his people. It, thus, appears from the above interpretations that the institution of chieftainship emerged out of the collective needs of group life which characterise tribal living. But there is no definite record when and how in the past, this institution took concrete shape. But it can be reasonably asserted that this happened at quite an early stage of evolution in their group life.[1] In this regard, it is further mentioned that the institution of chieftainship may be traced to biological origin. Zahmuaka being brave and strong was the first chief during migration period, who had six sturdy sons and all of them became chiefs. Thangura was one of the six. Thangura had two sons. Thangmanga was one of them. Thangmanga had one son named Sailova. Sailova was the ancestor of the Sailo chiefs. Thus the Sailos of today trace their descent from Sailova. In the long run the Sailos became the most powerful chiefs and they ruled practically over the then Lushai Hills (Now Mizoram) except in Pawi-Lakher region at the time of the advent of the British. Pawis and Lakhers had their own chiefs who ruled the south-eastern part of the Lushai Hills. They did not follow the Sailo chiefs.[2] There were Sailo and non-Sailo chiefs. The non-Sailo chiefs were known as *Hnamchawm* (Commoners) The Sailo chiefs formed upper clan among the Mizos.

Though the Sailo chiefs commanded more respect than others, all the chiefs enjoyed the same powers, functions and privileges. The British rulers did not make any distinction between them. They recognised them as independent chiefs but subject to their control. Really, when the British rulers encountered them, they were, rather, surprised to see a large number of indigenous institutions for the administration of local or village affairs running independently of one another by the autocratic chief of immense local standing. The institution of chieftainship was, thus, autocratic. There was a complete concentration of powers in the hands of village chiefs and their council of elders, who used to control and regulate all aspects of the village life in accordance with the customs. Shakespear described the chiefs as despotic heads of small independent states. Similarly Captain T.N. Lewin, who was the first British to know the Lushais/Mizos intimately described the village system among the Lushais as a number of petty states, each under a dictator or president.[3] Thus the Mizo chiefs in the beginning opposed the British rule and so fought the British rulers with all might at their command. The British rulers, somehow, annexed the then Lushai Hills (Mizoram) in 1890 and thereby normalised their strained relations with the main opponent-chiefs after appeasing them with the gifts of their wise statemanship. They divided the territory into two administrative wings, viz., the North Lushai Hills District, a part of Assam and the South Lushai Hills District, a part of Bengal. But they also decided in 1898 to merge the two districts into a single district—the Lushai Hills District, a part of Assam under a Superintendent. The same year marked the beginning of settled administration in the district. The British made the chieftainship hereditary. Because it guaranteed political stability and loyalty of the chiefs to the government. In 1898, a system of Land Settlement was introduced. Accordingly, each chief was given a certain area of land to administer. The British superintendent, thus, used the chiefs in such way that they became the main plank of the alien rule over their own people. They laid the foundation on which the edifice of the British rule was erected. The chiefs were made representatives of the British Government in their own land. In fact, the British superintendent and the chiefs ruled the people autocratically.

Each chief had territorial jurisdiction of his own, consisting of one or more villages. In fact, the chief owned all that was in the villages. The chief, before the annexation of the Lushai Hills exercised life and death powers, though these powers and functions were not precise and definite. He was, at the same time, the supreme administrator, the chief justice, the protector and guardian of his villagers. In running village administration, he was assisted/advised by a council of village elders called *Upas* in Mizo language. The elders were generally men of the chief's choice, nominated or selected without considering the opinion of the villagers. Most of them were either opportunists from among the well-to-do sections of the society or royal clan. But they held office during his pleasure. The chief and his council of elders discussed all matters of the village, and settled all disputes in the village. They received fees called *salam* from the villager who lost the case. Those fees were their only remuneration. Besides they had the privilege to select suitable land for cultivation, construction of house and not to pay taxes *(Fathang)*. The chief, after the annexation, also executed the orders and directions of the British superintendent heading the district. Briefly the chief was responsible for the control of the village, and had wide powers in the village administration.

Besides the *Upas*, the chief also appointed some village officials to assist him as well as to carry out the village administration smoothly and efficiently for the welfare of the villagers. They were such as *Ramhuals* (expert *Jhum* cultivation), *Tlangau* (village courier/crier), *Thirdeng* (blacksmith), *Puithiam* (priest), and *Khawchhiar* (village writer). The *Ramhuals* were the advisers on *jhum*. The *Tlangaus* were to proclaim chiefs orders. The *Thirdeng* was the village blacksmith. His main task was to make or repair tools and implements for agriculture, house construction and other work connected with daily life of the villagers. The *Puithiam* was the village priest who performed all kinds of ceremonies. But with the introduction of Christianity, the position of the village priest has substantially deteriorated. The *Khawchhiar* was the villager writer who has an important link between the chief and the Superintendent, and between the chief on the one hand and the villagers on the other hand. He used to maintain vital statistics, registers, and record of all the tried cases by the chief, births, deaths, village house list, roster of people in the village to be called for cooli's work and a list of all guns in the village. However, for their services, the village officials used to receive remuneration—mostly in kind directly from the villagers. For all these works, the village officials were exempted from cooli work, *fathang* and house tax.[4] The village officials had different duties entrusted to them by the chief, which they were to carry out individually for the welfare of the rural masses. Thus, the chief with the help of the council of elders and the village officials used to run the village administration. The British rulers also thought it fit and experienced to continue the chieftainship for village administration. Since non-interference in the internal administration of the chief was the general policy of the British superintendent, he often, upheld the decisions and acts of the chief. Although, the chief was the real repository of power, yet he seldom ignored the advice of his elders and well-being of the villagers. He hardly interfered with the findings of the elders in the trial of disputes and cases. He, thus, tried to give it the semblance of people's government in the governance of his village through the council of elders.[5] Theoretically, the chief was all powerful and despotic ruler. But his powers were actually circumscribed by the fact that his villagers could easily emigrate to another village in the jurisdiction of some other chief. So every chief had to use tact as well as force. A strong chief, who ruled his people according to custom, could do anything he liked without losing his villagers, but a weak chief, who behaved tyrannically, soon found himself without any villagers. But the social mores were so shaped through the process of evolution that he could seldom afford to exercise unrestricted powers over his people.

The *Pawis* and *Lakhers* in the South Lushai Hills (Mizoram) had their own chiefs. The chieftainship among the Pawis was the same as among the Mizos. The Lakher chieftainship was, however, a little different. Shakespear found the Lakhers in common with the Chins, as less democratic than the Lushais. The power of the chiefs was greater, and the chiefs' relatives and other wealthy people formed a kind of peerage.[6] The Lakhers had no single royal clan like the Sailo clan among the Lushais. Each Lakher tribe had its own royal clan. The chief had full power over the villagers. He could impose fines and, in the extreme case, turn a villager out of the village. The Lakher chieftainship was hereditary, the eldest son succeeding the father.[7]

Succession

The principle of primogeniture was not followed in the beginning. Later it was recognised but made applicable to the chiefs and not to headmen. The eldest son succeeded his father. Before the Lushai Hills was annexed, the chief had the right to appoint all his trusted sons as chiefs by dividing his territory among them. The youngest son inherited his father's lands and properties. This custom was changed by the British ruler. The principle of primogeniture was made in vogue/recognised. Thus the eldest son of ruling chief, unless he was a minor or physically or mentally unfit, inherited the lands of his father. If the eldest son was a minor, the Superintendent could appoint his mother and the customary council as the guardians provided the widow observed such customary rules, which she must observe by the Lushai customs or the Superintendent might appoint for life the nearest male heir who should ordinarily be the eldest surviving brother of the deceased chief or the eldest legitimate son of such brother.

The nearest male heir who became the chief on account of the youth of the legitimate heir held the chieftainship for life after his death, it returned to the original line. From the above, it is obvious that when a minor became a major, he was not entitled to chieftainship. The motive behind this customary rule is not clear. Normally the chieftainship should be held until the minor became a major. This rule was not observed in the Mizo Hills (Mizoram).

If the eldest legitimate son of the deceased chief suffered from permanent mental or physical disability or imbecile as to make him incapable of holding chieftainship, the superintendent did not allow him to become the chief. It was passed on to the nearest male heir. But it should return to the original line after the death of the existing chief provided there was a male heir in the line, capable of discharging his duties.

If the chief died without legitimate sons, the illegitimate sons if any were permitted to succeed. This was decided on the merits of the case by the Superintendent. The claims of the illegitimate sons must be settled before the claims of others. If the eldest son settled in an independent village and died without a son, the property and the chieftainship of the village reverted to his father.

A chief could also approach the Superintendent to disinherit his son, who was normally entitled to chieftainship. In that case the Superintendent must call for a Panchayat, consisting of fellow chiefs of the same clan—five in number, of whom two were the nominees of the chief, two of the aggrieved son and the fifth the nominee of the Superintendent. The Panchayat submitted its report to the Superintendent. The Superintendent made his recommendation on the report and sent to the Commissioner of the Division, whose decision was final. From this, it is clear that the chief had no right to disinherit his legitimate son. The son had a voice in the settlement of the dispute between himself and his father as regards inheritance. Thus the other sons became commoners due to the changed method of succession. Although, chieftainship was hereditary, the Government of Assam acting through the Deputy Commissioner had power to dismiss a chief and appoint a subsitute. This power was, however, rarely exercised.[8] Further the Mizo Society does not accept succession by daughters, because the succession to the chieftainship is from the male side.

Powers and Functions

As regards the executive and jucidial powers, privileges and status of the Mizo chief, he had wide powers and considerable privilege in holding and administering the Lushai Hills District (Now Mizoram). He was practically independent and real centre of authority in the village administration. He exercised autocratic powers and extracted more than what was due from the villagers. Some of the chiefs treated the villagers as their servants and reduced some to absolute slavery. The British Superintendent did not interfere in the internal administration of the chief except in the cases of murder and very serious matters. Heinous offences like murder and kidnapping had to be reported to the Superintendent. He often upheld the authority of the chief in his own village and over his own people. The political system was such that none could dare speak against his activities or criticise any act of his. Though in theory, his role was autocratic, in fact, he was guided entirely by customs as regards the exercise of his powers. His rule could not be malevolent as the villagers could always migrate from one village to another. Briefly the power exercised by the chief dependent on his personality and calibre, a strong chief controlling practically everything while a weak chief was guided almost entirely by his council of elders. All the time, he could not afford to be autocratic or indifferent to the opinions of the council of elders and the general well-being of the villagers.

Executive Powers

Apart from the power of appointing a number of village officials such as council of elders, village crier; blacksmith, village priest, village writer and *Ramhuals* (experts of *jhum* cultivation), the chief had tremendous executive powers in the village administration. He owned all lands in his village, but distributed the land among his people for cultivation. Definite boundaries were laid down for the different chiefs. No private ownership of land was recognised by the Mizo Society. The chief and his council of elders discussed all matters connected with village, assisted and advised him in the discharge of his duties. He presided over the meeting of the council. He often got his decisions accepted by them because elders were men of his individual choice. The chief had also the right to dismiss the elders, but he could never show his whims and fancies in the exercise of his prerogative. The chief helped the villages in their difficulties and adversities, encouraged them in all ways possible and also rewarded them in their achievements. He was, in fact, the administrator, the protector and the guardian of his village. Hence, the villagers, in their turn, had to obey chief's orders and carry out duties assigned to them individually and collectively. They helped the chief in all possible ways. Before the annexation of the then Lushai Hills by the British, the chief had extensive powers of owning all lands in his village, ordering capital punishment, seizing store and property of the villagers—intending to migrate to some other village, taxing traders doing business within the area of the chief's jurisdiction, appointing his sons as chiefs in his own jurisdiction and attaching the property of the villagers. Perhaps, this was the most severe punishment which could be inflicted on the villagers by the chief and his elders. After the advent of the British, the chief used to resort to the same without any substantial ground and consequently the above mentioned traditional rights of the chiefs and the infliction of such punishment were abolished by the District Superintendent. Besides, lands were taken over by the government and redistributed among the chiefs. The chiefs gradually ceased to be the absolute owners of land and became only the settlement holders. However, the British government allowed the chieftainship to continue in order to maintain the supremacy of its rule in the district, though gradually there was an erosion in the powers and privileges of the chiefs.

The chief was responsible for supervising the work of his village writer and compiling all district stranding orders communicated to him by the Superintendent. He also maintained the records of births and deaths, movement of people in or out of the village and all changes in licensed guns. He was also responsible for maintaining inter-village paths and communications in his village, constructing and repairing/maintaining *zawlbuk,* (bachelor's dormitory) signing the register for the house tax assessment prepared by the circle interpreters and reporting to the superintendent or his Assistants all epidemics, heinous crimes, violent deaths and, serious accidents occurring within the jurisdiction. Besides, he was at liberty to stop the sales of good stuffs from his village owing to general shortage, reporting his decision to the district headquarters. He asked the villagers to do *Hnatlang* (voluntary work) for constructing and repairing teacher's house, clearing jungle in an around the village, clearing and fencing water supply point and constructing bridges over rivers crossing the village. He occasionally called for the meeting of the council of elders to formulate policies for village administration, to chalk out programmes/activities concerning the village, to foster *Tlawmngaihna,* to maintain all accounts of fines imposed and to keep records of proceedings through his village writer.[9] He protected the fugitives seeking refuse in his house. Thus the village administration was left to the chiefs, though the Superintendent laid down some duties of the chiefs in order to check arbitrary rule.

Judicial Powers

The chief administered justice according to the customary law of the Mizos. The chief and his council of elders constituted as the village court and decided all cases and disputes. The jurisdiction of the chief's court was his village. The chief's court was more or less a bench system, of what we have today and the courtroom was the chief's house where cases were tried. Thus, the chief was the only court of justice in the village. Originally he had the power of life and death. His decisions were final. There was no appeal against his decision. But successful litigant found a way of getting his case retried.[10]

In a dispute, unless both the parties compromised themselves, the one, who was found guilty, was punished by a fine. The punishment differed depending upon the severity of the offence. A fine was imposed, which varied from Re. 1 to Rs. 5 known as '*Salam*'. In theft case, restitution of the articles stolen was always demanded. If a case was a severe one, a fine of one mithun or Rs. 40 per cent could be imposed. If a man killed another of the same village and for fear of being killed in retaliation, came to the chief's house for refuge, the chief would protect him and after no one would dare to take revenge against the murderer. The judicial supremacy of the chiefs remained as such till the British subjugated them in 1890.[11] The British Government reduced the supremacy of the chiefs after annexing the Lushai Hills District but could not do away with the chiefship. The government recognised the chiefs and their courts. But the British brought about two changes in the chief's administration of justice by curtailing their judicial powers. Firstly, an appeal against the decisions of the chief could be taken to the Superintendent. But no appeal against the decisions of the chief in petty cases was to be admitted. In order to maintain the general principle of non-interference, the Super intendent seldom changed the decision of the chief. He always upheld the authority of the chief. Secondly, he had no power to sentence anyone for death. He could not try cases of murder, offences concerning government property, suicide, rape, other heinous crimes and disputes between people of different villages. Such cases/offences were tried by the Superintendent. If the person fined proved to be very difficult to be handled by the chief, his decisions and order were enforced by the Superintendent. The proceedings of all cases/disputes tried by the chief's court were recorded and maintained by the village writer. Thus the chief and his council of elders were the highest court of justice among the Mizos. Briefly the policy of non-interference by the British in the customs of the tribes, and also in the decisions of the chief really paid a rich dividend in the smooth administration of then Lushai Hills without much expenditure. But after the abolition of the chiefship, this judicial power has been invested with the democratically elected village council, which administer justice according to the customary law of the Mizos.

Privileges and Statue

The chief, as a token of respect for his high status, was entitled to certain privileges. He was entitled to free labour from the villagers for the construction and repair of the house. He received *fathang,* one to three baskets of paddy from every household per year in the village. Later the Superintendent fixed it at a uniform rate of six kerosene tins of paddy. He was also entitled to *sachhiah* (meat tax). Any villager, who killed or trapped a wild animal, had to give the chief its left foreleg. He had the right to get *khuaichhiah*—(bee tax) one, who collected wild honey from a jungle within his jurisdiction, had to give the chief a portion of it. He also got *chichhiah* (salt tax) one-tenth of the quantity collected from a villager who collected salt from well or spring within his village. He was entitled to a position of the fish caught by the villages. Besides, the *Ramhuals* used to offer greater *fathang* to the chief. The chief and his council of elders received Rs. 5 out of every fine imposed on the person. The chief also expected material benefits from the earnings of the villagers from horticulture and cultivation other than agriculture. He had the right to seize half of the paddy produced by the villagers who migrated to another village without his permission. He received free portage for visiting a neighbouring village.

The Lakher chief had the right to receive two days labour from each household per year for cultivating his lands. He was also entitled to a basket of cotton from each family every year. But all these privileges of the Mizo chiefs, the Pawi chiefs and the Lakher chiefs, were, however, abolished on I April, 1955 and 15 April, 1956 respectively. After the abolition of chiefships in the areas covered by the *Mizo* District Council and the Pawi Lakher Regional Council, the administration of the village affairs has been entrusted to the village councils.

It, thus, appears from the above that the chief and his counsellors formed a royal or upper class, who lived on the villagers. It was so despite the fact that the Mizo society was classless and not caste-ridden unlike the plains areas. Although the chief had inter-clan marriage and free inter-course with other clan unlike the plains zamindars/landlords, he hardly worked even for his own necessaries. The institution of the chieftainship may be, to an extent compared with the plains landlords, no doubt, but they differed in many respects. For instance, the plains landlords/ zamindars, before the abolition of zamindari system, used to collect revenue both in cash and kind from the peasants and thereby became wealthy or rich due to accumulation of wealth. They hardly bothered for the welfare of the villagers/cultivators. But the Mizo chiefs had no scope at all of accumulating wealth because the Mizo society was egalitarian. So the chiefs were not affluent. They received support from their subjects through their offerings in kind and labour. Even the village officials, who worked for him, were not paid directly by him but were to receive subsistence and remuneration from the villagers mostly their position as people's servants. The chief with his village officials had to perform a lot of welfare functions and also to help implementation of welfare functions and schemes at village level. He was also spokesman for his villagers on all issues as well as prominent social, and religious gatherings and festivals of the village. He acted as a link between the villagers and the British superintendent. In fact, the chiefs became the local representatives of the alien government after the people settled down at fixed places, giving up their migratory habit, So the British traditionally supported/safeguarded the chieftainship whereas the first political party Mizo Union urged the people not to obey the government and instigated the common people to stone the chiefs.[12] The party even directed the common masses not to pay their dues. This situation lent support to the common people in their struggle against the chiefs.

As regards the abolition of the chieftainship. some possible reasons may be offered.

It has been experienced from the vast powers and privileges of the chiefs that some of the chiefs had become real despots and acted in a very cruel manner towards the Mizo Commoners, which was unbearable. As the remains true, the chiefs were practically sovereigns. The British Superintendent never interfered with their administration. Rather he often upheld the authority/decisions of the chiefs. The Superintendent and the chiefs used to rule the people as virtual dictators. The people were fed up with this situation.

The chiefs exercised autocratic powers and extracted more than what was due from the villagers. They treated the villagers as their servants and reduced some of them to absolute slavery. Naturally the people resisted this position of the autocratic institution of chiefship. They also opposed to the British rule. The educated and politically conscious Mizo Youths never desired for the handing over of powers to the Chiefs by the British, after India attained independence.

This development of opposing to the chiefs and the British rule was exactly analogous to what happened in Africa. Education was the key to the world outside the village and chiefdom. It led to employment in the police, the courts, the teaching profession and the church. As these men came to know of democracy, they interpreted the maintenance of the chief's authority as a denial of human rights. The attitude of the European rulers was, on the contrary, to keep up the authority of the chiefs and move against the chiefs was regarded as an undesirable creation of trouble making politicians, "so opposition to rule by the chiefs comes to be linked with opposition to rule by Europeans."[13] Besides, many of the young Mizos had been to outside the territory as army personnel during the first and the second world wars who could not accept the archaic rule by the chiefs, as they saw continuing unchange in their home district.

However, the resentment of the common people against the autocratic chiefs, being one of the reasons, led the Mizo youths to organise themselves into the first political party, Mizo Union in 1946, The party had economic programme of fighting the vested interests of the chiefs. So it was determined to abolish this autocratic/exploitative institution of chiefship. The Mizo Hills District Council for the Mizo and the Regional Councils for Pawi, Lakher and Chakma tribes were set up in 1952 and 1953 respectively. The Mizo union fought the elections to the Assam Legislative Assembly on the Mizo Hills District Council issue: The party succeeded in both the elections. As a result, the party held the reigns of the Mizo District Council and so persuaded government of Assam to abolish the chieftainship. Accordingly, the Government enacted the Assam Lushai Hills District (Acquisition of Chiefs' Rights) Act 1954 and abolished the chieftainship in the area covered by the Mizo District Council. Similarly, the chiefship in the Pawi Lakher region was also abolished by the same act. The chiefs were paid compensation in cash.

As regards the justification for the abolition of the chieftainship, some scholarship/politicians/church leader of the region opined that there was no justification for abolishing the chieftainship. It could have been modernised by limiting its powers/rights/privileges. The abolition of chieftainship created new problems. It helped emergence of discontented community, the chiefs and their dependants. It also alienated the chiefs from the government and thereby created ill will towards the government. All the disgruntled elements joined the force to oppose the government. One of the responsible factors for the outbreak of the Mizo National Front insurgency was the abolition of chiefship. If the chieftainship had been there, the MNF would not have come into existence at all.[14] This may be true to an extent.

However, the author is of the view that the abolition of this autocratic institution of chieftainship by the Mizo Union was fully justified in keeping with the fulfilment of the democratic aspirations of the common Mizos. In view of this, it was not desirable at all, on the part of the democratically elected members of the Mizo District Council and the Pawi Lakher Regional Council to leave the village administration to the hereditary autocratic chiefs. Because to allow the village administration to be carried out by the hereditary chiefs was contrary to the democratic provision of the Sixth Schedule to the Constitution of India and economic programme of fighting the vested interests of the chiefs as alleged by the Mizo Union. So the abolition of chieftainship became an expedient and as a result, it was done away with. This step was appreciated by the Mizo Commoners. There was no hue and cry made by the common masses against it. The abolition of chieftainship has definitely provided opportunities to a larger number of Mizos to participate in decision making. Although a few disgruntled chiefs joined the Mizo National Front, it did not mean that the MNF insurgency broke out partly because of the abolition of chieftainship. There were other important reasons for the rise of the MNF rebellion.[15]

REFERENCES

1. R.N. Prasad, *Government and Politics in Mizoram,* New Delhi, Northern Book Centre, p. 49.
2. *Ibid*, pp. 49-50.
3. Animesh Ray, *Mizoram Dynamics of Change,* Calcutta, Pearl Publishers, p. 30.
4. R.N. Prasad, *op. cit.*, pp. 50-51.
5. R.N. Prasad, A Study of Village Administration in Mizoram (IN) *The Indian Journal of Public Administration,* Vol. XXIX, No. 4, October-December, 1983.
6. J. Shakespear, *The Lushai Kuki Clans,* London, Macmillan & Co. Ltd. 1912, p. 216.

7. N.E. Parry, *The Lakhers,* London, Macmillan & Co. Ltd., p. 248.
8. R.N. Prasad, *op. cit.*, pp. 52, 53, 54.
9. *Ibid.*, pp. 56, 57.
10. R.N. Prasad, Administration of Justice in Mizoram (IN) *The Indian Journal of Public Administration,* Vol. XXXVII, No. I, January-March, 1991, p. 112, Quarterly Journal of I.I.P.A., New Delhi.
11. *Ibid.*, p. 3.
12. R.N. Prasad, See No. 1, pp. 60, 61 and 62.
13. Anirrlesh Ray, *op. cit.*, pp. 40-41.
14. V. Venkata Rao, H.Thansanga and Niru Hazarika, *A Century of Government and Politics in North-East India,* Vol. III, Mizoram, pp. 70-71.
15. R.N. Prasad, *op. cit.*, p. 62.

25

The Pace of Socio-Economic and Political Developments

Responses to British Colonialism and the Emergence of the Mizo Minority Nationality in Indian Politics

Zothantluanga Ralte

In any attempt to analyse developmental processes, it is necessary to present facts in terms of statistical figures and data. Here, this applies to the socio-economic and political aspects—the institutionalized forms and types practised, the more reformative years, the resultant features, etc. It is unfortunate that these are regrettably lacking and wanting in the case of the region concerned especially during British colonialism—a fact presented by the ignorance and backwardness of the inhabitants of the region. This lack of data may also be ascribed to the negligence of the British authorities who seem to be rather reluctant and hesitant at assessing and analysing the then prevailing conditions. It may also be mentioned that there are two differing opinions on the attitude of the British towards the economic and political development of Mizoram. Whatever the case may be, it is sincerely hoped that this chapter presents an unbiased observation of the state of the Mizos as a consequence of British policy.

In this review then, the author will not pretend and attempt an analysis of the production of economic goods. The stress will be rather on the narrative aspect of the Mizo socio-economic and political milieu and the response elicited by the British occupation. The attempt will thus be in trying to assess the responsibilities of the British government and the Missions and their effects on the traditional life of the Mizos. It also will attempt to investigate and enquire into the evolution of the political acumen of the Mizo people. It is regretted that lack of more reliable sources and data prevents the presentation from being more comprehensive and enlightening, explicit and specific—the outcome of a serious academic disappointment at the absence of archival documents. However, with existing sources and data, an attempt is made here with many a shortcoming and unsatisfactory presentation.

The Socio-Economic Milieu

When Mizoram formerly known as the Lushai Hills District was officially annexed by the British in 1890, they introduced various laws, rules and regulations such as the annual land tax, rice tax, taxes on licensed guns; etc. These taxation laws were met with a silent consent because the vanquished Mizo tribals were not in a position to bargain. The Mizos were, at that time, cultivators and hunters and had no need of cash money As such, money in the form of cash was a rare and scarce commodity. Moreover, the system of rice cultivation—*jhuming*—was primitive and taxing on land forcing the tribals to migrate and resort to headhunting raids so as to acquire new lands for cultivation. Also, road conditions were pitifully bad for the Commissariat General did not consider the construction of new roads necessary after the 1989-90 Chin Expedition with the result that there were no all-weather roads worth mentioning in the region during British rule. Thus, in such a setting, the common Mizo male had to depend on his energy, fortitude and intelligence so as to profit from his produce in exchange of cash which his Government demands in a poor agricultural region. To meet the annual land tax of even Re. 1, he had to earn a cash wage by carrying heavy loads far away from his home and family. Also, on the demand of the Government, he had to work as a labourer with a meagre cash payment, while on the other hand, he had to meet the social obligations of working free on various village developmental projects.

Trade with the neighbouring plains existed but on a very small-scale and was also inconsistent. The Mizo then had to apply his genius to meet his needs and requirements for daily utilization. With annexation and the adoption of Christianity as the main religion, imports increased and goods from outside became more easily acquired thus sharply decreasing the demand for indigenous products. This decline in indigenous crafts is usually attributed to the repressive nature of the teachings of the missionaries which, according to A.G. McCall, is unfair and incorrect. He asserts that the Mizos were in a period of transition, living only for the satisfaction of their immediate needs reinforced by their desire to acquire exotic substitutes from foreign sources. However, the problem of cash money remained a stark reality and the problem of its acquisition ushered in a hitherto unknown capitalistic outlook.

Initially, the Mizos were greatly affected by the sudden change of events with the advent of the British and the consequent governance and administration. They were paralysed because all the power and freedom they had enjoyed and desired so much for themselves was totally shattered. They, moreover, were confused and bewildered by the double-pronged onset of the British Government on the one hand, and on the other, the proselytizing missionaries. The former did their best to maintain law and order while the latter aimed at pacifying and taming the wild headhunters into a brotherhood based on love and genuine concern for one another. However, it is important to note that these agencies of control had their limitations in the sense that they hampered the natural and primordial growth of the Mizos. Moreover, the Government policy of enforcing the Inner Line Regulation prevented other social and cultural influences to nature the social milieu of the Mizos.

The impact of such a forceful British presence was tremendous. The change it brought about in the total outlook of the common Mizo was, as we have said, confusing yet it was drastic in its own way. This is so because its effects were positive for many as they were brought towards more civilized attitudes, thought and mode of living. Critics are, however, not unanimous at this juncture. Some maintain that the British occupation and administration was responsible for the complete severing of the hitherto existing social, cultural and kinship ties with the people of Cachar. They also blame and criticise the Missions for their attacks on and repression of traditional and indigenous practices, which were, so they maintain, a form of self-sufficiency in traditional economic system of production. They further blame the Missions for their role in the field of education. This last argument cannot be refuted nor ignored because the Missions were entrusted with the task of educating the Mizos. For this purpose, grants-in-aid of small amounts were made. However, local educational practice took such a turn that Mizos came to believe that education and Christianity necessarily entailed the securing of 'salaried jobs' thus substituting the grind of cultivating a hard agricultural land. As such, the educated Mizos realised the advantages of the 'salaried jobs' in place of a hard agricultural life thereby seeking employment outside and denying the land of their birth the benefits and fruits of their learning. Thus the aims of education did not result in the application of knowledge for the upliftment of the masses. Since the educational curriculum neither fulfilled nor met the needs of the Mizos. Further, the attainment of salaried jobs led to what A.G. McCall terms as 'blackcoatism' monthly salaried jobs providing the Mizo the opportunity to escape from the traditional life of hard work. This resulted in material independence creating a new phenomenon the salaried 'rich' who now has the power and the means to secure middle and higher education for his children whereas, to do this, the villager had the difficult task of producing surplus crops and the equally difficult task of converting these into enough cash within an economy which did not provide facilities for exports or profitable marketing facilities.

In a short time, the salaried 'blackcoatism' phenomenon produced a distinct class of experts and intellectuals which did not have any specific role in the indigenous society of Mizos. However, with the declining of traditionalism and the sudden rise of capitalistic and materialistic thinking, this new class attained the status of being oligarchical, transforming and reversing the *status quo* in the existing condition, thus, destroying the traditional communal equality and security.

It can be ascertained then that the transformation of the social life of the Mizos was brought about by the work of the Missions. This can be safely said because political changes that the British Government brought about were controlled and designed to protect the traditional Mizo society. On the other hand, the Missions offered conversion to Christianity as a protection from the government. Also, from the economic point of view, the new religion did not demand costly sacrifices and obligations and it was inevitable that Christianity would be conducive in an economy of hard labour. The salaried Christian then became materially independent and sometimes even surpassed the village chief in wealth.

Another impact of the Missions was on the age-old tradition of the *zawlbuk*—an important institution of the Mizos. Here, various problematic social matters and issues are dealt with, for instance, the extension of help to widows and the disabled in times of tilling the soil and in harvesting, helping the poorer sections of the village, etc. This important and socially useful institution was gradually viewed by the converts as detrimental to the growth of a healthy and morally law abiding society because its very nature of being a bachelors' dormitory entailed many a vulgar and bawdy talk opposed to Christian teaching. Moreover, with the spread of education and school attendance, young boys could no longer spare their time to perform the chores demanded by the *zawlbuk*. Counsequently, the great Revivals of 1919 and 1923 respectively, with the aforesaid factors, began to undermine and weaken the foundation of this institution.

Whatever impact the Missions have had on the traditional life of the Mizos, the British Government, on the other hand, tried to preserve it. It also tried to develop the deplorable Mizo economy by introducing various economic measures such as the tilling of the Champhai plain, promoting and financially assisting the rearing of livestock, planting and cultivation of beverages, vegetables, fruits and rubber, the last one of which unfortunately failed. Also, during 1908-09, an agricultural farming complex was established at Chite with a view to teaching and instructing the masses the benefits and techniques of crop production which consequently became a great success. The Government also established a public bazar at Aizawl and also a retail market in 1910 which facilitated business and commercial enterprises to flourish. In 1939, The Lushai Hills Cottage Industries was introduced by the Government so as to foster more income for the masses and also for a healthy competition.

All these economic measures greatly benefited the Mizos especially those living at and near Aizawl. However, the backwardness of the people did not enable them to exploit the opportunities and the pace of economic growth was thus slow. Also, the bulk of the Mizos living in the rural areas could not benefit very much from these facilities and privileges. On the one hand, there was little scope for realising revenue from the traditional Mizos. The Frontier Transit Regulation 1880 exempted the Mizos from paying normal taxes. The Assam Government, initially, was not very keen in taking over the administration of the Lushai Hills because, taking over would mean the incurring of additional finances. Moreover, the fact that the Lushai Hills were constituted as Excluded Area meant that no economic reforms were possible. As such, in economic terms, the economic condition of Mizoram was unstable and unproductive during British rule.

The Evolution of Political Awareness in Mizoram

When Mizoram came under the British rule in 1890, the chief administrator was the Political Officer (later changed to Superintendent) in whose hands the entire power of administration was centralized. The 1917 Montagu-Chelmsford Report declared that it was to be excluded totally from reform schemes and legislation was given entirely to the Governor-in-Council under Section 71 of the Government of India Act 1915. On 3rd January, 1921, it was declared as a backward area under Section 52 of the Government of India Act 1919 and, further, on 3rd March, 1936, an Order-in-Council declared the Lushai Hills as an

Excluded area. In this way, the Lushai Hills were not represented in the Assam Legislative Council and thus no legislation can be enacted and no resolution can be passed on it. Further, suggestions were made by various eminent persons that the Lushais were not ready to be included in the Reformed Constitution and that even the most educated Mizos were not competent to be in a Legislature. This was the political condition of the Lushai Hills during the first forty years of British administration.

One observes that the attitude of the Government towards the Mizos was negative although it recognised the fact that they had progressed significantly under the guidance and influence of the Missions. The percentage of literacy was higher than that of the Plains although the quality of education acquired was not satisfactory especially in technological areas. However, it was clear that the Mizos possessed enough intelligence required to govern and administer themselves, though one may wonder at the efficiency and wisdom of such an undertaking.

Much to the consternation of a few people, problems of administration and internal politics had been discerned by a small section of Mizos as early as 1925 when Telela Ralte and some persons approached the Superintendent Perry requesting for Mizos to participate in the Assam politics. The Superintendent was furious at this suggestion. Telela and Chawngbawiha then went to Shillong to consult the Rev. J.J.M. Nichols Roy on the political and administrative problems of the Mizos. However, on their return to Aizawl, they were arrested after delivering a few public speeches and were released after a severe reprimand. As such, the first politically motivated movement was controlled and contained. It is evident that education had given rise to an intellectual and political minded class which challenged the elitism of the traditional chiefs necessitating the occurrence of a political clash. This new class thus mobilized themselves against the practices and traditionalism of the chiefs and attempted to instigate public opinion against them.

Political awareness was also a result of the great wars in which many Mizo men and women volunteered. In these wars, the Mizos came into contact with the outside world and this caused many to view life in a different perspective, motivated by the questions and ideas of freedom and liberty and becoming more and more conscious of their own political problems. At the same time, the Indian National Movement which demanded independence from British rule began to form a more concrete idea of their own situation. Some of the more informed felt that the Mizos would be left in the lurch if India secedes from British and that they might have to face the undesirable and unwelcome aspect of returning to the past life of barbaric head-hunting. Thus, to gain for themselves a better bargain in the scheme of things, the Mizos felt that the formulation and founding of a strong and united political party was necessary and essential.

As a result, the Mizo Union was conceived of and founded by R. Vanlawma in 1946. He desired that the common Mizos should have a strong voice in the party and also wanted political relations between the commoners and the chiefs to improve through the party. With such aims and objectives, the Mizos Union was born on the 9th of April, 1946.

The Mizo Union was very popular with the common people. The chiefs, on the other hand, refrained from joining the party. A conference of the party was held where its aims and objectives were resolved. However, radicalism soon set in into the party because some members began to mount severe opposition against the institution of the traditional chiefs who were considered despotic and autocratic. A split occurred in the party—a Left Wing and a Right Wing which both submitted memorandums to the visiting Bordoloi Committee in 1947. However, after careful and serious consultations and the recommendations of the Committee, both the members of the split Mizo Union compromised and opted for the inclusion of the Lushai Hills in the Indian Union. As a result, the Lushai Hills was allotted three seats in the Assam Legislative Assembly in accordance to the Constitution of India. This marked the active political participation of the Mizos in Indian national politics.

The Mizo Union won the 1952 elections—the outcome of which was the abolition of the institution of chieftainship in April 1954. After winning the elections of 1962 again, the Mizo Union, however, declined in popularity because of intra-party policy differences. The result was that it was badly beaten by the Mizo National Front in the 1963 elections. It, however, won a majority at the first general elections held in 1972 forming the first ministry. It was then invited to merge with the Indian National Congress and, after the General Assembly resolved to dissolve the party, the Mizo Union merged itself with the I.N.C. on 23rd January, 1974.

In the manner, the Mizos entered into the mainstream of Indian politics and, with the growth of the Congress party in the region, the masses have been more active in participating in national as well as regional politics, resulting in the founding of various political parties all claiming to the region's recognition on what they decree as the best policy for the Mizos.

26

Effect of Self-Confrontation Strategy on Democratic Value Systems of Mizo Adolescents across Introversion-Extraversion

A. Bhushan

The research evidences tend to reveal that the basic psychological mechanism underlying the value self-confrontation strategy is the affective state of self-dissatisfaction the generates durable changes in different values (Hamid & Flay, 1974; Rokeach, 1979; Rokeach & Grube, 1979; and Sanders & Atwood, 1979) and also induces enduring changes in some values subsequently leading long-term changes in related behaviours (Rokeach, 1971; Greenstein, 1979; Conroy, 1979; Thousaranond, 1987; Sawa & Sawa, 1988 and Schwartz and Inbar-saban, 1988). However, the strategic effect of the self-confrontation exclusively on democratic values has not yet been reported degree. Similarly, conducting a study on Jungian personality typology and Rekeach's values, Snyder (1989) suggested that the personality contributes to the individual's value-set; but no research evidence was traced by the investigators on it. The present study, thus has made a pioneering attempt to explore the field (i) investigating the effect of self-confrontation strategy on democratic values with respect to Eysenck's (1947) introversion-extraverson which is the first among the five robust-dimensions of personality (Digman, 1990); and (ii) concentrating upon the Mizo adolescents who differ socially to a greater extent from their other Indian counterparts.

The objectives of the study are (i) to determine the democratic value systems of Mizo adolescents with varying personality types; and (ii) to examine the effect of self-confrontation strategy on democratic value changes of adolescent introverts and extraverts.

On the basis of review of literature it is hypothesized that the self-confrontation strategy induces durable changes in democratic values of adolescent introverts and extraverts.

Method

Subjects

A total of 300 sixteen to seventeen years old adolescents were originally studied, consisting of final year Pre-university students of P.U. College, Government Aizawl College and Zirtiri Women's College in the Aizawl town of Mizoram. From this population, the final sample (N=88) of introverts (N=46) and extraverts (N=42) were selected on the basis of Kundu Introversion Extraversion Inventory (KIEI).

Measures

1. *Democratic Value Survey*: In order to study the democratic value systems, a DEMOCRATIC VALUE SURVEY was developed on the basis of the Preamble of the Constitution of India and the review of literature (Nehru,1954; Mookerjea, 1956; Barnes, 1962; Solomon *et al.*, 1972; Eliot, 1978; Mahindroo, 1978; and Avinashilingam, 1983). It was designed after the Rokeach VALUE SURVEY (1973) which is extensively used in the area of value study due to ease of administration and clear exhibition of value preferences. Of course, the need was felt later on to develop a democratic measure at the commitment level (Chinara, 1991). On the basis of modifications, the Democratic Value Survey finally contained seven democratic values (REGARDS FOR THE DIGNITY OF INDIVIDUAL, EQUALITY OF STATUS AND OPPORTUNITY, SYMPATHY WITH EVERYONE, OPENNESS TO REASON, TOLERANCE FOR DIFFERENCES IN OPINIONS, RESPONSIBILITY AND COOPERATIVE DECISION-MAKING) and four distractors (Cultural preservation, service for needy and depressed, Loyalty to authority and self-progress) which were arranged concentrically from the nucleus to the outer orbits in order of importance to them. In order to obtain stability measures for each of the eleven values; the Survey was administered over 35 Pre-University students of P.U. College, Aizawl and the computed test-retest reliability coefficients were found to be .90, .90, .97, .90, .92, .93, .89, .86, .80, .95 and .90 for the above

stated democratic values and distractors respectively. In this measure, each value is required to be ranked in order of its importance as a guiding principle in one's life. The lower the number which the student ascribes to a given value, the more importance is presumed to be attributed to it. The possible ranks range from 1 to 11 for the total eleven values.

2. *Value Self-Confrontation Instrument*; Th Self-Confrontation Strategy was originally developed by Rokeach (1973) in the form of THE VALUE CHANGE instrument. This instrument was adopted in the form of VALUE SELF CONFRONTATION INSTRUMENT in which the Terminal Values were replaced by previously stated seven Democratic Values and four distractors. The instrument was validated in terms of answers given by 50 Pre-University students of Government Aizawl College to two separate questions concerning the understanding of interpretations of the ranks given by the democratic teachers and dissatisfaction to the ranks individually assigned by them. It was found that 75 per cent subjects agreed strongly with the interpretation made about the master-ranks to the eleven values, 16 per cent were not able to decide and 9 per cent strongly disagreed. It showed that interpretations were understood by the students. Similarly, out of the same 50 students, 20 per cent were found extremely satisfied, 70 per cent were extremely dissatisfied and 10 per cent were in-between about their ranks assigned to the eleven values. It indicated that the instrument has successfully induced the state of self-dissatisfaction which subsequently may bring changes in their values.
3. *Kundu Introversion-Extraversion Inventory*: KIEI (1976) was used to obtain reliable measure of introversion extraversion dimension of adolescent personality.

Procedure

In order to determine the sample, responses to the KIEI were obtained personally from 300 students who were studied section-wise. They on the average took 40 minutes to answer all the items. On the basis of the selection criteria given in the manual, 46 subjects securing a score of 179 or more were selected as introverts and 42 with a score of 122 or less as extraverts who together constitute the experimental sample. Conduct of the Experiment:

The experiment was conducted at three different phases.

Phase I: In this pre-test phase, each of the selected 88 subjects were served individually with a copy of Democratic Value Survey. The subjects took 8 to 10 minutes to give their responses. By early June, 1990, the pre-test responses were obtained.

Phase II: Following the pre-test, all the subjects of the experimental sample except one extravert who was found absent during data collection were individually given Value Self-Confrontation Instrument. It took almost a month to serve the value treatment. Each subject took 30 to 40 minutes to complete it in all respects.

Phase III: After completion of written responses to the Value Self-Confrontation Instrument, the post-test responses to the Democratic Value Survey were obtained frontation Instrument, the post-test responses to the Democratic Value Survey were obtained individually from the subjects twice: after a gap of (i) one week and (ii) two weeks from the date of treatment.

Table 26.1: Master-ranks on Pre-Test Scores of the Democratic Values across Introversion-Extraversion.

Values	*Reg.*	*Equa.*	*Symp.*	*Open.*	*Toler.*	*Resp.*	*Coop.*
I	5 (–202)	2 (–249)	1 (–276)	6 (–193)	7 (–187)	4 (–239)	3 (–247)
E	2 (–221)	4 (–217)	1 (–259)	7 (–172)	6 (I76)	5 (–199)	3 (–220)

W = .86; X2 = 10.32; X^2_6 (.05) = 12.59; X^2_6 (.01) =16.81

Results and Discussion

In order to determine the democratic value systems for both the *I* (Introverts) and *E* (Extraverts) groups, the ranks assigned to the seven democratic values by the subject during pre-test and post tests (*A* and *B*) were pulled up and the normalised master-ranks along with the co-efficient of concordance (*W*) were computed and have been recorded in Table 26.1 and 26.2 respectively. The value systems of both the groups with respect to the pre-test and post-tests (*A* and *B*) have been graphically depicted through pattern graphs (Figs. 26.1, 26.2 and 26.3). The results and discussion have been carried out in three different ways: Pre-test, Post-Test (*A*) Post-Test (*B*).

Pre-Test

The graphical presentation of the computed master-ranks of both the groups for the democratic values gave rise to two different patterns.

Table 26.2: Master-Ranks on Post-Tests (A and B) Scores of the Democratic Values across the Self-Confrontation Strategy and Introversion-Extraversion

Democratic Value	*Self–Confrontation*			
	Post–test (A)		*Post–test (B)*	
	I	*E*	*I*	*E*
Regards	5 (209)	6.5 (193)	6 (180)	5 (209)
Equality	1 (281)	1 (236)	1 (279)	1 (256)
Sympathy	2 (269)	3 (224)	4 (215)	6 (191)
Openness	7 (203)	5 (201)	5 (197)	7 (185)
Tolerance	b (206)	6.5 (193)	2 (261)	4 (223)
Responsibility	3 (260)	4 (215)	3 (240)	3 (234)
Cooperation	4 (250)	2 (235)	7 (172)	2 (235)
	W= .88; X^2_6 (.05) = 12.59;	X^2= 10.56	W=.66;	X^2 = 7.92 X^2_6 (.01) = 16.81

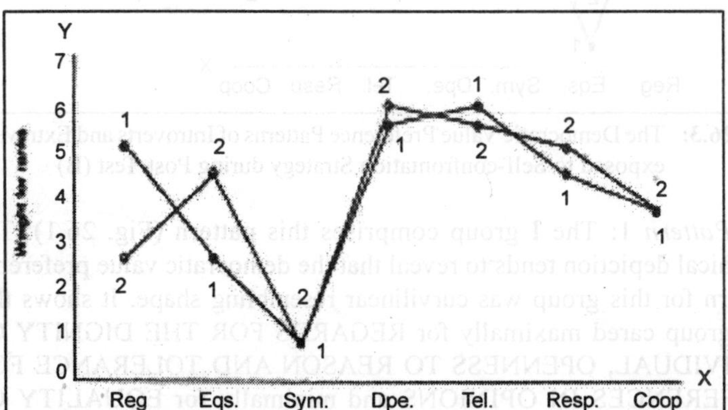

Fig. 26.1: The Domestic Value Preference Patterns of Introverts and Extraverts during Pre-Test

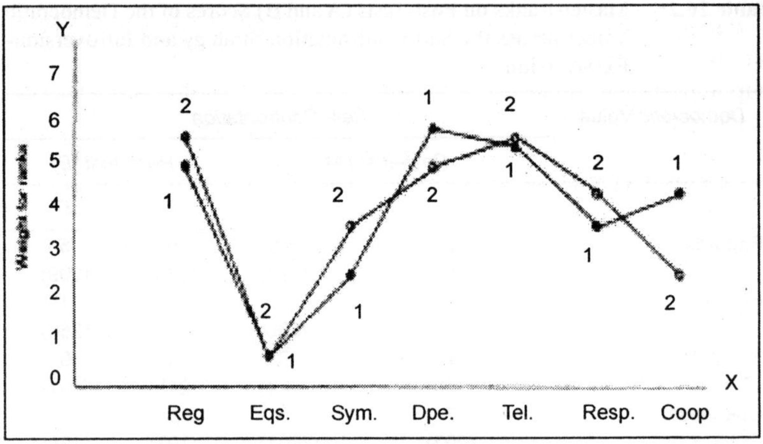

Fig. 26.2: The Democratic Value Preference Patterns of Introverts and Extraverts exposed to Self-confrontation Strategy during Post-Test (A)

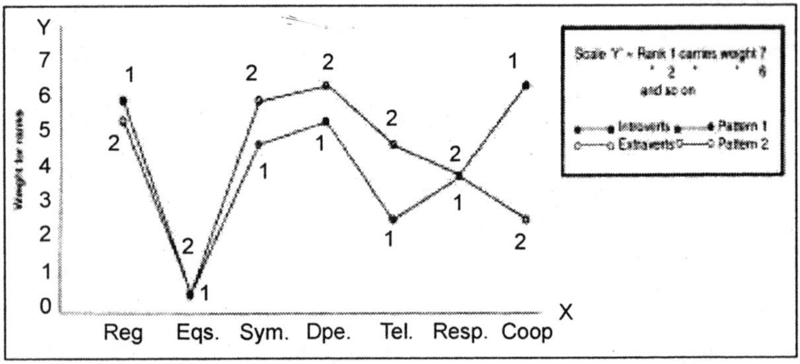

Fig. 26.3: The Democratic Value Preference Patterns of Introverts and Extraverts exposed to Self-confrontation Strategy during Post-Test (B)

Pattern 1: The I group comprises this pattern (Fig. 26.1). The graphical depiction tends to reveal that the democratic value preference pattern for this group was curvilinear resembling shape. It shows that this group cared maximally for REGARDS FOR THE DIGNITY OF INDIVIDUAL, OPENNESS TO REASON AND TOLERANCE FOR DIFFERENCES IN OPINIONS and minimally for EQUALITY OF STATUS AND OPPORTUNITY, SYMPATHY WITH EVERYONE and COOPERATIVE DECISION-MAKING. The value RESPONSIBILITY was ranked moderately.

Pattern 2: The democratic value preferences of *E* group comprise Pattern-2 (Fig. 26.1). The graph indicates that the value pattern for this group appears curvilinear which resembles *M* in structure. It suggests that the group assigned top three ranks to OPENNESS, TOLERANCE and RESPONSIBILITY and bottom three ranks to sympathy, REGARDS and COOPERATION. EQUALITY as a middle-rank value apparently seems not a matter to be bothered about much.

The agreement between the value systems of *I* and *E* groups was tested by the co-efficients of concordance (W=.86). The obtained (χ^2) value of 10.32 was not significant even at the .05 level. It shows that the value systems of the personality groups are independent from each other. This tends to indicate that the respective democratic value system appears to be the exclusive characteristic of the respective group. However, the graphs reveal that values SYMPATHY and COOPERATION were ranked identically and hence, both the systems are dependent on each other partially.

Post-Test (A)

Two different patterns emerged when the master-ranks of *I* and *E* groups were drawn graphically.

Pattern I: The group I comprises this pattern (Fig. 26.2). The preference graph shows that the value pattern is *W* in form. It indicates that the group valued REGARDS, OPENNESS and TOLERANCE very high and EQUALITY, SYMPATHY and RESPONSIBILITY very low. COOPERATION was neither among the most important nor among the least important values.

Pattern 2: The *E* group comprises the Pattern-2 (Fig.26.2). The graph suggests that the value pattern followed by the group was curvilinear which resembles *N*-shape. It shows that the group considered REGARDS, OPENNESS and TOLERANCE more important and EQUALITY, SYMPATHY and COOPERATION less important. RESPONSIBILITY was given a moderate rank.

The two value patterns of *I* and *E* groups exposed to the self-confrontation strategy do not show any kind of agreement as demonstrated by chi-square (W = .88; χ^2 = 10.56<.05) in Table 26.2. It means the value patterns of both the groups may be considered independent from each other. Assignment of different ranks to the democratic values except Equality by the *I* and *E* groups may be ascribed to the fact that personality types determine the value systems of Mizo adolescents.

An examination of the four preference graphs of *I* and *E* groups in respect of pre-test and post-test (*A*) suggests the following: (i) Discrepancies between both the systems comprising the seven democratic values of the groups exposed to the self-confrontation strategy have been widened further than what were reflected by pre-test responses. The two values (SYMPATHY and COOPERATION) common to both the groups have turned to be one (Equality) in case of the same groups following in value treatment. (ii) EQUALITY which was second among the three bottom-ranked values became the first for the groups after the treatment. (iii) The value pattern resembling *P*-shape turn into a meaningful shape of *w* in the case of introverts while for extraverts the *P*-shape appears to be *N* in appearance. In brief, the post-test (*A*) responses to Value Survey reveals that self-confrontation strategy has become effective by differentiating the groups further in terms of their democratic value systems.

Post-Test (B)

The calculated master-ranks showed two different patterns for *I* and *E* groups.

Pattern 1: The I group comprises this pattern (Fig. 26.3). The graphical description reveals that the value pattern appears curvilinear which resembles *w* in shape. The value continuum containing the democratic values in descending order of importance indicates that this group ranked both the extreme values (REGARDS and COOPERATION) including OPENNESS as most important guiding principles of life. The group did not bother much about SYMPATHY. Among the three bottom-ranked values (EQUALITY, TOLERANCE and RESPONSIBILITY) the group lived much with EQUALITY;

Pattern 2: The group *E* comprises that pattern (Fig. 26.3). The preference graph indicates that the pattern was curvilinear resembling *N*-shape. It tends to suggest that the group showed maximum concern for REGARDS, SYMPATHY and OPENNESS and minimum concern for EQUALITY, RESPONSIBILITY and COOPERATION. TOLERANCE was ranked in between top and bottom ranked values.

The two value patterns displayed by *I* and *E* groups exposed to the self-confrontation strategy do not show any kind of agreement between them as indicated by chi-square (W=.66; $\chi^2 = 7.92 < .05$) in Table 26.2. It means that the value systems of both the groups are independent. This finding further substantiates to the fact that values have been consolidated in the innermost orbit of the psycho-social systems of Mizo adolescents' personalities.

A perusal of the four pattern graphs of *I* and *E* groups in regard to post-tests (*A*) and (*B*) indicates the following: (i) EQUALITY was rate as the least important value by the groups; (ii) The value systems emerging out of the responses given by the *I* group appears to be closed not only in structure resembling *w*-shape but also in terms of assignment of identical ranks to EQUALITY and RESPONSIBILITY. Assignment of low ranks suggests that the adolescent introverts live with these values; and (iii) Identically ranked values of EQUALITY and COOPERATION reveal that the value systems of *E* group seem *N* in form. It suggests that the adolescent extraverts accept these two values as guiding principles in their lives. In sum, the self-confrontation strategy generates enduring changes in EQUALITY for both adolescent introverts and extraverts, in RESPONSIBILITY for adolescent introverts and in COOPERATION for adolescent extraverts.

The above stated findings lead to an inference that the hypothesis— "The self-confrontation strategy induces durable changes in democratic values of adolescent introverts and extraverts"was retained partially.

NOTES

Avinashilingam, T.S.: Inculcation of Social, Ethical and Spiritual Values in Education. *Journal of Educational Research and Extension*, July, 1983, 20 (11), 8.

Barnes, D.L.: Dimension of Democracy and Education. *Education*, July 1962, (7), 15-18.

Chinara, B.D.: Need Assessment of Research "Fools on Democratic Values. *NEHU Journal of Social Sciences and Humanities*, 1991, IX(3), 51-58.

Conroy, W.J.: Human Values, Smoking Behaviour and Public Health Programme. In M. Rekeach (ed.) *Understanding Human Values: Individual and Societal*; N.Y., The Free Press, 1979, 199-209.

Digman, J.M: Personality Structure: Emergence of the Five-Factor Model. *Annual Review of Psychology*, 1990, 41; 417-440.

Eliot, T.S.: *To Criticize the Critic and other Writings*. London; Faber and Faber, 1978.

Eysenck, H.J: *Dimension of Personality*. London: Routledge and Kegan Paul, 1947.

Greenstein, T.N.: Behaviour Change Through Value Self-Confrontation. A Field Experiment. *Journal of Personality and Social Psychology*, 1976, 34, 254-262.

Hamid, P.N. and Flay, Iv.R.: Changes in Locus of Control as a Function of Value Modification. *British Journal of Social and Clinical Psychology*, 1974, 13, 143-150.

Kundu, R.N.: *Kundu Introversion-Extraversion Inventory*. National Psychological Corporation, Agra, 1976.

Mahindroo, P.K.: Reconciling Freedom and Discipline as Educational Values. *Qest in Education*, January, 1978, XV (1), 62-69:

Mookerjea, S.: Democracy and Social Psychology. *Indian Journal of Psychology*, Vol. XXXI, Part III-IV, 1956, 113-120.

Nehru, J.: In a speech delivered during 1954.

Rokeach, M.: Long Range Experimental Modification of Values, Attitudes and Behaviours. *American Psychologists*, 1971, 26, 453-459.

Rokeach, M: *The Nature of Human Values*: N.Y:, The Free Press, 1973.

Rokeach, M: *Long Term Value Change initiated by Computer Feedback*. in M. Rokeach (ed.) *op. cit*. 210-219:

Rokeach, M. and Grube, J.W:: *Can Value be manipulated Arbitrarily* in M. Rokeach, (ed), *op. cit*., 226-240.

Sawa, S.L. and Sawa, G.H.: The Value Confrontation Approach to Enduring Behavioural Modification. *The Journal of Social Psychology*, 1988, 128(2), 207-215.

Schwartz, S.H. and Inbar-Sahan, N.: Value Self-Confrontation as a Method to Aid in Weight Loss. *Journal of Personality and Social Psychology*, 1988, 54(3), 396-404.

Sander, F.R.: A Study of Jungian Personality Typology and Values of Future Administration and Social Work Clinicians. 1988, Dissertation Abstracts International, 1989, 49 (10, 31b1-A.

Solomon, D.; Ali, F.A.; Kafir, D. Houlihan, K.A. and Yaeger, J.: The development of Democratic values and Behaviour among Mexican-American *Children: Child Development*, 1972,43(l),69-A.

Thousaranonad, D.: Self-Confrontation as a Means of Changing the Values and Behaviours of Cadets at Chulachomkiao Royal Military Academy, Thailand, 1987. Dissertation abstracts international, 1988, 48(12), 196197-A.

27

Evolution of the Chin Hills-Lushai Hills Boundary

Ranju Bezbaruah

When the North and South Lushai Hills were amalgamated in 1898[1] to form the Lushai Hills District under the Chief Commissioner of Assam, the new district inherited an ill-defined eastern, and undefined southern boundary. To the east of the new district was the Chin Hills, and to the south was an 'unadministered' * area[2] of about 1,000 square miles (between 92°4′ and 93°15′ east and 21°45′ and 22°20′ north bounded by Northern Arakan from the south, and the Chin Hills from the east). The Upper Kolodyne or Boinu river after making a long detour to the north turned south in about the same latitude as Lungleh and transected the tract. The full definition of the boundary between Chin Hills and Lushai Hills, therefore, was inseparably connected with the final disposal of this 'unadministered' tract. By 1898, the only clearly recognizable line of demarcation between the jurisdictions of the Chin Hills and the Lushai Hills was the one formed by Upper Kolodyne or Boinu, and the Tiau rivers. The northern extremity of the line was not spelt out until 1901. The boundary south of the most southernly point of the bend of the Boinu river towards the north, could be settled only in 1922 when the 'unadministered' tract was finally apportioned between Lushai Hills, Chin Hills and Arakan. Efforts will be made in this chapter to examine the different stages of the evolution of the Chin-Lushai boundary mainly on the basis of available primary materials.

---

* In this chapter the term 'unadministered' is used to mean 'outside the administrative control of the British'. This is not to describe complete lack of administration in any form.

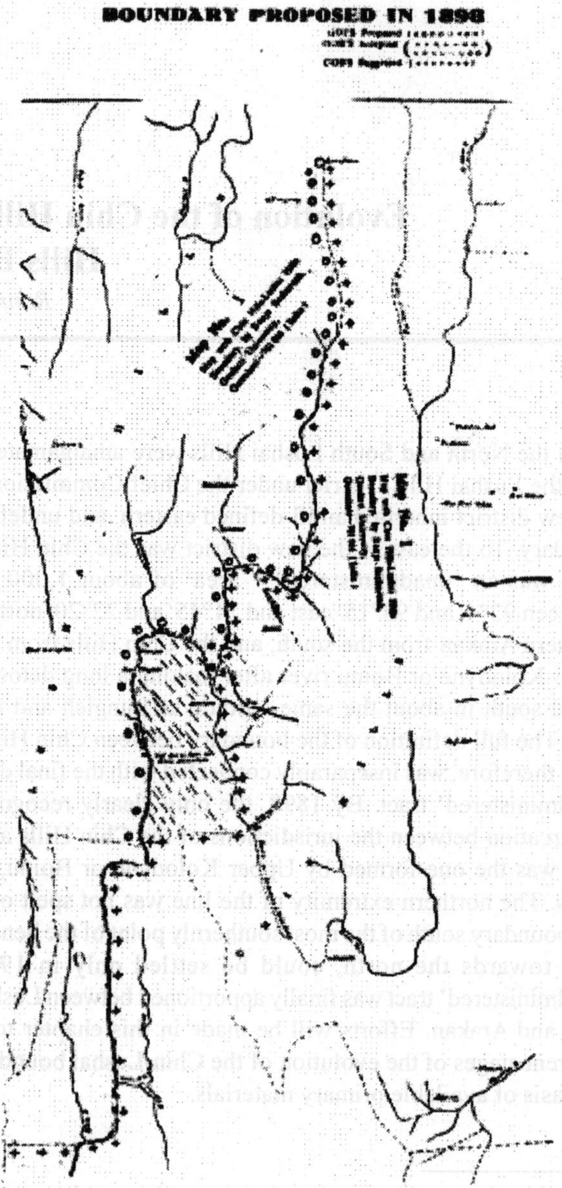

Map 27.1

Until the annexation of Upper Burma in 1885, the territory occupied by the Lushai tribes was regarded by the British as constituting the 'real frontier'. It was then thought in terms of 'lines of defence'[3] rather than a boundary. Since 1890-91, however, British administration in the Chin Hills was initiated from three centres—Fort White, Haka and Yawdin; and in 1892 the northern and central portions were tagged together under a Superintendent at Falam (with assistance at Haka and Tiddim)[4]. On the other hand, Lushai Hills territories, within the control of the British, too, were brought under administration through the tribal Chiefs. In North Lushai Hills, Aijal was selected as a permanent post in January 1890. South Lushai Hills were administered from Lungleh since December of the same year.[5] As a consequence of the 'Chin-Lushai Expedition', new areas were brought under British control in Lushai as well as Chin Hills. However, it was recognized that the Chins had nothing in common with the Lushais and their 'historic connection, tribal sympathies and practical interests' were with Burma.[6] In this context, while there could be no question of a defined political-boundary prior to the establishment of British control over the border tribes, ethnic line of separation did indeed exist. While narrating the military events of March 1890, Colonel L.W. Shakespear obviously meant Upper Kolodyne or Boinu as forming the 'boundary'between Chin and the Lushai Hills in the neighbourhood of the Tayo village,[7] strictly in ethnic, or at best, military sense. The fact was that the question of the boundary was not yet settled; it was still at a discussion stage.[8] On 13 February, 1892, however, a provisional boundary between the Chin Hills and Lushai Hills jurisdictions was decided by the Chin and Lushai Hills military officials during their meeting at Tao (Tayo).[9] While this boundary was 'not strictly defined' it was described as a line drawn due south from Lungleh through the Buljang peak to the western edge of the lake north-east of Tattun, which is supposed to be the source of the Tiau river; thence the Tiau river to its junction with the Boinu or Kolodyne; thence the Boinu to the most southernly point of its bend towards the north; thence a line drawn due south to Arakan boundary.[10] This boundary in effect recognized existing realities and cut across the claims of both Lushai and Chin (Haka and Thlantlang) villages. In the olden times Lushai tribes occupied the banks of the Lavar stream about 20 miles west of Haka. Eventually, however, the Hakas evicted the Lushais from their villages of Kwe Hring and Vizan on the western slopes of the Rongklang range and drove across the Tiau river. The Thlantlang Chiefs, too, asserted their influence as far as the Blue Mountains and the Tuipui river and north-westward. The TyaoBoinu line thus curtailed the territory of these tribes.[11]

In January 1892, the Chin-Lushai Conference, held at Calcutta and attended by the Lieutenant-Governor of Bengal and Chief Commissioners of Assam and Burma, resolved to the effect that the North and South Lushai Hills, 'with such portion of the Arakan Hill Tracts as might hereafter be determined' should be placed under the Assam Administration.[12] The Officiating Chief Commissioner of Burma, Sir Frederick Fryer, expressed the opinion that the whole 'unadministered area' nominally attached to the Arakan Hill Tracts should be made over to Assam.[13] The disposal of this 'unadministered' area would have occasioned the definition of the extended boundary of the Lushai Hills with Chin Hills. However, as it later turned out to be, neither the Lushai, nor the Chin, nor the Arakan Administration was willing to take additional responsibilities of a virtual *terra incognita*, even while recognizing the necessity for its being absorbed by the neighbouring counterparts.[14]

On 27 January, 1898, the Government of India (GOI) forwarded to the Government of Burma (GOB) a draft specification of the boundaries of the South Lushai Hills which were then about to be transferred from Bengal to Assam. GOB accepted the eastern portion of the boundary as correct 'although incomplete'. This accepted boundary was from north to south upto the Tiau Kolodyne junction. The western turn of the boundary thence, could not be accepted by GOB on the the ground that the 'Darzo loop', which was administered by the Lushai officials since 1890, would be left to the Burma (Chin) side of the boundary. The agreed boundary between the Lushai Hills and the Chin Hills ran 'from the Lunglen hill southwards in a straight line to the most northernly source of the Tiau river; thence down the Tiau river to its junction with the Kolodyne, i.e., the eastern or Upper Kolodyne (Map 27.l). From this agreed point, GOB proposed a new line leaving the 'Darzo loop' to the Lushai Hills. This line ran from the Tiau Kolodyne junction "Up the Kolodyne (Upper or Eastern section) to its junction with the La-aw-var; thence a straight line due west to the Kolodyne (Lower or Western section); thence down the Kolodyne (Lower or Western section) to its junction with the Kola stream"[15] (Map 27.2).

Thus the boundary between Chin Hills and Lushai Hills was not fully defined when the Lushai Hills District was formed in 1898. The defined boundary only covered the middle portion. The portion north of Lungleh hills, and south of Tiau-Kolodyne junction continued to be undefined.

In 1901, in accordance with the decision of GOI, a Commission which included W.C.M. Dundas and A.C. Bateman, demarcated the northern part of the Chin-Lushai boundary and reported thus:

> "The boundary commences at the confluence of the Tuipai and Tuisai streams. There is a chain and pillar No. 2 placed thereon the left bank of Tuisai and 5 yards from the confluence of the stream, marking the trijunctional point of Manipur, Lushai and Chin Hills. The boundary now goes up the stream of the Tuisai to where Tuimang meets it. This direction is due north and south thence up the Tuimong to a point where its tributary the Bapui Lui meets it, finally up the Bapuilui to its source below a pillar marked L/C.H/3 on Vai-khohmun, where is also the source of the Tiau, the recognized boundary between the Chin Hills and Lushai Hills districts".[16]

As result of this demarcation, the village of the Chief, Pumlala containing 386 houses, transferred from Manipur to Lushai Hills in the preceding year, was now left to the Chin Hills side. The new line was sanctioned by GOL.[17]

Thus by 1901, the Chin-Lushai boundary north of the Tiau-Kolodyne confluence was fully defined. A telegraphic description of this boundary by the Superintendent of Lushai Hills on 22 August, 1910, makes it appear as though the boundary was subsequently revised. The telegram read: "Eastern boundary of district commencing northern corner is junction of Tuisa (or Tuisai) with Tuivai (or Tuipai) thence up Tuisa and branch thereof to hill over source Tiau, thence down Tiau to Kolodyne and up Kolodyne to mouth of Maulve which is about due east of Thangkrangton as shown in old map boundary. South of this not defined as it is unadministered territory.[18] No evidence could be traced to show that the boundary beyond the Tiau-Koladyne junction was ever revised between 1901 and 1910. It is, therefore, possible that the Superintendent of Lushai Hills described the boundary on the basis of existing realities and his own reading of the old maps, rather than the line which was agreed in paper.

The interposition of the 'unadministered' tract to the south of Tiau-Kolodyne junction, on the other hand, resulted in the absence of a defined boundary between Chin Hills and Lushai Hills until this tract was absorbed. The eastern portion of the 'unadministered' tract to the west of Boinu or Kolodyne and east of Tuishi (Tish, Tishi, Tuipang, Wabling, Mi or Michang) river were the two Sabong (Sabong Tu and Sabong Pi), Sapi (Sepi), Satlong (Sa-klong or Saklong), Vaki (Baki), Taungbor (Daunbu),

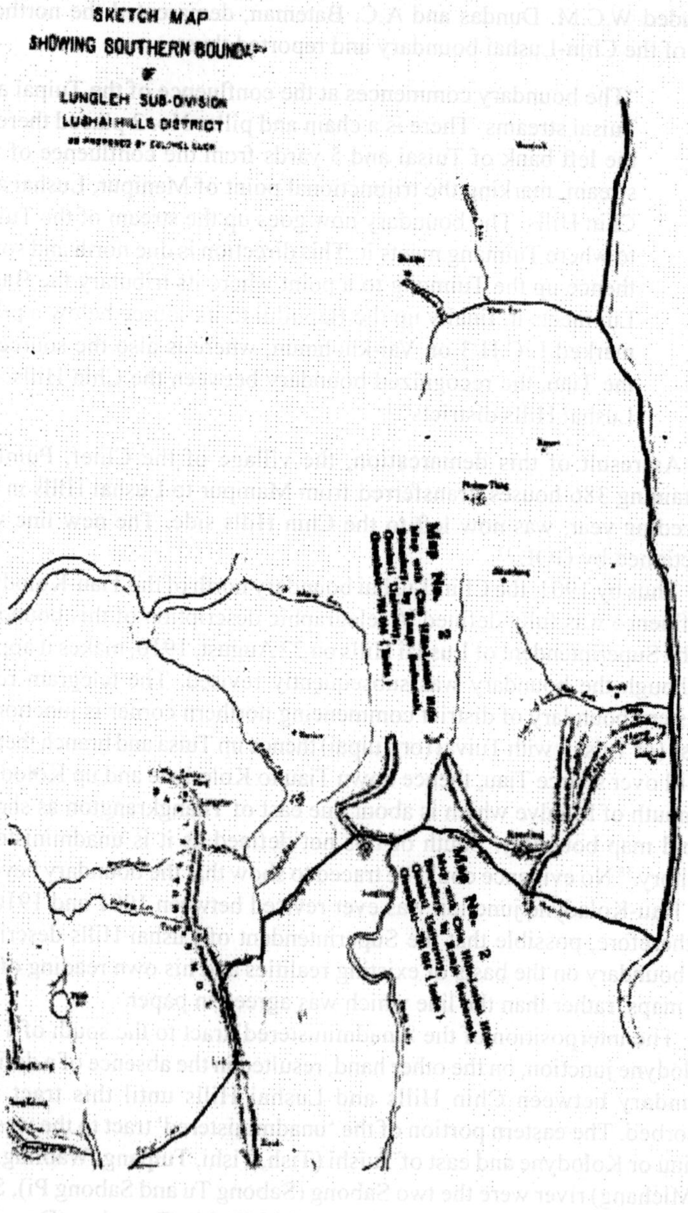
SKETCH MAP
SHOWING SOUTHERN BOUND
OF
LUNGLEH SUB-DIVISION
LUSHAI HILLS DISTRICT

Map 27.2

two Lalaoing (Lallaing) and three Ngapai villages. These villages were in contact with the neighbouring Chin villages of the Haka Subdivision of the Chin Hills. To the immediate east of the Tuishi (Tish, Tishi, Tuipang, Wabling, Mior Michang) river were the Shandu villages of Laki, Kuvi, Zongling (Yong Laing), Lake and Laki. They were in contact with the neighbouring Lakher and Poi villages of the Lungleh Subdivision of the Lushai Hills.[19]

Both the Chins and the Lushais from the adjoining districts had to pass through this 'unadministered' tract to Arakan for trade;[20] and lack of British control over this area created a situation inimical to peace. The overwhelming administrative problems arising from raid, abduction, murder, and encroachment within British territories committed by the 'unadministered' villages, called for a defined boundary. The situation could be clearly guessed from the following excerpt from a 1902 report from the Superintendent of Chin Hills:

> "Chins are well aware that Government protection does not extend to the unadministered tracts, and that so long as those tracts remain unadministered they enter them under certain risks. If Government is to take action on their behalf whenever they are molested in those tracts, it may be called on to do so frequently, and in each case a strong armed force would be necessary. I think the villagers in the unadministered tracts can be, and should be, taught that no acts of violence against our people will be permitted within our borders; but to teach them not to molest them across the borders might be a lengthy and expensive process. On the other hand, if the policy is to abstain from taking action on behalf of our people when molested in the unadministered tracts, our people may contend that acts of violence committed by them within those tracts should similarly pass unnoticed".[21]

The District Administrations on the immediate proximity of respective 'unadministered' villages had inferential responsibility to protect the 'administered' villagers even outside the 'administrative' boundary, particularly when the 'administered' villages were disarmed. Its only alternative seemed to be to allow the internecine inter-tribe feuds to continue unabated. This situation was made clear by a Chin Chief in a statement recorded by E.O. Fowler, Superintendent of Chin Hills, in May 1905, thus:

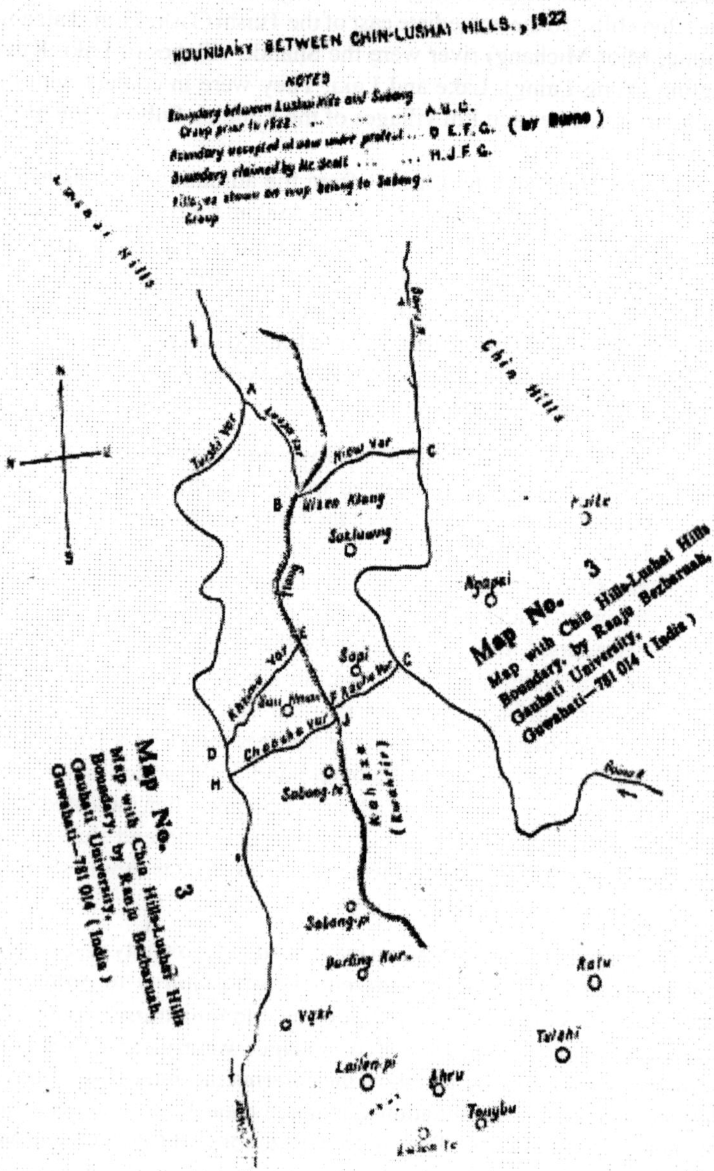
BOUNDARY BETWEEN CHIN-LUSHAI HILLS., 1922
NOTES
A.B.C.
D E.F.G. (by Burne)
H.J.F.G.
Chin Hills
Niew Var
Sakluang
Ngopai
Sopi
Chhoshe Var
Sabang-te
Sabang-pi
Vazai
Ralu
Tuiahi
Lailen-pi
Ahru
Tangbu
Map No. 3
Map with Chin Hills-Lushai Hills Boundary, by Ranju Bezbaruah, Gauhati University, Guwahati—781 014 (India)
Map No. 3
Map with Chin Hills-Lushai Hills Boundary, by Ranju Bezbaruah, Gauhati University, Guwahati—781 014 (India)

Map 27.3

> "We have been disarmed and made to conform to law and order and to pay tribute. In our endeavours to obtain the money wherewith to pay the tribute we run the risk of losing our lives and property. (Unadministered) People are armed, pay no tribute, and can go where they like and do what they like. We do not know what they will do next. They have killed our people, taken our property on several occasions, and, for all we know, may raid our villages next. If Government won't protect us we must see what we can do for ourselves."[22]

The problem of the undefined boundary and of controlling the 'unadministered' tract attracted inevitable concern of the Chin, Lushai and Arakan authorities, when 26 people from the Sabong village (on the Chin side of the tract) was brutally killed (9 December 1906) at Bahe (on the Arakan side of the tract) by its villagers while the victims visited the village to collect tribute.[23]

In the wake of this 'Bahe-Sabong Affair', the Government of Eastern Bengal and Assam (GOEBA) proposed GOB that the Superintendent of Chin Hills and the Deputy Commissioner of Northern Arakan should meet the Superintendent of Lushai Hills to endeavour 'to arrive at a common understanding as to the broad lines to be followed in laying down the administrative boundary' between their jurisdictions.[24] GOB was agreeable to 'any line' which the Lushai Hills Officers 'deemed suitable' provided it 'did not include territory actually administered' by the Deputy Commissioner of the Arakan Hill Tracts or the Superintendent, Chin Hills. Further, GOB too thought it 'desirable' that the proposed line should be discussed by the officers concerned on the spot, and 'they should give their opinion on its suitability. "There may be reasons against the division of tribal limits or the inclusion in Eastern Bengal and Assam of tribes hitherto regarded as politically under the influence of Burma which should be investigated".[25] GOEBA was of the opinion that all the country lying between the 'administered' tracts in Lushai Hills and the similar tracts in Burma should be 'distributed between the several districts of the two provinces and the boundaries of the same modified accordingly".[26] GOEBA even suggested an 'Inner Line' bounding the area of regular administration, and beyond this a 'sphere of influence' through which occasional tours might be taken and administration gradually extended.[27]

---

* In this chapter the term 'unadministered' is used to mean 'outside the administrative control of the British'. This is not to describe complete lack of administration in any form.

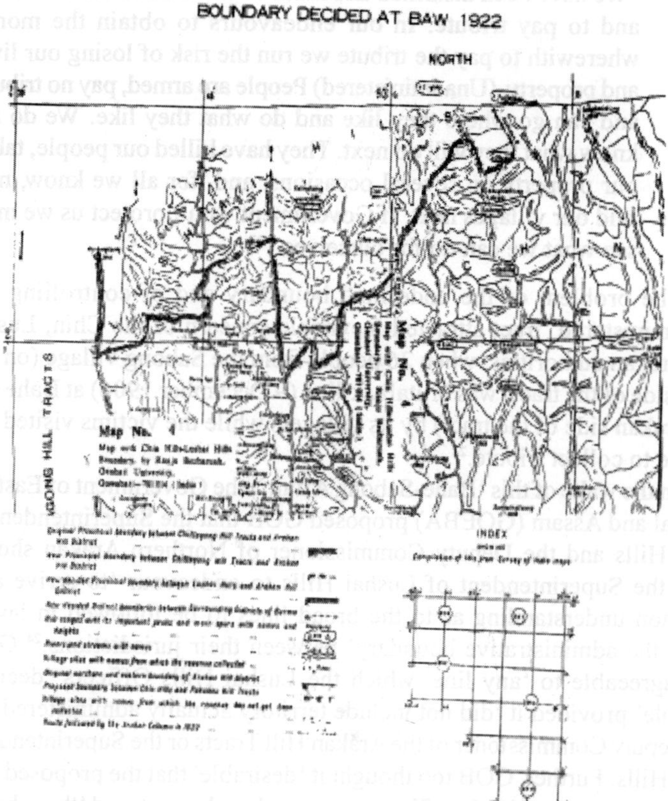

Map 27.4

With this backdrop, a meeting between the Superintendent of Lushai Hills (H.W.G. Cole), the Deputy Commissioner, Arakon (W.L. Thom), and the Superintendent of Chin Hills (W. Street) was arranged at Laki on 25 December, 1907. In a joint memorandum, signed by H.W.G. Cole, W.L. Thom, and W. Street. (January 1908), it was observed that the whole of the 'unadministered' tract (between 92°41′ and 93°15′ east and 21°41′ and 22°20′ north covering about 1,000 sq, miles) should be annexed. "Nothing short of annexation will assure the permanent pacification of the tribes . . . .", they observed. Referring to the principles on the basis of which the tract was to be apportioned, they observed:

We have considered the possibility of making a satisfactory ethnographical or of political division without arriving at any workable solution. In our opinion administrative convenience and economy are dominant factors, and it is quite clear that a boundary based on consideration of tribal and political connection could not be attained without their sacrifice. It is inevitable in view of the peculiar configuration of the country and the existing boundaries of the chiefs along the border which it is undesirable to disturb, that a border recognising existing rights and following natural features, must be some what irregular and lack the neatness on the map of arbitrary delimitation by imaginary lines connecting main points. But we are convinced that any boundary which cannot at once be recognised and accepted by the people themselves will be the cause of endless trouble and friction. The line we propose entirely follows natural features and will only require four boundary pillars at the points where the watersheds are crossed to complete its demarcation'[28]

The conference at Laki also defined the proposed southern boundary of Lushai Hills. The following section of the boundary line proposed to divide the 'unadministered' tract between the Lushai Hills and Chin Hills:

Thence up the Tishi river to where it receives the Luapa Lui, thence up this stream to its source just below Pillar No. 4 on the Missen Tlang. Crossing the range it follows the Niaw Lui from its source to where it discharges into the Upper Kolodyne which forms the existing eastern boundary of the Lushai Hills.[29] Acceptance of this boundary would have left the Sabong villages lying west of Boinu (Kolodyne) and east of Tishi (or Michaung) to the Chin Hills side of the border. This boundary also left Satlong or Saklong (20 houses), and Sapi or Sepi (60 houses) to the Chin side. However, G O I refused to accept the proposed boundary in the 'unadministered tracts'.[30]

In 1911, the Officiating Superintendent of Lushai Hills, Lieutenant-Colonel G.H. Loch proposed a provisional southern boundary between the 'unadministered' tract and Lushai Hills. The proposal, with certain amendments, was forwarded to the Commissioner, Surma Valley and Hill Districts. The proposed boundary was accepted by the Commissioner 'with the proviso that the boundary be subject to revision when the unadministered tract between Assam and Burma on this frontier is eventually absorbed."[31]

The portion of the line passing through the 'unadministered' tract between Lushai Hills and Chin Hills was:

(From the junction of the Tuisiluite with Tuisilui) Up the Tuisilui to the mouth of the Luapalui, up the Luapalui to its source on the Mawmang range (south of the Peak Missen Tlang). Across the saddle to the source of the Niawlui, down the Niawlui to its junction with the Kolodyne river,

LUSHAI-CHIN-ARAKAN BOUNDARY. EXTRACT

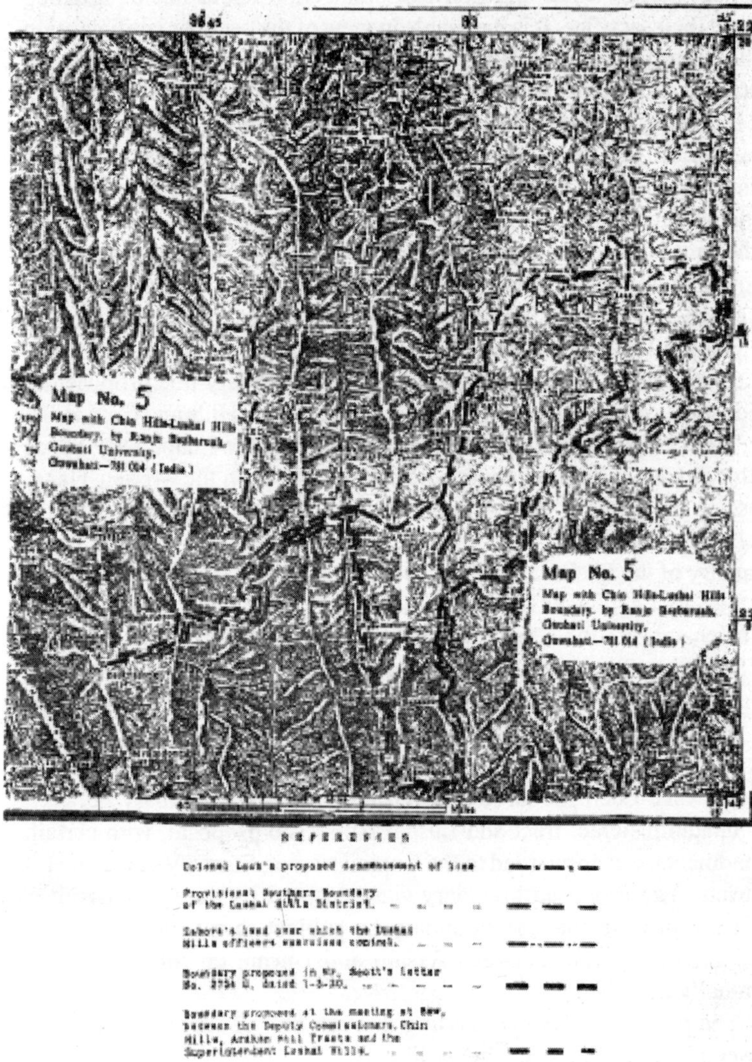

Map 27.5

which forms the accepted boundary between the Lushai and Chin Hills district (latitude 22° 99').[32]

This line, too, left Zongling, Laki, and their sub-villages outside the boundary of Lushai Hills.

The boundary thus defined was demarcated by Mr. Bradshaw, Sub-Divisional Officer, Lungleh, in the winter 1912-13.[33] This boundary was, however, 'intended only to be a provisional one adopted for the guidance of the local offices pending the permanent settlement of the question'. The Chief Commissioner of Assam proposed to address GoI on the question of the boundary 'after further consultation with the local officers'.[34] Further, as this boundary was not co-terminous with the boundaries of the province of Burma, the administrative difficulties arising from the existence of the intermediary 'unadministered' tract persisted.

Mean time, however, the 'Kami Sabong Affair"[35] of 1912-13 once more focussed attention on the problem of the 'unadministered' tract. The Commissioner of the Surma Valley and Hill Districts, for example, not only perceived the absorption of the tract as the 'real remedy', but also thought the 'Kami-Sabong Affair' as affording 'a good opportunity for obtaining the orders of GOI for absorption.[36] While this proposal was disapproved of by GOA (Government of Assam) at the moment, it was recognized that in order to obviate future difficulties in dealing with the tribes 'the first opportunity should be taken to note on the latest maps' all the available information, such as names and location of the villages, and natural features as they were known in Arakan, Chin Hills and Lushai Hills. It was also recognized that attempts should be made to improve both the Burma and the Assam maps so as to 'show clearly the boundaries of the unadministered territory' GOA proposed to this effect on 30 January, 1914.[37]

Accordingly, it was proposed to hold a meeting between the Superintendent of Lushai Hills, Superintendent of Chin Hills and the Deputy Commissioner, Northern Arakan at Laki on 1 March, 1915.[38]

The Superintendent of Lushai Hills, J. Hezlett, suggested that the proposed Laki Conference could also take up 'the whole question of dividing up the unadministered tract' between Burma and Assam.[39] According to him the Tuishi, Tish, Tuipang, Wabling, Mi or Michang) could be a good eastern boundary for Lushai Hills.

Acceptance of Hezlett's proposal would have meant inclusion in the Lushai Hills of the tract between the Sulla (Salo) and Tishi rivers containing the villages of Zongling or Yong Laing and Laki and their sub-villages. They included altogether five villages, containing about 200 houses.[40] This would also have meant Chin Hills taking over of the villages between the Tishi and the Upper Kolodyne or Boinu, known as the Sabong group, containing about 730 houses. They included Sabong Tu, Sabong Pi, Vaki or Baki, Ngapai, Sapi (Sepi) and Saklong (Satlong).[41]

The boundary proposed, was justified by Hezlett both 'ethnically and geographically'. The Zongling and Laki Chiefs belonged to the same clan of Lakhers as the administered Chief of Lushai Hills and spoke 'practically the same language'. The Sabong group of villages, on the other hand, belonged to the Chinzah clan and were connected in many ways with the Chins of the Haka subdivision.[42] Hezlett, therefore, argued that the Tishi formed a 'good natural boundary'. Accordingly Hezlett proposed to accept *mutatis mutandis* the existing provisional boundary as the extended Chin-Lushai boundary west of Boinu or Upper Kolodyne. According to his proposal, the Chin-Lushai portion of the boundary ran thus:

Tishi and up that river to where it meets the Damlui, then up the Damlui to its source of Mizen-Tlang, then along the range to the source of the Niawlui and down that river stream to its junction with the Boinu or Upper Kolodyne.[43]

Hezlett's proposed boundary east of the Tishi practically followed the existing provisional line except that it included the Khulu village, earlier 'administered' but by 1914 'apparently unadministered.'[44]

On the other hand, GOA was not in a favourable frame of mind to add to the territories of Lushai Hills unless it was absolutely necessary. The Commissioner, Surma Valley and Hill Districts was instructed that:

The Officers at the conference should consider the most suitable line for the boundary between Assam and Burma. The Superintendent of the Lushai Hills should be warned not to commit Government in any way and it should be pointed out to him that this Administration does not wish to take over more of the unproductive territory then is absolutely necessary.[45]

Neither was GOB desirous of assuming additional responsibilities. In 1915, in the context of the 'abnormal conditions' arising out of the First World War, GOB intimated to GOA its decision to keep in 'abeyance' the 'suggested extension' of territories.[46] And, constrained by the disturbances in the Kachin Hills, GOB even revoked its orders sanctioning the proposed meeting at Laki.[47]

While the 'precise run of the boundary' was regarded by GOA as a 'matter of minor importance,[48] the *raison d'etre* for urgent apportionment of the 'unadministered' tract nevertheless occurred as the frontier proved susceptible to tension. The insurgency of the Chins of the Haka Subdivision during 1917-1919 [49], precisely gave rise to such a situation. The impact of the insurgency could be soon felt in the border areas; and it seemed as though the neighbouring districts would be affected as well.

The Haka villages of Tangaw, Kwahrang, Shungner, Fantrem and Naring openly rebelled against the Chin Hills authorities. Several rebel Chiefs entered the 'unadministered' territory across the Boinu (Upper Kolodyne) River, where there were several offshoots from the rebel villages. Further, under threats from Tawng Ling, Chief of Tangaw, the villages of Lunsoi (Lungchawi), Ngapai, Paite, Leite, Leile and Laipi also proved recalcitrant.[50]

In 1918-1919, the Chin Hills disturbances led to troubles in the Lushai Hills. Several raids and murders were committed in the neighbourhood of South Vanlaiphai. Even the village of Vawmbuk near Lungleh, far removed from the Chin areas, sympathised with the rebels and refused to obey the orders of Sub-divisional Officer, Lungleh to supply coolies.[51] The Chin village of Longchawi was also deeply involved in encroachments in Lushai Hills territories. They cut *jhums* within the 'administered' areas and declined to pay dues to the Chief concerned.[52] Further, at the beginning of 1919, a group of villagers from Lungchawi raided the 'administered' village of Siata in the south of Lushai Hills district.[53] The raiders apparently came from the Chin Hills through the 'unadministered' tract.

To both GOB and GOA the solution seemed to be the absorption of the 'unadministered' tract by extending their respective 'administered' areas. On 8 September, 1919, GOB, and on 17 October, 1919, GOA proposed to GOI for establishment of 'loose-political control' over the 'unadministered' tract.[54] GOI accepted, in principle, the proposals for extension of 'political control' to the 'unadministered' tract between Arakan, Chin Hills and Lushai Hills on the condition that the actual extension of 'administered control' should wait till the open season of 1920-21. Further, GOI preferred to reserve sanction of the scheme pending the approval of the Secretary of State for India. GOI proposed to submit the proposal to the Secretary of State for India after detailed proposals of GOA and GOB were submitted following a meeting of Assam and Burma frontier Officials during the winter of 1919-20.[55] Accordingly, GOB proposed a meeting between the Chin, Arakan and Lushai Hills Officials at Maymyo in May 1920 to settle the boundaries of the respective 'districts'.[56]

The Maymyo Conference was held on 3 and 4 May, 1920.[57]

Shortly before the Maymyo Conference, Colonel L.W. Shakespear, Deputy Inspector General, Assam Rifles; in a letter to GOA, favoured the idea of Assam's taking over of the villages of Zongling, Laki, Chepi (Chapi), Saklong (Satlong), Sabong and Laikei. Shakespear was of the opinion that the administration of the tract would not necessitate a new post. Because none of the villages was far from the existing post of Tuipang and even the furthest of the villages, Sabong, could be reached in 2 or 3 days' march. Even if a new post was found to be 'desirable', it could be rationed from Arakan side *via* Sullawa and the Sulla river; and a track from the Sulla led to Laki and Sabong.[58]

The Superintendent of Lushai Hills, W.L. Scott, however, insisted on his district getting only Sepi (Sapi) and Saklong (Satlong) of the Sabong group of villages. He argued that the people of these two villages had become indistinguishable from the Lakhers (Shandus) of the Lushai Hills. He proposed that the provisional boundary of Lushai Hills should be revised so as to include these two villages, thus:

> "The Tuishi river to the mouth of the Chaocha stream; up the Chaocha stream to its source on the Kahsia Tlang; along the summit of the Kahsia Tlang north to the source of the Rapu stream; then down the Rapu stream then down the Rapu stream to the Boinu or Upper Kolodyne"[59]

At the Maymyo Conference, the Burma Officials did not object to the proposal of Assam absorbing Zongling, Laikei and Laki. But Chin Hills staked claims over Chapi and Satlong, leave alone Sabong, on the ground of their close relations with already 'administered' Chin villages. Arakan Officials, apart from claiming the Sullawa tongue; also objected the proposal for Tuipang being rationed through Arakan. They hunched that in that case the Assam authorities would have to be continually asking for assistance in coolies and other transport from Arakan.[60]

The Conferees of Maymyo reached the consensus that if the enclave on the Sulla river were allotted to Burma, the line proposed by W.L. Scott between the Tuishi and the Boinu rivers leaving Chapui and Satlong to the Lushai Hills should be accepted.[61] Between the Sulla enclave and the two Sabong villages (Chapi-Satlong), Scott preferred the latter; because Sullawa was 'too faraway to be easily reached by us', while it was necessary for the Northern Arakan Hill Tracts in managing the area proposed to be taken over.[62]

In this backdrop, the Governor General in Council intended to invite reconsideration of the policy of non-intervention vis-à-vis the 'unadministered' tract enunciated by Lord Morley in 1908.[63] In response to the proposal of GOI dated 27 January, 1921, the Secretary of State for India had sanctioned the proposal to extend over the 'unadministered' area a loose political control. The so-called 'loose political control' should be 'confined to tours of inspection by a civil officer every two years for the purpose of collecting tribute and settling disputes.[64]

In the context of the sanction, a meeting was arranged between the Deputy Commissioners of Chin Hill (L.E. Burne), Arakan Hills Tracts (W. Thom) and the Superintendent of Lushai Hills (S.N. Mackenzie) on 31 January, 1922 at Baw.[65]

While the basis for discussion at Baw, ought to have been the consensus reached at Maymyo in May 1920, the Deputy Commissioner of Chin Hills, L.E. Burne, insisted on the undesirability of separating Chapui and Satlong from the Sabong villages on the ground that all of them were originally founded from the 'Maram' villages of Paite and Ngapai, and that there was no administrative reasons for splitting the group, the Lushai Hills could take it *en bloc* along with the two Sabong villages, Boki (Baki or Vaki) and the three Lailen villages. The Lushai authorities, however, turned down the proposal on the ground that they were not authorised to take over villages other than Chapui and Satlong.[66] On the other hand, the Lushai Hills authorities insisted on getting Chapui and Satlong on the ground that the Lungleh subdivision being very sparsely populated, these villages could supply coolies for transport to ration the outposts of Tuipang and Sherkor.[67] Further it was already agreed at Maymyo by the Burma authorities to Ieave Chapui and Satlong to Lushai Hills in case of abdication by the Lushai Hills of its claim over the Sulla tongue.[68] In reply to objection raised by the Chin Hills authorities, the Superintendent of Lushai Hills, S.N. Mackenzie argued that Chapui and Satlong did not pay tribute to Sabong unless they cultivated in Sabong land. This was admitted by the Sabongs as well. Each of these villages had a clearly defined area, and even though the tribal group was broken up, Sabong thereby would not lose the "only tribute it could rightfully claim", i.e., tribute for cultivating Sabong land.[69] The Lushai Hills officials also laid stress on the fact that on being asked by Major Burne at Baw, whether he would like to be under the Chin Hills or the Lushai Hills, Ram Si, Chief of Chapui expressed his indifference.[70] Obviously referring to the phrase *divide et impera* (divide and rule), Mackenzie maintained: ".:. far from sharing the horror of the Deputy Commissioner, Chin Hills, at the idea of breaking up a tribal group of villages, I consider a powerful tribal group under a common head a source of danger. There is a very ancient Latin tag, which has its application here".[71]

Finally, however, Deputy Commissioner of Chin Hills, Burne, gave in and agreed to give up the claim over Chapui and Satlong to avoid a deadlock, but "under protest" and subject to the final acceptance of the proposal by GOB.[72]

The acceptance of the proposal to include Chapui and Satlong meant the endorsement of the boundary proposed by W.L. Scott at Maymyo. However, a minor deviation from the Scott's boundary had to be made when it was discovered that there was a Sabong settlement on a spur just north of the Chaccha river. It was decided to leave the area to Sabong rather than Zongling and boundary was moved slightly northward, to the Kheimu, which flowed into the Tuishi at the same point as the Chaccha.[73] The sole deviation from the Scott's boundary was the replacement of the Chaccha by the Kheimu to facilitate the transfer of this small area to the Sabongs.

The Chin-Lushai boundary as finally agreed upon by the conference at Baw ran thus:

Starting from the point of the Tuishi where the boundary between the Lushai Hills and the Arakan Hill Tracts terminates; up the Tuishi to the mouth of the Kheimu, up the Kheimu to its source on the Kahria Tlang down the summit of the Kahria Tlang to the source of the Raphu, then down the Raphu to the Bionu or Upper Kaladan, which is the recognized boundary between the Lushai Hills and the Chin Hills.[74]

Since the new boundary was based on the principles agreed at Maymyo in 1920, GOB intimated GOA that it was, not in a position to object.[75]

Thus the new boundary between the Tuishi and the Boinu, left the Sabong villages of Sabong Ti and Sabong Pi, Vaki (Baki), two Lalaoing (Lallaing) and three Nagapai villages to the Chin Hills side of the Chin-Lushai boundary, and Chapi and Satlong to the Lushai Hills side. The boundary fixed at Baw was in accord with the one agreed at Maymyo in 1920 with the singular exception of the replacement of the Chaccha by the Kheimu.

REFERENCES

1. With effect from 1 April, 1895. Annual Report on the Native States and Frontier Tribes of Assam, for the year 1898-99, 28.
2. The problems created by the interposition of the tract are discussed in, Ranju Bezboruah, "Problem of the 'Unadministered' Tract and the Evolution of the Lushai Hills—Northern Arrakan Boundary, 1898-1931",

paper presented at the XII Annual Session of North-East India History Association, November 1991.

3. See, H.K.Barpujari, *Problems of the Hill Tribes, North-East Frontier, 1873-1962*, Vol. III, Gauhati, 1981, p. 90.
4. C.U. Aitchison, comp., *A Collection of Treaties, Engagements and Sanads relating to India and Neighbouring Countries*, Vol. XII, Delhi 1983 (reprint), pp. 218-219.
5. Barpujari, n 3, *op. cit.*, p. 98.
6. *Ibid.*, pp., 90,105.
7. Colonel L.W. Shakespear, *History of the Assam Rifles*, Gauhati 1980 (reprint), p. 92.
8. For example, Foreign Department letter No. 139 IE., dated 3 July, 1890, to the Chief Commissioner of Assam; Foreign Dept letter No. 1396 E., dt. 3 July, 1890, to the Govt. of Bengal; and Burma political letter No. 787-26-14, dt. 28, July 1893. Cited in Bertram S. Carey and H.N. Tuck, *The Chin Hills*, Vol. I, Aizawal, 1976 (reprint), p. 5. (f.n. 2).
9. *Ibid.*, p. 63.
10. *Ibid.*, p. 5 read with f.n. 2.
11. *Ibid.*, pp. 153-160.
12. Assam Secretariat Proceedings, political-A (ASPPA), June 1906, No. 321 A-2 C.-1, Govt. of Burma political Dept., F.C. Gates to Chief Secy. to Govt. of E. Bengal and Assam, dt. 18 October 1905.
13. *Ibid.*
14. Ranju Bezbaruah, n 3 *op. cit.*, n 2.
15. ASPPA, Feb. 1908, No. 24.
16. Suhas Chatterjee, *Mizoram under the British Rule*, Delhi, 1985, pp. 137-138.
17. *Annual Report on the Native States and Frontier Tribes of Assam*, for the year 1900-1901, p. 14.
18. ASPPA, Jan. 1911, No. 41. Tele. No. 165 G., dt.Aijal 22 Aug. 1912, from Suptd. Lushai Hills to Secy. Govt of E. Bengal and Assam Pol. Dept.
19. ASPPA, Mar. 1908, Nos. 18, 19.
20. For the importance of this trade route, see Major H.W.G. Cole's (Officiating Superintendent of Lushai Hills) views, excerpted in *Annual Report on the Administration of the Lushai Hills*, for the year 1910-1911, pp. 5-6.
21. ASPPA, June, 1906, F.C. Gates' letter, dt. 18 July, 1905, No. 743-2c-9. Govt. of Burma, Political Dept.
22. ASPPA, June 1906, E.O. Fowler to Chief Secy., Govt. of Burma, No. 211 C, dt. 14 May, 1905.
23. ASPPA, Feb. 1908, Nos. 38, 60.
24. ASPPA, Feb. 1908, No. 26.
25. ASPPA, Feb. 1908, No. 37.
26. ASPPA, Feb. 1908, No. 42.
27. ASPPA, Feb. 1908, No. 42.

28. ASPPA, Mar. 1908, No. 18.
29. ASPPA, Mar. 1908, No. 20.
30. Proposals regarding the 'unadministered tract' was submitted to Govt. of India in Hughes-Butler's letter No. 5500 J, dt. 21 Dec. 1908. GOI through letter No. 41 E.C., dt. 9 Jan. 1909, stated that the proposals could not be considered. Cited in B.C. Allen's letter to Govt. of India, dt. 27 May, 1916. ASPPA, May 1916, No. 44. Also, ASPPA, Jan. 1911, No. 42.
31. ASPPA, Jan. 1912, No. 7.
32. ASPPA, Jan. 1912, Encl. (2) to progs: No. 7.
33. ASPPA, Sept. 1915, No. Also ASPPA, Mar. 1914, No. 10.
34. ASPPA, Mar. 1914; No. 10, para 3, 4.
35. Ranju Bezbaruah, "Kami-Sabong Affair: Question of British Intervention in the`Unadministered' Tract between Burma and Assam (paper to be presented at the Delhi session of the Indian History Congress, 1992) gives details.
36: ASPPA, Mar. 1914, No. 15.
37. ASPPA, Mar. 1914, No. 16; also ASPPA, May 1916, No. 44.
38. ASPPA, Sept. 1915, No. 4, 5, 6.
39. ASPPA, Sept. 1915, No. 5.
40. ASPPA, Sept. 1915, No. 5.
41. ASPPA, Sept. 1915, No. 5 read with ASPPA, Mar. 1908, No. 19.
42. ASPPA, Sept. 1915, No. 5.
43. ASPPA, Sept. 1915, No. 5.
44. ASPPA, Sept. 1915, No. 5.
45. ASPPA, Sept. 1915, No. 6. B.C. Allen's letter, dt. 16 Oct. 1914. Emphases added.
46. ASPPA, June 1916, No. 70.
47. ASPPA, Sept 1915, No. 7, Govt. of Burma's Tele. dt. 5 Feb. 1915; Also ASPPA, May 1916, No. 41. Govt. of Burma's. Tele. dt 14. Jan. 1916.
48. ASPPA, May 1916, No. 44, B.C. Allen's letter. dt. 27 May 1916.
49. *See*, C.U. Aitchinson, *op. cit.*, p. 219.
50. ASPPA, June 1921, No. 24.
51. Annual Report on the Frontier Tribes of Assam, for the year 1918-19, p. 5.
52. *Ibid.*
53. *Ibid.*; ASPPA, June 1921, No. 24.
54. ASPPA, June 1921, Nos. 6, 3.
55. ASPPA, June 1921, No. 6.
56. ASPPA, June 1921, No. 14.
57. ASPPA, June 1921, No. 38.
58. ASPPA, June 1921, No. 25. Tuipang post was built in 1907.
59. ASPPA, Mar, 1924, No. 42.
60. ASPPA, June 1921, No. 38.
61. ASPPA, Mar. 1924, No. 41.

62. ASPPA, June 1921, No. 38.
63. Lord Morley's Political despatch No. 128 dt. 13 Nov. 1908 cited in ASPPA, March, 1924, No. 2.
64. ASPPA, Mar. 1924, No. 2.
65. ASPPA, Mar. 1924, Nos. 42, 41, 34.
66. ASPPA, Mar. 1924, Nos. 42, 45, 34.
67. ASPPA, Mat 1924, Nos. 42, 45.
68. ASPPA, Mar. 1924, No. 42.
69. ASPPA, Mar. 1924, No. 33.
70. ASPPA, Mar. 1924, Nos. 42, 45, 34.
71. ASPPA, Mar. 1924, No. 33.
72. ASPPA, Mar. 1924, Nos. 42, 33, 34.
73. ASPPA, Mar. 1924, No. 33.,
74. ASPPA, Mar. 1924, Nos. 34, 45, 59.
75. ASPPA, Mar. 1924, No. 41.

28

Inner Line (Mizoram) : A Study in Historical Perspective

Lalrimawia

Formerly there was unrestricted intercourse between British subjects in the plains of Assam and the wild tribes living across the frontier. But there broke out frequent quarrels and, sometimes, serious disturbances between the former and the latter. This was particularly the case in connection with the traffic in rubber brought down by the tribes, for which there was great competition. The extension of tea gardens, as mentioned earlier, beyond the border line also frequently involved the Government in troublesome disputes with the hillmen. To obviate frictions Government of India decided that certain special rules should be laid down by taking up special powers. Accordingly, in 1872, the provisions of Act XXXIII Vict., Cap.3, section 1, was made applicable with effect from the 1 January, 1873, in Cachar and Chittagong Hill Tracts. Subsequently, Bengal Eastern Frontier Regulation 1 of 1873 was passed for the frontier districts. This Regulation had given power to the Lieutenant Governor to prescribe a line, to be called the "Inner Line" in each of the tribal areas beyond which no British subjects or those of specified classes could pass without a licence! Accordingly Inner Line started on the southern frontier of the District of Cachar, from the site of the outposts established during the Lushai Expedition of 1871-72:

. . . . to the outposts of Chatter Choora and Jhalnacherra; thence along the Dullessur River . . . . to the south-west corner of the Jhalnacherra grant, ... along the southern boundary of the Jhalnacherra grant, across the Jhalnacherra Khal . . . . to Barooncherra grant . . . . . From the north-eastern corner of the Barooncherra grant, ... to the Rengti Pahar range; thence—along the ridge of the Rengti Pahar range in a northern direction, ... range bifurcates into two . . . . one leading to the Clave house, the other to the Bara Jalinga grant, ... From the point of bifurcation . . . . along the Jalinga River to the south-east corner of the Sonacherragrant; . . . . it follows the police road to the Rukni River . . . . to the western boundary of the Monierkhal grant; . . . . to the river Sonai . . . . to Mynadhur . . . . to the River Barak.[2]

Under this Regulation the local authorities were empowered to prohibit British subjects from beyond the Inner Line without a pass issued by the Deputy Commissioner of Cachar. However, a pass could be issued subject to such condition and limitation, as might appear necessary. The line laid down did not necessarily indicate the territorial frontier but only the limits of the administered area. Neither it decided the sovereignty of the territory beyond.[3]

Under the same provisions, the Inner Line of the Chittagong Hill Tracts was also notified in June 1879 as follows: This line of boundary commences at the hill station marked *S*, south of Betting Sib (Behliang Chhip) 2234, on the Jampoi range . . . . along the whole course of the "Tulenpui" or "Sujjuk" River to its junction with the Karnafuli River . . . . to the junction of the "Tui Chong" River . . . . to . . . . Opihum No. 5 . . . . joins the Thega Khall . . . . follows the watershed of the Weybong . . . . meets . . . . Keokradong . . . . meets . . . . portion of the Arakan Hill Tracts . . . . [4]

The Inner Line was strictly in force till 1895[5] The Political Officer, North Lushai Hills, however, proposed in 1895 that it should be allowed to fall into destitute as it effected the free egress and ingress of all people from the districts of Cachar and Silent (Syhlet) into the Lushai Hills. When both the Deputy Commissioner of Silent (Syhlet) and Cachar raised no objection, the Chief Commissioner of Assam sanctioned the proposal. Theoretically no pass was required to enter the Lushai Hills district from Cachar. Yet many persons continued to approach the Deputy Commissioner, Cachar, for a pass, and in such case a pass was issued. The question of pass did not arise with the district of Silent (Syhlet) since there was no direct communication with the district. Foreigners were allowed to proceed upto the first police outpost in the Lushai Hills with or without a pass. In case of travel by rivers, the outpost was Sairang on the Dhaleswari river, and if the travel was by road, the outpost was Kolasib on the Aijal-Silchar road. In these outposts, foreigners, going to Aijal, were detained until the permission of the Superintendent or Assistant Superintendent was obtained to proceed to Aijal, unless as in many cases, permission was previously obtained. The former had to report themselves to the latter as soon as they arrived at Aijal, and then a pass was issued for residence, temporary' or semi-temporary as the case might be in the Lushai Hills. A pass for temporary residence was seldom refused. Only when the character of the applicant was known to be bad, or the purpose of his visit questionable then pass was not issued to the person concerned. Traders, shopkeepers and the like, including their agents were freely given passes for semi-permanent residence. Telegraphic communication was maintained effectively between Aijal and the outposts. Similar procedure was followed in the case of Lungleh Sub-Division; passes were still required to enter the district. Any person who arrived at Demagiri, the outpost on the Karnaphuli river, reported himself to Sub-Divisional Officer, Lungleh, who then issued a pass.[6]

As a matter of fact the Inner Line legally in force in the Lushai Hills district was the Inner Line of the Cachar District. It was only the Deputy Commissioner, Cachar not Superintendent, Lushai Hills, who was competent to issue passes for crossing the Inner Line. To legalise the position the Governor in Council considered that the last course would be to replace the Cachar Inner Line for the Lushai Hills district. This would give the Superintendent the necessary legal authority to control entry into the Lushai Hills.[7]

Cachar Inner Line replaced by that of Lushai Hills

In June 1930, W.A. Cosgrave, Officiating Chief Secretary to the Government of Assam, explained to the Government of India that hitherto Lushai Hills was not an administered British district but a *terra incognita* inhabited by savage tribes. Lands were leased out for tea in the Cachar district near its boundary with the Lushai Hills and, therefore, it was necessary to prevent adventurous planters, traders and *shikaris* or hunters from making excursions across the boundary line which might lead to political complications. Secondly, the Lushai Hills became an administered district under resident British Officers in 1890. The Lushais soon proved themselves more civilised than any other hill tribes on the North-East Frontier, and the necessity for the Old Cachar Inner Line diminished. In 1895, under the order of the Chief Commissioner, the Inner Line was allowed to fall into destitute, so far as it affected and free egress and ingress of all natives of India from the districts of Cachar and Silent (Syhlet) into the Lushai Hills. Simultaneously, orders were passed that all Lushais should be required to take out passes before going to the plains or to the Manipur state. It is not certain whether the Government of India were informed of these orders. In spite of all these, the old Inner Line of the Cachar district had never been formally abolished.[8]

Cosgrave made it clear that the Lushai Hills became one of the most peaceful districts in Assam after a few years of British occupation. It is, therefore, necessary to protect the Lushais against the immigration of undesirable foreigners. These foreigners were divided into two classes—Bengali shopkeepers and Nepali graziers. In case of the former bazar sites were small and not capable of extension, and they were already over populated. The problem of water supply, sanitation and fuel supply were becoming increasingly difficult. Besides, it was feared that if the Bengali shopkeepers were allowed to enter the Lushai without control, they would probably indulge in illicit trade, such as arms and ammunition, drugs and possibly also procuration of women: In the past unlicensed guns used to reach the Lushai Hills *via* Chittagong Port, and so the Governor-in-Council wanted that there should be some measure of control over the entry of Bengali shopkeepers into the Lushai Hills. As regards to Nepalis, they usually came to see their alleged relatives in the First Assam Rifles, which is permanently stationed at Aijal, the headquarters of the Lushai Hills. The Nepal Darbar represented frequently that Nepalis should not be encouraged to settle in Assam. The Lushais, who is dependent on the *jhuming* system of cultivation disliked the Nepali grazier with his herd of buffaloes, which damaged the bamboo forest.[9]

In Lushai Hills district, the Bengal Eastern Frontier Regulation of 1873 had never been extended. But for the last twenty years, successive Superintendents had, by executive orders, endeavoured to control the ingress of foreigners into the district, and had punished disobedience to these orders under section 188 I.P.C. It was pointed out that similar control over the ingress of foreigners had been exercised by the Deputy Commissioner, Naga Hills, and the Political Officer, Sadiya Frontier Tract. There had been an Inner Line in respect of both these areas.[10]

In consideration of these facts the Government of Assam submitted in September 1930 three draft notifications for consideration of the Government of India; viz. :

(i) the extension of the Bengal Eastern Frontier Regulation (V of 1873) to the Lushai Hills;

(ii) the prescription of the northern boundaries of the Lushai Hills district as the inner line of the district under this Regulation; and

(iii) the abolition of the inner line of the Cachar district.[11]

The Government of India approved the notifications.[12] Accordingly, the Government of Assam prohibited all persons passing through the

Lushai Hills district other than officers on government duty, from going beyond the 'Inner Line' without a pass under the hand and seal of the Superintendent, Lushai Hills. However, foreigners who have been permitted to reside in the district and indigenous inhabitants of the district were exempted from the prohibition against crossing the Inner Line.[13]

The Government of India suggested one consolidated Inner Line for the Lushai Hills district and a fresh notification superseding the earlier one.[14] Accordingly the Governor-in-Council issued a notification prescribing the line as the "Inner Line" of the Lushai Hills district.

Till today, the notification, regarding the Inner Line of the Lushai Hills district, issued by the Assam Government, continue to be the Inner Line of the district. So far no modifications had been made as regards to the disputed point nor any survey undertaken.

Needless to say, the Lushai Hills Inner Line had been an effective instruments in checking large scale immigration of undesirable foreigners into the district. Had not been this Regulation introduced, the district might have been completely infiltrated, like those of Tripura and Assam and in a lesser degree, Meghalaya and Manipur. Fortunately, the Hills had been safeguarded and foreigner's problem has not been a serious issue like most of the North Eastern States. At present, the numbers of foreigners are almost negligible throughout the district, but the Chakmas of Chittagong Hill Tract have been in the habit of immigrating into Chakma Autonomous district area in the South Mizoram, which had considerably increased their numbers recently. If this is not checked effectively, there is every possibility of large scale influx of these tribes into Mizoram. Since the issue of permit for entry and residential passes had been restricted, there are only a few Bengali families of shopkeepers who had been in possession of a residential house of their own within the district. Nonetheless, there exists a number of Nepalese who had been settling and acquiring land of theirs in different parts of the district. Even this is not a serious problem. The material result of all this is that, not like the Assam, Meghalaya and Tripura, most of the rich business people and big contractors belong to Mizo community themselves.

REFERENCES

1. Aitchinson, *Eastern Bengal and Assam*, 11, Part III, p. 132.
2. A. Mackenzie, *History of the Relations with the British Government with the Frontier Tribes of N.E.India,* 1884, Appendix B, p. 395.

IV-Notification by the Government of India, Foreign Department No. 2299 p., 20 August 1875 as modified under 19 June, 1878.

3. E.A. Gait, *A History of Assam*, Reprint, 1967, p. 387.
4. A. Mackenzie, *op.cit.*, p. 397. V-Notification by the Government of Bengal, dated the 30 June 1879.
5. A.S., For A, January 1896, Nos. 7-14.
6. AS., No. 33; The Superintendent of Lushai Hills, 18 March, 1929 to Under Secretary to the Government of Assam.
7. AS., Pol A, December. 1930, No. 34; Chief Secretary to the Government of Assam, 14 May, 1929 to the Commissioner, Surma Valley and Hill Division.
8. *Ibid.*, No. 52; Cosgrave, Officiating Chief Secretary to the Government of Assam, to the Government of India, 4 June, 1930.
9. *Ibid.*
10. *Ibid.*
11. AS., Pol. A, December 1930, Nos. 58-60; Notification 9 September, 1930.
12. *Ibid.*, No. 57; Government of India. For. and Pol. Department, 25 July, 1930 to Chief Secretary. For the prescribed "Inner Line", Vide the Government of Assam's description of the northern boundary of Lushai Hills as revised by the Director of Survey.
13. *Ibid.*, No. 61; Notification 28 August, 1930.
14. *Ibid.*, Government of India's, Foreign Pol. Department, 24 February 1933 to the Chief Secretary to the Government. of Assam.

29

The Mizo Identity and Mizoram

L.B. Thanga IAS

The terms Mizo and Mizoram are now in the Statute books of the country and will remain so perhaps for generations. To begin first with the latter, namely Mizoram, Pu K. Zawla, aged about 90 years now but still mentally alert and physically active, is one of the most prolific writers on the lives, folk lores and traditions of the Mizos of old. His book, the MIZO PI PUTE LEH AN THLAHTE (The Mizos, their ancestors and descendants), first published in 1964, is one of the most exhaustives on the hitherto unrecorded ancient past of the Mizos, and could be one of the most authoritatives on the subject. Sometime ago, Pu Zawla said to me somewhat nonchalantly but in a very matter of fact manner that but for LALSAVUNGA the Mizoram of today would not be what it is but would have comprised of the land west of Tlawng (Dhaleswari) river only. When I asked him if he had propounded this fact of immense historical importance in any of his earlier expositions for future research by modern scholars, he was apologetic. However, one could see that he did not view with quite fervour the urge to call someone or another of the present day politicians as the Mizo *Hnam Pa* (Father of the Mizos). It is not like the case of Mahatma Gandhi who is universally accepted as the Father of the Nation by everybody inhabiting *Bharat,* that is India.

In all the publications of the Government of Mizoram, the total geographical area of Mizoram is given as 21,081 sq. km. and its location as Degree is 92° 20′ to 93° 29′ E (longitude) and 20° 21′ to 24° 27′ N (latitude). The entire length of the eastern and southern Mizoram is bounded by Burma (now Myanmar). Three-fourth approximately of the western Mizoram is bounded by Bangaladesh, and it is only in the remaining one-fourth and the northern tip of Mizoram that it is contiguous to the rest of India. The strategic importance of Mizoram could thus be appreciated. With respect to its size, as in the case of Nagaland, Meghalaya or Arunachal Pradesh who were all parts of Assam constitutionally at the time of independence, Mizoram also has claims of certain tracts in the adjoining Cachar of Assam: However, since no territorial jurisdiction of State can be too rigid, being subjected to changes for a number of reasons, for our present exercise the area of Mizoram as given by the Government could be taken. Thus far for the term MIZORAM.

In the annals of the reigns of the Tripura and the Manipur kings.[1] We find mention of wild hill tribes commonly called KUKIS after the post-East India Company's period only, and these Kukis lived partly in the hills and the plains. From the RAJMALA (the history of the ancient kings of Tripura by Babu Kailash Chandra Sinha, the erstwhile prime minister of Maharaja Birendra Kishore (1909-1923), the independent kingdoms of Cachar, Manipur and Tripura were contiguous to one another before the Britishers conquered them. However, we find no mention whether any of them had suzereignty over the hills now known as Mizoram; and when some of these hillmen attacked the people in the plains of Barak and Surma valleys and the British India advised the Maharaja of Tripura to restrain them assuming that they were his subjects, the Maharaja disowned them.[2]

Who then were the original inhabitants of today's Mizoram? Who also was/were the original owner/owners of the land or was it a no-man's land before the Britishers came? When and how did the Mizos come and possess the land? Finally, who are these Mizos?

From the time of their first contact with the inhabitants of the present day Mizoram towards the close of the eighteenth. century, the Britishers had consistently refused to acknowledge or recognise the Mizos or Mizoram. These two terms were simply non-existent in their terminology. They first chose the KUKI appellation, then the LUSEI-KUKI and finally LUSHAI by corrupting the original LUSEI. After annexation of the land, they gave to it the name of the LUSHAI HILLS DISTRICT within the then province of Assam. The inhabitants were called LUSHAIS. On the other hand, the missionaries who came from the United Kingdom almost simultaneously with the annexation of the Mizo land preferred to call themselves ZOSAP, meaning White-Zo thereby signifying that their difference with the local people was only in their colour while they identified themselves with them wholly in all other respects. The immense dividends obtained by the missionaries in this regard are now part of the modern history. If only those in the then government were as discerning as these missionaries were, much of the acrimonious debates in later years and continuing till today as to whether MIZO or ZOMI or simple ZO is the most appropriate name of this non-Indo-Aryan stock of people living in what was once the unknown and unfriendly hills sandwitched between the Chindwin valley of Burma in the east and the Cachar-Sylhet plains in the west could have been largely lessened if not altogether avoided.

I have in the above used the term 'non Indo-Aryan' with a significance. I have often heard educated Mizos, both young as well as some elderly, explaining to non-Mizo friends that MIZO simply means a highlander by translating MI as man and ZO as highland or hill. This is too simplistic an explanation and is not only inexcusable but also obnoxious smacking of ignorance. It is all the more execrable when such an interpretation is given in official or other august functions like the one organised, say, to welcome the distinguished members of the Senate of the Serampore University who for once held their Convocation at Aizawl when a number of distinguished scholars and renowned theologians from all over the country and outside came to Mizoram. I was shuddered as I had always been proud to be a Mizo and cherish all the Mizoism that goes with it.

There is a distinct stock of people who could indisputably be called belonging to one ethnic group, Mongoloid in all respects, speaking closely allied dialects of the Indo-Tibetan origin. This ethnic group of people are known by the name of ZO. This is confirmed by T.H. Lewin when he wrote, "The generic name of the whole nation is DZO."[3] I had earlier referred to the stubborn refusal of the British to use to terms Mizo or Mizoram. However, there were few among their officers who were understanding and Col. Lewin was one of them and the Mizos lovingly called him THANGLIANA.

One of the best documented accounts of the ZO I have so far come across is the one by Dr. Vumson.[4] To better understand the relationship between the various groups of Zo people, Dr. Vumson categorized them into six major groups, namely, Asho, Masho, Sho, Laimi, Mizo and Zomi. All Zo people living in Arakan and on the Burmese plains except those in the Kale-Kabaw-Myittha valleys as well as the Khyangs in the Chittagong Hill Tract are the Ashos. The Masho includes the Mru, Khami and Khumi, and dwell in the Paletwa area, the eastern hilly region of Chittagong and in the northern Arakan. The Shos are in Mindat-Kanpetlet and south Matupi. The Laimi which includes the Pawis are in Matupi, Falam, Haka and the Pawi-Lakher region of Mizoram. The Zomi includes Paite and a number of tribes akin to Kukis in Manipur. The Mizo and Zomi might be said to be closest.

Pastor Vanchhunga was one of the first evangelists amongst the Mizos. He was an ardent student of the Mizo history. He served the Welsh Presbyterian Mission in Mizoram and Manipur from 1903 for over thirty years. He travelled widely on foot not only the length and breadth of Mizoram and Manipur but also deep into Burma to study the past history of the Mizos. It is believed that the Zos led a peaceful life during their settlement in the Chindwin valley, but afterwards they moved west into the rugged hills in the west which spread over a number of years, contacts between them became rarer developing thereby differences in dialects and habits. The Luseis had the reputation of absorbing the smaller language groups into Lusei speaking people and those called by the Luseis as AWZIA (meaning indistinct speakers) such as Chawhte, Ngente, Khawlhring, Vangchhia, Pautu, Rawite, Tlau, Renthlei, Zawngte, Khiangte and quite a few others had given up the use of their distinctive dialects in favour of Lusei. On the other hand, the Ralte, Hmar, Paite and Pawi continue to retain their respective dialects. At the same time, Pastor Vanchhunga asserted that all of them collectively call themselves Mizos and the Lusei dialect, also called DUHLIAN, was known by all as MIZO TAWNG (Mizo Language).[5]

Reverting back to Dr. Vumson, in establishing that the word "Lushai", a corruption of "Lusei", is often wrongly interpreted as "headhunter" by translating the Mizo word LU as head and SHAI as shoot, Dr. Vumson traced the genealogy of the ZO clan showing a close link between the Lusei, Hualngo and Songthu (Chawngthu) clans. He recorded Songthu and Ngaite as brothers at the fourth generation from Zo. Luseia in turn was the grandson of Ngaite. Descended from Luseia in the fifth generation was one Hualthan who had two sons, namely Hualnam and Hualngo. The Mizos of today's Mizoram are their descendants while the Zomis and few others who still go by the name of Kukis in Manipur are from the Songthu line.

Now that we know who the Mizos are and their habitat in earlier days was in the Chindwin-Irrawady valleys of Burma, our next exercise would be how they came to their present habitat of Mizoram. Here again, absence of any written records is our greatest handicap. Fortunately, however, all the Mizos are reputed for their love of music and songs. Many folk lores, songs and tales, some of them as old as the beginning of the Christian era or even earlier, were passed down by words of mouths generations after generations. It has, therefore, been possible to establish fairly accurately that in a series of migrations beginning from the North by the Hmars, the Hualngos in the south and the Luseis in the centre, they began occupying the present day Mizoram before the close of the fifteenth. century. Mizo historians like Pastor Liangkhaia,[6] Pu Zatluanga,[7] Pu V.L.

Siama[8] besides Pastor Vanchhunga and Pu K. Zawla [9] agreed with this. No doubt, some like Prof. G.H. Luce[10] placed the Mizo migration of India from Burma during the sixteenth. century. Pu Zawla was quite specific and put 1466 AD as the time the Mizos came to settle at Lentlang. In any case, the series of migrations could have spread over a period of years while the fact remains that the Mizos have been in the present day Mizoram for not less than four hundred years; and this, by any standard, is long enough to call the land as their own.

I had earlier briefly mentioned about the continuing acrimonious debates as to which of the two names, MIZO or ZOMI, is correct. It is human nature that no one would like to accept a name other than the one he/she calls himself/herself. In this, the Britishers had made a grievous mistake of forcibly clubbing all the Mizos under Lushai and calling their land Lushai Hills. The revulsion of the Mizo people to this was so intense that soon after independence they were changed to the present Mizo and Mizo Hills to become Mizoram on the attainment of statehood. When the Mizo Union, the first political party in Mizoram, was established on the eve of the Independence, all other offshoots of Zo origin outside Mizoram would have readily accepted Mizo as their common name. I know that the Mizo Union was heartily welcomed in Manipur, Tripura and the Chittagong Hill Tracts and units of this party were organised in many villages. They had high hopes in the Mizo Union leadership to fulfil their aspiration for unification of all Zo people under a unified administration. Perhaps the leaders of the Mizo Union and other politicians of Mizoram were too busy sorting out their problems with the Government of Assam and had belied the hopes and aspirations of their brethren in the adjoining areas of Mizoram. Such a situation cannot last and the political scenario soon changed because the urge to uphold one's identity cannot remain suspended. The Chins in Burma had always believed that the name Chin could encompass all the divergent Zo people. The Pawi specially those in Mizoram who hardly distinguish themselves from the Mizos now call themselves LAI, obviously abbreviating from the original Laimi. We have the Paite National Council, the Hmar People Convention and many others, each with one or more demands. It is hoped that all these would, at least in some degree, help studies of the MIZOS in the right perspectives.

REFERENCES

1. (a) *Manipur*—A Study, Prof. N. Tombi Singh, Rajesh Printing Press, Delhi-6, 1972.

(b) *Progressive Tripura*, Apurba Chandra Bhattacharyya, Sudha Press, 198-1, Cornwallis Street, Calcutta, 1930.

2. *The North-East Frontier of India*, Alexander Mackenzie, First published in 1884 entitled "History of the Relation of the Government with the Hill Tribes of the North-East Frontier of Bengal. "Reprinted 1978.
3. *A Fly on a Wheel or flow I helped to govern India*, Lieut. Col. Thomas H. Lewin, W.H. Allen & Co., 13 Waterloo Place, London, 1885.
4. *Zo History*, Vumson C/o N.T. Thawnga, Venghlui, Aizawl, Mizoram.
5. *Lusei Leh a Vela Ilnam Dangte*, Pastor Vanchhunga, Zoram Printing Press, Aizawl, 1955.
6. *Mizo Chanchin Bu* 1, Rev. Liangkhaia, Hmingliana & Sons, Zoram Printing Press, Aizawl, 1957.
7. *Mizo Chanchin*, Zatluanga, Mizo Academy of Letters, Aizawl and Khuma Printing Press, Aizawl, 1966.
8. *Mizo History*, V.L. Siama, Sialhawk, Lalrinliana, Bara Bazar, Aizawl, 19[illegible]3.
9. *Mizo Pi Pute leh and Thlahte Chanchin*, K. Zawla, Modern Printing Press, Aizawl, 1964.
10. Note on the People of Burma in the 12-13th. century AD, Census of India, 1931, 11, 1, App. F., G.H. Luce.

30
Emergence of Mizo Nationality

B.K. Roy Burman

Mizo is a generic name and stands for several major tribes and sub-tribes in Mizo Hills. The major tribes consistently committed to Mizo identity are Lushai, Ralte, and Pawi. Eleven sub-tribes, Chawngthu, Chawhte, Ngente, Khawlhring, Khiangte, Pautu, Rawite, Renthlei, Tlau, Vangchhia and Zawngte are known under the common name Awzia. The tribes and sub-tribes preferred to identify themselves as Mizos and this was formalised when "The Lushai Hills District (change of name) Act 1954 was passed by the Parliament. Under the Act the name of the erstwhile Lushai Hill District was changed to Mizo District with effect form 29th April, 1954.

"The term 'Mizo' appears to have been derived from two Lushai words '*Mi*' and '*Zo*'. '*Mi*' in Lusei means man, scholars do not agree on the meaning and connotation of '*zo*'. According to one view *zo* means highland. So Mizo means highlanders or people living on high hills. '*Zo*' may also mean 'cold region' and, therefore, 'Mizo' signifies people of cold region. Another explanation says that the people were so called after the name of the habitation area they built around 1765.

The Lushai tribe settled in the central area around the administrative centres of Aizawl and Lungleh, form the predominant population. To the north live the Hmars who claim to be autochthones; but Hmars who live in the Central region identify themselves as Mizo. To the south are the Pawi or Lai, and to the south-east, the Lakher or Mara. Some small but important tribes, such as the Renthlei and Ralte who historically have been different from the Lusei are gradually accepting the generic name of Lusei or Mizo, although they retain their separate endogamous units also. The Chakma and a few tribes from Tripura inhabit the western border of the Mizo Hlls. Lack of close linguistic cultural and religious affinities have kept the Chakmas largely away from the socio-political movement of the Lushai Hills. Many of the tribes living in Churachandpur area of neighbouring Manipur State are culturally and linguistically akin to most of the Mizo tribes. However, they have had a different historical experience, coming into contact with the Luseis only occasionally, through wars or migration, before the annexation of the area of the British.

Legends and folklores suggest that these tribes were driven out from their original habitation in Chin Hills of Burma and came in waves of migration. They Drove away the Thado Kuki from Lushai Hills and made a series of raids into neighbouring area, under the leadership of despotic chiefs. In 1871, the Lushai people raided a tea garden in Cachar, killed the British proprietor. In retaliation the British made a two pronged expedition into the hills and establish a tenouos rule within a year, which was later on consolidated by 1897.

The majority of the traditional chiefs belonged to the Sailo lineage of the Thangur clan of the Lushei tribe. Each chief ruled his own territory or *ram* and the people living in that territory. The chief used to take best plots and the next best were taken by the *ramhual* and *zalens*, who were required to pay higher tributes to the chief. The chief allowed the people to cultivate their land and in return took tributes in kind. Anybody dissatisfied with the chief was free to leave the village.

The British administered the district through the chief on whom they conferred even greater power than they enjoyed traditionally. Later on a representative body of twenty-two chiefs was elected to form the chief's council, which was considered by the administrators to represent the people. The British administration also put an end to inter-tribal wars and consolidation of administration was coupled with intensive Christian missionary activities. The Lusei dialect was reduced into writing. The Bible was translated; schools and dispensaries were set up and within a few decades almost the entire population embraced Christianity, except the Chakmas, who are Budhists.

In 1935, the Lushai Hills District was declared in Excluded Area. The first political party, established in the Lushai Hills, the Mizo Union, started informal activities at about this time. Ultimately in April 1946, the party was formally etablished with the consent of the District Superintendent. On their demand, the British Superintendent of Lushai Hills, decided to incorporate the commoners' representatives in the chiefs' council. This seems to reflect the strained relationship between the chiefs and the common people even at that time.

In the wake of India's independence in 1947, the British administration started canvassing in favour of Prof. Coupland's plan to create a Crown Colony of Eastern Agency, free from the political control of either India or Burma and directly under the British Government. It would comprise the hill districts of Assam and adjoining Burma. On 5th July, 1946, the chief s formed a political party, the United Mizo Freedom Organisation (UMFO) which wanted to merge the Mizo area with the Union of Burma. But the leaders of the Mizo Union took inspiration from the activities of the Indian national leaders and favoured remaining within India, with a certain amount of autonomy. The leaders of Mizo Union also demanded the return of the Mizo areas of Manipur and Burma to the district.

The Sixth Schedule of the Constitution of India was promulgated to safeguard and traditions, customs and practices of the hill tribes of North East India and to protect them from outside traders and exploiters. The Lushai Hills District Council was constituted in 1952. To satisfy the minority aspirations, the Pawi-Lakher Autonomous Region was carved out of the Lushai Hills District in 1953. In 1954, the Assam Lushai Hills District (Acquisition of Chiefs' Rights Act) was enacted and the rights and responsibilities of 259 Mizo Chiefs and 50 Pawi Lakher Chiefs were vested in Government. The administration of land was transferred to the District and Regional Councils from the Chiefs. With the passing of these Acts that traditional leadership pattern and the elite structure yielded place to a new order. The former chiefs' party UMFO lost its hold. They formed another, Easter India Tribal Union (EITU). When Assam Government decided to introduce Assamese as the State language, and the tribes of Mizo District as also other hill areas of Asam "were scared of losing their linguistic identity and minority rights. They were also dissatisfied at the way the money given for tribal welfare was used by the Government of Assam without much apparent benefit to the Mizo Hills. The economic condition of the Mizo Hills was precarious in the mid 1960s after the famine or *mautam* which lasted a few years. This led to the movement for the formation of a Hill State in 1961, initiated by All Party Hill Leaders' Conference (APHLC) which included both EITU and Mizo Union. The movement rapidly gained popularity. At the same time, a third political force whch later led to the Mizo insurgency emerged. On 22nd November 1961, a political party, called the Mizo National Front (MNF) was established under the leadership of Laldenga. By 1964, the demand for separate statehood for the Mizo Hills had gained momentum and when this was not conceded the MNF started its insurgent activities on 28th February, 1966.

Laldenga has systematically mobilised the people focussing their attention on the need for unity among the Mizos. On 15th and 16th January, 1965, he met the Kuki-Chin leader of Churachandpur in Manipur and resolved to demand a bigger Mizo state including Kuki areas of Manipur. The former chiefs who were unhappy with the Mizo Union and Mizo Congress, also supported Laldenga. Besides, as Laldenga belonged to Pawi tribe, most of his tribemen supported his activities. They set up units in every village to recruit volunteers and raise funds.

Following the outbreak of insurgency, large scale regrouping of villages was resorted to, as a counter-insurgency measure. This was done by phases, starting in early 1967. The forced displacement of the majority population from their villages and their habits which was introduced by the imperialists in Malaysia in the 1950s has been criticised by many in India, as a misconceived one, incompatible with the democratic ethos of the country. While in the grouping centres many amenities were provided, these were not found viable for sustaining autogenous economic activities over a length of time. By mid 70s, the rigour of enforcement of the operation was considerable relaxed and a good number of persons started to go back to the old village sites. The new villages which have come up on the old sites are called Thlawhbawk or temporary dwelling places. As these are not oficially recognised, these villages do not have any statutory village council. However, in many cases the villagers have formed informal village committees.

Another development that deserves special mention, is that, in 1972 Mizo Hills district was delinked from Assam and Mizoram was constituted as a separate Union Territory.

The brief ethno-history of the Mizos and situational appraisal about Mizoram raises several important issues:

(i) A number of identifiable ethnic entities are considered to constitute the unified Mizo ethnic formation. Are all the constituent entities committed to the unified Mizo formation to the same extent and in the same manner? Is there any locus of shift in their commitment?

(ii) Some of the constituent entities have their counterparts outside India in Burma and Bangladesh and inside India in Manipur, Assam and Tripura apart from Mizoram. How do the diversities of political boundaries affect the identity structures of the constituent entities?

(iii) To what extent the Mizos perceive identity of interests with other population of the Third World Countries in the struggle for peace and for improvement of the conditions of life, in the contemporary world situation?

(iv) To what extent the existing political arrangement in India satisfy the urges of the Mizos for self-expression and for participation in crucial decision-making processes, concerning them?

(v) To what extent, the economic, social and cultural policies pursued by the ruling elites in India satisfy the aspiration and modern vision of the Mizos?

(vi) At the micro-level, what identity and dilemmas, strains and new possibilities are being felt by the Mizos in the wake of regrouping of villages?

Goswami has reported that while a Hmar living in the central belt of Mizoram calls himself a Mizo, a Hmar living in Manipur will not do so (p. 23). During the demarcation of the boundaries in 1948, the Mizo Union also is reported not to have pressed for the Hmar areas to be included in the Lushai Hills District. In 1950, a Hmar Mongolian Federation was formed. The Lakhers are also khown as Mairam in Haka sub-division in Chin Hills and as Shendus, Khongsai and Zou in various part of Burma. Till 1930, the Lakhers were not administered by the British. In 1945, the Lakher chiefs protested against their inclusion in the Lushai Hills Chiefs' Council (p. 60). The Pawi people have cultural similarities with the Lakher as well as with the Mizo (Lushai). Though through Christianity they have come nearer to the Mizos. In 1965, a section of them organised a political party called Chin National Front, which shows that they have identity dilemmas. There are some Paites in Mizoram, but the majority live in Manipur. Those of them who live in the central part of Mizoram have forgotten their language. This, however, is not equally true about those living in Manipur or in its border areas with Mizoram. The Paite National Council with its headquarters to Churachandpur is reported to have opened a number of political units in the Paite villages of Mizoram. In the 1950s, the clamoured for the establishment of a Chinland by taking out areas from India, Burma and the then East Pakistan. In 1969, however, the Paite National Council pressed for constituting autonomous districts in the tribal areas of Manipur (p. 67-68).

Another development also deserves mention. Some of the ethnic formations which were considered part of some of Mizo tribes have shifted their identity and are now claming to be Nagas. For instance though Buite is considered to be a section of Zou tribe included in Mizo group, many

Buites now indentify themselves with the Nagas. Such identity shift seems to be related to the ideology of political organisation and of control of resources. In parts of the country, elected chiefship and free access to the land resources of the community are considered to be distinctive features of the Nagas; on the other hand hereditary chiefship and some sort of ownership right of the Chief over the resources are associated with the Mizo-Kuki group. The switch over to Naga identity is related to the assertion of rights by the commoners against the chiefs in some areas outside Mizoram.

In view of the foregoing facts, it is very difficult to say that a stable Mizo identity has crystallised, particularly outside Mizoram. It appears that the constituent entities are subjected to pulls and pressures from two directions. One is the aspiration of the broad mass of the population to have access to the resources and to be directly involved in crucial matters relating to resource management. The other is the ambition of the traditional as well as the modern elite, (who have emerged through spread of education and incorporation in bureaucratic machinery through reservation in services) to enjoy share of State power in the context of the functioning of the parliamentary democracy. The crystallisation and consolidation of Mizo identity inside Mizoram and outside, will depend on the convergence of the goals at these two levels. Such convergence, however, does not appear to be taking place. The first step taken after the abolition of chief-appears to be the point of departure. On abolition of the chiefship the ownership and control of land did not devolve to the village community; it was transferred to the District Council. Later on, abolition of the Mizo Hills District Council, the same was passed on to the State. As the autonomous District Council came into existence through the mobilisation of the tribals for self management and for preservation and development of their traditional rights, this had the potential to assume the character of a supratribal entity. But as the resources for social and production infrastructure and extending various social services were with the State, the latter tended to transform the District Council into subordinate organ of the State. The District Council also was assailed by force which could draw upon the primordial loyalties at the village level. This explains the conflict between the Mizo Union and the Congress in the late 50s and the recovery of political relevance of the chief to a certain extent at that time. Also this accounts for the alleged tacit understanding between Laldenga and B.P. Chaliha, in their common confrontation against Mizo Union.

As regard share of State power, the ambition of the Mizo elite has been only partly satisfied. Union Territory administration falls for a short of the half-way between political management and administrative management, in the existing pattern of Centre-State relations, even full fledged States have limited power to absorb endogenous political processes, if the same are not derived from or are avowedly in harmony with the political processes at the all India level. As regards the endogenous political processes of the Mizos, two dynamic elements of Mizo culture are to be kept in view "In the grim struggle for survival against nature and enemies, the Mizos have developed a code of conduct called *tlawmngaihna*, which literally means unwillingness to be defeated. In practice it took the shape of an obligation to be unselfish and to be helpful to other".

2. The world viewed of *tlawmngaihna* is also to be considered in the context of lineage, clan and local community basis of access to resources.

The second dynamic element is the concept of Vai[3] or outsider. But it appears that all non-Mizos are not Vais. Indian, other than tribals of Assam are outsiders. It follows that there are two categories of non-Mizo, one category consisting of non-Vai non-Mizo; the other consisting of Vai-non-Mizo. Existence of the two polar extreme represented by *tlawmngaihna* and Vai respectively, in the culture, generates a deeper psychic need for a synthesis. Satisfaction of such need can take different forms. One such form has been described by Jaim Castillo, the principal idologist of Latin American Christian Democracy in his famous write-up and Communitarian society[4] "Individualism holds and erroneous conception of human rights—they are considered as rights of man against society—in circumstances which required that they be oriented toward the community". "Collectivism was a reaction, but at the same time a fundamental value was involved, in the reassertion of the fact that individual cannot realise himself except in the community". "Communitarianism results from the realisation that by applying proper categories of analysis we can succeed in harmonising the extremes". "These ideas can be expressed with some precision in two formulas. One is that Maritain, "the community of free man". This sums up our ideological goal, many individuals of free men in a community with highest degree of freedom.

The second formula is that Toniolo "a community of communities". Here one can see what the political and social organisation of communitarian society would be. There would be a multiplicity of organisations which implies a greater possibility of realising freedom that if the society were reduced to a single social segment". Though Castillo has expressed the political credo of Christian Democracy in a somewhat different idiom, it is very much in line with the Gandhian ethos of self-propelling humanism embedded in national cultures. Obviously it is this fundamental unity in the world-view and ethos, that prevailed, in persuading the Mizos in identifying themselves with India, rather than with Burma or from going in for a crown colony, as desired by the colonial officials, at the time of withdrawal of the British rule from the subcontinent. But has the identification with the rest of India fulfilled the expectations and aspirations to the Mizos? Do the Mizo have a sense of fulfilment in their Indian Identity?

For an answer to this question, one is to look into two processes; psychic and socio-political. As with any other citizen, there would be ups and downs in the psychic aspect of the sense of fulfilment. In contrast socio-political aspect is not just a question of mind; it is a matter of analytical appraisal of a situation and of consequential action. If as early as 1947, the dominant political leadership of the Mizo appreciated the significance of the freedom struggle of India and decided to tie up the destiny of the Mizos with the rest of the country, there is no reason to think that they would remain indifferent to the struggle of the Third World Countries to keep themselves free from the long term-goals and strategies of enticing neo-colonialism. Also they cannot be unaware of the vanguard role of the national leadership of India in this matter.

One can, therefore, assume that in the world order context, Indian identity is a matter of satisfaction to a large number of Mizos. But there are many in the country who feel disturbed with the growing linkage of Indian economy with the world capitalist system.[5] Many also feel that this is subverting the self-reliant growth of the nation and promoting the process of extortion of resources from the outlying regions in the interest of the capitalist entrepreneurs. A logical corollary of this analysis is that these regions from where extortion of resources is not immediately possible for lack of requisite infrastructure, are more likely to suffer, are more likely to suffer from cruel neglect; in spite of all pious talks about balanced regional development. The traumatic experience of the famine in early 1960s and the subsequent miscarriages of many development efforts have created a coral reef of distrust in the minds of the Mizos. If they fail to preceive that the rest of the countrymen also equally share the frustration, the same heaps of disrupted dreams, the blame is not entirely theirs. Perception in creating a common future, depends largely on the perception of a common past. It is often complained that a communion into the past is not possible, is the Mizo and other hill-dwellers had remained aloof from the common freedom struggle. In fact the boot is in the other leg. The people of the plains have till today failed to recognise the anti-colonial nature of the confrontation of the hill men wth the British. They were junior partners of the benefits of colonial expansion to the hills and, hence, have been too ready to accept the version of the colonial administrators that the confrontation was between barbarism and civilisation. The academics who mainly hail from the plains have also failed to come out of the mire of myopic vision. If the rest of India fails to make the past of the Mizos a bit of its own past, the Mizos cannot be expected to be effectively tied-up with the future of the rest of the nation.

It is a case of crisis of identity of the nation as a whole. The democratic elite of the nation has failed to define the dimensions of identity in respect of the people with whom common political and economic ties were forged mainly during the colonial rule. To a considerable extent, the identity crisis of the Mizo and similarly placed ethnic entities is a by-product of this much larger identity crisis. One lacuna in India's politico-legal frame-work also deserves special mention. Anderson[6] used to designate the group of people who regard itself as the original inhabitants of an area into which others have migrated, as Charter group of the community. The Charger group often develop a typical orientation, no matter whether they are in dominant or subordinate status. They conceive of themselves as the people who "really" belong to the area; others are either quests or unwanted intruders. Because of their identification with the territory, they feel a special responsibility for looking after it. They are the ones who become concerned about the exploitation of the resources. Whether in historical fact they are the first to occupy the territory does not matter; what is important is that they believe the land is theirs[7].

While the Sixth Schedule of the Constitution took care of the historical prerogatives and psychic needs of the Charter groups like the Mizos, its functional erosion during actual application, has further aggravated their identity crisis[8]. The grouping of villages as a counter insurgency measure again is a complete disregard of the effective cognitive processes cherished by the Charter members of the Mizo social formation at the micro-level. It has blurred the perception of humanistic nationalism, to which Gandhi committed the nation through his life and more so, through his death; and it has strained the articulation of the proto-nationalism,[9] of the Mizos with the multi-dimensional nation building process of India. There are, however, many flexibilities at the operational level in such matters; and because of the same, it can be expected that the strain will be overcome over a length of time.

REFERENCES

1. Goswami B.B., 1979: *The Mizo Unrest*: Aalekh Publishers, Jaipur
2. Goswami B.B. and Mukherjee, D.P., 1972: The Mizo Political Movement in *Tribal Movement in India* (ed), K.S. Singh, Manohar, New Delhi, p. 131.
3. *Ibid.*, p. 138.
4. Castillo Jaim, 1966: Property and the Communitarian Society: Excerpt published in—*Ideologies of the Developing Nations* (ed.) P.E. Sigmund, Praeger Publishers, New York, 1972.
5. Bagchi, Amiya Kumar, 1982: The New International Economic Order and India 1982: paper presented at the colloquium on endogenous groups in world development, organised by ICSSR and Bernaled Centre.
6. Anderson, L., 1937: We Americans, Harvard University Press: Referred to in *Ethnic Stratification*: Tamotsu Shibutani and Kiau M. Kwan: McMillan Co., 1965, p. 219.
7. Tamotsu Shibutani and Kiau M. Kwan, 1965: *Ethnic Stratification*, McMillan & Co.
8. Roy Burman, B.K., 1980: North East India—An Overview: *Mainstream*, 6th December, 1980.
9. Roy Burman, B.K., 1983: Transformation of Tribes and Analogous Social Formations. *Economic and Political Weekly*, Vol. XVIII, No. 27, 2nd July, 1983.

SOCIO-CULTURAL HISTORY

31

The Mizo Value (As Reflected in Oral Traditions)

R.L.Thanmawia

Man has continually searched for, and rendered efforts towards the creation of an ideal world. In the process he has constructed homes, slowly improved architectural designs, and developed social skills. Social values have, therefore, been central and they have distinguished man from other aspects of creation. All social institutions, down the ages, have held life to be sacred. As such values have been cherished in terms of festivals, religions and social activities.

Mizos are a very distinctive people endowed with age-old traditions, cultures and heritages. Their values and beliefs along with the various social religious practices that interspersed their pattern of life gave them a distinct Mizo identity.[1] In recognizing the values, the two social institutions such as the court of village Chief and the *zawlbuk* (bachelors' dormitory) tradition, fostered a system of honouring great deeds performed by individuals as well as groups of individuals in their day to day life. The Mizo values are depicted in their oral traditions, especially in their folk songs and folk narratives.

Bravery

One of the forces which shaped Mizo life for nearly three hundred centuries were the frequent wars with neighbouring tribes or the wars among themselves. Whenever a male child was born in a village, the elders would bless him so that he would be endowed with bravery in order to kill enemies and wild animals. A Mizo youth christened to be brave as this was desired of him by the elders in the society. All the young men were expected to stay at night at *zawlbuk*. *zawlbuk* played an important role in the life of the village, and the community as a whole. It acted as a village guard room. This was obvious for a hunting and warring people. They had to occasionally fight to protect their village against external aggression from the neighbouring villages. Internecine feuds were frequent; men of a village needed to remain alert to fight as and when situations demanded. The noted chivalry among the youngsters is honoured by offering *nopui*, a special cup for rice beer. Thus, all the young men try to attain *nopui* at least once in their life time.

As such, the Mizos have several war chants (*bawhhla*) and songs on the triumph over their enemies. If the Mizo *pasaltha*, (the warrior) killed his enemy, he had to trample the dead body under his foot, declaring his own name and would chant *bawhhla*. After doing this, the soul of the enemy would no longer frighten him, and even when he dies, the soul of the enemy would escort his soul to the *pialral*.[1] The killer would bring the head of the enemy to his home, and hold a group dance in celebration of the head taken in the raid, this is called *rallulam*. *Bawhhla* or war-chant mainly expressed their superiority over their enemies.

There are several songs on this theme. One of the most popular folksongs is termed *zopui zai*, a song commemorating the massacre of Thlanrawn people, is the triumphant song of the clever Chief Lallula. He sang about the event with all the sarcasm and mockery for the defeated foe.[2] Lallula was one of the most powerful chiefs of the Sailo clan, ruling at Zopui village. A very barbaric tribe called Pawis or Thlanrawns, who were living the Chin Hills of Burma in the east, used to undertake raids upon the villages mostly inhabited by Mizos in the west. These included the villages under Sailo Chiefs. It is said that Lallula cleverly invited the Thlanrawn tribesmen to collect tributes from them. When the Thlanrawn chief and his warriors arrived at Zopui village, Lallula and his men by subterfuge brutally massacred all except two, who made a narrow escape. The heroic action of the Zopui villagers was praised in tune. Examples may be taken from Zopui Zai as follows:

> Phunthanga demanded ivory,
> Thanchhuma is locked in the stock,
> Oh, what a sombre sight.
> Blame not my Zopui village,
> Where we chopped off Thlanrawns' head,
> Commemorated with trophy posts in rows.[3]

(Here Phunthanga was the chief of Thlanrawn and Thanruma, his famous warrior.) Adoration of the heroes is widely reflected in their folk narratives also. One example may be taken from the story of a famous legendary character called Chhura. Once upon a time there was an evil and ferocious spirit called Phungpuinu (a female demon with children) who would always terrify people. One day his neighbour called Nahaia was badly terrified by this demon while he was in his *jhum* plot shooing away birds from feeding on the ripened paddy. Even though Nahaia knew that cowardice was greatly condemned by the society, he shamelessly ran away from the terror and approached Chhura to whom he fervently pleaded for an exchange of *Jhum* plot. Understanding Nahaia's plight; Chhura conceded to his request. Thereupon he received the same threat from the she-demon. Immediately Chhura devised a plot to capture the demon. He made a swing in the farm hut and pretended as if he was going home, while actually hiding himself on the roof of the hut. After some time, Phungpuinu came to the *jhum* hut and sat on the swing thinking that Chhura had gone home, and began to swing and sing happily.

Chhura then suddenly pounced on the demon firmly catching hold of her hair and told her that he would take her home for village children to make fun of her or make her to dance. The demon dared not face those whom she had always terrified in the past. She then made offer of her most precious possession, a magic horn called Sekibuhchhuak (a horn containing an inexhaustible supply of meat and cooked rice) for her freedom. According to Siamkima, Chhura was a great hero in the same mould as Hercules, Ulysses, Beowulf, Hector, Achilles, Promutheus and Durga. He concluded that "if Chhura were in Greece, he would have been in the Elysium".[4]

Hunter

Hunting was the favourite pastime of the menfolk among the Mizos. The society honoured *pasaltha* or successful hunters. When a male child was born, elders would bless him so that he would grow up to be able to attain the status of *pasaltha*. They had plenty of *hlado* or chants raised by successful hunters, and Salulam zai, that is songs usually sung in celebration of animals killed by the hunters. Some few examples may be taken out from the lines of *hlado*, as follows:

> Chhawl thing e, thliak na ngai e,
> Mangnghin e, thạnhawl ka vak liau ve;
> Chhawlhnawm e, rak tho ulaw,
> Valan nghovari zalna e.

(Being a brave hunter, I go out hunting,
Now remove the leaves with which
I had covered the wild boar I bagged)

The chanting would be immediately followed by a volley of gun fire. *Hlado* was a means to revere successful hunters who were held in high esteem. Every male youth would aspire to become a successful hunter. A young hunter after a successful hunt would proudly chant the following lines:

Chun nun e, a tir che maw,
Uai hnianga ram va tuan chu e,
Kei chu e, changram te nen,
Tlangah e, thliten ka her liai e.

(Languidly you go to work in the *jhum* under the dictate of your mother,
As for me, I take my gun and
Hunt over the hills after wild animals).

Hlado sometimes would indicate the pride and fame that an ordinary man in the village can attain due to his success in hunting and in the process he would compare himself as standing on equal footing with the privileged rich man in the village who had attained the status of Thangchhuah. Such chanting would be like this:

Lianchhung e, an than ni'n e,
Tualah hnumkhuang a ri e,
Rairah e, kan than ni'n e,
Tlangan e, kan lo au lai rih e.

(One day the rich man performs a grand feast, the village resounds with joy,
We poor men achieve fame, the hill echoes with our victory chants).[5]

Tlawmngaihna

Among the qualities that the Mizo fostered in their life, was the spirit of Tlawmngaihna which eludes literal translation. The nearest translation in English according to K.C. Lalvunga is, "an ideal of life in which a man could not be outdone in doing well to others. When a man is Tlawmngai, one cannot defeat him in doing well to others, and that self-sacrifice sometimes demands life itself"[6]. Every Mizo was expected to abide by this code of conduct. If a villager was sick and was unable to look after his plot of land, his neighbours would readily come forward to help. If a villager was short of rice, those having plenty would readily share the same with him. Sympathy, compassion, fellow-feeling were the traits very fondly cherished by a Mizo Therefore, due to Tlawmngaihna, Chhura was able to go for Nahaia in order to face the ferocious demon called Phungpuinu. Due to this undaunted spirit, Chhura was able to catch the demon. We have seen many legendary men who are endowed with this attribute, men such as Vanapa, Taitesena, Chawngbawla, Khuangchera, and others.

One interesting story is that one day a man called Vanzema dived into the deep water in the river where there was a horrible monster who warned him not to come back. Unfortunately no one believed Vanzema when he told what he had seen inside the deep water. As he could not convince his companions, Vanzema told them that he would enter into the deep water again, and that they should pull him out of water immediately when he made signal with the long rope tied on his ankle. He again entered the water, but the horrible monster got hold of him and he lost his life. Before he entered water for the second time, Vanzema knew that he would surely lose his life, but due to his spirit of Tlawmngaihna, he wanted truth to triumph at the cost of his own life.

Vanapa, a famous Mizo legendary hero in real life is another case in point. One fine day a group of young hunters went hunting under his leadership. After roaming around the thick jungle the entire day, they became tired and hungry. Vanapa then located a fig tree laden with ripe fruits. He then summoned the hungry youngsters who happily ran after him, and a particular youngster jumped to the tree and immediately started feeding on the fruit. Whereupon Vanapa admonished him telling that he himself had not taken a single fruit in order that all would share the fruits equally. In this way, the youngster learnt a bitter lesson on one aspect relating to Tlawmngaihna which equally applied to others in the group. Decent and courteous behaviour with others was one of the many facets of Tlawmngaihna, and was considered of value for everyone. Act of decency and courtesy, especially to the elder people were considered to form norms of good conduct and as such were valued in the society.

Physical Strength

Apart from bravery, persons endowed with physical strength and power were held in high esteem in the society. We have seen such extraordinary men in their folk narratives. Few examples may be taken from their legends. There was a famous Mualzavata who could clear jungles in hundreds of hillocks for cultivation in a single day. There was another man called Saikhaia who could lift up a full grown elephant with his hands, and Pangpuielhtliaka who could easily break a large tree with his bare hands. Aihniara was famous for his lightning speed that he could cross the whole Mizoram from east to west in a day. When he travelled leading a goat by a rope, the goat had no chance to touch the ground with its legs but would simply hang in the air due to the super speed of its owner. There are several of other legendary heroes laced with humorous elements.

Music

Mizos loved music that some people remarked them as a singing tribe. They cherished both good singers and good composers. There is one popular Mizo saying, "*Khuang lova chai ang*" which means 'dancing in festivity without drum' and this saying shows that without music the life of the Mizos is incomplete. B. Thanmawia says, "Music to the Mizos, is as indispensable as air is to man and beasts" [7]. They sing in all occasions both happy and sad. When condoling bereaved families, they sing songs of condolence; they sing songs of joy when attending marriage party.[8] They even sing or hum tunes while working or walking on the road. A story is told that once, while villagers were proceeding towards their *jhum* plots to work, they happened to hear the sweet song of a *cicada* which sat on a tree overlooking the main pathway to the village *jhum* fields. The sweet song had captivated all the village folks passing on the path and everyone stopped to listen. The villagers continued to gather on the spot waiting for Saikuti, the born-poetess of the village. When Saikuti arrived, she was requested to compose a befitting song. Complying to their request, she spontaneously recited the following verse:

> Oh, thou cicada of the wood,
> Your sweet voice sans rhythmic drum,
> Was enough to enchant people from their works.[9]

On hearing this verse, all the villagers went back home and sang together the whole day in celebration of the new song of Saikuti.

A very important social institution of the Mizo in the olden days was the school of *zawlbuk*, the bachelors' dormitory in which all the young men who attained puberty were required to sleep. The main function of *zawlbuk* was in terms of village defence. Apart from this, it served as a school of instructions for the youths. They learnt innumerable lessons from the elders such as good manners, obedience to elders, discipline, art of warfare, wrestling and other sports. It was a place where iron discipline was taught in practical ways. It was a place where youths learnt bravery and all aspects related to the concept of Tlawmngaihna. It was a place where the elder people passed on the history of the nation, myths and legends of the tribe, stories of their ancestors, etc. It occupied an important position in the life of the village community as a whole. Although *zawlbuk* served the community so many ways in the olden days, modern life being deprived of any similar institution has suffered from this void. The Spartan discipline binding the Mizo youths is gradually collapsing, and the *nopui* no longer attracts the younger generations. Diligence, honesty, respect for the elders and above all the spirit of Tlawmngaihna has gradually declined. Mizos need to revive their old values in order to inject fresh impetus to Mizo entity.

REFÉRENCES

1. K. Zawla, *Mizo Pipute leh An thlahte Chanchin*: Gosen Press, Aizawl,1986, p. 82.
2. Lalruanga, A study of Mizo Folk Literature, unpublished Thesis, Gauhati University, 1984, p. 74.
3. R.L.Thanmawia, *Mizo Poetry*, Franco Press, Elecric veng, Aizawl, 1998, p. 46.
4. Siamkima Khawlhring, *Zalenna Ram*, p. 86.
5. R.L. Thanmawia, *op. cit.* p. 47.
6. K.C. Lalvunga, The heritage we received from our forefathers, A seminar Paper, published by Directorate of Higher and Technical Education, Government of Mizoram, p. 32.
7. B. Thanmawia, Mizos and Music, *Mizoram News Magazine*, Autumn Issue 1985, p. 12.
8. Kathryn McKenzie, *Chhinlung Magazine*, Vol. II, 1986, p. 19.
9. R.L. Thanmawia, *op. cit.*, p. 30.

32

The Marriage Customs of the Maras before the Advent of the British in the Maraland

K. Zohra

The Maras constituted a distinct tribal group in south Mizoram. They were very rich in customs and traditions. Their marriage customs were different from their neighbouring tribes. The area where they lived previously was known as "Lakher land". This was coined by the Lakher Pioneer Mission, which was founded in the year 1907. At present it is commonly known as "Maraland". The Maras were brought under the British control in 1923. Their customs and traditions were reformed and several changes were introduced by the Lakher Pioneer Mission, supplemented by the administration of the British rule.

In marriage, the Maras followed a tradition of monogamy or the marriage of a single spouse was in vogue. However, the person belonging to the chiefly clans and wealthy families, in earlier days, could marry two or more wives as there was no rigid usage about marriage.

The first major wife was known as *Nobei* and the second major wife *Notho.* Among the Maras polyandry or the marriage of two or more husbands by a woman was not prevalent. A widow or a divorced wife could remarry freely any one either a widower or a divorced husband or a young man. A widower or a divorced husband also could remarry any woman. Marriage was usually patrilateral in which the son might marry the daughter of his mother's brother. This was not legally binding but it was believed that marriage with the daughter of the mother's brother brought good fortune for a man. The prescriptive matrilateral alliance was widely prevalent. Generally it improved the prestige of the wife-taker's family. In earlier days the young man and girl had no choice in marriage. Marriage arrangement were made by their parents. Marriage generally took place long after the boy and girl attained puberty. This system of marriage may be described as "Marriage first and love afterwards", contrary to the modern system of "Love first and marriage".

The marriage system had some restrictions imposed on the choice of a wife. Among the Maras, marriage within or without the group or clan was equally permissible. The system of inter-marriage among and between the different clans was widely prevalent. There was a definite social gulf between the three clans: (1) the chiefly clans; (2) the patrician or middle class clans; and (3) the plebian or the lower class clans.

The woman of the chiefly clans had higher marriage price than those of lower clans. Among the Maras, a high status household or chiefly family felt rather that it ought to marry its daughter only to another chiefly or wealthy house. The rank of a Mara family did not; however, depend upon the rank of the wife-giver. Marriage could not change the original rank and lineage of the clans but raised the status of the wife-taker, who belonged to the lower clan, through matrilineal alliance. The wife-giver was the *Pato* and the wife taker was the *nazua.* The wife giver or the *Pato* had received the *puma,* one of the main bride's price of the *nazua's* daughters. A person belonging to a lower clan sought to raise his status by marrying a wife belonging to a clan higher than his own.

In-marriage, the eldest son was the guardian of his sisters and could arrange their marriages in case the household father was dead or become a poor aged man. If the sisters had no father or brother, the father's brother or his son could arrange their marriages. Various household families of the same clan helped and supported each other in the marriage arrangement. The maternal relatives were also involved in the marriage of their *nazua's* daughter or son. The paternal relatives must, as a rule, shoulder together the price of wife. A young man or widower could not marry his own sister or his father's brother's daughter.

Children of the same father but different mothers could not marry whereas children of the same mother but different fathers could marry each other. A father could marry his deceased son's widow but a son could not marry his deceased father's widow. The marriage of a maternal uncle to his niece, and nephew to the widow of his maternal uncle were not allowed. The two sisters of the same parents, who married about the same time, after performing the *amakia* ceremony but before intercourse with their husband, could exchange their husbands if each husband mutually accepted the proposed term.

Widower/Widow Remarriage

Among the Maras there was no bar or restriction against a widow and a widower in marrying again. The widow could remarry to any male person either a young man or a widower who responded to her amorous glances. Remarriage of widows was customarily free but dependent on the age, personal attractions and industry of the woman. The remarriage usually took place after the erection of the memorial stone of the deceased husband or wife. Before performing the *lopheiparai* ceremony, a widow was usually confined in her deceased husband's house. Among the Maras, there were three types of remarriage. Firstly, the remarriage between a widow and her deceased husband's brother. This form of remarriage was known as *lapinokhu.* The parents of the widow could not raise additional price beyond an extra price known as the *Abanaso*.

This was a handsome price, usually consisting a gong of eight spans. There was no formal marriage celebration and feast. This form of marriage usually took place after performing the *lopheiparai* ceremony. Secondly, a widower could marry one of his deceased wife's sisters, locally known as the *akeipa* which usually took place after the *lopheiparai* ceremony. The wife-taker must give the marriage price to the girl's parents. The custom of *akeipa* was not obligatory. A widower could, after the erection of the memorial stone of the deceased wife, can marry any woman. A widow could also marry any person freely, solely depended on the will of her parents but usually after the erection of the memorial stone of her deceased husband, and before which she confined herself in her husband's house. The third system was ordinary widow remarriage. The widow or divorced wife could freely remarry any male person a young or a widower or a divorced husband. Under this form of remarriage, the parents of the wife-taker must first send and convey to the girl's parents to woo their favourable willingness. No sooner did both parties reach mutual agreement than the marriage was arranged and the price was claimed. There was no marriage celebration.

The widow could remarry freely if her deceased husband's brother refused to marry her or deceased husband had no brother. A widower could remarry freely if his deceased wife's sister refused to marry him, or deceased wife had no sister. The widow or *nohmei* who had outlived three husband was called *maluso,* and was likely to outlive a fourth. The Maras were very shy of marrying a *maluso.*

Ordinary Marriage

The ordinary marriage was the most prominent system of marriage among the Maras. A young man whose hair became long enough to tie up in a knot over his forehead could become *satlia.* A girl who could dress her hair in a ball low down on the nape of the neck became *laisa*; and when a boy had attained the status of *satlia,* he was allowed to join the young man in *laisacharei* or courting the girl who became the *laisa.* A *satlia* never confined in his parents' house at night but slept in the girl's house selected for the *laipho* when the parents had found a girl who was delightful as a bridge for their son. They sent a woman to the girl's parents to have preliminary discussion on the contemplation of the boy's parents and thereby she drew the attitude of the girl's parents. If a woman reported favourably, the boy's parents appointed an intermediary, known as the *lyuchapa.* The *lyuchapa* was sent to present the girl's parents with a *dao* as engagement called *thuaso* The boy's parents again sent the *lyuchapa* to the girl's parents to discuss about the price. As soon as the price had been agreed on, the wedding day was fixed. There was, however, no season for marriages among the Maras, but *Chhiepa* (June) and *Thlazo* (August) months were considered unfavourable.

On the marriage day, their respective relatives and friends had gathered in the house of the bride and bridegroom. The persons who were entitled to the bride's price had killed pigs, cows and mithuns. Each party prepared a great feast. On the whole day, the marriage price was discussed between the two parties through the envoy, *lyuchapa.* After settling preliminary price satisfactorily, the bride and her aunt started their procession to the bridegroom's house, known as the *amakia* headed by a cupbearer or the *sahmaphaopa,* then followed by the bride's friends. The *amakia* usually took place either on wedding day or before or after the marriage ceremony. The *amakia* feasts which took place after the wedding day lasted for three days. The first day was the *awruabawna* day, and the bride's parent killed pigs. The next day the bride price was claimed, on the third day, a feast was held, the *amakia,* the bride's marriage procession to her bridegroom's house the bride's aunt claimed the *tini* price which consisted of several number of small dues. This was followed by the actual marriage ceremony. The bride and bridegroom took seats near the rice beer pot. The *lyuchapa* took first a cup of rice beer, dip his brass hairpin in it, gave some beer from the hairpin to the bride and bridegroom to drink and wished them many children, long life and prosperity. This ceremony called *tipani* must be performed before the first cock crew. The ceremony was followed by drinking and singing, and finally the bride returned to her parents house.

On the next day the bride's parents with the bride and some friends went to the bridegroom's house with a pot of rice beer. The bridegroom and his *lyuchapa* were asked to pay the marriage price. They spent the whole day in feasting and drinking. In the evening, the bride's party moved to her parent's house. On the third day, they all met again in the bridegroom's house, and asked him to give presents called *ahla* on the next day, the bride finally moved to the bridegroom's house, which followed by *miapati* sacrifice, killing a white cock to cast out the spirits of the pigs which had been killed on the wedding day, and to ensure good crops. The bride remained in her husband's house.

In marriage custom, there were two slight variations. Firstly, among the chiefly families, the *okiasanie* was performed, the bridegroom paid the *okia* to the bride's parents. This was usually done before the *amakia* ceremony. The *okiasanie* feast was followed by the marriage ceremony. Secondly, among the common people, the *sisazi* was paid in advance for which the bride's parents killed a pig, this was followed by usual marriage ceremony.

Child Marriage

Among the Maras, there was a custom of child marriage, called *no apahaw* which was solely arranged by the parents of the two families, the wife-taker and the wife-giver. This form of marriage usually took place when a boy and a girl were below the age of puberty, or else either of them had not yet reach the age of puberty. There were also cases, a young man of marriageable age married a girl child, or a girl who had attained puberty, a boy much younger than herself. The parents who contemplated to such marriage sent a woman to woo the girl's parent. If there was an explicit response, a male envoy called the *lyuchapa* was deputed to present a *pumtek* beard to the girl's father as an ear-ring to be worm by the girl, known as *nachipaba*. The *lyuchapa* was entertained with rice beer. This stage was soon followed by marriage engagement called *thuaso* presenting a *dao* or a pot to the girl's parents through the *lyuchapa*. The match was finally settled, fixing the marriage price. If the man broke off the engagement, eloping or jilting a girl, he must pay the *okia* or a *hmiatla* to the girl's parents. If a girl broke off the engagement her parents must pay a *vaopia* to the man's parents, and the engagement *thuaso-chatlai*. If a man broke off the same, his parents must pay *vaopia* to the girl's parents as *thuaso chatlao*, and the *thuaso* was returned back. When the girl called *Amakia* took place, pigs were killed by both parties and the price was claimed.

The couple must wait each other till either of them or both of them had attained puberty. A husband who forcibly slept or had intercourse with his wife before attaining puberty must pay a fine, known as *Hmiatla* or offering of a *racha* a large earthenware pot or any other equivalent household article. A wife who had connected with another man before her husband had attained puberty was treated as an adulteress and was subject to penalties incurred by adultery. If a husband refused to consummate his wife, after attaining puberty, the case was treated as divorce and the marriage price could not be refunded. If a wife rejected her husband's persuasion, her father must tie her hands and feet for free connection with her husband. Child-marriage was commonly prevalent among the chiefly and wealthy families.

33
Questions on the Mizo Kinship System

B.B. Goswami

One of the least discussed topic of ethnographic concern about the erstwhile Lushai and presently the Mizo people is the kinship system. Shakespear (1912) devoted a section on marriage dealing with bride-price, divorce and widow remarriage under Law and Customs. About one and a half decade after him, Parry (1928) wrote *"a monograph on the Lushai customs and ceremonies"* giving details of marriage practices, bride-price and affairs connected with family and marriage. These two books are important milestones on the Mizo ethnography. McCall's (1949) book describes the diachronic situation but nothing on the kinship system.

Shakespear wrote the book in two parts describing the Lushei and related people under the title *The Lushei Kuki Clans*. In the first part he used the term Lushai approximately in the same generic sense as the Mizo is used today. The word Lushei meant only a clan which had many families and branches (*ibid.*, 125). In the second part he described non-Lushei clans *(ibid.,* 129) whose habits, customs and beliefs though different had similarities with the Lushe i. He, however, did not attempt to work out the theoretical basis of their structural affinity. Parry's account *(ibid.)* has gone more into the descriptive details about the Lushai people. The account was so much convincing to the people that during the post- Independence period, the Mizo District Council summarized the book (*Mizo Hnam Dan*) considering the same as authoritative law for the use of Village Courts and District Council Court for handling issues pertaining to the customary laws. Parry (1932) also wrote a detailed monograph on the Lakhers of Mizoram which received a lot of attention from the scholars who were involved in comparing societies for building up theories of social structure. Due to these scholars like Leach (1957), Loffler (1960), Levi-Strauss (1969), etc. referred to the Lakher kinship and social structure in building up their arguments. The Lushais (Mizo) were not discussed. One of the reason was that Shakespeare, Parry and McCall (*ibid.*) did not write on the kinship terminology. It is not understood why Parry did so, for he had made a very good attempt in collecting the terms of relationship of the Lakher (1932: 240). In the recent years Lehman (1963: 137) has analysed the kin terms and related the same to the social structure of the Chins of Myanmar.

It should, however, be kept in mind that there were problems regarding ethnic identity of the Mizos, when Shakespear collected his data. In the general terms Lehman has given succinct observation regarding the past Mizo scene, "in the course of wars, famines, population growth and migration, there had been definitely a great deal of change of tribal or ethnic or even linguistic identity, for instance, the Ralte seem certainly to have started out as a distinct dialect group, a sort of tribe or sub-tribe. But some of them either joined Sailo's Mizo or were conquered by them, and these Ralte, soon adopting a Mizo dialect, became in a Mizo context, merely a clan, although at least until recently, there have been, outside of Mizoram proper, Ralte speaking their own language or dialect and in fact divided into several distinct and inter-marrying clans. The attempt made by many writers. to find out, e.g., whether Ralte is really a tribe or a clan, is a spacious scholarship." (1979: 22). Grierson (1967: 74) raised such doubts about the Ralte long back.[2] So Shakespear was very much troubled about this fact. He observed that due to the nomadic nature of the Mizos, since their western trek about 275 years ago and due to the process of ejection and absorption of groups in a realm of a chief most of the people were not conscious of their clan affinity. There was a lot of ambiguity and looseness in the nomenclature. "During the Census of 1901 an unsuccessful attempt was made to get a complete list of clan, families and branches. The causes of the failure were the ignorance of the people themselves as to what clan or family they belonged to and the *tendency to claim* to be true Lushais (*emphasis mine*, Shakespear 1912: 42). Shakespear conjectured that "before the Thangur chiefs had risen to their present predominant position there were many consanguineous communities scattered over the hills, living under headman of their own and each using a dialect of its own. Some of these communities appear to have had separate corporate existence for long periods and in consequence to have been subdivided into many families and branches. "(emphasis mine, *ibid.* 42-43). Shakespear and Grierson both mentioned the factors of war and slave system among the tribes resulting to the absorption of people from one group to the other forging the identity. The ongoing process of absorption continued during the advent of the British rule which received further fillip when the converted Christians ignored the facts of clan and lineage. Many of the traditional markers of the clans such as sacrifices, the position occupied by the corpse at the funeral feast, dialects, etc., lost their cultural importance and significance. The transformation was fast. Finally, after *Mizo unrest* (Goswami 1979) the ties of alliance related to descent further loosened due to village regrouping, migration and miscegenation.

It may be clear by now that the Mizo society, since its entry into Mizoram, is in flux (Goswami 1987). The present identity is a consequence of the above stated socio-historical processes through which the people of the cultural region is going through. They are not the pristine, nascent, homogeneous settled group of people. Because of this reason the earlier authors probably made no attempt to characterise the principles of the society by either looking into descent and marital alliances or by persuing kinship terms.

In 1958, I read out a paper on the Lushai kinship terminology in a meeting of the Assam Anthropological Society, Gauhati, a revised version of which was published by the Anthropological Survey of India (Goswami, 1960). Therein I hypothesised Mizo social structure having tripartite categorisation following matrilateral cousin marriage. The villages where I carried out the field work are no more in existence at the same place and form. Even at that time the ethnic forging was continuing in those villages; the term Mizo in place of Lushai was becoming popular; ethnic groups were not endogamous, and villagers were oblivious of any other ethnic dialects excepting Mizo (for detail see Goswami, 1979). I think for developing my arguments I should place a summary of my findings.

A word before I do so. It is necessary to keep in mind the social usefulness of kin terms used in a society. This can be viewed in two dimensions. One is to see in terms of 'social conditions' which mattered for the emergence of terminologies and another is the 'bearing' which the terminologies have upon the nature of social relations. The issue for consideration are not only the social conditions which give rise to a type of terminology but also the question of how the terminologies contribute to social interaction. A society acts on terminology and terminology acts back on society (Makilney, 1971).

The Mizo (Lushai) kinship terminology has twenty two terms to denote the pattern of relationships. Within the circle of close kin the kinship system discloses the principle of bifurcate merger. The sex of the kin addressed is distinguished in all the cases except in the case of the brother and sister when they are addressed by their siblings. Sex of the speaker is disclosed in terms like *tu*, *vah* and *laizawn*. Wide range of terms applied to relations of the paternal side indicate their greater intimacy when compared with the kin of the mother's side. Age distinction within a single generation are observed only when the terminology is applied to one's own siblings. Range of terminology is limited to two generations above and two generations below. As a general rule one does not address a person younger than him by kinship term.

In the Mizo kinship terminology the 'principle of unity of lineage' is playing a significant part. The whole system appears to be based on the importance of one's own lineage. The overall structural principles which govern categorisation of relations are:

(i) All the females going out of one's lineage through marriage are grouped together and their husbands also stand as a group in relation to ego (*makpa* group),

(ii) The offspring of the above also form one group and are known by the same kinship term making only a distinction of sex (*tu* group),

(iii) The females who come into the agnatic group of ego form a group (*pu* group).

The above principles give rise to tripartite categories of the people in alliance, viz., ego's group, wife-taker group (*makpa*) and wife-giver group (*pu*).

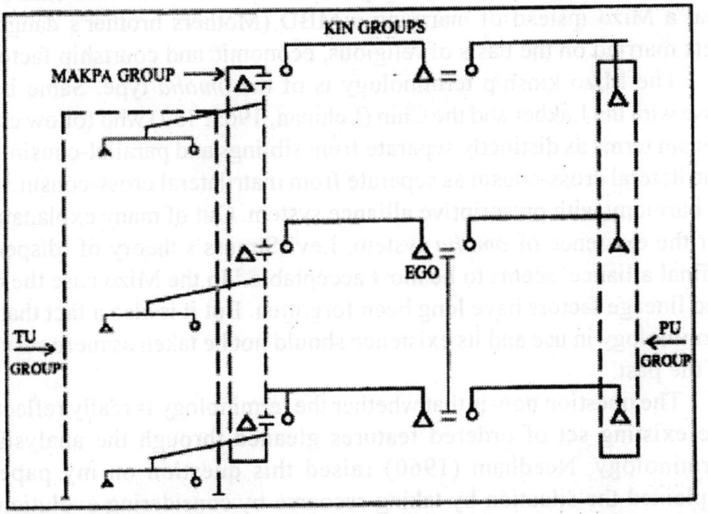

The diagram shows that the grand children categorisation only happens to form with the Children of the wife-taker (*tu*).

There is an inherent mechanism in the Mizo alliance system to take case of the kin categories even living widely dispersed, of bride price and certain associated rituals.

The attitude towards relatives through the women that are married in one's own family is one of deference and consideration which is clearly reflected in certain traditional custom, whether they are still followed or not is a different issue about which I shall comment after some time. According to the tradition, when any animal like *mithun* or pig is cut, it is essential to give the hind leg of the animal to his matrilateral kin, i.e., *pu* (*pusa*). On the other hand, one is not obliged to pay anything to the wife-taking group, i.e., father's sister's husband or sister's husband. As a matter of fact ceremonial cutting of the animal is to be done by *makpa*. It may be noted that if the *pu-tu* relationship remains unrecognised the flow of goods and reciprocal relationship of obligations between the above stated groups will stop.

The Mizo society is patrilineal but prescription for marriage is matrilateral. Certain expression also indicate that marriage with matrilateral cousin should be indulged.

Needham calls such marriages as prescriptive. Levi-Strauss relates elementary social structures with obligatory prescriptive marriage system. But the fact is I could not come across a single case of cross-cousin marriage during the tenure of my fieldwork. Observational data show that a Mizo instead of marrying a MBD (Mothers brother's daughter) gets married on the basis of religious, economic and courtship factors.

The Mizo kinship terminology is of the *omaha* type. Same is the case with the Lakher and the Chin (Lehman, 1963: 137) who follow cross-cousin terms as distinctly separate from siblings and parallel-cousin, and patrilateral cross-cousin as separate from matrilateral cross-cousin.[3] It is in harmony with prescriptive alliance system. Out of many explanations for the existence of *omaha* system, Levi-Strauss's theory of 'dispersed affinal alliance' seems to be most acceptable.[4] In the Mizo case the clan and lineage factors have long been forgotten. But it is also a fact that the terminology in use and its existence should not be taken as mere survival of the past.

The question now is that whether the terminology is really reflecting the existing set of ordered features gleaned through the analysis of terminology. Needham (1960) raised this question on my paper. I explained the situation by taking recourse by considering evolutionary historical processes (Goswami 1973). My conviction is that the terminology should act also as per the demand of new emerging situation.

The process involved in this matter has to be looked into through fresh fieldwork.

Levi-Strauss asserted the 'integrative' feature of prescriptive system related with matrilateral cross-cousin marriage. On this matter let me quote him "marriage with father's sister's daughter is less frequent than with the mother's brother's daughter, it is because the second not only permits but favours a better integration of the group." (emphasis mine). To him such marriage system generates a greater organic solidarity. In a patrilineal society the mechanical solidarity between the brothers who grow together and are responsible for states and power of the family is obvious. But the development of organic solidarity between unrelated individuals and their kins definitely generate integration and consequent enlargement of the solidarity axis. As such classificatory category such as MBD (Mothers brother's daughter) helps. While analysing the data collected by Das on the Purum, Needham wrote, "So far as the social order is concerned, the same tripartite categorisation orders relations between individuals, between descent groups and between the componant local descent groups of the village and creates ties between the politically independent villages" (1962: 82).[5]

One of the important dimension of development in Mizoram is the solidarity movement of the people. The fact of lineage unity has weakened over time but alliance through marriage is liberal and integrative. The idea of Mauss that the exchange of women are gift items probably is working as latent idea. If the kinship system in a society is a product of the social organisation it should have considerable linkages with the existing system. We do not know anything about this including bride-price paid during marriage and other subsequent presentations. The difference between theory and practices should be evaluated qualitatively and quantitatively. I propose that certain points need careful attention in the contemporary situation by those who are interested in the study of social structure and alliance system. (Goswami, 1988) These are: nature of relationship of a person with the mother's brother (*pu*), nature of relationship between parents in law and children in law, nature of marriages (even courtship marriages) in cultural and political groupings away from urban and market centres, justification of marrying parties in terms of kin relationship, contemporary function and role of *pu* and *makpa*, and changes in the bride-price system and material presentations especially gift exchanges, viz., meat and goods. It may be noted that meat and bride price moves in one direction and material goods in another.[6]

All this will classify the the structural categorisation in reality. The ideal was delineated by me 35 years ago, but the present day reality and operation need fresh examination.

REFERENCES

1. That was the time when Needham (1958) ably analysed the data on the Purum, showing the terms of relationship in accordance with the rules of descent and marriage prescription to fall in line with Levi-Strauss's theory of elementary kinship system (1969). That was also the time when Lehman wrote that "the Lushai have no prescriptive marriage alliance" (1963: 122), and Homans and Schnlider that the Lakhers are 'non-prescriptive' concerning marriage (Needham 1962: 55). I have already shown that the Lakher system follow matrilateral prescriptive marriage contradicting Homans and Schneider's observation. Lehman's inference has been contradicted by my data 35 years ago.
2. The Mizos are not much ranked as the Lakhers, Hakachins or Kachins are. Status and rank differentiation was, however, there. Between chiefs and slaves there were number of status positions. Their rights and privileges differed in matters of life in this and beyond the world. In marriage status of clan and lineage was reflected in the number of *mithun's* to be received by the wife-giver. This has been also the practice among the Lakher where status and rank was more marked and occasionally fluid. For example, status of a family among the Lakher could be changed if the females married to the family were of higher clan in three ascending generations (Parry 1932: 230).
3. See my paper on the Lakher kinship system wherein I have shown that in some marriages though the MBD was not in reality, a geneologically placed MBD, but she was classified in a manner that could be viewed so. Parry repeatedly stated the existence of MBD marriages in his monograph. "In the Zeuhang villages child marriage is practised only in the case of marriages between cross-cousins, that is to say, when a man marries with mother's brother's daughter. Marriage between these relations are much favoured in Savang" (*ibid*: 310).
4. Most Omaha societies are patrilineal (81 per cent) (McKilney), i.e., following unilineal descent. Morgan was the first to note that certain terminologies disregard generational distinction between cross-cousin was less advanced than other kinship system. Radcliffe-Brown (1952), the most important structuralist, argued that the Omana kinship system is the reflection of the principle of unity of lineage group. Leslie White (1939) pointed out that in the evolutionary scheme of unilineal descent group *omaha* system appeared at quite a later stage. And then there are formal semantic analysts who through formal analysis comment upon the

existence of rule such as lineage unity for the emergence of term. McKilney (*ibid.*) while arguing with the view point of Levi-Strauss "that the terminology acts as a formula for prohibiting successive marriages between the same two descent lines" raised the question of "ideological role" played by terminology. Levi-S trauss has limited the issue of ideological role by looking for consistency.

5. "Matrilateral alliance can be regarded as a simple and effective way of creating and maintaining counterfissive relationships in a segmentary society" (Needham, 1962: 97).
6. Lehman (1963) criticises Needham by saying two classes of goods which are channelised in social exchange as simplistic derivations. His views are 'heuristic'.

NOTES

1932, *The Lakhers*, Macmillan & Co. Ltd., London.

1979 Book Review. In *Thu Leh Hla*, September, Aizawl.

A.G. McCall, 1949 *Lushai Chrysalis*, Luzac & Co. Ltd., London.

A.R. Radcliffe-Brown, 1952, *Structure and Function in Primitive Society*. Free Press, New York.

B.B. Goswami, 1960, Explanatory note on prescriptive alliance and the Purnm, *American Anthropologist*, 66, 1385-86.

——1960, Kinship System among the Lushai. Bulletin of the *Anthropological Survey of India*, Vol. No. 9, No. 2. Calcutta.

——1973, Structural Phenomenon of Kinship with regard to the Lushai. In *Tribe, Caste and Peasantry*, Ethnographic and Folk Culture Society, Lucknow.

——1979, The *Mizo Unrest—A Study of Politicisation of Culture*, Aalekh Publishers. Jaipur.

——1987, Mizo in the Context of State Formation. In *State Formation in Eastern India*, edited by S.C. Sinha, K.P. Bagchi, Calcutta.

——1988, Structural, issues regarding the Maring of Manipur. *Journal of the Indian Anthropological Society*, Vol. 23.

C. Levi-Strauss, 1969 *The Elementary Structures of Kinship*, Becon Press, Boston, Second printing).

E.R. Leach 1957 Aspects of Bridewealth and marriage stability among the Kachin and Lakher. *Man.*, No. 59.

F.K. Lehman, 1963 *The Structure of Chin Society*, The University of Illinois Press, Urbana.

G Lorenz. Loffler, 1960, Patrilateral lineation in Transition: The Kinship System of the Lakher (Mara), *Ethnos*.

G.A. Grierson, 1967 (reprinted) *Linguistic Survey of India*, Vol. I, Part 1. Manoharlal Banarsi Das, Delhi.

J. Shakespear, 1912, *Lushei Kuki Clans*, MaMillan & Co. Ltd., London.

Leslie White, 1939, *A Problem of Kinship Terminology*, American Anthropologist, Vo1.41.

N.E. Parry, 1928 *A Monograph on Lushei Customs and Ceremonies*, Assam Government Press, Shillong.

Robert McKilney, 1971, Why do Crow and Omaha kinship terminologies exist? A Sociology of Knowledge Interpretation. *Man*. Vol. 6, No. 3.

Rodney Needham, 1958, A Structural Analysis of Purum Society. *American Anthropologist*, Vol. IX.

Rodney, Needham,1960, Explanatory Note on Prescriptive Alliance and the Purnm, *American Anthropologist*, 66, 1385-86.

——1962, *Structure and Sentiment*, The University of Chicago Press, Chicago.

34
On Cultural Policy

J.V. Hluna

Definitions

Culture is an all-pervading concept. Put simply it means the way 'an individual is' or 'a group of people are'. Language, literature, aesthetics, values, folkways and other such aspects of life are involved in the concept of culture. Hence, any discussion, debate or policy on culture has to take into account all these important aspects of a collective life.

British Cultural Policy

During the colonial period, the British cultural policy in India was guided by British colonial interests. Till 1813, they followed a policy which was changed as it was felt that to faster the interest of the British industrial capitalism the rigid social and cultural structure had to be liberalised. By 1800, moreover the conservative attitude in England was fast giving way to a new attitude which was sharply critical of Indian society and culture. Indian civilisation was viewed as static and decadent. This thinking was encouraged by the rise of the doctrine of humanism, rationalism and reason in Europe. By this time some honest and philanthropic Englishmen also influenced the British cultural policy in India. The policy of modernising Indian society and culture was also encouraged by Christian Missionaries and religious minded persons such as William Wilberforce and Charles Grant. The Missionaries were critical of the Indian cultural practices. They were supported by some paternalistic and utilitarian English administrators as well as some radical Indian reformers like Ram Mohan Roy. Thus we find the abolition of the *sati* system, Female infanticide, widow remarriage, introduction of the age of consent Bill and the introduction of modern education in India by the Britain. Although these reforms were considered unwanted interference of the outsiders by some, others did welcome them.

To sum up the overall policy of the British as far as culture is concerned was of careful non-interference but at the same time slow and gradual modernisation of Indian culture according to English/European parameters. Its "divide and rule" policy helped to keep the people of India culturally divided but on the other hand a kind of culturally homogeneity was also brought about among the urban educated Indians through anglicisation.

Cultural Policy of India after Independence

After Independence, the National Government followed a policy of non-interference also. But after the initial hesitation 'Hindi' was attempted to be made into national language but due to the violent opposition from the Southern as well as Eastern States the policy had to be given up. But the Central policy is still to slowly and gradually encouraged the use of the Hindi Language in public as well as private life through legislation, T.V., Radio and Films. A subtle attempt to Hindi is the entire country is being carried out in the name of mainstream culture. It is preparing the way for declaring Hindi as the national language. The attempts of Hindisation is slowly being carried out in the non-Hindi-speaking States of the South, Bengal, Assam and the North-East.

Apart from language, the audio-visual media tries to carry the message that all life in India is centred around Hindu religion. An attempt has also been made to show that Christianity is not a religion of Indians. Since it professes secularism and most of the cultural activities of the people are related to religions, the Government cannot have a strict cultural policy.

The Central Front has a Film and Video Censor Board as a part of its cultural policy which acts as a moral guardian of the people. It decides what kind of films and video films can be seen by the people of India, Violence, sex, vulgarity, oppression on woman, etc., were considered taboo on screen. Therefore, movies depicting these are not passed. But the central front is handicapped as it can censor only Indian and legal western pictures. But the smuggled/illegal western pictures-movies that are flooding the Indian markets cannot be dealt with by this Censor Board.

Suggestions

(a) The Government of India should have a sound and *solid* Cultural Policy.

(b) It should be based on rationalism, humanism and tolerance.

(c) It should foster nationalism, but not impose the majority culture on minorities.

(d) Small minorities and tribal culture should be protected.

(e) While formulating cultural policies the interest of these small minorities and tribal group interests should be taken into account. They should be consulted too.

(f) There should be free intermixture between people of different regions on friendly basis and mutual exchange of cultural programmes so that each be made aware of the other culture.

(g) Minorities and Tribals should be encouraged and provided financial concessions to travel to other parts of India and, if willing, settle in any part of the country.

(h) There should not be any imposition of either language or culture on each other.

(i) Provisions/legislations should be made for free development of every culture.

(j) The underlying unity in diversity should be emphasised upon.

(k) The State should profess secular attitude as far as culture is concerned and should not favour any particular religion or culture

35
Mizo Culture

H.S. Luaia

Origin of the Mizos

Oral tradition says that Mozos are of eastern origin. Our elders say we came out of 'Chhinlung', hence, Mizos are of Chhinlung origin. This stock includes parhaps all mongoloids. The time of our birth from Chhinlung, as recorded by Pu Buanga (Rev. J.H. Lorrain, Dictionary of the Lushai Language, p. 80) was after what is called 'Thim zing', meaning thick darkness which lasted seven days and seven nights ridden with monsters. (*Cf.* Lt. Col. John Shakespere, the Lushai Kuki Clan, p. 93). Some like V.L. Sanglura (Lal Elshadaia, Lamka) have identified Chhinlung with the Great Wall of China. And there our ancestors might have cohabited with Jews of the Dispersal of the Christian era. For there is a strange but universal knowledge of the name of Pawla (St. Paul?) whose arrows never miss those who did not love a girl during their life on earth.

> Pawla shoots at those who did not love,
> I've escaped his dart should I go that way
> For I have my shawl which covered me with my love.

It looked very much like a parody or misconception of the teaching of St. Paul on Love. Some household articles like the gin, the spinning wheel bears the stamp of artisanship in the long past when we were a member of a bigger family of a cvilized race.

Social Administration of the Mizos:

The following account is based on my own observations as the son of a Chief's Councillor, Lal upa. The Chief's (of a tribe, or of a village or a group of village) administration looked somehow like that of the British monarch's. The Chief has a circle of councillors, a priest or sacrifice-performer and also a village crier. Besides these close circle, there are a number of ablebodied families called *Ramhual* who were given special choice of *jhum* land, thus securing economic security for the entire community. When a person finds life difficult and wanted to try his luck elsewhere he is withheld by means of supplying him rice form the surplus of *Ramhual* family. My host in England told me of how the British Commonwealth worked. Beggary was not allowed, and a local committee saw to it that even the lowest from the employment had a salary compatible with the market price for the sustenance of the family. The rich paid taxes in proportion to their capital. The Mizo Chiefs jealously conserved the *jhum* land under their control. Forest fires were quickly and efficiently extinguished by the young men who cleared a fire path and the girls backed them up with gourd full of water and packets of food. On their return the Chief treated them with a rich feast. This showed the goodwill that existed in the Chief's community. The rich and poor lived without social restraint; the rich supported the poor in every possible ways. To me the old Mizo society was like a big family. The Chief and his councillors were given due respect, but not like the awe and fear with which the rest of the world regarded kings and lords.

Discipline of the Young

For young people constituted the popular image of the community, and are the backbone of the Chief's administration. The young men with the *zawlbuk* as their Office and Training Camp were much respected and feared by the Chief and his subjects, avoiding their displeasure as much as they could; for without their popular support the community had no real defence. *zawlbuk* was built at the centre of the village. A fire roared in the middle fed with firewood collected involuntarily by the boys. The young men slept all around the fire. I spent all my boyhood and youth-time in the *zawlbuk*, and I found the administration of the boys and the youth without equal in maintaining a stable and happy society in the context of constant danger from beasts and foes. A senior gentlemen normally took the responsibility, and he was much respected by his charges, perhaps even more than they would the Chief himself. The boys were under the guidance of a young man given the charge of firewood collection. A boy who failed to collect firewood for the *zawlbuk* was punished. The young men were permitted to go out courting only after the girls were ready to sit with them with their spinnings. And they were not to stay over-long as the girls had to get up early for the next day's chores. If a girl happens *inleng* might help her upto three *sai* or bunch of cotton. Exceeding this the young man would have his cloth torn in half by his friends and the girl would be expected to give him a new one.

Zawlbuk was where *Tlawmngaihna,* the spirit of service before self reigned. The young men competed to be the first to run after the tiger when it snatched a pig or to carry message to another village.

Care for Children

Mizos were not much given to caring for the welfare of children. The new born baby was fed the yolk of boiled egg and cooked rice, and then blessed with a sacrifice of a young chick. When the child grew up, every one treated him/her as a tireless servant, saying. 'Children and gourds grow up soon enough, why spare them.' When someone celebrates his blessings by performing the *Sechhun* plenty of porridge was prepared for the children who, according to custom, demanded their portion by crying, "We want porridge, we want porridge", and beating and shaking the house from under. They were then served outside. Before this day the boys cut lengths of vines from the jungle with which they played with the bull-mithun, beating it mercilessly. I enjoyed the game as a boy too. But the missionaries started a school in my village, and our teachers prohibited taking part in such cruel sport.

Lot of Girls: Women occupied a very low place in the Mizo society. 'Women and crabs have no religion' is how they were classed, which means they were regarded no better than a marriage commodity. The unmarried girls '*nula*' worked very hard, getting up at dawn to draw water, husk rice, and go to *jhum* after breakfast. After a gruelling day's work they stayed awake (or do they?) while the young men courted them till late at night. When the *jhum* work is over they spent the time in weaving clothes in preparation for the bridal property/dowry. They never drink except a sip or two on festival days. Virtuous girls were expected to be wise and conscientious. It was impossible to know whether they love a particular young man; because they showed their favour equally to all who courted them. Some young men, just to prove their mettle, would bring a half-witted person with them, watching how she treats such a person. The wise girl would never be duped by such stratagem. It was not nice to address married persons without the proper term for calling a relative. They would ask their parents how this or that person should be addressed by her. They do not dress ostentatiously, they do not laugh like libertine in front of men. Manners was valued more than looks. Such girls honour the Chief and their parents.

Religion

Although Mizos were classed as animists, a deeper study of their life and culture would reveal that they worship a Supreme Being, and that the sacrifices made to spirits were made only to appease their anger when they became ill. They trusted the heavens for the fruit of the field and for the rains and sunshine. They believed in a Heavenly Father whom they call '*Pu Vana*' or '*Khuanu*' or '*Khua leh vang*'. In the story of Liandova we see Liandova consoling his younger brother in their poverty: "Do not cry, God above in heaven looks at us on his belly". God was believed to be omnipotent, omniscient, onipresent and creator of all things. There are a number of superstitious codes of conduct which could have only been meaningful in the presence of a universal and an eternal God. Some of them are almost parallel to the *Bible*:

1. Murder is a curse unto generation.
2. Adultery is punished by a tiger or by lightning.
3. Stolen hoe or axe will dig the thief's grave.
4. A curse on other come back.
5. Dornications bar the gate of birth.
6. Cruelty to creatures is punished just before death.
7. A house blocking public path produces corpse.
8. Divide and live, keep and die.

That God blesses the good but punished the bad was celarly inculcated by their elders. My father did not accept Chirstianity until I became a young man, yet the way he guided me lacked very little of Chirstian upbringing because he was a very religious minded father. And as a Christian he outshone us all. Once at a Summer School I was asked to speak to two hundred English young people about the Mizo life. When I mentioned our old life and superstitious beliefs, one of the Professors of Serampore Theological College blurted out: "Now I can understand why the Mizos have always impressed me as being distinctive from other communities". We worshipped God, but know very little about Him. Our ancestors talked about our 'Book' being eaten by a dog could well have been the *Bible* written in leather scroll ! It is surprising how the entire community have come to accept Christianity in such little time after the advent of the white Missionaries.

Entertainment

Mizos had very few forms of entertainment in comparison with other neighbouring tribes. The biggest occasions are the '*Kut*' or festivals. We had three such '*Kut*' in a year.

1. Chapchar Kut

It was celebrated after completion of the *lovah* or *jhum*-cutting. The most entertaining part of this festival was '*Chai*' or group-dancing. Young men and women stood in a circle, the young men putting their arm on the girls' shoulders on either side. The girls just hang their arms down. It was begun on the eve of the festival day, and it must continue all through the night; for if they do not, they would not be allowed to '*chai*' the rest of the festival. Thus they danced on and on in the Chief's yard, the drummer and horn blower in the centre reciting the songs endlessly. Children offered them honey or beer in glass bottles, while they sang:

> Yonder southern wild our hunting field
> Our spears lifted high amidst cries of long tuskers.

This song is our only informant that they had hunted elephants with spears even before they had guns. Girls wore crowns of feathers called *vakiria* and put on their best clothes. The young men, including married men, also dressed to match the girls. Children loved the very sight of them. On the eve of the festival, before sunset, children with their mothers gathered at the memorial ground (a place at the approach of the village where memorial stones were erected) bringing with them various articles of food on decorated plates. Mothers wore brief skirts and big shawls. They put meat, eggs and rice in one another's mouth, chasing each other. It was an enjoyable moment, which even as a Christian youth I found it hard not to envy.

'*Chai*' is not the name of a dance; a variety of dances were performed in it. Since they had this festival only once a year, and it being the only festival meant for sheer celebration, they were loath to end it, but carried on for days together, depending on their store of grain. Once Chawngtui village carried on till harvest time, and when a parrot flying over them dropped an ear of paddy they recovered to find that they had no more rice, and so the village dispersed, as the tale goes.

2. Pawl Kut

It is held after the year's harvest. Victuals was the main item of this festival.

The men hunted and trapped games for the festival. Some had collective fishing. The fatted pig was reserved for this occasion. The Lusai and *lu tawi* killed pigs on different nights. The pig, after being caught was tied front and hind legs with the pounding stick between the legs and taken up to the threshold where it lay helpless and groaning. The priest (sadawt) appeared at dusk, and mumbled the sacrificial vow which was considered an ideal wife. Such a time and the society we remenber new as in a dream.

It must be the first duty of the new generation to keep up what is best of the old life so that we may become once more a self-sufficing, independent people in our beautiful hills.

36

Mizo Women and Human Rights

Kunja Medhi

The Mizo women have enjoyed human rights as enshrined in the Charter of the United Nations and the Constitution of India. These rights as incorporated in the Constitution of India have been the Rights to six freedoms; namely, the Right to Equality (Articles 14 to 18); Right to Freedom (Articles 19 to 22); Right against Exploitation (Articles 23 to 24); Right to Freedom of Religion (Articles 25 to 28); Cultural and Educational Rights (Articles 29 to 30) and the Right to Constitutional Remedies (Articles 32 to 35).

Certain time-honoured and salutary customs and practices have enabled the Mizo women to enjoy the status of dignity, equality and the human rights when their counterparts all over the world clamoured for getting recognition as "individuals". The recognition of man and woman as complementary to each other in the Mizo society and the hailing of the birth of a girl child as a perpetuating factor of human race have sustained social stability. The overall balancing role of the society also has shaped the customs and practices to ensure in honourable position for the women. The overwhelmingly dominant role of the group life in the social structure has been such that no woman has been left alone to suffer inferiority, indignity and exploitation at the whims and caprices of the male. The girl child who continues to play a significant role in the family has still been regarded as the harbinger of good fortune since through her marriage relations the parents find prospect of gaining new support. The freedom of the girls to free courting or "*nula rim*" and choosing the groom is respected by the parents. This socially accepted system recognises the women's inherent right to choose her life partner. The equal treatment meted out to both boys and girls has saved the latter from derogatory and discriminatory situations unlike their counterparts in the plain areas of India.

Recognition of Unwed Mothers

The acceptance of and recognition to the unwed mothers by the society is another hallmark which has recognised the human rights of the Mizo women. Freedom for pre-marital relationship between the boys and the girls testifies their equal status. Moreover, the provisions for severe punishment for committing adultery has not only made the society disciplined and moral, but it has also provided protection for the exploited women. The custom for which the bride has to take with her the *Zawlpuan* a piece of cloth woven by her to her hunband's home is another feature of equality of women. The cloth is meant to cover the husband's body after his death.

The marriage system by service or paying the bride's price also gives an important position to the Mizo women. "The payment for a bride, has tended to emphasize the influence of women, their ability to hold their own, the esteem in which they are held and their important roles in the social life" (Evans-Pritchard, 1965). Provisions for widow marriage, easy procedure of divorce, social protection for the marriage woman and her children abandoned by her husband and the customary details in handling the different situation in the life of the women have shown that the Mizo women enjoy high status in the society. The society's special concern for the *thisen pal* (those who have children) and the *thisen pal lo* (barren or childless), concubine's position and her claim to the same financial provisions in the case of her separation from the male like that of a married woman also testify the high value and importance of the Mizo women.

Political Consciousness and Mizo Women

With the spread of education political consciousness among the Mizo women has increased considerably. The turnout of the women voters in the election shows their involvement in the political process and the democratic culture. Even in the primeval period some women of this State exercised political and administrative powers with success. They could declare war, make peace and receive foreign dignitaries. Before the advent of the British rule the practice of succeeding the chieftain by his wife was a well-recognised custom. The wife of Vanhnuailiana, a Chief of the Eastern Lushai clan who succeeded her husband after his death made peace with Lushai Expedition of 1871. Pibuk, the queen of Western Lushai clan was another powerful female Chief. She exercised all the political and administrative powers except for guiding the Lushai militia in the battle field. In that capacity she could hold meetings in the *Zawlbuk* (the bachelors' dormitory) which was generally a forbidden area for the female. Rani Banai Thangpuii held meeting with Major Boyd, the Deputy Commissioner of Cachar at a *zawlbuk* in 1884. The British considered Rani Laponi Leni to be a formidable enemy and after her arrest by the British she was sent to a jail in Chittagong (Bengal). Even after the annexation of the Lushai Hills by the British the succession of the female to the post of the Chieftain continued.

Customary Law and Mizo Women

Mizoram which was placed within a purview of the Assam Chieftain Act, the protective provisions of the Government of India Act of 1935 and subsequently the Constitution of India, had the privilege of coming into contact with the Christian Missionaries. Within half a century of the arrival of the Christian Missionaries the people attained comparatively high rate of literacy. Mass conversion into Christianity also helped them to replace the ancient tribal customs with modern practices in different fields of life. However, unlike in other States of India where the Indian Succession Act and the Civil Code prevail, in Mizoram customary laws were also accepted in principle by the Mizoram Peace Accord of 1986. The local Church leaders who replaced the foreign Missionaries after the Independence of India as well as the Mizo District Council favoured the revival of the old customary laws, culture, folk dances and music. Although the educate males still favour the retention of the customary laws, the Mizo women have been slightly at a disadvantaged position in regard to property, divorce and maintenance under the same. The steps taken by the Mizo Young Women Association (MHIP) and the Mizo Women Christian Association for the adoption of the Civil Code in the State have been noteworthy.

Role of Christianity and the Mizo Women

Christianity has played a revolutionary role in emancipating the women of Mizoram as well transforming the society. Increased access to formal education associated with conversion, creation of posts in the government offices and the Mission Organisations provided the necessary incentives to both the male and the female. Moreover singing of hymns in the churches required literate people. Principles of equality achieved through Christian baptism raised the status of people beyond the distinction of sexes. Spread of literacy went hand in hand with conversion. Education thus became the largest single factor to improve the status of women. It changed the pattern of thinking of people also. There is evidence of a strong correlation between the educational level and employment rate of women. The educated women have started seeing the marriage as a partnership where the family life becomes a co-operative venture. The gradually increasing number of Middle English Schools, High Schools and Colleges like 343, 134 and 12 respectively by 1982 explains the rate of rapid spread of education in Mizoram. There is no discrimination against the girls in terms of education and employment.

Traditions have gradually been replaced by modernity. The *zawlbuk* has fast been losing its former position since the educated young boys do not favour it as they used to do prior to their exposure to Christianity and formal education. People now prefer modern medical facilities, formal education, English language and a richer material life to the customary practices. The rapid changes of the society have made the modern educated Mizo women more conscious about their rights and simultaneously capable of facing the new challenges of life.

ECONOMICS AND DEVELOPMENT HISTORY

37

Environmental Aspects of Land Use Pattern and Rural Economy with Special Reference to Mizoram

Chandralekha Raghuwanshi

1. Introduction

The modernization process under way in North-East India has been causing changes in the land use pattern both because of the introduction of new laws and restrictions by government and because of some internal forces of change. As a system the region is mainly based on wet rice cultivation and the tribes on shifting cultivation. Results of experiments on land and water resource management in the area indicate possibility of slow conversion of substantial part of *jhum* land into terrace fields for mixed farming. Our knowledge of the most effective land use in these heavy rainfall areas is still fragmentary.

High altitude areas have received little scientific attention. Ecological conditions vary greatly even within short distances in these areas, depending upon aspect; latitude, altitude, slope, soil depth and distances from the plains. Large variations in temperature and rainfall occur and the length of growing season is controlled by the time of occurrence of snow in winter and its disappearance in the spring. Erosion is a serious problem and in several of these areas.

2. General Environment of Mizoram

Mizoram or Lushai hills, as it was known formerly, is situated between 22°-24° SN latitudes and 92° 26′-93°4′ E longitudes. It is bordered on the North by Assam, Manipur on the east, on the south by Burma and on the west by Tripura and Bangladesh. The entire State presents a mountainous terrain with more or less parallel hill ranges running in North-South direction averaging 700-1300 m in altitude. However, the isolated peaks, attain height over 1,900 m with the Phawngpui tlang in the Blue mountains being the highest peak (2400 m) followed by Lengteng tlang, Ngur tlang. The State covers a total area of 21,081 sq.km of which 12,233 sq. km or 57 per cent is under forest cover, both primary as well as secondary comprising diverse vegetation of tropical, sub-tropical and temperate type. The territory receives an annual rainfall between 2000-3600 mm from both north east and south-west monsoons, which together with conducive range of temperature 20°-30°C during summer and 11°C to 21° C in winter and high humidity help in a considerably rich growth of orchids, both in luxuriance and diversity.

3. Land Use Pattern and Economy

Although it is well known that the protection of mountain ecosystems is essential for the economic wellbeing of not only the people living in the hills, but also in the plains, considerable deforestation is taking place in all our hill areas and Mizoram no exception. The problem is also aggravated due to wrong agricultural practices causing serious soil erosion. The erosion of soil ultimately undermine the renewable base of agriculture. It has brought misery to the local population which used to thrive and live so happily in their own surroundings in the past.

In spite of the low density of population in the hilly areas there is scarcity of good cultivable land. The tribal people depend primarily upon the shifting cultivation which is the most primitive system of crop production.

It is a fact that the population density in tribal areas is even lower. But it may be noticed that shifting cultivation or *jhuming* has evil effect on ecological setting. Besides, in certain areas the economy of the people depending on this type of cultivation has already reached a critical point because of the shortening of the *jhum* cycle due to pressure of population.

Because of the rapid loss of fertility due to soil erosion the *jhum* land is abandoned after the harvest. In the *rabi* season also the plot is not used for cultivation. Thus, the system is an extensive nature of land use. In the *jhum* cycle the interval is mainly dependent upon the density of population of a particular area and the availability of suitable hill slopes for *jhum* cultivation. In Mizo hills of Mizoram the *jhum* cycle is of 5 years.

Studies have shown that *jhum* cultivation cannot feed a dense population. Saha (1970) estimated that between 3 to 9 persons per sq. km. can be maintained depending upon the quality of land through *jhuming* at a subsistence level at the existing level of productivity, provided 50 per cent of the total areas are available for cultivation and 15-20 years are provided for *jhum* cycle. In case of Mizoram the population density has already exceeded the carrying capacity resulting in extreme poverty of the shifting cultivators.

4. Suggestions for Potential Utilization

The following suggestions may be granted for the better use of land resource:

(i) Correct and proper management of the land on the basis of its capability is a must for best land utilization. As such land may be classified into two major classes:
   (a) land suitable for cultivation, and
   (b) land not suitable for cultivation.
   These two classes can be further divided into other sub-classes according to their morphometric conditions, and productivity.

(ii) To check erosion, terracing must be adopted. For best cultivation on steep slope, bench terraces are quite suitable.

(iii) For the conservation of soil and water, special crops with high conservation efficiency should be grown.

(iv) Utilisation of postures must be regularised to check soil erosion.

(v) Economic condition of the people can improve through effective development of horticulture, vegetable production; social forestry; soil conservation programmes, and animal husbandry. Vast scope exists for the development of forest based industries.

(vi) Large-scale and appropriate afforestation programmes for the establishment of forests should be taken up.

(vii) Detailed studies should be made on watersheds, catchments and land capabilities for better planning and management programmes.

38

Change in Source Pattern and Distribution of Income and its Effect on Society in Rural Mizoram

P.K. Das

Mizoram is situated in the north-eastern corner of India. It was one of the districts in Assam till 1972 when it was made a Union Territory (21st January, 1972) as a part of the major reorganisation of the State of Assam, under the North Eastern Areas (Reorganisation) Act of 1971. Mizoram was given a status of full-fledged statehood in 1987 and is now the 24th State of the Union of India.

The Mizos came for settlement to the present Mizoram around 1700 A.D. when they crossed the Tiau river and reached the place now known as Mizoram. It is now widely believed that the Mizos belonged to the Tibeto-Burman sub-group of the Tibeto-Chinese family and were placed together with *Naga, Sak, Burman, Kachin, Lalo,* etc. But in course of time the Mizos departed from other groups in their southward movement from north-west China to the Upper Chindwin Division of Burma and ultimately to the present Mizoram.

The Mizos were head-hunting savages with primitive customs and faith. They also knew the art of *jhum* farming and after final settlement in present Mizoram, *jhum* farming has become their main occupation. The distinct feature of the society was the existence of *bawiship, zawlbuk, Tlawmngaihna*, etc. *Bawiship* implies the practice of surrendering people themselves to the chief for any reason, economical, political or social. *zawlbuk* is the quarters for bachelors where the young people used to learn discipline through the senior inmates of the *zawlbuk. Zawlbuk* was regarded as the nerve-centre of the Mizo society. *Tlawmngaihna,* on other hand, is a value system, an unwritten code of etiquette which guides the people in their interpersonal relations demanding selflessness in any needed situation. *Tlawmngaihna* demands people to be helpful. hospitable and kind to others even at the cost of self-sacrifice. Besides, the society was characterised by the chief as the head of the society, existence of good and evil spirits, *Pialral* and *Mithikhua* the two abodes of life, after death, lower status of women in the society, etc.

Jhum farming was the only source of income with little scope for subsidiary sources of income. People in the society were more or less independent with minimum division of labour. Society was less stratified and existence of poverty was obscured within the framework of community ownership of land and *tlawmngaihna*, the value system, in Mizo society. The presence of egalitarian relationship and absence of authoritarian rule created a sense of cohesion and equality among the people in the society.

But the introduction of British rule and arrival of Christian Missionaries in the hills had brought about remarkable changes in the social and cultural life of the people within a short period of time. The sincere effort of Missionaries made it possible to convert the Mizos, the followers of animistic rites, into Christians to the extent of more than 96 per cent within a life time of one generation. On the pattern of western culture the Mizo society was converted into a Christian-oriented society. Under the influence of Christianity, the customs and faiths like head-hunting, *zawlbuk*, *bawiship*, believe in good and evil spirit, etc., disappeared gradually. With Christianity the Mizos gained education, modern ways of life, western culture, etc., but in exchange of the transformation of their own social life, good old customs, practices, habits, faiths, etc., to a considerable extent. More and more inclination to westerrn culture, western pattern of life, modern facilities and comforts created more and more social instability as there were no social obligations or laws to curb this unimaginative social transformation. Such a blind attraction to western pattern of life and modern comforts sowed the seeds of self-interest or egoism among the Mizo people in the society.

After independence, the Lushei Hills became one of the hill districts of Assam and this Lushei Hills district was upgraded to Assam Union Territory and renamed and Mizoram on January 21, 1972. Up to 1972 the Lushei Hills district figured in the Five Year Plans and Annual Plans of Assam only and as such had no direct implication on plans. The Mizos even at the later part of the twentieth century were economically very backward as economic development in the modern sense of the term was still in an embryonic stage. It was only after attaining the status of Union Territory in 1972, that the development programmes could be undertaken in Mizoram with an expenditure of Rs. 9.31 crores during the last two years of the Fourth Plan. Since then there have been a significant increase in development and non-development expenditure under various schemes. But most of this expenditure were in the nature of initial or 'threshold' investment to create minimum infrastructural facilities while the rural economy of Mizoram failed to receive the least attention for its own development. The concentration of development activities in and around the town areas lured the villagers to migrate themselves to town areas with an intention to earn more. As a result, there have been a speedy urbanisation and about one-fourth of the total rural population migrated to town areas especially in and around the capital town of Aizawl by the end of 1980.

The concentration of development and non-development expenditure in urban centres under Five Year Plans and various Central sponsored schemes not only resulted in large scale urbanisation but also jeopardised the system in urban Mizo society to a great extent. Continuous and heavy inflow of central aids, grants, loans, etc., resulted in the extension and penetration of exchange relations in Mizoram and to the same extent there emerged an affluent or elite class mainly representing administrative bureaucrats, Class I contractors, etc., characterised by conspicuous consumption. The process of extension and penetration of exchange relations while resulted in the emergence of capitalistic forces, automatically gave birth to a middle class also to be differentiated in terms of asset holding from the bottom as well as from the top. This middle class includes in Mizoram all clerical supervisors, Government officials, teachers, small producers, independent professional people, etc.

The situation in rural areas of Mizoram during the earlier part of 1980s were found to be much worse. Rural people had no alternative other than to practice the primitive, wasteful and less remunerative *jhum* farming and, therefore, was found to be the most deprived class in Mizoram.

With a view to reducing the difference between urban and rural areas and thereby readjust the situation, quite a number of plans, programmes and schemes both at Central and State level have been undertaken in Mizoram in addition to the existing ones since 1980-81. Programmes like IRDP, NREP, RLEGP, House Construction schemes, etc., have been implemented on priority basis to improve the living standard in rural areas by creating more employment opportunities. State Government of Mizoram also aimed at shifting 60,000 *jhummia* families from shifting cultivation to settled or permanent cultivation by 1994. By the end of 1990, the State Government succeeded to reduce the number of *jhummia* families to about 40,000. Programmes like development of irrigation potentiality, generation of electricity and village electrification, land reforms, supply of safe drinking water, women and children welfare, sufficient number of fair price shops, biogas plants and a number of other poverty alleviation programmes also have been implemented in Mizoram.

All these efforts have brought about remarkable changes in the socio-economic front of rural areas in Mizoram. Over the ten years period from 1980-81 to 1990-91, remarkable change also can be noticed in the source pattern of income in rural Mizoram. With increased Government efforts, loans, grants, aids, etc., a large variety of alternative sources of income have cropped up in rural areas. In the primary sector, subsidiary source of income like settled cultivation, horticulture, piggery, poultry farming, dairy/livestock farming, forestry, etc., are becoming more popular. Trade, transport, casual hiring out of labour, etc., have become the most important sources of income in the tertiary sector while sources of income in the secondary sector still awaiting for proper exploitation.

On the basis of the pattern of occupation in rural areas, four different occupational categories may be found in rural Mizoram. Those categories are *jhum* group, Salary group, Casual labour group and Trade group. At present less than 40,000 families, which accounts for roughly 44 per cent of families in rural Mizoram, are still engaged in *jhum* farming. In rural Mizoram about 14 per cent of families depends on hiring of casual labour, 20 per cent of total households are engaged in trade, transport, etc., and the rest 22 per cent of rural families are salaried families in various government and semi-government departments in and outside the village.

But in terms of total work force in both main and subsidiary employment it can be observed that *jhum* workers constitute nearly 41 per cent of the total work force followed by casual workers (20 per cent), traders (12 per cent) and salaried people (9 per cent) while the rest 18 per cent of the total work force in rural areas are engaged in transport, settled cultivation, dairy/livestock farming, piggery and poultry farming, horticulture, forestry, etc. Therefore, it can be said that though people in rural areas are getting themselves engaged more and more in various subsidiary occupations in both primary and tertiary sectors, yet shifting cultivation is still to be considered the major source of employment in rural areas since it covers 44 per cent of families in rural areas and 41 per cent of total work force of rural Mizoram.

Although *jhum* farming is the major source of employment in rural Mizoram, it cannot be said to be the major source of income. Looking into the sectoral income generation one can find that *jhum* cultivation contributes less than 10 per cent of the total income of rural areas while trade together with transport contributes roughly 43 per cent of rural income and salaried employment contributes roughly 19 per cent of the total income. About six per cent of the rural income comes from hiring out of casual labour and the rest of the rural income comes from other subsidiary occupations like settled cultivation; piggery farming, poultry farming, dairy/livestock farming, house-letting, etc. Basing on this pattern of sectoral income generation where *jhum* farming contributes even less than 10 per cent of the total income in rural areas, it cannot be said that *jhum* cultivation is the major source of income in rural Mizoram although it is the major source of employment.

Looking into the size of income of occupational categories from different sources it can be seen that the trade group in the rural Mizoram is the richest group among all occupational groups. The trade group in rural areas contributes roughly 44 per cent of the total income of rural areas. The second position is occupied by the *Jhum* group and nearly 27 per cent of the total rural income comes from this group. The *jhum* group is followed by the salaried group with 27 per cent share of the total rural income while the casual labour group contributes only seven per cent of the total rural income.

If we look into the income of the *jhum* group itself it can be seen that it derives less than 25 per cent of its total income from *jhum* farming. Roughly 14 per cent of the total income of this group comes from settled farming while the rest more than 61 per cent of the total income of this group comes from a good number of other subsidiary sources like trade, transport, piggery and poultry farming, etc. Although the *jhummia* families constitute the largest occupational group in rural areas and *jhum* farming is still the single largest source of income, yet it contributes less than one-fourth of the total income of this *jhum* group. Therefore, it can be said that the *jhummias* are dependent of *jhum* only for one-fourth of their total income. This can definitely be termed as a positive change in the picture of rural economy compared to the situation prevailing during the earlier part of 1980s. Incomes of *jhum* families have increased manifolds during the last ten years and the *jhummias* are earning at present from shifting cultivation as well as from other subsidiary sources. In fact subsidiary sources together contributes more than three times the income derived by the *jhummias* from the cultivation of *jhum* lands. Similarly, the casual labour group earns roughly 40 per cent of their total income are wages earned as casual labour. Rest of the income of this group comes from large number of other subsidiary sources like settled and *jhum* cultivation, forestry, trade etc. Trade, and salary group, on the other hand, can be found to be better off compared to *jhum* and casual labour group. Comparatively well built houses in rural areas are occupied by the two groups and also by those earning good income from *jhum* and settled cultivation and from other allied services. Most of those houses in rural areas are located quite close to the main road or market with sanitation provision and easy access to basic facilities. Salary and trade group earn sufficient income from their main occupation and, therefore, look less to the alternative sources of income.

On the basis of income earned by occupational groups the rural households can conveniently be divided into three classes—rich, middle and poor. The trade group being the richest group have roughly a per capita income of Rs. 6,000. The salary group with a per capita income of Rs. 2,900 can be termed as middle class while the *jhum* and casual labour group will fall in the poor class with roughly a per capita income of Rs.1,900 and Rs.1,500 respectively. However, it is also not true that the per capita income shown above are uniformly available to all members of the respective occupational group. A *jhummia* may earn much higher or much less than the average per capita income of the *jhum* group and the same is true in case of other occupational groups also. In fact, within each occupational group clear demarcation can further be made on the basis of the size of income earned by the families.

The consumption pattern of rural households also reflects this class distinction. If we consider the expenditure of occupational groups on food alone it can be seen that both *jhum* group and casual labour group spend roughly 66 to 68 per cent of their total income on food alone. On the other hand, in the case of salary and trade group it can be seen that the salary group spends nearly 42 per cent of their total income on foodgrains alone and the trade group spends even less than 20 per cent of their total income on foodgrains. But even then the per capita expenditure, saving and investment of the salary group are much higher compared to *jhum* or casual labour group and the per capita expenditure, saving and investment of the trade group is still higher compared to service group. And it is natural that the poor people will have to spend a higher percentage of their total income on food compared to the people who are economically more sound. The existing pattern of consumption in rural areas simply confirms the existence of economical class distinction in rural areas.

After the attainment of Union Territory status the force of Central aids, loans, etc., which under Five Year Plans extended and penetrated the exchange relations and to the same extent gave birth to capitalistic and middle class groups in urban areas, the same force in later years affected in the same manner the socio-economic position in rural areas also. On an average 35 to 40 per cent of families in rural areas are living either below or very close to the poverty line. The State Government has undertaken a large number of programmes and schemes to raise the living standard of the rural population to reasonable standard. But most of the poverty alleviation programmes and other development schemes very often failed to assist the targetted groups due to the non-existence of proper action plan, skilled and honest manpower, banking facilities, transport and communication problems, proper monitoring system, etc. Despite the implementation of a large number of poverty alleviation programmes, a large number of households in rural areas are still struggling just below the poverty line.

Although class contradictions are not yet much felt within the society, a careful observation by an outsider will clearly show the existence of wide gap in income of different households in both urban and rural areas of Mizoram. But the existence of the value system related to *tlawmngaihna,* to which the society as a whole is committed, although to a lesser extent, restricts the internal class relations juxtaposing to one another. So far, neither social reforms have been found to be organised by the middle or poor class in the society nor any notable effort has been made by the Government for the rectification of the social ills, which is most urgent, before they go deep into the soil of Mizoram. However, social reformation movement in Mizoram would not be possible so long as ethnic considerations and sub-national aspirations outweighs the sentiment of the people of Mizoram.

But the State machinery cannot ignore its responsibility in the rectification of socio-economic imbalances in the society. The Government should undertake new development programmes and continue the implementation of the programmes, undertaken already to alleviate poverty, more vigorously as little more concentrated efforts would be able to push a large number of households up the poverty line.

At the same time, the Government should also be more cautious in the selection and implementation of programmes so that the targetted group actually receives the benefit. Otherwise the existing inequalities of income will be widened further which in its turn will lead to concentration of wealth in few hands pushing down further the people in large number below the poverty line.

NOTES

A. Mackenzie, *The North East Frontier of India,* Delhi, 1970, pp. 278-280.

A. Roy, *Dynamics of Change,* pp. 123-124.

A.G. McCall, *Lushai Chrysalis,* London, p. 211.

C.A. Soppitt, A *Short Account of the Kuki-Lushai Tribes on the North-East Frontier with an Outline Grammar of the Rangkhal Lushai Language, T.R.I.* Aizawl, reprint, pp. 7-8.

K. K: Upadhyaya, *Semi Primitive Economy of an Indian Village,* Delhi, 1989, pp. 80-81.

L.B. Thanga, *The Mizos,* Gauhati, pp. 32-33.

N. Chatterjee, *Status of Women in the Earlier Mizo Society,* TRI, Aizawl, 1975, p. 3.

N. Chatterjee, *Zawlbuk as Social Institution in the Mizo Society*, T.R.I. Aizawl, p. 5.

R.N. Prasad, *Government and Politics in Mizoram,* 1947-1986, New Delhi, 198' pp. 110-111.

S. Chatterjee, *Mizoram Under British Rule,* Appendix B, p. 206.

S.B. Saha, *Tribes of North East India,* Agartala, 1987, pp. 26-28.

T.H. Lewin, *Wild Race of South-Eastern India,* T.R.I., Aizawl, pp. 48-50.

39

Participation and Development in Mizoram

Jogamaya K.K. Saikia

The Land

Mizoram is a mountainous region which became the twenty-third State of the *Union of India* in February 1987. It is situated in the N.E. corner of India and bounded by Burma in the east and south, Bangladesh in the West. Towards the north are Assam and Manipur while in the west lies Tripura.

It has a 630 km long international boundary with Burma and Bangladesh. The total geographical area is 21,081 sq. km with a total population of 686,217 where the male: female ratio is 357: 329 according to 1991 census. Of the total population 93.58 are scheduled tribes which mainly belong to three groups known as Mizo, Pawi-Lakher and Ralte. Mizo is the dominant group, covering more than 80 per cent while Ralte is the least. The density of population is 73 per sq. km with a growth rate 56.86 per cent and sex ratio is 890 females per 1,000 males. There are 3 districts, i.e., Aizawl, Lunglei and Chhimtuipui, 9 sub-divisions and 20 development blocks and 6 towns. Out of these, Aizawl is classified size Class II (50,000-99,999) population, Lunglei falls under Class IV and the rest Kolasib, Champhai, Serchhip and Saiha fall in category of Class V urban area. The urban population consists of 317,040 which is 46.20 per cent of total population and ranks sixth in the country. In unbanization, Mizoram has made a rapid progress from 24.67 per cent in 1981 and hold 15th in rank by that time.

The topography of Mizoram is like other hill States. The hills in Mizoram run from North to South with the tendency to be higher in the east. The hills are steep and separated by rivers and deep gorges. The climate varies from 11°C to 21°C. Summer is wet with monsoonal rainfall with average 254 cm per annum. Winter is dry and rainfree.

Due to traditional kin-based economic organisation like shifting plot and shifting cultivation or *jhuming* involves cutting down the jungle and felling of trees. The cultivation system in cyclic order from 3-8 years of time is continued. As a result, the environmental ecology and the topographic climate variations are effected. The vegetation growth is insufficient to meet the need of the people. Hence, non-agricultural occupations are increasing, mostly in and around the urban areas. By and large, the plots of agricultural land is decreasing. With the increase of population, the fallow period becomes shorter, cultivable plots are becoming smaller and the harvest is insufficient.

With this background in view, Mizoram has to develop herself. As a newly born State, Mizoram needs all-round development. It requires full cooperation of the people of the land and their participation in different developmental sectors. This will indicate the people's aspiration and motivation towards development. This chapter will highlight the different developmental features and people's participation. Furthermore, it will focus the prospective areas for upliftment. It will examine the qualities of the people for aspiration to overcome the drawbacks of the area for development. Thereby, this chapter will ventilate outlets for planners to chalk out plans and programmes for bringing change and upliftment.

Methodology

Emic view: Longitudinal:

- born and brought up in greater Assam, where Mizoram was a district only;
- have closer interaction with the people of the land;
- have studied different Mizos in different areas as individual, small groups, large group in different aspects;
- as an anthropologist and sociologist, have better insight for developmental aspects;
- have knowledge of historical, political development of the area as a student of History;
- Micro-level treatment, keeping peoples' participation in different sectors, of development;
- carrying out interviews, free talks with administrators, Mizo researchers, elderly and experienced people of the land;

- Comparative studies through History, Socio-economic activities and active participation of the people in methodology; and
- developmental inputs and outputs with the help of Census Report and Economic Survey Report.

Findings

(A) *Features in Common*

1. The whole area is full of hills and inhabited by Mizos.
2. Boundaries are open to foreign countries, i.e., Burma and Bangladesh. Therefore, innerline/boundaries are to to be protected and should be under proper vigilance for security purpose.
3. Boundaries from Tripura, Assam and Manipur are under protection and innerline permit is required to enter into the land.
4. Interior areas are not easily accessible.
5. Except NH-54 and a few fair weather roads, the condition of the rest needs improvement.
6. Modern mass-media like T.V., radio have entered immensely, yet communication through telephone, telegraph, postal development are not adequate. There is only one post office per 65.01 km area in 1987.
7. Water resources are scanty and mostly at very low levels during dry seasons.
8. The medical attention is poor with only 1 doctor for 3,713 people.
9. Lack of industrialization. Raw materials and natural forest resources are plenty. Except weaving and a few cottage industry materials nothing has been developed.
10. No market for development of horticulture and vegetable farming. Orange, pineapples, squash, ginger, etc., grow abundantly, but due to absence of a ready market in and around the State, people market them at a low price and the economy suffers.
11. For urban market, the goods come only from outside the State. As Mizos do not produce finished goods, they are to buy them at high prices.
12. Trades are dominated by outsiders. (Grocery shops are run by *banias*).

(B) *Drawbacks and the Required Changes for Development*

Development requires mobilization. Mobilization of manpower and technologies of various kinds are required. Efficiency of the person concerned is the utmost need for handling the management and work. Therefore, mobilization of manpower does not mean the mobilization/migration of people, but his talents, knowledge, technical knowledge, know-hows, efficiency with managerial qualities which are the utmost need for any meaningful development.

Population and Literates in District by Residence and Sex, 1991.

State/Dist.		Population Person	Male	Female	Literates Person	Male	Female
Mizoram	Total	686217	356,672	329,545	462,246	250,962	211,284
	Rural.	369,177	192,729	176,454	215,570	120,265	95,305
	Urba.	317,040	163,949	153,091	246,676	130,697	115,979
Aizawl	Total	475,360	246,465	228,895	343,630	183,436	160,194
	Rural	216,511	113,346	103,165	141,210	76,992	64,218
	Urban	258,849	133,119	125,730	202,420	106,444	95,976
Lunglei	Total	111,209	58,229	52,980	71,466	39,842	31,624
	Rural	66,677	34,582	32,095	36,732	20,891	15.841
	Urban	44,532	23,647	20,885	34,734	18,951	15,783
Chimtuipui	Total	99,648	51,978	47,670	47,150	27,684	19,466
	Rural	85,989	44,795	41,194	37,628	22,382	15,246
	Urban	13,659	7,183	6,476	9,552	5,302	4,220

Source: Census 1991 (Provisional).

These developmental resources are possible to acquire only with education. Education in different fields open new prospects of development. These prospects are the basic needs of the State. To plan the scheme, to utilize the scheme in action and the action is to be managed through operational works and administration. Besides these, economic development, i.e., starting small or large scale industries, cottage industry, agro-based industries including fruit processing and preservation centres require good management. For all these, education as derivative should be boosted up in required direction. Physical efforts are worked out when skilled and educated people are aware about new schemes of development.

In this respect, it is observed that the State of Mizoram is in an advantageous position in the field of education. Here, the literacy rate is 81.23 per cent whereas male shares 84.06 per cent and female 78.09 per cent according to 1991 census. Table 39.1 will show the population and literates by residence and sex 1991.

In literacy, Mizoram leads with the highest number of male and female literates in North-East, whereas per capita budgeted expenditure on education is 400.81, the highest in North-East Region. From these information, it is clear that in Mizoram there is no dearth of educated people for carrying out new areas of development.

Mizos are sturdy and can work hard. Physically they are strong and can take manual labour. This is why to find labourer, skilled, semi-skilled or unskilled is not a problem in Mizoram. Technical persons too, given the proper facilities can be trained up as and when required.

Mizos have no class distinction. On ground of sex also there is no discrimination. They live in a free society, with no bar against joining any services. Government or private, self employment or co-operative undertakings. Therefore, their service can be utilized for developmental activities.

Ninety per cent Mizos are agriculturists. The total cultivators are 29.48 per cent and the ratio between males and females is 30.92 : 27.90. The total rural cultivators are 36.90 in which male cultivators (38.82%) are the highest number amongst the rural cultivators of North-East Region. Proportion of main workers to total population is 41.73, where men are 50.38 and women are 32.33. In this respect, it can be assessed that in agriculture, horticulture, the cultivators can be utilized from both the sexes.

Within a short span, Mizoram is developing urbanization in a fast manner. She ranks sixth in the country with the percentage of urban population to total population is 46.20 rising from 24.67 and ranks 15th position in the country in the 1981 Census. It further shows that rural population for education, employment, etc., rush towards urban area as facilities infrastructure is more and accommodation in nature in the beginning of the statehood. The prospects of individual upliftment with other facilities in urban areas attract people from rural areas. Rural areas cannot afford all these. Therefore, once rural people intigrate and settle with job, establish themselves in urban areas and never intend to go back. Their family members also accompany them. As a result the rural area has to lose a good number of educated, skilled, job holder population forever. For this reason the village economy suffers, agriculture and other allied activities dwindle. Due to the constant absence of educated, earning people, the rural areas cannot plan any developmental schemes. Even if the plan is made, there is hardly a few to take initiative, fund or offer physical help or supervision.

Lack of innovation for effective implication for opening new areas also happens to be a cause of backwardness. No individual and independent source has voluntarily started any industry to encourage the developmental well-being. If it would have been, by following them many of the youths would have been inspired to start their own. This lack of initiation amongst educated people is due to the high cost for transportation of the raw materials to the place of production or manufacture, lack of road and communication, etc. For these drawbacks none is interested to start work by spending huge amount right from infrastructure to manufacture.

Wrong person in wrong occupation is one of the cause of hindrances for development. As common people need employment, enter wherever job is found and as such lack interest for serving, but still continues for having as they cannot manage next employment of interest due to factors like education, experience, age, etc. As such the talents in person gradually decrease and on the other hand the work concern suffers heavily.

Linkage between the villages and remote areas, nearby urban areas in wet season is the cause of backwardness. Improvement in transport communication system can efficiently utilise the productive resources from agricultural fields, forest, cottage industries and others, with the help of local, talents and entrepreneurs.

(C) *Prospects of Development*

Development requires prospects. The prospective views give rise to inertia in man. The qualities and talents for developmental works and their operations are to be examined as potentials before we do plan for development. Here the qualities of Mizo, and their inner urge for the developmental prospects are observed as below:

1. Mizos can follow a profession of his/her interest and there is no restriction in it.
2. The people have definite geographical location with strong communal feeling of their tribes with social level and understanding.
3. Social acceptance, social utility having social beneficiaries, give security to them as an unique quality in the tribe.
4. Social values out of development are scrutinised before bringing social change through development.
5. In socio-economic spheres, men and women are equal.
6. In decision-making, they are independent.
7. There is no dearth of working population. According to physical capability, men and women work in agriculture and horticulture:

8. In management and administration, as Mizos are highly literate, they are capable of holding responsible jobs.
9. Trained people, are energetic and hence good response can be obtained.
10. Vocational, industrial training can improve their talents for handling industries and small industries like handloom, lain cloth weaving, cottage works and allied activities with the forest resources.
11. They are free and frank by nature and that quality in people make them understand and easy interaction with other groups of people.

These are the essential qualities amongst Mizos for any developmental work in any region. Topographical climate factors are congenial for health to conduct hard physical labour according to age and sex.

In a new born State like Mizoram which was neglected since British time till the recent past, made Mizos to rebel for a long time, when the rest of the country has already completed five years plan of development. After attaining Union Teritory in 1972 to full statehood in February 1987, Mizos have started democratic life by having a Legislative Assembly of 40 members with their own political leaders. Mizoram is now represented at the Parliament by two members of parliament; one in the Lok Sabha and the other in the Rajya Sabha. At present they are managing Mizoram Houses looked by Liaison officers at Silchar, Shillong, Guwahati, Calcutta and New Delhi. Now things are easier to contact. In other areas, Constitutional, political, administrative changes have brought tremendous developmental activities with peoples' participation from top to bottom. Along with the growth of urbanization, education, literacy growth rate make Mizos to prosper by opening new areas of development with job oriented tasks, future prospects with managerial and execution of works with operational perspectives. Manual or physical contribution for development is related to the actual operational part of the work with the co-operation and active participation of skilled, semi-skilled, unskilled manual labourer as manpower mobilization and migration from different areas of the State itself. It will provide them encouragement and mental satisfaction to carry out works when they obtain means of livelihood.

Development has to be made according to the needs and choice of economic priorities. Development is a way of organising and utilising resources from people and nature to maximum advantage. The plan shall be made in such a way that people will be satisfied from its beneficial results and to raise the standard of living, economy and transfer their mental remoteness from the rest of the country due to their geographical location. With the aid of potential resources available inside employment avenues should be made to characterise the integrated sectors of development, i.e., infrastructure, roads transport system, industry—large and small— and electricity for running industries as energy, water supply system to reach agriculture in dry season, improved methods of agriculture with HYV, and "grow more production" mission should be drived to supply the surplus and make money to finance other ancillaries. Manpower, natural resources should be mobilized for investment purpose with technology transfer from primitive to modern. If primitive methods can be utilised with modification, should be supplemented and encouraged.

In Mizoram, planning for development assumes significance and its successful implementation depends on the active participation of the inhabitants. They should be aware, alert and qualified physically, mentally with education an training in respective areas. The other methods of planning like financial, physical, structural, managerial, commercial, etc. will be in the hands of government, State and Centre with Planning Commission.

Development has no hindrance for lack of initiatives or participation from the locals in Mizoram. They are co-operative by nature. If any opportunity is opened, Mizos are there to get themselves involved. If developmental schemes are spread throughout the length and breadth of the State, the migration of the Mizos will be stopped and they will stay back in their respective areas which further enrich with education, skill, economy and other necessities to train the youngs to handle efficiently thereafter. Participants aspiration in the operation will be fruitful if the cause of backwardness or hindrances are focussed as remedial suggestions for improvement.

40

Agroforestry: A Stable Alternative of *Jhum* Cultivation for North-East India

L.K. Jha and *R.P. Tiwari*

The people in the hilly region have been practising *jhum* cultivation for centuries, was simple, self sustained and environmentally sound. The main cause of sustained income was limited population, vast land area, little daily needs. All these contributed the practice of shifting cultivation with long fallow period, allowing the abandoned *jhum* lands longer period till the natural fertility of the soil is restored. In this way system was providing social security to the hill people.

Presently, *jhum* cultivators are facing problem like poverty due to insufficient production of crops and putting more forest areas under *jhum* cultivation, with shorter rotation period. The reduced period has decreased production potential and created environmental hazards like soil erosion, water loss, loss of fertility, degradation of land and finally threatens the ecological balance of the region.

Present Status of Forest Covers in Mizoram and its Impact on *jhum* Cultivation

The people of North-Eastern States participated in the promotion of afforestation programme after enjoying several inducement, but unfortunately the forest area seems dwindling in the past years. When we observe comparative situation of forest area in the year 1982 and 1987 we find that in Mizoram there is decrease of forest cover by 914 sq. km (4.78 percentage change). At the same time three States of north-eastern belt (Arunachal Pradesh, Manipur and Nagaland) show increase in forest cover (Table 40.1). It is essential to mention that the State Forest Report, Government of India (1989) indicate that Mizoram State possesses 86.2

Table 40.1: Forest Cover Comparative Situation (1987-1989)

Sl. No.	*State/UTs*	*Geographical*	*1987 assessment based on imagery 98-99*	*Forest cover assessment 1989 assessment based on imagery 1985-1987*	*Actual cover as % geographical 1985-1987*	*Difference in sq. km.*	*Percentage change*
1.	Arunachal Pradesh	83580	60500	68763	82.3	+8263	+13.6
2.	Assam	78520	26386	26058	33.2	–328	–1.2
3.	Manipur	22360	17679	17885	80.0	+206	–1.66
4.	Meghalaya	22490	16511	15690	69.8	–821	–4.97
5.	Mizoram	21090	19092	18178	86.2	–914	–4.78
6.	Nagaland	16530	14351	14356	86.8	+005	–0.03
7.	Tripura	10480	5743	5325	50.08	–418	–7.2
	Total India	3287797	642041	640134	19.47	–1907	0.29

Source: The State of Forest Report, 1989.

per cent forest Progress Report of Forestry in Mizoram (1990) published by Department of Environment and Forest, Government of Mizoram indicates that forest area in Mizoram is approximately 40.33 per cent and the actual area on the ground is very much less than that. The report says the main factors leading to deforestation are political upheaval during 1966 and continued practice of shifting cultivation. (Table 40.2). It is apparent that there are great discrepancy in the area covered by forest projected by Forest Survey of India and Department of Environment and Forest, Government of Mizoram. We think data projected by Forest Survey of India appears more reliable.

If we visualise the forest area density class-wise in Mizoram State, dense forest area has increased (945 sq. km) and there is decrease in area affected by shifting cultivation in the North-Eastern Hill States. The area under shifting cultivation has reduced from 73,410 sq. km to 62,854 sq. km during the period of 9 years, i.e., 1975 to 1984. It is interesting to note that in Arunachal Pradesh and Assam, area under shifting cultivation has increased 7.3 and 74.9 per cent respectively. In the rest 5 States, area under shifting cultivation has decreased. In Mizoram in 1975, area under shifting cultivation was 16,110 sq. km. It decreased to 22.8 per cent, i.e., 12,442 sq. km as recorded in 1984 (Table 40.3).

The decrease in practice of *Jhum* cultivation is happy situation but one question strikes our mind is "*Are farmer's gradually leaving jhum cultivation wilfully with great zeal*"

In our opinion answer is *No*. This question should be discussed at length because these farmers are backbone of the State economy. We feel the reason is socio-economic, and bio-physical causes of the land. Today we can see long range of barren hills. The family once dependent on *Jhum* cultivation are now facing problem in maintenance of their family due to various ecological and socio-psychological problem. Now they are migrating in the urban areas in search of jobs.

In this chapter, authors try to venture how *jhum* farmers can be settled by introducing intergrated land use management programme, i.e., agroforestry. Successful implementation of this system will help *jhumia* in the following ways:

- Farmer will get regular sustained income from their farm land and also regular employment.
- Regular employment in their farm land.
- Protection of *jhum* land from soil erosion, more moisture conservation, fertility status will remain balanced.
- No further extension of *jhum* land.

Table 40.2: District-wise Data on Legal Status of Forest Area in Mizoram (Area in Sq. Km.)

Sl. No.	*Categories of Forests*	*Aizawl District*	*Lunglei District*	*Chhimtapui District*	*Total*
1.	Protected Reserved Forest	1444.00	3.40	–	1447.40
2.	Rivenine Reserved Forest	4023.00	432.96	–	4455.96
3.	Inner Line Reserved Forest	509.00	–	–	509.00
4.	Proposed Wildlife Sanctuary	–	–	145.00	145.00
5.	Road side Reserved Forest	158.00	–	–	158.00
6.	Safety & Supply Reserved	1354.00	–	131.00	1485.00
7.	Station Reserved	–	15.90	–	15.90
8.	Council Reserved Forest	–	–	290.00	290.00
	Grand Total	7488.00	452.26	566.00	8506.25

Source: Progress Report of Forest in Mizoram (1990).

Table 40.3: Comparative Situation by Density Class Assessed 1987 (Area: Sq. Km.)

Sl. No.	State	Dense Forest Based on 1981-83 Imagery	Based on 1985-87 Imagery	Open Forest	
				Based on 1981-83 Imagery	Based on 1985-87 Imagery
1.	Arunachal Pradesh	51096	54272	9404	14491
2.	Assam	18415	16688	7971	9370
3.	Manipur	4670	5060	13009	12825
4.	Meghalaya	5749	3427	10762	12263
5.	Mizoram	2938	3883	16154	14295
6.	Nagaland	6379	4632	7972	9724
7.	Tripura	330	1214	5403	4111
	Total India	361412	378470	276583	257409

Source: The State Forest Report, 1989.

Characteristics of Ideal Multipurpose Tree Species

While selecting MPTS for agroforestry system, only such species should be introduced which show proper growth, with ability to increase productivity of site. A good MPTS should have following characteristics (Jha,1990):

1. Production of firewood, timber, green manure, fodder on sustained basis.
2. Fast growing and ability to produce a flush of fresh shoots when cut at ground level.
3. Minimum competition should be between crops and multipurpose tree species. The problem like sunlight penetration, etc., can be tackled by judicious canopy management.
4. Tree species having nutritious and palatable leaves are preferred, to supplement leaf fodder during lean period.
5. MPTS having ability to fix nitrogen in addition to other productive benefits should be preferred.

In selecting the crops to be grown in the interspace attention must be given to the points mentioned below:

1. The crop should not exhaust the soil.
2. Spacing of the main tree crop and interspace should be planned according to their requirements.
3. Intercrop may be utilised as green manure for maintaining organic matter content of the soil. This will also check weed, control soil erosion and help in enriching nitrogen content of the soil.
4. Combination should be such so that soil nutrients can be maintained and soil erosion can be minimised.
5. Intercrop may be utilised as mulch. This is very common in tropical and sub-tropical conditions. The mulch acts as a surface barrier preventing evaporation, suppressing weed growth the decrease soil temperature.

   The best mulch absorb little moisture and permit the rainfall to move downwards rapidly into the soil. This helps in improving the soil structure.

   During summer soil moisture is considerably reduced which cause severe fruit drop in citrus. If trees are not irrigated frequently, mulch can solve this problem. Mulching with leaves, as a standard practice for citrus orchard are followed to tide over a high soil moisture and rapid evaporation of soil moisture during high atmospheric temperature and low humidity.

6. Farmers should always keep in mind that grain forming timing of the crop should not coincide with flower by differentiation in fruit trees. In non-bearing orchards farmers can grow any crop.

Comparative Analysis of Shifting Cultivation and Improved Technology

The shortening of the *jhum* cycle, does not allow the soil fertility to build up. Thus farmers needed larger areas to be cultivated for same quantity of produce. Many Research centres have been carrying experiments to tackle the problems of shifting cultivation.

Soil Loss, Surface Runoff and Water Conservation

ICAR publication (1983) specially pointed out that the average soil loss due to shifting cultivation has been recorded to be 40.9 tonnes/ha in a study at Meghalaya. The highest sediment yield, however, was 76.9 tonnes/ha/yr. The annual loss of soil was computed by taking into account an average soil loss of 40.0 tonnes/ha/yr. Report also indicate that annual soil loss due to shifting cultivation in the region was about 15.5 million tonnes. Jha and Rather (1981) mention that erosion ratios of Orissa soils under shifting cultivation were 18.03 and 18.78 in the surface and 6.5 and 11.4 in the subsurface as compared to erosion ratio of soils under shifting cultivation of 10.7 and 10.8 in the surface and 3.7 and 11.7 in subsurface soils. Erosion ratios were higher in the upper layer than in the lower layers. Soils under shifting cultivation had high erosion ratios, while soils not under shifting cultivation within the safety limits of erodibility. Borthakur *et al.* (1978) studied that surface runoff under shifting cultivation was about 11.40 mm partial terracing reduced surface runoff further to 32.8 mm. This study indicates that physical barriers considerably reduces surface runoff.

In recent decades, continuous cropping have accelerated the soil erosion and condition is gradually deteriorated. In most of the shifting cultivation areas wrong soil tillage practices also played important role in increasing rate of runoff and soil erosion. In these areas luxurious vegetation (Grass species) makes people to consider, that the soil extremely rich, but this impression is misleading. In fact soils are poor and heavy rain destroy them within few months or few brief years.

Young (1989) mentions that trees are responsible for erosion control. This is achieved in two ways with trees acting as barriers or as cover. The barrier function in the conventional approach to erosion control by checking runoff of water and cover reduced the rain drop impact. Reynolds *et al.* (1983). Mention that on slopping land, when leguminous tree species planted along the contour, the trees limit soil erosion, Tree foliage can be used as mulch and fertilizer for food crops.

Nutrient Status

Mishra and Ramkrishna (1983) studied the effect of *jhum* on soil fertility at high elevations of Meghalaya using 15,10 and 5 years *jhum* cycle and terrace system. Soil nitrogen concentration under a five = year cycle was significantly lower than under the 10 and 15 = year cycle, The concentration of this nutrient declined sharply after the burn in the surface layers and was attributed to volatilization. The degree of volatilization is dependent on the intensity of the burn and, therefore, the nitrogen decline is lower in a five = years cycle than in longer cycles. Nitrogen concentration in the soil improved at the end of one year under all cycles, but such an improvement was observed only under 10 and 15 = year cycles.

Under terrace cultivation nitrogen losses continued up to the end of two years. Available *P* (phosphorus) was generally lower under a five = year cycle than 10 and 15 = year cycle. Available P under the three-year *jhum* cycle declined significantly after the burn. Recovery occurred after 30 days under 10 and 15 years cycle and, after 100 days for the five = years cycle with subsequent decline during cropping. In the terrace system, the available P declined during cropping, after an initial increase. The concentration and total quantities of allocation on the surface soil layers under the three-year *jhum* cycles improved markedly after the burn owing to releases through ash, but subsequently declined sharply. The decline is partly due to absorption by the developing crop. Large quantities of allocations were released under 10 and 15 = year. *Jhum* cycles owing to greater quantities of slash burned than that under 15 = year cycle. Starting from a lower level in a zero year fallow, the recovery of C, N and available P occurred in older fallow of 5 and 10 years with a slight decline in a 15 = year fallows, longer fallows gave greater improvement in humus and nutrients in order to sustain slash and burn agriculture. A *jhum* cycle of 5 years is definitely short as far as nutrient recovery is concerned.

Longer cycle of 10 years are preferred. A terrace system does not offer a better alternative to short cycle because it cannot sustain continuously cropping without heavy fertilizer inputs. Chauhan (1990) in his paper also cited result of report of ICAR Research Complex (1983) that when the forest canopy of virgin land is slashed and burnt for shifting cultivation, there is very likelihood that organic matter of the surface soil is also oxidised. This may cause a decrease in the level of soil organic matter. The decrease in organic matter will be more pronounced particularly when the temperature during burning exceeds 150°C. Both erosion and cultivations caused a decrease in the organic matter content of the soil. He has also reported that in North-Eastern region, the annual loss of soil and crop yield due to shifting cultivation was estimated to be 15.5 million tonnes and 52.23 thousand tonnes respectively. The on-site cost of soil degradation was computed to be Rs. 980.6 ha/yr which was 36.6 per cent of the value of the crop produce harvested. In regional basis, the on-site cost of soil degradation amounted to a loss of Rs. 37.9 crores/year. The crop yield loss, plant nutrient loss and land depreciation contributed 48.2, 39.6 and 12.2 per cent, respectively towards the on-site cost of soil degradation. Among the plant nutrient, nitrogen contributed maximum (29.2) followed by phosphorus (97.8%), potassium (1.6%) and sulphate (1-0%).

Under agroforestry system, hedge rows may be utilised as green manure or mulch. Nutrients are released in the soil when incorporated into the soil. Under alley cropping system moderate fertilizer of F.Y.M. may be the best solution to yield stability and increased production under modified shifting cultivation models.

In the *jhum* cultivation, villagers cut and clear and strip of forest three to four metres wide all around the *jhum* plot as fire line before they set fire to the area and scrupulously guard against fire escaping outside the area. The control on protection of the forest is gone and no more damage to vegetation is caused by escaping *jhum* fire than the actual practice of *jhuming* cultivation itself. The sprouting young vegetation covering the left over *jhum* area is destroyed year after year till the land becomes completely devoid of vegetative cover worth the name (Status report, AFCL, 1989).

In this practice, increase in temperature also destroys beneficial micro-organisms. Besides, there are some positive effect of control burning. The smoke liberated in the slash and burn cultivation, killed pathogens and pests.

A Look into Future

Before implementation of modern technology, we should study in depth the psyco-socio-cultural profiles, particularly the social organisation, social behaviour and social cognitions associated with shifting cultivation and permanent settlement pattern by employing standard psychometric and sociometric parameters. The finding of above study would provide empirical foundations to formulate strategies for cognitive and behaviour modification of individuals and community orientation programmes for planned elimination (minimization) of *jhuming* and to facilitate a permanent settlement patterns relating to agriculture forestry and animal husbandry, hence meeting the objective means rehabilitation of the shifting cultivation area for the rehabilitation of the people.

It is apparent from above discussion that the approach of *jhum* cultivation should be need based and location oriented. This practice can be only modified by studying existing agriculture practices and utilising its natural resources, keeping in mind the psyco-socio-economic problems of the area.

Several design/models have been suggested to solve the problems of shifting cultivation. The three-tier system suggested by the ICAR, Shillong, i.e., cultivation of trees at the hill top, cultivation of horticulture crops in the middle portion of the hill slopes and opening of terraces at the lower portion of the hill slopes and opening of terraces at the lower portion for cultivation of field crops. Pandey and Singh (1984) suggested the tree rotation shifting cultivation. Each of these methods as alternative to shifting cultivation has limitations.

In our opinion any alternative models can only be adopted by local people if it suits to local environmental condition and meet the needs and constraint of farmers. Besides this, the model should be similar to traditional practices with minor alterations. The above problem can be tackled by developing appropriate agroforestry model agroclimatic zone (different altitude, aspect, etc.). Introduction of all the three components, i.e., agronomy, forestry and animal husbandry will help in minimising the soil erosion, conservation of moisture, increase in infiltration rate, decrease in evaporation from soil and balance nutrient status and finally help in land remaining productive on a sustained basis.

Here we would like to say that in agroforestry if we will depend on on-station experimental station. We generally try to transfer the technology in the farmers field without considering biophysical and pyso-socio-economic problems of the farmers. Farmers never accept imposed technology under above circumstances impact remains for short period. In our opinion we should not spend our time in on-station trial. Our extension worker/scientist should work along with farmers to examine requirements of the farmers and biophysical causes. We should conduct on-farm trial (in the farmers field) with collaboration of farmers on model basis in 5 or 10 village in first phase. Here again we would like to mention that this practice cannot be successfully introduced by any single department. To this programme personnel of agricultural, forestry, soil conservation, Social Science and Animal Husbandry Department should work under one umbrella.

Thus, proposed agri-silviculture, agri-silvi-horticulture or agri-horticulture practice may be the best solution for rehabilitation of *jhum* land.

Suggested Models for the Rehabilitation of *Jhum* Land

We have not discussed about the slope and nature of crops to be tried in particular zone, because farmers generally practice *jhum* cultivation within permissible level of slope. Percentage of slope will help in computing the alley width under agro-forestry system. Extension worker, scientist should be careful in computing the alley width. Agricultural crops, tree species vary in different agro-climatic zone. In each agro-climatic zones models must be tried with local species as well exotics. The proposed model of agro-forestry systems are as follows:

Model-1: Intensive Hedgerow (Alley) Cropping on the Jhum Land

Objective

- This model improves fertility status and other properties of soil.
- Conserve more moisture and less soil erosion.
- Maximum utility of site by increasing productivity.

Alley cropping involves planting of rows of trees or shrubs, along contours and food crops, cover crops are grown in between the rows. The trees will limit soil erosion, decrease rate of run off and tree foliage can be used as mulch or fertilizer for agricultural crops/or for animal feeds. Tree foliage is used to maintain and improve soil fertility, while cropping is in progress, similar to natural process that occur during the traditional fallow period, thus increasing land use efficiency.

Suggestions

(1) Government is trying to change the *jhum* cultivation into settled scientific cultivation. In the hilly areas still their is no shortage

of land. Government should allot land permanently to the *jhumia's,* individually or community basis, so that they can think that permanent reclamation of *jhum* land is their own development or their development is directly related with reclamation of *jhum* land and they will not get new area for this practice.

(2) Establishment of network of alternative models in each zone similar to their traditional practice and their demonstration to the *juhims*.

(3) As the system is multidisciplinary, separate education and training for development management and extension of agro-forestry system at different level is required.

(4) Most *of jhumias* are below the poverty line. Moreover, in spite of the efforts made during our five years plans, infrastructure in our *jhum* belts is not up to the mark. The facilities for education; drinking water, transport and communication, institutional credit, etc., are lagging far behind. Under these circumstances we cannot expert voluntary involvement of *jhumias* to settle scientific cultivation.

(5) Vigilance cell consisting of *jhumia's* representative, should be formed at remote village, so that *jhumias* may avail themselves of timely benefits granted by the Government.

For proper implementation of rehabilitation programmes of *jhumias* Senior Officers should be posted for longer times

Jhumia's Co-Operative Society

Needless to say co-operatives can play a pivotal role in accelerating the tempo of rehabilitation of *jhum* land or *jhumias*. The *jhumias* are the weaker sections of our society. It is apparent that proper functioning of *jhumias* co-operatives society would reduce their economic exploitation and will raise their socio-economic status. Presently utmost emphasis is laid for the rehabilitation of *jhum* land to increase productivity and sustainability of the *jhum* land. This will improve overall quality of life of *jhumias*.

The co-operative society will create awareness among the farmers and motivate them to implement rehabilitation programmes of *jhum* land. The society will co-ordinate technical expert/extension workers to guide and provide latest technical know-how for successful rehabilitation of *jhum* land. The *jhumias* co-operative society will arrange timely short, medium and long-term of credit. Credit will be provided for consumption purpose during the lean period of the year to eliminate exploitation or in the initial years of settled cultivation. The *jhumias* will get technical guidance from the expert through society. Marketing of produce of members will be exclusively done by primaries. Consequently, exploitation by the intermediaries will be eliminated, processing and marketing of the produce of the members by the society will also facilitate the timely recovery of loans and hence the problem of overdues will be automatically solved. Thus it is apparent that co-operative society can solve the problems of *jhumias* and will help in improving the overall quality of life of *jhum* cultivators and help in the formation of egalitarian social order.

(8) Thus in our opinion to reclaim *jhum* land first phase is permanent allotment of land to *jhum cultivators*; and second phase is creation of awarness, motivation, technical know-how, financial assistance, etc., to *jhum* farmers. Farmers may be provided above incentives through co-operative societies or any suitable agencies. The farmers can utilise available space and resources by introducing agro-forestry model. Suppose farmers have been allotted 10 hec. land planning should be such that after construction of house, kitchen, pig and cowshed, compost pit, *Gobar* gas plant, water harvesting tank, etc., rest area may be put under different cropping system as per need of farmers. Border area of the allotted land should be planted by bamboos. One portion of plot may be put under high density of plantation, i.e., timber species at 10 × 10 metres spacing and fuelwood/nitrogen fixing tree species at 2 × 2 metres spacing or as suggested by the experts. The hedge rows with perennial grasses species may be established to protect the field from soil erosion problem. In second plot, farmers can plant fruit trees at 8 × 8 metres or 10 × 10 metres spacing or as suggested by extension worker and in the interspace agricultural crop, vegetables may be grown. Hedgerows should be formed at required interval. In the third plot farmers can plant only tree species to fulfil the requirements of fuelwood of silk host plant may be planted. This will also assist in raising the income of farmers after 4 years and lops and tops of host plant can be used as fuelwood. Farmers can put their third plot under multicropping system. Fruit trees at large spacing 12 m × 12 m space or as suggested by experts, in between the papaya, banana or any other fruit species may be planted. In the interspace agricultural crop, species, vegetables, etc., can be grown as per their requirements and demand of local market. Farmers can grow perennial flower or seasonal flower in a small part of his field and can practice Apiculture to increase their income. The hedgerows foilage can be utilised as green manure of fodder. As we discussed earlier under Government financial help farmer should be provided cow/pig/goat, etc.

The grass species and foliage of nitrogen fixing tree species can be used as fodder. The farmers can use farmyard manure of his compost pit in his crop field and rearing of cows/pig/goat/etc., will improve their side income. It is apparent that under agroforestry system interaction and co-ordination of all the three departments, i.e., Agriculturer Forestry and Animal husbandry is essential. Finally this system will improve the economic status of *jhum* cultivation and loan provided by the Government can be recovered in instalments. In the initial year *jhum* cultivators will maintain their family from the loan provided by the Government, concerned efforts are to be made by all to enthusiastic *jhumias* for voluntary and mass involvement, so that, economic stability may be a reality (Jha, 1990).

REFERENCES

1. A.F.C.L. (1989). Status Report on Dhaleswari Catchment, MIZORAM, Department of Agriculture, Government of Mizoram.
2. Borthakur, P., *et al* (1978). Cited by R.K. Gupta, (1981). Ecological consequences of irrigation land uses in loss of productivity soil. In (T. Tingsanhall and Eggers, ed.,), II. *Southeast Asain Regional Symposium on Problems of Soil Erosion and Sedimentation*, Bangkok, Thailand, pp. 27-29.
3. Chauhan, B.S. (1990). On site degradation due to shifting cultivation in North Eastern region NEHU, *Journal of Social Sciences and Humanities*, Vol. VIII, No. 3, pp. 5-8.
4. Cole, Z.A. (1990). Cassia alley cropping in the Gambia. *AFNETAN Newsletter*, Vol. 2, No. 2, pp. 6.

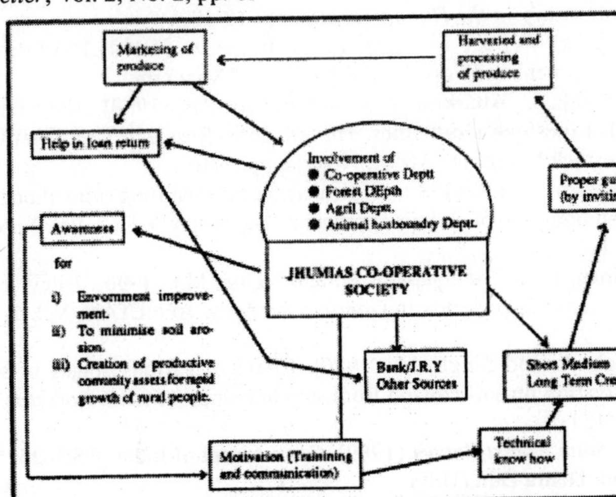

Fig. 1

5. Getahum, A and Rashid, K (1988). *Agroforestry in Kenya*, A field guide, Rural afforestation extension, Forest Department, Ministry of Environment and Natural Resources in collaboration with the Swiss Development Co-operation, pp. 1-59.
6. I.C.A.R. (1983). *Shifting Cultivation in Northeastern India*, Research complex for North Eastern Region, Shillong, Meghalaya, India, pp. 35-40.
7. Singh, J. and Pandey, M.C. (1989). Some measures to improve shifting cultivation, NEHU, *Journal of Social Sciences*, Vol. V, No. 4, pp. 9-12.
8. Jha, L.K. (1990). Rehabilitation of *jhum* land through Social Forestry S.F.S.O.; Shillong p.
9. Jha, L.K. (1991) *Social/Agroforestry as an Important Component in the Development of Tribal Villages: A Case Study*. Mendal, 6 (3-4), pp. 487-490.
10. Jha, M. and Singh M. (1980). Effect of various stages of shifting cultivation on soil erosion from steep hill slopes. *Indian Forestor*, Vol, 107(5), pp. 310-313.
11. Jha, M. and Rathore, R. (1981). Erodability of soil in shifting cultivation areas of Tripura and Orissa. *Indian Forestor*, Vol. 107(5), pp. 310-313.
12. Kokewe, M. (1990). On farm agroforestry trial in Luapula province Zambia, AFNETAN, *Newsletter*, Vol. 2, No. 2, pp. 6-7.
13. Lundgrean, B. and Raintree, J.B. (1983). Sustained agroforestry In (B. Nestel Ed.). Agricultural research for development: Potential and Challenges in Asia. The Hauge, *ISNAR*, pp. 37-39.
14. Mishra, B.K. and Ramkrishnan, P.S. (1983). Slash and burn agriculture at higher elevation in North Eastern India. Soil fertility changes *Agric. Eco-system and Environment*, pp. 83-96. Cited by R.E. de Cruz and N.T. Vergara. Protective and ameoliorative roles of agroforestry—*An Overview. Agroforestry in the Humid Tropics*, pp. 18-19.
15. *Progress Report of Forestry in Mizoram* (1990).Department of Environment and Forests, Government of Mizoram.
16. Reynolds, L., Atta-krah, A.N. and Francis, P.A. (1988). Alley Farming with Livestock Guidelines. Humid Zone Research site, International Livestock Centre for Africa, Nigeria, pp. 1-30.
17. Roy Burman, B.K. (1989). Critical appraisal of shifting cultivation farming technology and of various approaches, *Journal of N.E.C.*, Vol. X, No. 2-3, pp. 1-4.
18. Shanan, D.A. Kabaluapa, K.N. and Ngoyi, M.L. (990). Alley cropping stabilizes maize yields in *Gandhiji ka Zaire*, AFNETAN, Vol. 2, No. 1, pp. 8-9.
19. Singh, A. and Singh, M. (1980). Effect of various stages of shifting cultivation on soil erosion from step hill slopes. *Indian Forestor*, 16(2): 116-121.
20. *The State Forest Report* (1989). Government of India. F.S.I. 25, Subash Road, Dehra Dun (U.P.)

21. Young, A. (1989). 10 Hypothesis for all agroforestry research *Agroforestry Today*, Vol. 1(1), pp. 13-16.
22. Young, A. (1990). Agroforestry environment and sustainability, *Outlook on Agriculture*, Vol. 19, pp. 155-160.

HISTORY OF NORTH-EAST OTHER THAN MIZO

41
Ahom Myths of Origin
A Contextual and Regional Analysis

B.J. Terwiel

Myths relating the origin of mankind have fascinated all generations of anthropologists. In order to explain the inexplicable such myths resort to improbable imagery. Therefore, they have incited the formulation of bold universal hypotheses. These origin myths present a particular material that seems to link all peoples together, across language and cultural achievement, presenting a storehouse of symbols that beg for further analysis. They have, therfore, been particularly fruitful in fields such as comparative economic systems analysis and the study of symbolism and less than conscious patterns of thought.[1] In this essay no attempt is made to make statements that expand on hypotheses of transcultural and universal symbolism, traces of which can be found in most cosmogonic mythology. On the contrary, the analysis concentrates itself largely upon the local and regional level, fields which may hitherto have been neglected in favour or broader cross cultural comparison.

There are two specific reasons for singling out Ahom origin myths as a subject for study. In the first place, the Ahoms occupy such a remarkable position among the Tai-speaking peoples, that any study throwing light upon aspects of Ahom culture is relevant to the study of Tai peoples in general. Probably in the second-half of the eleventh century A.D., Tai peoples began to move from their homelands in what is now the Chinese Province of Guangxi into mainland South-east Asia. In the following two hundred years Tai people spread over large parts of mainland South-east Asia. The Ahoms constitute the westernmost group of this migration. It is generally accepted that at the beginning of the thirteenth century the Ahoms broke away from their fellow Tais in the Hukawng Valley in Upper Burma, crossed a series mountain ranges and descended into Upper Brahmaputra Valley. After gaining a foothold through conquest and diplomacy, over the following centuries they managed to expand their influence until then were the masters of an area that more or less coincides with the present State of Assam. In order to effectively rule in such a large area the Ahoms adopted the local Indo-germanic *lingua franca*. Ironically, their political success may have led to the gradual disuse of their own language and unique script. Ahom gradually became a religious sacerdotal language. Francis Buchanan (Hamilton), who collected his information in 1808 and 1809, noted that Ahom was then already 'a dead language', 'only studies by those who follow the old worship'.[2] This was confirmed in 1837 when it was reported that the Ahom priest who was employed as a teacher did not seem to possess a very perfect knowledge of the Ahom language, and that the same was true of the Ahoms in general, who for the most part had lost all knowledge of their original tongue.[3] While the assumption that for almost seven hundred years the Ahom culture remained completely isolated from other Tai people is untenable, it cannot be denied that the language displays certain archaic features, and that knowledge of the Ahom culture will be of value for a deeper understanding of Tai cultures in general.

The second reason for examining Ahom origin myths is the curious circumstance that most of the publications that are concerned with Ahom documents happen either to be devoted exclusively to this sort of myths of origin, or they include samples of such myths.

After having read all available literature on the subject it became clear that in Ahom texts there can be discerned two quite distinct types of origin myths. The first and best-known of these invariably begins with a description of the primordial time, before life existed. We shall call stories that begin this was Type 1 and shortly indicate the different publications that contain such Type 1 texts.

PART A: TYPE 1

PUBLISHED TYPE 1 TEXTS

The very first description of the Ahom language in 1837 by the Reverend N. Brown was accompanied by a lithograph of twelve lines of Ahom text,[4] which, later that same year, was translated and was discovered to be myth of origin.[5] With the advantage of hindsight we can now identify the text as being merely the opening lines of Type 1 relation of the first beginnings of the universe. The number of characters of the fragment is not inconsistent with the idea that Brown was given a transcript of both sides of only the first page of a Type 1 document. More than sixty years later, when Grierson prepared his monumental Linguistic Survey and chose to include a description of the Ahom language, he decided to take these twelve opening lines as one of his three language specimens.[6] Grierson must have been quite satisfied with the whole Ahom section of his Linguistic Survey because he extracted it and published it also separately in the form of a lengthy article.[7]

A much expanded version of the opening part of a Type 1 myth appeared two years later, also under Grierson's name.[8] It comprised sixty-four lines of Ahom, a transcription, a word-by-word translation as well as a free translation. The text covered the gist of the 1837 fragment, albeit in a different wording and pushed the story a little further, to include the generation of number of creatures. To those familiar with south-western Tai languages it is obvious that this version contains a number of mistakes in the Ahom and that the translation is often fanciful and demonstrably incorrect. Cochrane, who worked among Shan people, was particularly critical of the treatment of the text fragment and, with the help of a Khamti and a Shan informant, he published a poetic translation that pushes the story much further, to where the world is divided up into various realms. Unfortunately Cochrane refrained from publishing the original document and many of his more puzzling phrases can, therefore, not be checked against the original.[9]

The latest, and most complete publication of a Type 1 text occurred in 1930. It comprises the whole first chapter of Golap Chandra Barua's Ahom Buranji.[10] The publication includes not only the English translation, but provides a transcript of an original Ahom manuscript. In this version the text continues beyond the division of the universe to the sending down of various deities to teach the rules of behaviour, the celestial ancestry of the first rulers, Khun Lung and Khun Lai and an enumeration of number of their respective offspring.

A comparison of these publications reveals that these various texts are all closely related to one another, whole phrases of the one text can be found another. The myth gradually unfolds as the texts are read in the sequence of when they were first published. On first sight the Ahom Type 1 myth is thus admirably represented in publications. No less than four separate indigenous texts were used, and three of the cases involve the reproduction of text or text fragments in the original Ahom script. However, when this impressive documentation is scrutinised much of the apparent solidity proves illusionary. In the first place each of the three separate Ahom texts reproduced was based on a single document. During the last two hundred years Ahom texts have been copied by people who had at best a very incomplete knowledge of the language and as a result copying errors did multiply. This renders it unadvisable to rely upon a single version of a text. Secondly, the Ahom writing system, like the older Shan writing system, does not indicate tones, so that even if a perfect copy of a text were available, the would be translator must be prepared to consider a range of possible meanings for each syllable before deciding which translation is the better. It follows that anyone who wishes to translate Ahom Texts must have a good grasp of grammatical constructions in Tai languages. Jenkins, Grierson and Barua demonstrably did not fulfil this criterion. Even Cochrane, whose informants were native Tai speakers, shows, as far as can be determined, an utter disrespect for Tai grammar. The four texts and text fragments must, therefore, be checked with original manuscripts and the translations must be critically examined before the myth may be analysed. Thus in order to avoid false imagery, such as occurred in *Bible* translations where a "ship's rope" was mistranslated as 'camel'—causing countless preachers to wrack their brains as to imagine how difficult it was for a camel to pass through the eye of a needle—it was decided to consult various original manuscripts.

INTRODUCING UNPUBLISHED TYPE 1 TEXT MATERIAL

Among the photocopies of original Ahom documents acquired over the last ten years six manuscripts were found that contain the myth. Two of these are almost word-for-word identical with the lengthy text published in 1930 as Chapter 1 of *Ahom Buranji.*

The acquaintance with a series of original manuscripts containing the Type 1 myth brought an unexpected new insight. A comparison of the unpublished manuscripts with the published texts of the origin myth reveals that the manuscripts differ from the publications in two significant respects. Firstly, while the published versions carry titles such as "An Ahom Cosmogony" (Grierson, 1902, 1966). "The Great Creation" (Grierson 1904) or "The Creation" (Barua 1930), the unpublished texts commence without such a heading. Secondly, the published versions present the myth as an independent text whose purpose is to relate the first beginnings, while in the manuscripts the origin myth is invariably invoked in a wider context, it is the introduction to a different theme.

In our opinion, these two differences are related to each other. By calling the document "A Cosmogony" or "The Creation", the authors imply that the text was written for the purpose of revealing the first origin of all things. The title assumes that we deal here with a revelation, a sacred book, the Ahom equivalent of the first book of the Christian *Bible*. This pervades also the style of translation. As an example we can take a few lines from the 1930 "Creation" (p. l, paragraphs 2,3 and the beginning of 4):

> There was only one omniponent being, the Great God. He remained suspended in the sky like a swarm of bees in a hive. He had no head and no legs to walk. He had no mouth to speak. He resembled a lump of flesh hanging in the sky. Then God thought of changing His shape, otherwise no one would praise His name. Thus a long time passed. God suddenly opened His eyes and could see nothing attractive and charming. He created a deity, known as KHUNTHEUKHAM, from His breast.[11]

This sample suffices to indicate the sonorous language and impressive imagery, apparently inspired by sacred literature. In this Barua followed the tradition set by Grierson and Cochrane.

In order to demonstrate how fanciful, and uncertain even this most recent effort to translate the origin myth is, it was decided to present the parallel Ahom text as well as a word-by-word tentative translation.[12]

Some of the differences between Barua's rendering and the one preferred here can be explained by the idiosyncrasy of Ahom script: lacking tone-marks, the translator has with most syllables a wide choice of possible meanings which he can only narrow down by a knowledge of Ahom sentence construction and by taking the context into account. Sometimes it is clear how Barua chose his translation. *'Nang phu'ng'* may indeed be read as 'like bees' (and then it was apparently further embellished to 'like a swarm of bees in a hive). *'Nang'* is, however, also "to sit", and *"phu'ng"* can mean "collected". While Barua has grasped the gist of the story, it is maintained here that many of his expressions are rather doubtful and some appear to be simply unwarranted. There is no cause to introduce lumps of flesh. Nothing in the text indicates the spirit pondering to change its shape. Barua gratuitously presents *Khun Thiw Kham* with the epithet 'deity'. The title *Khun* does, however, not necessarily imply godliness. Barua chose *Khun Thiw Kham* to come out of the first spirit's breast. The text is absolutely clear that it was from the "*chaw*", which corresponds with the Thai *chai.*[13] This word is known among all Tai languages and admittedly is difficult to translate. It is usually taken to mean "the heart, the mind or the spirit (in the figurative sense)".[14]

[illegible]
Later on a spirit holding rule and power stayed

[illegible]
Without misfortune in the middle of space [he] sat collected.

[illegible]
Not yet possessed a head or foundation for speaking or saying.

[illegible]
Not yet [he] possessed a mouth to utter sound.

[illegible]
[he was] free and loose there was no contact,

[illegible]
[he remained alone there was no contact, [13]

[illegible]
He then [in] darkness rested [but] darkness changed to glitter.

[illegible]
Anyone not looked at [his] shining body.

[illegible]
Later on the spirit then rose up

[illegible]
Opened [his eyes not saw good [not] saw beauty.

[illegible]
And then from [his] heart Khun Thiw Kham [he] took out.

While Barua may have upgraded Khun Thiw Kham to godly status, Cochrane (1911, 1915) was much further off the mark. Apparently taking '*Khun*' to mean'god', '*Thiw*' to mean 'row; line', and '*Kham*' to mean 'word and disregarding the rules of Tai grammar, he conjured up an image of 'words that changed themselves into shining gods'. Or in the style adopted for such an important myth: 'the sovereign God, from meditation. brought forth bright words [that] radiantly from his heart came forth afar as shining gods.[15] In his analysis of the passage Cochrane alludes to the imagery of 'words' which issued from the 'mind' of the God as world-gods bowing before their Sovereign, which almost reminds him of the Hebrew conception that the "worlds have been framed by the word of God".[16] It is not difficult to demostrate that Cochrane had allowed himself to be carried away by biblical analogies. The manuscripts clearly indicate that *Khun Thiw Kham* is a single character, for in the following paragraphs we read repeatedly of the founder-spirit and *Khun Thiw Kham* as 'both of them' *(song ra)*. Moreover, while a final epithet *Kham* may be derived from *khwam*, 'words' or 'language, it also could mean 'golden', 'sojourn', 'to step', 'to exceed', 'to shut in', or 'evening', to mention some possibilities. Without the guidance of tonal signs the translation of Ahom proper names is a hazardous exercise. Cochrane's translation must have been largely guided by his Christian presuppositions.

The two examples above show that even though Ahom myths have been widely published in translation, we may not use these publications as if they represent authoritative authentic Ahom material. There is need to re-examine the original manuscripts. It does not lie in my intention here to produce a critical text analysis of the various manuscripts that related to the Type 1 myth. Since this would involve the introduction of a considerable number of documents, such a study would easily fill a monograph. It was decided to limit the study to a close examination of two manuscripts that contained texts that apparently underly the Ahom text that was published as Chapter 1 in *Barua's Ahom Buranji.* This must be regarded as a much needed check upon the published version, which clarifies obscure passages and eliminates some of the scribal errors. To produce a full text analysis of this particular version of Myth 1 would still be too ambitious, for the purposes of this chapter it suffices to present the myth in its barest outline:

> In the beginning there were neither spirits nor men, no living beings, no firmament. Afterwards as yet unformed spirit arises. This spirit creates out of its own self another being, Khun Thiw Kham, with whom to converse. A lotus plant sprouts forth out of a navel and subsequently is created a world upholding crab, a tortoise, a coiled serpent, an elephant with curved tusks, a white lump of rock to unhold the world, posts were set up in the four directions. Then the spirit and Khun Thiw Kham create a huge spider. The latter goes to and fro in the sky and weaves in the firmament a golden throne. The spirit then divides itself into a

> male and female half for the purpose of procreation, a number of golden yolks (*mo'n kham*) result and a certain and a certain. Thaw Lung is given the task of hatching them. At first the yolks would not hatch, but eventually, with the help of the elixir Nya Pu Lok the yolks break and the spirit's offspring are born. The care of the universe is then divided among this heavenly brood (Chaw Ai Ko; Sing Cho Pha Pha Kham; Sing Kam Pha; and Ngi Ngeu Kham). Sing Kam Pha did not obey his ancestor and after death became a spirit. His son Ring Ko Pha became the guardian spirit of houses. The founder spirit then notices the lack of guidance in the world and creates Pu Phi Su'a, Phu Chet Khing and Kun Khwam Ngam, who gave the sheets of rules. Pu Phi Su'a, who lives at the *pipal* tree, then chose Pha But Rum (Sang Nam), to be ruler of Keng Khru'w, and his son Pha Si Up (Sang Ning) went to rule Pha Kaw Khru'w. He had four sons, of whom the youngest, Chaw Da Kham went to be ruler of Mu'ng Lai. He is the ancestor of Khun Lung and Khun Lai, the ruler who came down from heaven by way of a metallic ladder to govern mankind.

Then follows the genealogy of Khun Lai: *his son Chaw Chang Bun, his son Chaw Khun Nyew [Khun Chang Nyeu], his younger brother Chaw Tai Pha, his son Chaw Phan Long Yu'ng (Chaw Phan Kong Yu'ng Kong Rai, his son Ngi Tow Saen Nga, his son Taw Nga Ku'w, his son Taw Khun Ming, his son Taw Khun Kum, the ruler of Mu'ng Ri Mu'ng Ram, then Chaw Tai Pha of Mu'ng Maw came down to be king, Pa Miw Pu'ng of Mu'ng Mit became king, then Phu Chang Khang was king.*

At this point the manuscripts continue simply with a list of all Ahom kings:

- Su'w Ka Pha, Su'w Teu Pha, Su'w Bin Pha, Su'w Khang Pha, Su'w Kham Pha, Su'w Tu'w Pha, Taw Kham Thi, Su'w Dang Pha, Su'w Yang Pha, Su'w Phu' k Pha, Su'w Saen Pha Tammra, Su'w Kan Pha Tammra, Su'w Pim Pha Tammra, Su'w Hum Pha Tammra, Su'w Ku'n Pha Tammra, Su'w Kham Pha Tammra, Su'w Sing Pha Tammra, Su'w Rom Pha Tammra, Su'w Ching Pha Tammra, Su'w Tam Pha Tammra, Su'w Pu'ng Mu'ng Pha Tammra, Su'w Kon Pha Tammra, Su'w Hung Pha Tammra, Su'w Nyot Pha, Chaw Su'w Kham Yang, Su'w Yin Pha Tammra, Su'w Lik Pha Tammra, Su'w Pat Phat Tammra, Su'w Khung Pha Tammra, Su'w Ton Pha Tammra, Su'w Naen Pha Tammra, Su'w

Reum Pha Tammra, Su'w Nyeu Pha Taṃmra, Su'w Hit Pu'ng Pha Tammra.

The Local Context of Myth Type I

When we compare the two manuscripts with the Ahom column of the 1930 chapter 'The Creation' the first thing that becomes apparent is that the 1930 text follows the manuscripts practically verbatim until it stops short with the reign of Phu Chang Khang, the father of Su'w Ka Pha. It is of course possible that Barua's copy was incomplete, but in view of the liberties he took with the translation it seems possible that he deliberately refrained from presenting the royal genealogy. He may have felt that the genealogy did not 'belong' in the story of the first creation, it carries the reader much too far in time right up to the late eighteenth century. By omitting the final section of the manuscript Barua may well have made it possible to present Chapter 2, which deals with an episode of the mythology, as a natural sequel.[17] Whether Barua deliberately excised the last part of the document or had access only to an incomplete version will probably never be established with certainty.

It is crucial, however, to take note of the original documents as a whole; for only then can the apparent purpose of this particular recitation of the Type 1 myth be established and a beginning be made to place the text in its historical context. While the Ahom religion, with its priests and astrologers, its sacrifices and rituals, developed as the Ahom polity grew in size and power, this traditional religion and its practitioners were increasingly challenged by the Hindu religion. Su'w Tam Pha (Jayadhvaj Singha) in the mid-seventeenth century was the first Ahom king to accept Vaisnavism as his personal faith, thus causing serious competition between the old state religion with its sanguine animal sacrifices and an anti-sacrificial form of Hinduism. Su'w Pat Pha (Gadadhar Singha. 1681-1696) adopted the more pro-sacrificial Tantric or Sakta form of Hinduism and encouraged a general plunder of Vaisnava property. By the late eighteenth century the Ahom kings had generally favoured the Sakta faith for more than a century, but not without occasional support for Vaisnavites and maintaining some of the old Ahom rituals and priesthood. To complicate matters, an unorthodox, anti-Brahmanic form of Hinduism, usually called the Moamaria sect, had found widespread support among the common people. In 1769, the Moamarias rebelled and from that time onwards the country was often in a state of civil war. In 1782, Su'w Hit pu'ng Pha put down one Moamaria attack, but in 1786 they rose up once more. For the remainder of his reign the country was in uproar. The position of Ahom priests at this time may safely be described as precarious. They had been losing out to their various Hindu counterparts and their role in court ritual was no longer safe.

The myth Type 1 can be looked at in the context of this longstanding bitter religious rivalry. The opening paragraphs of the text are in pure Ahom, not a single Hindu loan word can be found, the names of the characters, including the founder-spirit are all in pure Tai. Even in the closing list of kings, the recent monarchs who had also taken Hindu names are only referred to by their Tai names. While the language and script are maintained in their classical form, at the same time it is apparent that the ideas are mostly derived from Indian thought. This may be taken as an indication of the extent of Hinduisation that had already taken place by the end of the eighteenth century. However much the imagery of the opening stages of creation owes to Hindu parallels, these ideas have been absorbed and are presented in their own Ahom fashion. Myth Type 1 must have been written as a Tai myth, a telling of the origin of Tai gods and kings. When the myth reaches Khun Lung and Khun Lai there is a confident, smooth run to the father of Su'w Ka Pha and the line of Ahom rulers. This part may not be seen as an appendix, to be discarded without violating the text, as Barua appears to have done. The genealogy must have been, to the reciting priests at least, an essential, indispensable section. It reminds the reigning king Su'w Hit Pu'ng Pha of his long line of predecessors, going back to the two first Tai kings, Khun Lung and Khun Lai, who had a mandate from heaven. While flattering the king by linking him with a heavenly lineage, at the same time the text must be seen as an affirmation that this lineage was Tai, not Indian.[18] The detailed knowledge of Khun Lung and Khun Lai's heavenly ancestry and the names of those who descended from them may have been quite recent among the Ahom priesthood, for it was during the same reign of Su'w Hit Pu'ng Pha that a commission of learned men was sent to Mogaung to examine the histories of their race and to work out the lineage between Khun Lung and Khun Lai and Su'w Ka Pha.[19]

The weakened court position of Ahom priests during the second half of the eighteenth century is underlined by the fact that they no longer monopolised the coronation ceremony. According to the Tungkhungia Buranji during the coronation of Su'a Hit Pu'ng Pha the new king was blessed by the heads of the major religious factions.[20] It so happens that the text chanted by the Ahom priests at this occasion has been preserved and published.[21] The important of Type 1 myths in the late eighteenth century is strongly underlined when it is noted that the Ahom priests' text commences with a summary version of this same cosmogony Type 1. Another summary Type 1 account was found as the introduction yet unpublished manuscript which tabulates earthquakes, the time of the year they may occur and the portent of these events. No doubt such a text was part of an astrologer's professional literature. The minimum function of Type 1 myths thus seems to be a legitimising one, an assertion by religious specialists that what they are to say rests upon the very foundations of creation. Its frequent use in documents some of which can be dated to the late eighteenth century may be regarded as a patent sign of the weakness of the Ahom priests at that time.

Cochrane is the only scholar who have attempted to date this myth. Since his Khamti and Shan assistants had difficulty reading the text he places it at a very early period, not long after the Ahoms had reached Assam. That argument is unconvincing, for the difficulties in reading an unfamiliar Tai genre in a script that omits tonal differences are formidable. There is nothing in this and other Type 1 texts at hand to suggest that they were written prior to the eighteenth century.

The Regional Context of Myth Type 1

This myth is full of interesting imagery and information. The general impression is that there are close parallels between some of the medical Indian religious literature and the Ahom Myth 1. The first setting, a beginning without gods, men or sky is reminiscent of the commencement of the description of the creation in many Indian religious texts, from the latest phase of the Vedic times to the *Puranas*.[22] If Barua's free translation is added that this world was surrounded by water, a sentence he apparently took from the 1904 version, but which is absent from the manuscripts and also from the Ahom text as reproduced by Barua himself. The primordial spirit out of whom emanates the various manifestations of life is a regular theme in Indian literature; it is Visnu or his demiurge *Brahma*, who creates out of his body a number of sons (just as Khun Thiw Kham and a number of cosmic animals are created out of the primordial spirit). The navel and lotus imagery also has direct parallel in Indian cosmology, with *Narayana* floating asleep on the water from whose navel the lotus emerges. The following scene is almost wholly inspired by a Vaisnavite cosmogony, which is usually known as a version of the story of the 'churning of the ocean' in order to win the *amrita* elixier. The cosmic tortoise is inspired by none other than *Visnu* and the snake by *Vasuki*. Also the elephant holding up the earth is a well-known Indian symbol.[23]

Establishing the most likely source of these ideas does of course not preclude further analysis. The Ahom choice of all these symbols in this sequence may be reinterpreted locally. The trio of crab, tortoise and serpent may well represent the amphibious in this Ahom cosmogony, that what lives in water, but which can sustain itself also out of the water. It may be regarded as an in between stage, before the introduction of the elephant and the rock. [24]

Then follows the interlude of the large spider. Barua (1930: 2) misled by the fact that the text says 'both of them (i.e., the original spirit and Khun Thiw Kham) created a large spider, mistakingly translated this as 'a pair of spiders'. The element of a weaving spider was not found in the available Indian literature. Grierson (1904: 182) already noted that with the introduction of the spider, there is a distinct break in the story, it consists of an element added to the Indian-style cosmogony, probably an autochthonous theme. The only regional reference to a cosmic weaving spider in the available literature came from the Shans.[25]

After the spider has finished weaving the sky the Puranic story is taken up again. The original spirit has exhausted his a sexual creation and—just like Brahma—he divides himself into man and woman who comply with the wishes of the creator and begin the work of [sexual] creation. [26] The golden yolks in the Ahom myth appear to have a parallel in the celestial egg which is prominent in various *Puranas*.[27] The Ahom myth then leaves the Purnaic tradition and introduces a number of characters from the Tai pantheon, Pu Phi Su a (possible literal translation: Grandfather Protective Spirit; the spirit in the *pipal* tree), Phu Chet Khing and Kun Khwam Nagam (possible literal translation: Man of Excellent Words; the author of the books of rules). This section, from the apear-ance of Pu Phi Su'a to that of Kun Khwam Ngam appears to be but a summary, a compressed account.

This is followed by the ancestry of the legendary Khun Lung and Khun Lai, who, in various Shan chronicles, are regarded as founders. Khun Lung and Khun Lai are invariably described as envoys from the gods who descended from heaven by way of what Barua translated as an iron ladder.[28] The story of the decent, the gods' instructions, the intervention by a trickster character and the quarrel between Khun Lung and Khun Lai is well-developed in Ahom mythology and worthy of further scrutiny, but since it is taken for granted in our myth Type 1 an analysis shall await another occasion.

Only ten generations of rulers are given between Khun Lai and Phu Chang Khang, the father of Su'w Ka Pha. When this list is compared to various Shan genealogies it is found to coincide in broad outline with only that part of the Mu'ng Mao royal genealogy that Elias dated between the late eleventh century and the early thirteenth century A.D.[29] The Ahom list takes Chaw Chang Bun to be the son of Khun Lai, while in the Elias list there are another seventeen rulers between these two.

The final part of the text is a list of all Ahom kings from Su'w Ka Pha who led the first group of Tais into Assam in the early thirteenth century till Su'w Hit Pu'ng Pha, also known as Gaurinath Singha. The absence of any further royal names between Su'w Hit Pu'ng Pha and the colophon may be taken as an indication that the document was written during that reign, some time between 1780 and the end of 1794.

The Universal Dimension

While the purpose of this chapter is to demonstrate the importance of a myth's contextual and regional cadre, it is by no means my intention to belittle the achievements of those who have analysed the universal structures and meaning behind mythology. They have charted a sophisticated and convincing framework of conceptual oppositions and oft hidden layers of meaning of many sysmbols. How useful can be a recourse to universal analysis will be indicated in a single short example from our Type 1 Ahom myth. To illustrate the point I have chosen the striking imagery of the spider weaving the sky.

Cochrane already noted the curious fact that such a spider myth is also found among some of the American Indians of Arizona and new Mexico. With the boldness of an early twentieth century diffusionist he points out that the American Indians may have come originally from what is now eastern China or Korea, not so far from the early home of the Shans.[30] In order to understand the spider story, however, it is relevant to quote Eliade:

> The moon, however, simply because she is mistress of all living things and sure guide of the dead, has "woven" all destinies. Not for nothing is she envisaged in myth as an immense spider—an image you will find used by a great many peoples. For to weave is not merely to predestine (anthropologically), and to join together different realities (cosmologically) but also to create, to make something of one's own substance as the spider does in spinning its web.[31]

If the link between the weaving spider and the moon as assumed by Eliade were not yet convincing, the ending of the segment with the image of the creation of a heavenly golden throne should convince the sceptic that indeed the Ahom weaving spider concerns the story of the creation of the moon. Its prominent insertion so early in the Ahom cosmogony is "an indication of the pre-eminent position of the moon in Ahom religion. In another as yet unpublished text we read the invocation to the chief heavenly bodies which begins with Ai Khun Nu'n, Ngi Khun Ban, or the Eldest, Lord Moon and the Second-Born Lord Sun.

PART B: TYPE 2

PUBLISHED TYPE 2 TEXTS

In Ahom literature there exists an origin myth that is quite different in a character from that described above under the rubric Type 1. The first published version of Type 2 Ahom origin myth appeared in 1894 as an article by E.A. Gait under the rather non-descript title "Abstract of the Contents of one of the Ahom Puihis."[32] A summary of the myth, which Gait gave the heading "The Ahom Story of Flood." is as follows:

Once the heat from the sun dried up all the water causing widespread death. The earth cracked and masses of boiling water killed all remaining life except the old man Thaw Lip Llng and a cow who were in a boat made of stone. The flood carried this boat to the mountain Iba in the north-east. The stench of rotting corpses caused the gods to send down fire. Thaw Lip Ling saved himself by killing the cow and hiding in its body. There he found the seed of a gourd, which he later planted. An immense plant emerged with branches in four directions. The northern branch was dead by the cold, the southern dead from heat, the western drowned, but the eastern branch thrived and grew a gigantic gourd which contained all types of life. The creatures inside cried and Indra's messenger, Pan Thoi heard them. Indra's eldest son Ai Pha Lan was sent to open the gourd by means of a flash of lightning. Wherever he aimed the creatures at that spot begged him to spare them. Finally, Thaw Lip Ling, who was sitting at the point where the flower had dried off from the gourd, offered to sacrifice himself. Thaw Lip Ling was killed and life escaped from the open gourd. Ai Pha Lan then taught the creatures their various skills. Thaw Lip Ling is still worshipped by the Ahom priests who make offerings to the man, but for whose act of self abnegation the gourd might have remained unbroken to the present day.[33]

Unfortunately, Gait did not supply a copy of the text in the original Ahom, and this account represents the contents as related to him by the owner of the manuscript. While the gist of the story is clear. It is, therefore, not certain if the name Indra was actually in the manuscript or whether it represents a translation of an Ahom name, such as Leng Don.

Cochrane reported a slightly different version of the story in great detail. The rendering of the Ahom names reveals how much he relies upon his Shan intermediaries. Instead of the Ahom Leng Don, he writes a Shan version: Linglawn. Similarly, Lao Khri is rendered as Lao-hki and the Ahom Mu'ng Ri becomes Mu'ng Hi. Before the flooding the sage Lip-long [Thaw Lip Ling] was told to prepare a raft. In pages of purple prose Cochrane describes Lip-long's heart-rending farewell to his family and the destruction by water. After the flood the stench of corpse is obliterated by a fire, Lip-long kills the cow and hides in its belly, finding the gourd seed. Of the resulting vines, one was scorched, another was overrun by water, but one grew bearing great gourds. Thunderbolts broke the gourds. In this version Cochrane tells that the creature sacrificing himself for mankind was a certain Sao Pang.[34]

Another version of myth Type 2 can be found near the beginning of Chapter 3 of Barua's Ahom Buranji.[35] Since Barua provides both an Ahom and an English text and because this text is also available in manuscript form it is possible to report the content with a measure of authority. It is written in a remarkably terse 'telegram' style:

> At that time water flooded the forest. In the 19th and 20th year of the 60-year cycle fire destroyed the world. In the 21st year there came down and was planted a gourd near the middle. Late that year [it] burst and became people. In the 22nd year new human seeds were sent sown. Late that year [they] burst and became people. Not sufficient for every town. In the 23rd year Lord Lan was ordered to go down to continue to seed humans. Late that year Thaw Lip Ling and [his] servant Thaw Man Sing were sent down to teach humans below in 30,000 towns. In the 23rd year towns were confused[?] and in the 29th year there was no overlord. This was discussed by Thaen Kham and Leng Don together with all kinds of Thaens [gods] from beyond the sky. There was no-one to rule the 30,000 towns. In the 30th year they placed Khun Lung and Khun Lai to be rulers.

The three accounts are obviously three versions of the same story. They refer to a world-wide flood that destroyed all life and the re-seeding of life *via* a gourd. Ai Pha Lan is undoubtedly the same character as Lord Lan, and in all stories Thaw Lip Ling occurs even though the taks allotted to him differ in the three versions. The 1930 version seems to be an extract of a much longer story, for what happened in the first 18 years of this (first) cycle has not been preserved in the available documents.

Type 2 Texts in Regional Context

Anyone familiar with the ethnography of mainland South-East Asia will confidently note that the Ahom share this Type 2 myth with many ethnic groups living further eastwards. The flood/gourd story is one of the most common episodes of mainland South-East Asian mythology. Versions of the theme have been recorded among a wide range of ethnic groups, particularly in the northern part of Vietnam, but also among the Chams, the Sre, the Ma, the Tai Nuea, the Tai Lao, the Khmu, the Lamet, the Lawa, the Karen, the Wa and others.[36] It is, therefore, not necessary to analyse details of the Type 2 Ahom myth in isolation, instead we can use the wider context to highlight in what details the Ahom versions differ from those recorded among other people, particularly from other Tais.[37]

First there are the named characters in the story. Lip Ling, Pan Thoi, Pha Lan, Sao Pang and Man Sing do not occur among the many names found in the standard recorded mythology of the other Tais. The account of Lip Ling and the cow, whom he killed in order to save himself from the fire is also not found in that form. In the Black Tai versions there are animals being let down on earth, including a cow, but this element seems to serve only to acquaint the audience with the reason of the forward curve of the cow's horns, which resulted because in its fear it slid down back to front. The closest parallel can be found in a Laotian variant where a buffalo works three years, dies and from whose nostrils emerges the plant that gives rise to the gourd.[38]

A most intriguing image from one of the Ahom Type 2 myths is that of the stone boat in which Lip Ling is saved. In mainland South-East Asian versions the survivors of the flood are usually saved in an ordinary boat, in a raft, in a drum (that is, a dug-out tree trunk), or more commonly in the gourd itself.[39] The Ahoms seem to be unique in assigning the stone element to the boat. The image of a weightless stone, just as a life-bringing stone, is the kind of image eminently suited to convey a key theme in cosmogony: how life came out of non-life.'[40]

Dating Type 2 Texts

Thematically Type 2 texts belong to the mainland South-East Asian tradition. It is quite likely that the various Tais who migrated to mainland South-East Asia in the eleventh and twelfth centuries A.D. absorbed the gourd origin myth from the local populations whom they subjugated. The absence of the myth among the Tais of Southern China and the Li of Hainan.[41] would render support to that idea. Less than two centuries after their invasion of mainland South-East Asia the Tai-Ahoms crossed the Patkoi ranges into the Brahmaputra Valley, and it could be argued that they took along with them a version of the gourd-myth in their earliest literature. If that were accepted the three versions of Type 2 myths could then be seen as the end result of a process of copying that spans all the centuries since their arrival in Assam. The fact that the three versions of Type 2 are rather dissimilar in style and content would support the hypothesis of lengthy local history of the myth.

If this scenario were accepted the Ahom Myth 2 versions—and all other versions that may still be encountered in the as yet untranslated Ahom manuscripts—may be regarded as particularly valuable, for their being copied for some seven hundred years in isolation from the many other people who share this myth, would be a historical find. It would establish the age during which the Tais first adopted the myth. Moreover, the elements that the different Tai versions, including the Ahom ones, have in common may be taken as direct pointers to the type of literature which the Tais met when they first arrived in mainland South-East Asia. The characters of Lip Ling, Pan Thoi, Pha Lan, Sao Pang and Man Sing would become all the more intriguing and warrant a search in the early legendary parts of a range of South-East Asian annals.

However, their is a much more recent possible path by which the Type 2 myth could have inserted itself, namely by a deliberate grafting of Shan legendary history onto the Ahom tradition. That certain Shan historical documents were studied and at least partially copied by late eighteenth century Ahom chroniclers has already been noted.

In order to choose between an early and a recent introduction it is necessary to closely examine Shan cosmogonies. In this examination no conclusions will be drawn from broad similarities: the occurrence of flood, a fire, or a large gourd is too vague and generalised and indeed can be found across the whole of mainland South-East Asia. Only if there are among these Shan Myths versions that resemble the Ahom Type 2 stories in specific detail, such as stone boat, or the appearance of characters such as Lip Ling, Pan Thoi, Pha Lan, Sao Pang or Man Sing, such commonalities may be taken as signs of a relatively recent borrowing.

The ensuring search covered the literature of important Shan groups such as Tai Yai, Tai Khoen and Tai Mao, but also Tai Lue. The flood/gourd story was often encountered, sometimes mixed with themes that obviously derived from Buddhist sources.[42] Not a trace of our Type 2 myths was found.

It was, therefore, with a measure of surprise when checking through a recently published collection of 35 cosmogonic stories, recorded mainly in the northern Thai provinces, a version was encountered that did not merely contain an indication of similarity, but presented what can only be described as a clear-cut Type 2 Ahom myth in striking detail. Apparently a high-ranking monk, Phrakhru Phrommathammakhun in Chiangrai Province told three cosmogonic stories which were compressed by an editor into a lengthy tale of which the relevant part is here given in translation:

> ....After the humans had offended the gods aflood overwhelmed the earth. Grandfather Land Choeng, Khun Dek and Khtut Khan made a raft on which they took wives and children, with the rising waters they reached the godly world and obtained forvigeness. When they wanted to go down to earth again the chief Taen gave them a buffalo to help prepare the fields. This buffalo worked for three years and died. They kept the carcass until only the bones were left. In these bones there was a seed of a gourd. A man named Thaw Li Ping took the seed, planted it and a plant as large as a mountain emerged, and on the gourd there was a small hole. Out of this hole came the incessant sound. Thaw Li Ping felt suspicion and tried to get up to the hole. When he stooped down he stumbled and fell in the hole. His body felt on soft floor of the gourd so that his fall was not dangerous. Then he saw that the gourd was full of various types of humans, animals and plants all trying to get out of the gourd. The sound reached the great Thaen. The Thaen wanted to open it with lightning, but did not know how to do so without accident to humans or animals. If he opened it where the humans were, they would die. If he did so where the animals were people would have no animals to help with the work, if he destroyed the plants there would be no food. Thaw Li Ping decided to sacrifice himself and allowed the gourd to be opened just where he was.

> After the gourd was opened for three days and three nights all the living things came out. The humans who emerged divided into Tai Li, Tai Chueng, Tai Lo and Tai Khwang. These peoples still worship Thaw Li Ping who sacrificed his life for all. When the people came out grand-father Lang Choeng taught how to tend the fields, weave cloth, the marriage ceremony.[43]

This story is exceptional in that it is only one outside Assam thus far encountered that represents a close parallel to the Ahom Type 2 myth. It becomes even more remarkable when we read the beginning of this same story of the creation of the world, for that describes nothing else but an Ahom myth Type 1. Step by step the Ahom story is followed. A great spirit out of whose self was created Khun Thiw Kham, then a crab floating on the water on which the earth rested. Then earth was created in the north. On top of mountains pillar were placed, a rope was bound and two golden spiders were created.

At this point there can no longer be any doubt as to the source of Phrakhru Phrommathammakhun's first story. The rope, pillars and the two spiders did not exist before 1930 when they were published as Golap Chandra Barua's somewhat fanciful translation of Ahom myth Type 1. Anthropologists tend to overlook the fact that some of the older literature has found its way back to the field and that such literature is bound to be assiduously studied and may have unforeseen effects.

Alerted by the fact that Phrakhru Phrommathammakhun used written sources from outside his direct region it was not too difficult to find the source of the opening paragraphs of the section translated above. grand-father Lang Choeng, Khun Dek and Khun Khan must have come from the Laotian Nithan Khun Bulom. In this well-known Lao chronicle they are known by the same names. The chronicle relates how they built a raft and with wives and children they rose upon the flood waters. The Laotian chronicle also records the buffalo that worked three years before dying and out of which the gigantic plant grew with the gourd. The three days and three nights' stream of life from the opened gourd, as well as the teaching role of grand-father Lang Soeng all come from this Lao source.[44]

There remains the character of Thao Li Ping who sacrificed himself to open the gourd. As was indicated above, he is not found in the Laotian annals or any other non-Ahom mythology. There can be little doubt but that Thao Li Ping is almost homophonous with the Ahom character Thaw Lip Ling[45] and Phrakhru Phrommathammakhun could have found him in Barua's Ahom Buranji but the story of his self-sacrifice does not occur in this work. There is thus a third source involved, one that mentions Thaw Lip Ling's death. The question remains whether Phrakhru Phrommathammakhun used a third published Ahom source—such as Gait (1894), or Cochrane (1915); or if he derived the Thao Li Ping story from a *bona fide* Shan source. If the answer to that question is the latter, this would strongly indicate a more recent dating of the Ahom myth Type 2. Until such a Shan source is found the question remains open.[45]

Comparative and General Remarks

Whether we can succeed in dating the introduction of the Type 1 myth to the eighteenth century and the Type 2 myth to the beginning of the second millennium or not, the fact remains that both types were being copied by Ahom priests in the nineteenth century. It is not so unusual in cosmogonies to find themes being repeated in various guises.[46] In the case of the Ahom the repetition forms part of a scheme quite common among Tai peoples. The Type 1 myths relate to the heavenly descent of royalty, while Type 2 tells of the gourd-origin of ordinary mankind. The Tais, who founded their position in South-East Asia by means of rapid conquest, maintained a social organisation that is characterised by strict hierarchical divisions. How essential this system of inequality has been is reflected in the way the Tais have kept the story of how the two brothers Khun Lung and Khun Lai—or whatever other names have been assigned to the first rulers among other Tai groups—were selected to rule by the gods themselves and descended from heaven, while the rest of humanity originated here on the earth.[47] This link between social stratification and myths of origin only becomes apparent through the framework of local and regional analysis.

Each of the two Ahom origin myth types has revealed a distinct story. Type 1 can best be understood by realising that the Ahom peoples had descended upon a huge valley with complex cultures, part and parcel of the Indian sphere of influence. By the eighteenth century Hinduism had so deeply penetrated Ahom culture that it had become usual for Ahom to belong to one of the various competing schools of Hindu thought. In the late eighteenth century the country was deeply divided and steeped in what may be described as a bitter sectarian civil war. The Type 1 myth reflects the extent to which the Ahoms had internalised principles of Hindu mythology. At the same time it indicates a conscious effort on behalf of the beleaguered Ahom priests to cast these thoughts in a Tai frame, to translate and thereby transform or at least attempt to Tai-ise Hindu thought.

Myth 1 may thus be seen as an instrument in the hands of these priests which serves to legitimate their role, to lay claims to resources, to remind the king of his age-old ancestry and duties towards the sacred Ahom tradition.

The adoption of the Type 2 myth may be seen as part of the cultural heritage of the South-Western groups of Tai peoples as a whole. Its occurrence among the Ahoms may be interpreted as an indication of the route through mainland South-East Asia taken by their progenitors. The fact that many versions of the gourd myth are known among South-Western Tais allows an interesting approach, often neglected in the study of myth, namely the collection of different regional variants of the same myth and attempting to account for the variations by taking note of specific historical and cultural circumstances. While this chapter is specifically concerned with Ahoms, the question of how the Ahom flood and ground myth differs from that of other Tai peoples is germane. While other South-Western Tais relate how, as a result of the effect of the lightning that broke the gourd, scorched, darker skinned autochthonous peoples came out first; followed by the lighter skinned Tais, the Ahom versions do not take up this theme. The reason for the absence of that theme lies probably in the fact that their situation *vis-à-vis* other ethnic groups in the Brahmaputra Valley does in no way reflect such a simple imagery. While in mainland South-East Asia folklore it is common to equate 'hill tribes' and subjugation with darker-skinned people, in Assam the hill peoples are often of lighter colour than the dominant valley dwellers. Taking the theme of the forceful opening of the gourd by lightning the Ahom version attaches the story of the sacrifice of Thaw Lip Ling, a theme not found in mainland South-East Asia. It is possible that the choice of this theme also reflects the local Assamese situation. The self-immolation of Lip Ling may have been inspired by the devotional form of Vaisnavism that won itself a large number of adherents.

This type of local and regional analysis is often overlooked by anthropologists who have learned to look at myths as a special genre of literature and have concentrated upon uncoding the myth's hidden messages. In this chapter it has been shown that an examination of the historical and cultural circumstances in which the myth is recited may lead to a fruitful understanding of particular local variants. To move directly from the recording of a myth to a universal analysis appears to me a hazy, if not hazardous undertaking. In my view the intermediate levels are prerequisite to a confident application of models of universal analysis.

Finally a word about sources. The Ahom myths of origin were traced in a number of nineteenth and early twentieth century sources, some of them even with a facsimile of the original Ahom text provided. Although they have the appearance of being exemplary primary sources, comparison with manuscripts has proven them to be flawed in, the reproduction and suspect in the translation. The fact that we deal with manuscripts written in an ill-understood language was not openly admitted by the researchers of a century ago. At that time there seems to be a tendency towards gloryfying scientific efforts and it does not seem to be quite the done thing to express one's doubts or ignorance in print.

More seriously, the authors who wrote and quoted Ahom cosmogonies have been shown to have selected from their manuscripts passages which have been deprived of their original context. In our opinion cosmological information has often been collected in such a manner as to introduce serious bias. In the first place many of accounts of origin were collected by agents of colonial regimes as part of their standard repertoire of gathering information of practical use to the government. In many of the older ethnographic works we read in a few tantalising lines that there are certain fabulous accounts, but that these do not establish any clear geographical indication of a tribe's original whereabouts.[48] The other likely nineteenth century recorder of cosmologies is the missionary who often felt unable to think about cosmology unless it was in comparison with the current European cosmological myths and, therefore, they felt compelled to cast the indigenous stories in a biblical framework. The fortunate circumstance that we have access to some of these myths in their original context and that we have been able to show how they have been deliberately quoted out of context should serve as a serious warning. How much of the vast literature on cosmogonic mythology is similarly flawed? How many recorded myths are based on mutilated accounts? How many mask the indigenous intentions?

One of the most obvious ways for the anthropological discipline to strengthen itself is to improve its older accounts through critical source analysis, assisted in this task by a thorough in-depth study of other cultures. When making analytical statements or engaging in theoretical debates we must be sure that our agreements are based upon statements made by those who have acquired real insight in a culture's language and history. Cross cultural comparison based upon flawed sources is bound to harm the discipline. Conversely, one of the most hopeful paths for our discipline to develop is that of the pursuit of regional in-depth studies.

REFERENCES

1. 'La pensee mythique, ... celle qui cree et administre les mythes, est intermediaire entre la pensee onirique et la pensee verbale, entre le reve, dont elle a le caractere illustre, dramatique et en general symbolique, et le discaurs, dont elle a le caractere lucide, articule et en general coherent. G. DurneAl, *Loki* [new, revised edition], Paris: Plammarion, 1986, p. 228.
2. F. Hamilton, *An Account of Assam, First Compiled in 1807-1814*, edited by S.K. Bhuyan, Gauhati: Department of Historical and Antiquarian Studies, 1963, p. 7.
3. N. Brown, '*Alphabets of the Tai Language*', *Journal of the Asiatic Society of Bengal,* Vol. 6, January, 1837, p. 17. I claim that the efforts by modern revivalists to resurrect Ahom are not based on the Ahom of old documents, but on a mixture of other Tai languages. What is being learnt in the 1980s and 1990s under the label of Ahom is written in the old script, but has little else in common with seventeenth century Ahom. It may hence be called Neo-Ahom.
4. "Specimen of the Ahom, or Assam, Character, from a manuscript volume presented to the Society by Capt. F. Jenkins", 1835, *Journal of the Asiatic Society of Bengal,* Vol 6, January, 1837, Plate IV. This Plate formed part of the article by Brown, 'Alphabet of the Tai language', mentioned above.
5. Major F. Jenkins, Commissioner in Assam, 'Interpretation of the Ahom extract, published as Plate IV of the January number of the present volume, Journal of *the Asiatic Society* of *Bengal,* Vol. 6, November 1837, pp. 980-983.
6. G.A. Grierson, (comp. and ed.) *Linguistic Survey of India, Vol. 1, Mon-Khmer and Siamese-Chinese Families (Includ ing Khassi and Tai),* Delhi: Motilal Banarsidass,1966 [reprint of the 1902 edition], pp. 118-119.
7. G.A. Grierson, 'Notes on Ahom', *Zeitschrift der Deutschen Morgenlan dischen Gesellschaft,* Vol. 56, 1902, pp. 1-59. Grierson comments scathingly on the Plate of 1837, in his opinion it was 'very incorrectly reproduced'. I do not share that opinion, it is a nicely produced and readable text Grierson's remark that the order of words was 'quite abnormal' also must be rejected. For details see B.J. Terwiel, Neo-Ahom and the Parable of the Prodigal Son', *Bijdragen tot de Taal, Land, en Volkenkunde,* Vol, 19, pp. 125-145.
8. G.A. Grierson, 'An Ahom Cosmogony, with a Translation and a Vocabulary of the Ahom Language', *Journal of the Royal Asiatic Society,* 1904, pp. 181-202.
9. W.W. Cochrane, 'An Ahom (Shan) Legend of Creation (From an Old MS)', *Journal of the Royal Asiatic Society,* NS Vol. 43,1911, p. 1132-42. An even more poetic rendering of the same text forms the beginning of his chapter 'Shan Religion (Mythological)' in *The Shans,* Vol 1, Rangoon: Superintendent, Government Printing, Burma, 1915, pp. 113-19.

10. Golap Chandra Barua (transl. and ed.) *Ahom-Buranji (with parallel English translation) From the Earliest Time to the End of Ahom Rule,* Calcutta: Baptist Mission Press, 1930, pp. 1-4. Gogoi's chapter on Ahom cosmology is basically a summary of Barua's translation, see P. Gogoi, *Tai-Ahom Religion and Customs,* Gauhati: Publications Board, Assam, 1976, pp. 1-4.
11. *Ahom Buranji,* p. l, paragraph 3 and the beginning of paragraph 4.
12. The Ahom lines that follow vary in some details from the published 1930 Ahom text. The reason for this is that I have relied upon two authentic manuscripts that do not show some of the irregular spellings that Barua provides.
    [The Ahom lines were in Ahom script in the manuscript and could not be printed here—Editors]
13. This sentence is omitted in Barua's Ahom column.
14. M. Haas (comp.), *Thai-English Student's Dictionary,* Kuala Lumpur: Oxford University Press, 1964, p. 126. Cushing calls it 'the mind; the most essential part; of anything', J.N. Cushing, A *Shan and English Dictionary,* Rangoon: American Baptist Mission Press, 1914, p. 198.
15. 'An Ahom Legend of Creation', p. 1135.
16. The Shans, Vol. 1, p. 116.
17. In fact, it would seem that three separate manuscripts have been cobbled together in *Ahom Buranji,* the manuscript under lying Chapter 1 was a document in its own right, Chapter 2 seems to be an extract from a religious documents written in a completely different style, and the beginning of Chapter 3 reads like yet another document. As a matter of fact, from Chapter 3 onward most of the published 1930 *Ahom Buranji* follows the famours 'Cobra manuscript', of which a copy rests at the British Library in London.
18. Rival Hindu priests relate how Ahom kings descended from Indra. See, for example *Assam Buranji* (S.K. Bhuyan ed.), Gauhati: Department of Historical and Antiquarian Studies, 1960, pp. 128-129.
19. Elias, *Introductory Sketch,* p. 10. See also the comments by L. Gogoi, *The Buranjis, Historical Literature of Assam (A Critical Survey),* New Delhi: Omsons, 1986, pp. 34-35.
20. E. Gait, *A History of Assam* (Third, revised edition), Calcutta: Thacker Spink, 1963, p. 290.
21. Ranoo Wichasin has published a transcription and translation into Thai of the most of the Ahom text, Unfortunately the photocopy of the opening page must have been illegible, the lack of it caused Acharn Ranoo to change the order of pages and to miss the fact that the beginning of this text consists of a summary of what has been described here as Myth 1.
22. See the Vedic Hymn of Creation, in A.L. Basham, *The Wonder that was India*, Fontana, 1971, pp. 249-250 and, for example, the *Agni Purana* [17.2].

23. For the navel of the earth, the lotus, the turtle and the snake, see V. McCeller, Symbolik des Hinduismus und des Jain ismus, Illustrations to Text Vol 4 in the Series Symbolik der Religionen (ed by F. Herrntann), Vol 19, Stuttgart: Iliersemann, 1974, Plate 56, p. 79. For the elephat as the carrier of the earth, see H. Zimmer, Mythes et Syrnboles dans l'art et la civilisation de l'Inde, Paris: Payot, 1951, pp. 103-105.
24. Such Indian symbolism pervades cosmologies much further east The world supporting elephant is also found in Tai Lue cosmology. See J.F. Hartmann, *Linguistic and Memory Structures in Tai Lue Oral Narratives*, Pacific Linguistics, Seris B No. 90. Canberra: The Australian National University, 1984, pp. 107-108. A cosmic crab at the bottom of the ocean is found among the White Hmong. See J. Mottin, Contes et legendes Nmong Blanc, Bangkok: Don Bosco Press, n.d., p. 23. Even as far east as the Philippines we find sometimes the world growing on top of a turtle, or another story of how the creator made a great eel (Kasili) a fish, snake like in appearance, which he "wound around the world". He also made the great crab (Kuyamang)'. See F. Demetrio,'Creation Myths amount the Early Filipinos', Asian Folklore Studies, Vol. 27, 1968, pp. 48 and 56.
25. L. Milne, *Shans at Home*, New York: Paragon, 1970 [reprint of the 1910 edition], p. 197.
26. See the Introduction to the *Siva Purana*, Vol. l, Delhi: Motilal Banarsidass, pp. xiv-xv.
27. *Linga Purana* [17.66-69], *Brahma Purana* [1.40-42] and *Padma Purana* [1.2.910]. In the *Garuda Purana* this celestial egg contains the celestials, *asuras* and humans.
28. *Ahom Buranji*, p. 4. I am not wholly satisfied with the'iron ladder. The Ahom manuscripts say that the pair came down *cha lik cha kha*, where indeed it is likely that *lik* means 'iron' and *kha* 'an alloy of iron and zinc'. The puzzling factor remains the word *cha*. The Ahom for 'ladder' is *kha nai*.
29. N. Elias, *Introductory Sketch of the History of the Shans in Upper Burma and Western Yunnan*, Calcutta: Foreign Department Press, 1876, pp. 26-27.
30. *An Ahom Legend of Creation*, p. 1134.
31. M. Eliade, *Patterns in Comparative Religion* (transl. by R. Sheed), Cleveland: Meridian Books, 1958, p. 181.
32. E.A. Gait, 'Abstract of the Contents of One of the Ahom Puthis', *Journal of the Asiatic Society of Bengal*, Vo1. 63, Part 1, No. 2, 1894, pp. 108-111.
33. 'Abstract', pp. 110-111. The spelling of Ahom names has been changed so as to conform with usage throughout this paper.
34. *The Shans*, pp. 120-126.
35. *Ahom Buranji*, p. 39. The passage can be found in manuscript version in the Buranji held at the British Library folio 14 recto.
36. For an overview of the distribution *see* J.W. Tschesnow, *Historische Ethnographie der Lander Indochinas*, Berlin: Akademie-Verlag, 1985, pp. 254-60.

37. A.Pavie, *Mission Pavie, Indochin* 1879-1895, *Etudes diverses II, Recherches sur l'histoire du Cambodge, du Laose et du Siam,* Paris: Leroux, 1898, pp. 10-I2; A. Bourlet, Zes Thay', Anthropos, Vol 2, 1907, pp. 921-926; L. Finot, Recherches sur la litterature laotienne', *Bulletin de 1 :EcoleFrancaise d'Extreme-orient,* Vol. 17, 1917, pp. 159-161; H. Roux, '*Quelques minorities ethniqus du Nord Indochine', France-Asie,* 1954, pp. 362-364, 375-385; C. Archaimbault, 'La naissance du monde selon les traditions lao; le mythe de Khun Bulom', in *Structures religieuses Lao (rites et mythes)*, Vientiane: Vithagna, 1973, pp. 97-130; J.F. Harmann, Computations on a Tai Dam Origin Myth', *Anthropological Linguistics*, Vol. 23, No. 4, 1981, pp. 183-202.
38. 'Phongsawdan Lan Chang', *Prachum Phongsawadan*, Vo12, Bangkok: Khurusapha, B.E. 2506 [1963], pp. 137-139. See also P. Levy, *Recherches prehistoriques dans la regions de MluPrei*, Hanoi, 1943, p. 322 as cited by Tschenow, *op. cit.*, p. 256; Finot, Recherches', pp. 159-160; Archaimbault, 'La naissance du monde selon les traditions lao', p. 99.
39. Tschenow, *op. cit.*, pp. 258-59. There are also other receptacles. Among the Tai Nung the two survivors drifted on the leaf of a sea-rose (*beoc-lin*). See G. Prunner, Die Religionen der Minderheiten mit Daischen Sprachen;, in *Die Religionen Sudostasiens, Die Religionen der Menschheit* (ed. by C.M. Schroder),, Stuttgart: Kohlhammer, Vol. 23, p. 181. citing Savina, *Dictonnarie etymologique francais-nung-chinois*, Hongkong,1924, p. 489 ff. One of the hill peoples in the southern part of Vietnam relates that it was a big storage chest. See H. Maitre, *Les jungles Moi*, Paris; E. Larose, 1912, p. 417.
40. It is, therefore, not surprising that the image of life coming out of stone is widely recorded. For references see M.S. Laubscher, *Schopfungsmythik ostindonesischer Ethnien*, Basler Beitrage zur Ethnologie, Vol 10, Basel: Pharos-Verlag, 1971, p. 152.
41. For accounts of the sorts of myths found among Tai-speaking peoples in China, see H. Maspero, *Le Taoisme et les religions chnoises*, Paris: Gallimard, *1971, pp. 254-267.* See also Prunner, '*Die Religionen der Minderheiten mit Daischen Sprachen*; pp. *183-185.*
42. Shan cosmology is reported in C.R. Macgregor, *Military Report on the Khampti-Singpho Countries,1887*, p. 69, [reprinted in V. Elwin, *India's Northeast Frontier in the Nineteenth Century,* Oxford: Oxford University Press, 1959, pp. 380-381; W.R. Hillier, 'Notes on the Manners, Customs, Religion, and Superstitions of the Tribes inhabiting the Shan States', *The Indian Antiquary,* April 1892, pp. 120-121; J.G. Scott and J.P. Hardiman (comps.), *Gazetteer of Upper Burma and the Shan States,* Part 1, Vol 1, Rangoon: Superintendent, Government Printing, Burma, *1900* pp. 329-330; L. Milne, *Shans at Home,* Chapter 16; Hartmann, *Linguistic and Memory Structures.* Particularly valuable is the vast collection of folk stories published in Thai, edited by Vagn Plenge, *Duai Panya tae*

Khwamrak, Nithan Chaw Mueang Neua, Bangkok: Siam Society and Samakhom Sangkhomsathaeng PrathetThai, B.E. 2519 [1976].

43. Phra Thammathatto and Ph. na Pramuanman, *Tamnan Ton Phi Thai,* Bangkok: Amarin, B.E. 2533 [1990], pp. 88-90.
44. Phongsawadan Lan Chang', *op. cit.,* pp. 137-139; Archaimbault, '*La naissance du monde selon less traditions lao*', pp. 98-100.
45. It is possible that Phrakhru Phommathammakhun took Barua's spelling Thaolipling and in order to write it in Thai, split the name up into Thao Li Pling, which then was simplified into Thao Li Ping.
46. See, for example E. Leach, 'Genesis in Myth' in J. Middleton (ed.), *Myth and Cosmos; Readings in Mythology and Symbolism,* New York: The Natural History Press, 1967, pp. 1-13.
47. This social stratification is apparent also in Khamti mythology. See Macgregor, *Military Report,* p. 69. See also G. Con dominas, *L'espace social a propos de Asia du Sud-est,* Paris: Flarttmarion, 1980, p. 299.
48. In a long list of prepared questions by the Ethnographical Survey of Burma, questions *3* and *4* are respectively: 'What is known of the actual (as apart from legendary) origin of the tribe?' and: 'What legendary remembrance has the tribe of its original home?'

42

A Short Comparison between the Dai of the Burmese Border (Yunnan) and the Dong (in Guangxi), with reference to the Tai in India

Jean Berlie

Turung (speaking a mixed Lai/Singho-Kacdhin-lingpo languages are not studied here.

Dai, Khamti and Phake languages belong to the Western linguistic sub-group of the Tai languages. Dong is placed in the Eastern sub-group of this important South-East Asian family. In the last group, I include Zhuang, the closest culturalo-linguistic group to the Dong. In passing, I shall mention the other Tai related Memories of China: Buyi, Gelab, Li, Maonan, Mulao and Shui. The Li are "Culturally" less closely connected with the other Tai Minorities of China and their language includes many different dialects of the Haipan Special Economic zone.)

General Setting

The Dai of the Sino-Burmese border are divided into two sub-groups of which the Neua have the largest population. More than 300,000 Neua are living in the extreme Western part of Yunnan, namely in the following: districts: Baoshan, Longchuan, Longling, Luxi, Tengchong and Yingjiang. The Dai are paddy cultivators. To give an example of their setting in the hilly part of Dehong, in April 1991, I surveyed a village near Mangshi (administrative city of Dehong prefecture) which gave the following data: a total of 65 households of 359 Neua villagers had 420 *mu* (29.4 ha). Their physical capital base included 15 hand-tractors *(shoufutuolaji)* (I use thepinyin Chinese system of transcription), 61 buffaloes to plough the rice-fields, 145 hogs, 68 bicycles and 23 TV sets.

The Neua have a particular type of housing around a courtyard. The houses on stilts and bamboo walls of the Dai Mao have some similarities with the Phake traditional housing style in Upper Assam. The Mao live in the flat plain around Ruili, a very important market place linking Myanmar in particular Mandalay and China. They are less numerous around Longdao, commercially connected with the city of Nam Kham (in Myanmar), another Mao market. Today, the Chinese and the Burmese dominate the commercial exchanges between China and Myanmar. In parallel with the ethno-linguistic complexity of this border (eight languages are currently used in Ruili), it should be mentioned that Sinicization and Burmecization play an important part in this far away region of China.

In total, the present population of the Dong is over two and a half million with an impressive official increase of 76 per cent between 1982 and 1990. On the mosaic Tai chessboard, the Dong live farthest to the East. The Minorities of China have special privileges, their members are not obliged to compel with the one child family size policy and do have advantages in education, for example, special lists for the admission in universities. The sudden 1982-1990 increase of the Dong population is presumably related to these special privileges. In South-Eastern Guizhou there is a Dong autonomous district, Xinhuang and other less important districts for this Minority such as Jianhe, Jingping and Sansui. In the districts of Yuping, Jingzhou and Tongdao in south-western Hunan, the Dong are numerous.

But here, in relation with my fieldwork, I only try to give a short definition of the 400,000 Dong in Guangxi. In Sanjiang (district of the "Three Rivers") are kept their unique cultural markers such as the covered bridges "wind and rain bridges" *(fengyu qiao ch.)* and bronze drums towers. The other districts where Dong are present are Longsheng, head of a Dong Cultural Association and Rongan and Rongshui, linked by road and train to the big industrial city of Luizhou.

Encompassed 127 households and its population was 628 inhabitants in August 1991. Their tangible property included 30 hand-tractors used for their transportation and 20 TV sets. The State subsidize pig raising, I noted down 600 of them in a village of 110 households, and in this village my data gave 260 hogs. Almost all the households had one bullock to plough the rice-fields (130 bullocks in the village). For comparative studies, like the Ahom of Sibsagar, the Dong of Fulu (Sanjiang) keep the paddy in sheaves in their granaries, threshing is only done when rice is needed. Ahom and Dong threshing is sometimes done by bullocks.

Religion is an important cultural marker. Buddhism is attested in Dali, in Western Yunnan, by the Qianxum Pagoda ("Thousand Feet pagoda") built in 836 AD and by an old *stupa* called *guangmu* South of Ruili. The principal religion of the Dai is Hinyana Buddhism. Sometimes polytheist, the Dong are also "Mahayanist". They follow the Chinese Buddhism through the medium of the Chinese characters. Contrarily to the Neua and Mao who have their own different scripts, the Dong have originally no script to transcribe their language.

The Dong are also rice cultivators (as the other Tai) and have compact villages along rivers. Their majestic houses in firwood are erected symbolically with the trees planted by the parents when a child is born. After the marriage, generally in winter when there is less work in the paddy fields, fir trees and other trees such as pine trees are felled and the new house is built. An ordinary surveyed village encompassed 127 households and its population was 628 inhabitants in August 1991. Their tangible property included 30 hand-tractors used for their transportation and 20 TV sets. The state subsidise pig raising, I noted down 600 data gave 260 hogs. Almost all the households had one bullock to plough the rice-fields (130 bullocks in the village). For comparative studies, like the Ahom of Sibsagar, the Dong of Fulu (Sanjiang) keep the paddy in sheaves in their granaries, threshing is only done when rice is needed. Ahom and Dong threshing is sometimes done by bullocks.

History

The archaelogical research could certainly help to find the origin of the Tai, but there is still a series of unsettled controversies. In the museum of Nanning is found one of the best collection of Zhuang and also Dong bronze drums. Around Kunming and Dali, in Yannan, the discovered bronze drums are also related with the Bai Yue culture. The Tai are linked to these numerous Yue principalities which existed around two thousand years before. But it is difficult and Dong and the peoples of these principalities. The Tai in general have certainly a strong ability to build a society by eventually assimilating other ethnic groups thanks to their politico-cultural system. Assam is a good example of a ceeded in maintaining their power for six hundred years Ahom princes Khunlung ang Khunlai do exist in the chronicles of the Dai Mao and in Chinese the two brothers are called Genlun and Genlun.

Historical research on the Sino-Myanmar border show the importance of the Shan (see the article on the origin of the Tai, in *Dongnanya Xuekan*

7, published in December 1990 by the Institute of South-East Asia in Canton). The Shan and the Tai most probably are descendants of the Bai Yue peoples. In the eleventh century, the Mao of the present Dehong were united with the Shan-Mao of Shengwei (Hsenwi), Xinggu and Xingse (Dao 1990: 580). The Dai certainly played an important historical and economical role along the Burmese road. Their traditional system to hold a market in rotation every five days in different towns *wankat* is still in use in the Dehong autonomous prefecture and the some other districts of Yunnan. One important historical challenge is to know if the Dai played a part in the government of the Nanzhao kingdom. It must be noticed that Professor Chen Lufan only said that the Tai did not find this kingdom, but he never wrote that they were not present among the numerous ethnic-nationalities of this kingdom.

The present old Dong people of Piaoli in Guangxi where I conducted my fieldwork said that they came from Hunan province five hundreds years before only. The Chinese sources trace the Dong called *Qiandong Man* ("The barbarians of Guizhou") as far back as the Qin dynasty (221-207 BC}. They are believed to be a branch of the ancient Luo Yue. Like the Dong, the Baiman of Nanzhao had a particular veneration for the fir and pine trees (Chen 1990: 225). This similarity of symbolic concepts between the Dong and the peoples of the Nanzhao kingdom could only be easily understood if Tai people, called Jinchi ("Gold Teeth"), were present among these Nationalities. In the 860s, during the Nanzhao's three years expedition in North Vietnam (Annam), the Zhuang and the Dong helped the Nanzha armies. According to the *Man shu* ("The Book of the Barbarians"), the Tai were present in this expedition, they were not called Shan but *Jinchi.* According to the *Yunnan tongshi* ("Yunnan General History," chap. 199), Yi Mouxun was a king of Nanzhao *(Manshu* chapter 3) and after he fought the "barbarians", the *Jinchi* were weakened. The presence of Tai in the kingdom of Nanthao is difficult to deny.

According to Vietnamese writers and Bas Terwiel, the Tay of Vietnam construct big water wheels powered by the force of the stream lifting the water to a system of bamboo tubes. Among the Dong, such water wheels are still used today around Chegyang (Guangxi). In some Khamti villages of Assam such irrigation machineries are also seen. Toponymy also helps to understand better former Tai settlements, the names *Meng* and *Mang* coming from *Mucng* ("principalities") in Dai, are used to designate present time place names in the districts South of Dali. Now in this part of Yunan the Muslims (Hui) are numerous, they entered in Yunnan for the first time with Kublai Khan. Only after the fall of the Nanzhao kingdom in

1253 did the Yuan dynasty start to really control the formerly remote Yunnan and Guangxq. More research is needed, but the historical relationship between the Nanzhao kingdom and the old Tai kingdom of Mengmao called Zardandan ("Gold Teeth") by Marco Polo, cannot be denied. The indirect political control of the borders of Yunnan and Guangxi, was implemented with the help of the Minority chieftains (*Tusi*) during the Yuan, Ming and Qing dynasties. The former Burmese indirect administration with Sawbwa was a similar system. This socio-political organization of the Chinese border lasted more than 500 years, with some change after 1911, up to the establishment of the PRC (1949).

Languages

According to Chinese linguists, the Dong language is included in the Dong-Sui-Mulao-Maonan family. In 1958, a romanized Dong alphabet was developed. Presently, informations from the Institute of Nationalities of Guangxi give me the impression that this romanization is only a transition which will not last long. Familiarity with Chinese is on the increase especially among young people. The television programmes make a significant contribution to the publicity of Minority cultures, but public education and television programmes are done in standard Chinese *(putonghua)*. Fifteen per cent of the households (and more in a near future) in a Dong village do had TV sets, so it could happen, in the coming years, that bilinguism (Dong/Chinese) will predominate with more emphasis on Dong inside the family and on Chinese outside. The Dong language is noteworthy for its extraordinary large number of tone distinctions. It is said that some dialects have fifteen tones. I cannot say if it is really true. In Guangxi, I was able to hear six "checked" tones and voicing contrasts. According to Chinese linguists, the Dong language, like Mulam has no voiced stops. Compared to a six tone language like the Dai Ya spoken in Mengyang; the pronunciation of certain words is anyway sometimes more difficult in Dong than in Ya (both groups have no script).

The Dai Mao of Myanmar, around Nam Kham, and in China, around Ruili and Longdao use the same script. Many Mao in China know the old common script better than the new Dai Dehong script introduced in the late 1950s. I noticed that the Dai teachers were not very proficient in the new Dai Dehong script because they teach mainly in Chinese, so we can expect that in a few years they may simply forget to make the short introduction to the Dai new script in the first year of primary education. The Dai Dehong script is supposed to be studied for one or two months.

A short vocabulary of a part of the tools used for paddy cultivation by the Dong and the Dai is given in the following table. Equivalent words are given in Chinese and English. There are six "checked" tones in Dong (here is noted the dialect of Piaoli in Guangxi), and Dai (*N* stand for the spoken Neua in Mangshi and *M* for the spoken Mao in Longdao). In Mandarin there are four tones. All tones are marked, whenever it is possible by a number after the transcription of the word (between 1 and 4 for the Mandarin Chinese and 1 and 6 for the Cantonese and Dong). The "*g*" is pronounced as the French "*k*" Ji, a well known Ahom word for "barn or store" is also presently used by the Dai Mao with the same meaning.

DONG	DAI	ENGLISH	CHINESE
gan3	*gan2* (N/M)	*carrying pole*	*gan*
lim !	*kieul* (N)	sickle	*lian 2-daol*
(*lim*4 in			
Cantonese)	*lian2*	*hieul* (M)	
siu2	hoe	*chu2* (*chutou2*)	
te-i4	*ta-i2* (N/M)	plough	*li2*

These examples prove a similarity for only one Tai word in the very useful agricultural vocabulary of the Dai and Dong languages. The influence of the Chinese language (Putonghua and Cantonese) is particularly important for the modern technical words such as hand-tractor and threshing machine. A bigger glossary and more comparative research is needed.

Briefly, I shall conclude. Although numerous these have been published concerning the brilliant Tai culture, there are still a number of historical and linguistic problems to be solved. For the promotion of social sciences, the assistance of China and India is decisively needed to improve our knowledge of the Tai and the Minority Nationalities of Asia.

NOTES

Barua Rai Sahib Golap Chandra (ed.). *Ahom Buranji. From the Earliest Time to the End of Ahom Rule.* Guwahati, Spectrum Publication, 1985, pp. vii+388.

Berlie, jean, *Les Dai de Chine,* Metz, CCRL, 1991, p. 138.

Buragohain Romesh, "The Tais in Northeast India . In: *Proceedings of the* Fourth *Conference on Thai Studies.* Vol. 4 (CTS 4/4). Kunming, May 11-13, 1990, pp. 358-375.

Chen Lufan. *Whence Came the Thai Race—An Inquiry.* Kunming, International Culture Edition, 1990, pp. vi + 319.

Dao Anju. "The Social and Economic Development of the Dai Community in Dehong Prefecture since the Founding of the PRC". CTS 4/4. Kunming, 1990, pp. 578-587.

Jiang Yingliang, *Daizu Shi* ("A History of the Dai"). Chengdu, Sichuan People's Press, 1983. pp. xvi+652.

43

Chin Padi and their Association with the Chins of Myanmar

Virginia M. Di Crocco

Ancient and new beads of etched agate and onyx bead onyx design with patterns of white on black are called Chin Padi (Chin Beads) in Myanmar. The term Chin Padi appears to apply to both etched agate and onyx beads with designs of white etched on black and fossilized wood beads with applied black and white colours which copy them. Chin Padi have been discovered in and near walled cities associated with the Pyus which Myanmar archaeologists have dated from the first through the early ninth century A.D., and in Burial 1 at Taungthaman in modern Amarapura, dated *C.* 460 B.C. The Chin Padi discovered there are etched onyx beads (Stargardt, 1990, p. 25). Thus archaeological evidence suggests Chin Padi in the form 95 of etched beads may date in Myanmar as far back as the fifth century B.C. Other archaeological evidence indicates that their fossilized wood imitations made at Wati (latitude 21° 25′N and longitude 95°41′E) (Figure 43.1) date as early as the fifth to seventh century A.D.

This chapter will present evidence of the making at Wati during Pyu times of fossilized wood beads bearing the white on black designs common to agate and onyx etched beads, evidence that imitations in fossilized wood were made in the area in the twentieth century, evidence of ancient etched beads in Myanmar and adjacent areas, and evidence of a relationship of design between those etched beads and the fossilized wood beads made in the Wati area and the reason beads of this design are called Chin Padi, and will suggest why they have been sought after by the Chins.

Evidence of ancient manufacture of beads of fossilized wood was first discovered in 1904 near the Pyu walled city of Wati, about five miles south-East of the sizeable town of Natogyi and near Payagyi and Kyigan Villages in north central Myanmar. Beads, both finished ones

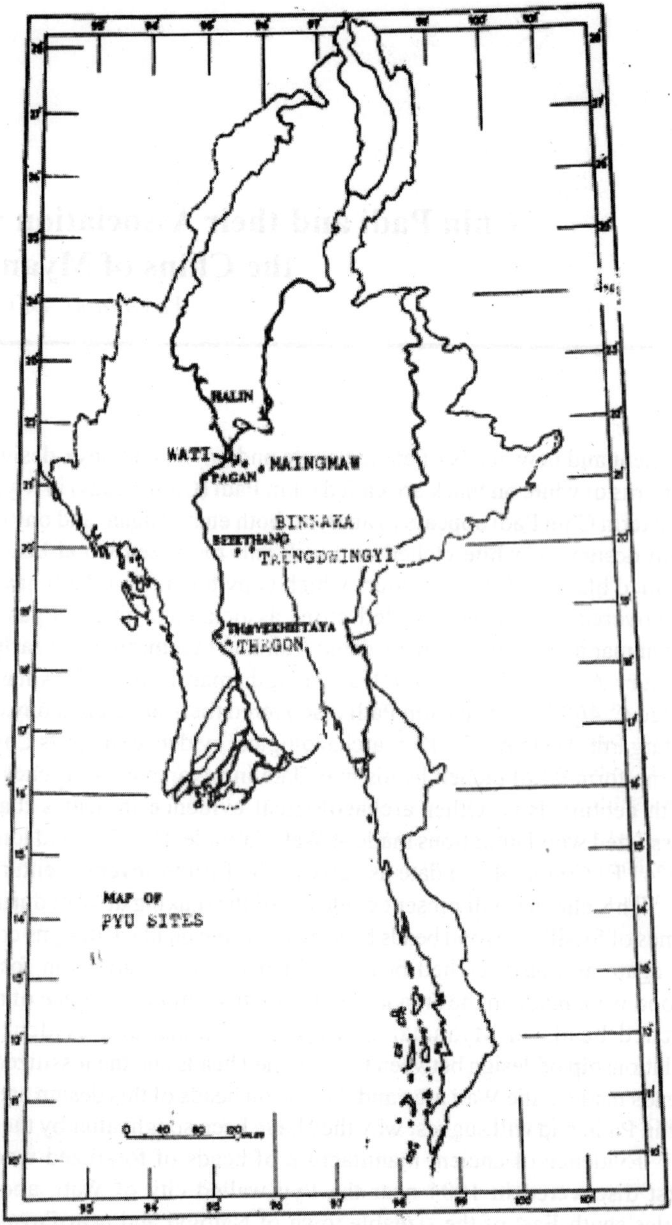

Figure 43.1: Archaeological places Evidence of fossilized wood beads

Figure 43.2: After Aung Myint 1979

and blanks which suggest local manufacture, were illegally excavated at a place called the Red Earth Pit, a graveyard on a mound north-west of the Wati city wall. Some of the beads were found within burial urns of a type associated with Pyu burials. This plus the discovery in the area of bricks bearing markings such as those found on bricks in sites already established as Pyu has led to the identification of Wati as a Pyu settlement. This settlement had been destroyed at a still unknown time and thus the bead manufacture had stopped.

The beads made of local fossilized wood *(eingyin kyaukpyu)* have designs emulating those on etched agate and onyx beads. The decoration is in white on a black background, cream on coffee, and amber as well. Eleven different patterns emulating those on etched beads have been reported (Figure 43.2). These were given specific names by the locals so that their Chin customers could order them. Beads of other materials were found with the fossilized wood beads including beads of amber, gold, and green and white stone. Of particular interest are green stone beads made in the forms of elephants and what may be pigs, dogs and rats (Figure 43.3). Clay beads, a clay ear-plug and red stone or crystal ear-plugs were excavated as well.

Trade in the beads became very popular. Shops were set up and Chins flocked from the western highlands to buy the ancient beads. The ones

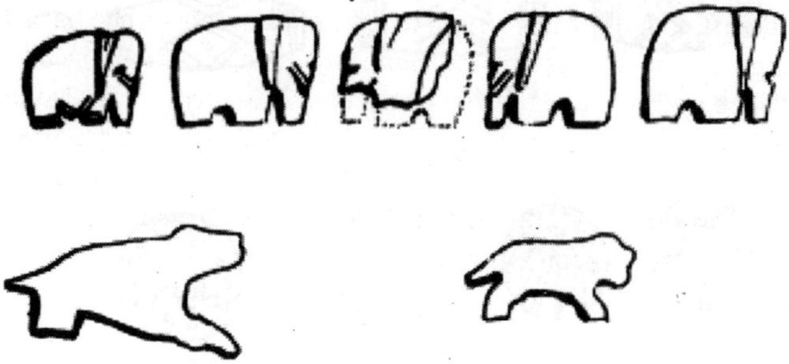

Figure 43.3: After Aung Myint 1979

which they liked the most were those bearing white designs on a black background like those on etched agate and onyx beads. Thus beads of this type of design came to be called Chin Padi.

A similar scenario occurred at the nearby walled Pyu city, Maingmaw (21° 17′N, 96° 12′E), at the same time. Trade was so brisk that shops are said to have sprung up as if at a festival.

After a time the supply of excavated beads ran out, and to supply the Chin demand for more, villagers of Payagyi and Kyigan began to make Chin Padi from fossilized wood which they searched out within the old city of Wati and their own area. They experimented with local materials until they were able to develop good black and white colours with which they coated them. The sizes and shapes of the beads and their designs were like those of the ancient ones. The workmanship was excellent and the Chins came to purchase the locally manufactured ones.

During World War II there was no trade. It resumed after the war and then stopped after 1950 when the Chins no longer came to buy the beads. The villagers felt the reason was that the Chins had become more modern and fashions had changed (Aung Myint 1979, pp. 1-39).

In the 1980s, the author found newly made fossilized wood beads of Chin Padi designs in shops in Rangoon. They were being offered to tourists as ancient beads. By the late 80s they were being imported into Thailand and sold in the antique shops of Bangkok. It would appear that the making of fossilized beads had been resumed in Myanmar, perhaps in Wati, as a result of tourist and foreign demand.

Pyu cities other than Wati where Chin Padi have been reported found are Hanlin, Beikthano, Thayekhettaya (Srikshetra), Maingmaw, Taungdwingyi and Thegon (Aung Myint 1984, Plate 8). The last named is situated west of the Yangon-Pyay railway at latitude 18°38′ N and longitude 19°24′E. Both Thegon and Taungdwingyi have only recently been identified by U Aung Myint as Pyu settlements on the basis that the markings on the bricks are the same as those on bricks in cities long established as Pyu, i.e., Beikthano and Thayekhettaya (Aung Myint 1984, p. 124-27). In all sites except Thegon, Chin Padi were reported found with green stone elephant beads. Whether there were Chin Padi made of fossilized wood at all the other six sites as at Wati is not clear from his report. However, specific mention has been made in reports by other researchers of the discovery of etched agate and onyx beads at the following sites in Myanmar:

At the prehistoric Taungthaman site, round polished onyx beads etched with lateral white beads were found in Burial 1 dated *c.* 460 B.C. (Stargardt 1990, p. 24-25, Plate 6 c.). Etched agate beads with similar white lateral markings were discovered at the prehistoric sites of Ban Chiang and north-eastern Thailand and the Tambon Caves, Philippines (Stargardt *ibid.*).

One etched agate bead was reported discovered at Beikthano. It is Dikshit's type II where the black background has been whitened and the design is etched in black. This cylinder bead has black chevrons on a white surface [Dikshit, 1949, p. 11 and Aung Thaw 1968, p. 49 Figure 76 (1)].

Round etched beads with a design of white vertical stripes on a black background and a barrel-shaped bead with a horizontal white chevron pattern were excavated at Hanlin (Myint Aung 1970, p. 61, Plate 7). An etched bead of the same design type was found in Taoila and dated "first century A.D.?" (Dikshit 1949, p. 58, Plate IX, Figure 10). More beads of the type were excavated at Ban Don Ta Phet, Kanchanaburi Province, West Central Thailand. The most recent radio carbon date for the site is 2190± 300 B.P. (Glover 1989, p. 23, Figure 14).

Sein Maung U, Head of the Myanmar Archaeological Division, Mandalay, has reported that in 1926 a cemetery outside of the walled Pyu city of Maingmaw was dug up by villagers in order to collect etched onyx beads, which were highly prized by the Chins. The etched beads were found inside burial urns (Sein Muang U, 21 January 1981, p. 5).

An elephant-shaped bead of the type found with the Chin Padi at Wati had been discovered by the Department of Archaeology in the relic chamber of the Khin Ba mound at Thayekhettaya in 1926. Among the other important finds in that chamber were gold manuscript plates with script ascribed as fifth to sixth century A.D. (Aung Thaw 1972, p. 31) and sixth century A.D. (Sein Maung U, 3 February 1981, p. 5.)

Furthermore, an elephant-shaped bead was unearthed in a silver bowl at U-hnaunggon Village, Myinmu Township, west of Sagaing. The silver bowl bears a one-line inscription in Pyu letters dated epigraphically to the sixth century A.D. Another elephant of the same stylistic type was excavated at Nern Makok, north-east of Lopburi, Central Thailand with finds dated fifth to seventh century A.D. (Department of Archaeology, Thailand 1989, p. 58 and 85). The dating of the elephant beads found elsewhere to the fifth to seventh century A.D. would suggest that fossilized wood beads discovered with elephant beads at Wati were made as of the fifth to seventh century A.D.

The designs of the fossilized wood Chin Padi made and excavated at Wati (Figure 43.2) are similar to the following etched onyx and agate beads found in Myanmar and neighbouring areas:

Figure 43.2, line 1, a — This barrel bead with a vertical chevron design (white on black) is similar in design to etched agate beads found at Ban Don Ta Phet, Thailand dated *2190± 300* B.P. (Glover, 1989, p. 23, Figure *14)* but it is not exactly the same in that the number of stripes in the centre and at the end differ.

Figure 43.2, line 1, a — This barrel bead with horizontal chevron design (white on black) is like thaton an etched bead excavated at Hanlin (Myint Aung, 1970, p. 61, Plate 7).

Figure 43.2, line 2, a — This round bead with vertical stripes (white on black) is virtually identical to etched beads found at Ban Don Tha Phet (Glover *ibid.*), Hanlin (Myint Aung, 1970, p. 61, Plate 7) and an etched bead (white on black) from Khao Sam Keo, Chumphon, a port on the eastern coast of Thailand, 1st century B.C.-A.D. lst century (Srisuchat 1990, Plate 9).

Figure 43.2, line 3, a — This round bead with lateral stripes (white on black) is like etched beads reported at Taungthaman (Stargardt, 1990, p. 25-26, Figure, 6c) and Khao Sam Kaeo, Chumphon (Srisuchat, 1990, Plate 9).

Figure 43.2, line 3, b — This round bead with *chinlon* design (design of a rattan bail used to play the game *chinlon* in

Myanmar) (White on black) is like that of etched beads from Khao Sam Keo, (Srisuchat *ibid.*).

Figure 43.2, line 3, c — This square flat bead with the disign of a cross (white on black) is similar to one in the holdings of the Indian Museum, Calcutta (Diskshit, 1949, p. 58, Plate XIX, Figure 14).

The provenance of etched beads found in Central Myanmar and in Thailand is not yet known. The Chins' connection with ancient etched and fossilized wood beads also is not clear. However, the fact that the Chins rushed to purchase both types of beads found in and around the Pyu walled cities indicate that the beads were already known to the Chins and had been significant to their culture for some time, perhaps as talismans dating from the Pyu period or earlier. Prior to the Mongol invasion of Myanmar at the end of the thirteenth century A.D. the Chins are reported to have lived in upper Central Burma and thus would have had access to the early etched beads and to their fossilized wood copies made at Wati as of the fifth to the seventh century (Luce 1985, pp. 80-81).

NOTES

Archaelogical Department, Thailand 1989 Nern Makok, Bangkok: The Fine Arts Department.

Myint Aung, 1979, *Preliminary Investigational Research and Study of the Ancient City of Wati, Document No. 6* (in Burmese), unpublished.

Aung Myint, 1984 "Excavations of Ancient Pyu Cities Still Underway and Excavations Not Performed," *Journal of Yangon University* in Burmese), 1.2.

Aung Thaw 1968 *Report on Excavations at Beikthano,* Yangon: Ministry of Union Culture.

Aung Thaw ,1972 *Historical Sites in Burma.* Yangon: Ministry of Union Culture.

Dikshit, M.G., 1949 *Etched Beads in India,* Poona: Deccan College.

Glover, I.C. 1989 *Early Trade Between India* and *Asia,* London: The University of Hull Centre for South-East Asian Studies.

Luce, Gordon H. 1985 *Phases of Pre-Pagan Burma, Language and History,* I, Oxford: Oxford University Press.

Myint Aung, 1970 "The Excavations at Halin, *Journal of the Burma Research Society,* LIII, ii.

Sein Maung U., 1981 "Mongmao: A Forgotten City II, Archaeological remains brought to light," *The Working People's Daily,* 3 February, p. 5.

Srisuchart, Amara 1990 "Significant Archaeological Objects in Thailand Associated with Maritime Trade, "*The Silpakorn Journal,* 33, 6, p. 24-34, Plates 1-19.

Stargardt, Janice 1990 *The Ancient Pyu of Burma,* I, Singapore: PACSEA CAMBRIDGE in association with The Institute of Southeast Asian Studies, Singapore.

This talk will be accompanied by slides.

APPENDIX-I

Census of India 1901

B.C. Allen

Composition of the Population

The population of the district is, with the exception of a very few immigrants, all of one race. The people, however, recognize a number of divisions and sub-divisions. My enquiries have led me to the conclusion that each of these divisions and sub-divisions bears the name of some famous man who distinguished himself in former days, and from whom the majority of those bearing the name now are descended (or the whole of a family may have adopted the name of some very distinguished member). Old men tell me that, in their father's time the various clans lived in separate villages ruled over by Chiefs of their own clan. Prominent men in each clan founded families which were called after them, and these families have been further sub-divided as in course of time other prominent men have arisen, whose descendants were proud to adopt their names. In each case, the connection with the original clan is carefully preserved, thus a man will say that he belongs to the Lian-nghor branch of the Pachuao family of the Lushai clan.

During the last 200 years these clans have been very much broken up and in some cases there is much difficulty in finding out whether a name is that of a clan or only of a family. In some cases the clan had formerly a separate corporate existence, which was broken up so long ago that its few remaining members, living among other clans for so long, have been practically absorbed. This tendency of the clan to disappear has been increased by the extraordinary way in which certain Lushei families have come to the front and have asserted a claim to be Chiefs, and have got this claim recognized, not only by the Lushais, but by almost all the other clans as well. At the present time nearly every village is ruled by a Chief of one of the five royal Lushai families. It is, therefore, only natural for members of less distinguished clans to try to get themselves recognized as Lushai. The amount of variation between the different clans is by no means constant. The Ralte, Paithe, Thado and Lakher are easily distinguishable, and a very brief acquaintance with them would make it apparent that they were not Lusheis; and the same applies to the clans which have been grouped under the names of Hmar and Poi. The remaining clans are so much alike that one might live a long time in the hills without being aware that there were any differences between them. It may be as well here to explain what the people themselves consider the marks of a different clan. The most important is the method of performing the domestic sacrificial ceremonies. This is almost conclusive proof that these clans are really only enlarged families. The other sign of difference of clan is a difference in dialect; but in many cases the dialect has been lost entirely, while the sacrificial rites have been kept intact. It was manifestly both impossible and unnecessary to classify the population according to all the minor divisions and, therefore, I directed that the population should be grouped under the following 15 heads:

> Lushei, Ralte, Paithe, Pante, Ngente,
> Khawlhring, Kiangte, Royte, Renthlei, Chongthu,
> Thado, Lakher, Darlong, Poi, Hmar.

With the exception of Poi and Hmar, all these are true clan names. Poi is the term used by the Lushais, and other original inhabitants of the present Lushai Hills district, for all the people living in what we call the Chin Hills, except one or two small communities. Among these Pois or Chins there are a great many clans and families, and I was unable to collect information about them all, nor did my enumerators know enough to enable them to distinguish them and I, therefore, decided to adopt the custom of the district and classify all these people as Poi. Regarding them and their customs, I propose to say but little, as they are merely immigrants from the Chin Hills, and will be fully dealt with in the Census Report of that district.

Hmar which means 'north', is used by the rest of the inhabitants of the district to denote immigrants into the districts from the Manipur State. These mostly belong to clans which are very closely allied together, and speaks much the same dialect, but I was unable to find a more suitable name under which to group them.

Of the remaining 13 divisions into which I divided the population, all except the Ralte, Paithe and Lakher are becoming more and more alike every year.

The Rise of the Lushai Chief

Some 200 years ago there lived a man, Thangurra by name, who distinguished himself above his fellows and become a powerful Chief, and to him all the present Chiefs trace their pedigrees. At Thangurra's time, there is but little doubt that the hills were dotted over with little hamlets, in which lived people all more or less closely connected. Thangurra's descendants, by their prowess in war and wisdom in governing, gradually established their rule from one end of the hills to the other, and their authority now is undisputed, even by the other clans. The most powerful branch of Thangurra's family is the Sailo, so named from Sailova. In old correspondence, the Sylu tribe is frequently spoken of. By this term was meant the villages of Chiefs of the Sailo family, these villages frequently containing hardly any Sailo except the Chief and his family.

General description of people and their mode of life—As I have already stated, the people of this district are undoubtedly all of the same race. They are distinctly Mongolian. Though the different clans have various customs, yet even between those that vary most, there is a strong resemblance. I propose now to briefly describe the manner of life of the majority of the people, and then to point out in what respects that of different clans varies from it.

General Appearance

The race is distinctly a short one, the men being from 5 feet 2 inches to 5 feet 6 inches, while the women seldom reach 5 feet 2 inches. Both men and women are stoutly built and have a very muscular legs. The men seldom have any hair on their faces, and if a man can grow a moustache he generally pulls out all the hairs, except those growing at the corner of his mouth. The women pierce their ears when young, and insert discs of baked clay, which are continually increased in size till the lobe of the ear is distended, so that a ring $1\frac{1}{2}$ inches in diameter can be inserted. In this hole an ivory ring is worn. On a woman being left a widow, she removes her ear-rings, and when she definitely gives up all idea of remarrying she slits the lobe of her ears. The men sometimes wear very small wooden or bone studs in the lobes of their ears.

The hair of both sexes is drawn straight back and tied in a knot behind. In this knot pins of various shapes and materials are worn. Widows wear their hair loose. It is considered unwise for males who have reached the age of puberty to cut their hair, as doing so is sure to bring on ill health.

All children run about naked for the first-two or three years of their lives. The clothing of the men consists of a coat which reaches below the waist, but is only fastened at the throat, and a single cloth, which is worn thus,—one corner is held in the left hand and the cloth is passed over the left shoulder behind the back under the right arm, and the corner thrown over the left shoulder again. When working in hot weather, the coat is generally dispensed with, and the cloth simply rolled round the waist with the ends loosely knotted hanging down in front. Men sometimes wear turbans. Both body cloths and turbans are generally white, but dark blue cloths with coloured stripes are worn by the better-off people. There is a particular pattern which only men who have killed two metna to feast the village are allowed to wear. The women wear coats and cloths like the men, and in addition a short dark blue petticoat reaching just to the knee. Both sexes are fond of ornaments. Amber necklaces are very popular, and some of these are valued very highly, being passed down from father to son through several generations. Rough uncut cornelian are also much prized, these are either worn in a necklace or suspended from the lobe of the ear.

Constitution of Society

The people live in villages, each of which is ruled by a Chief, who is entirely independent. Even a young son will not admit his father's right to influence him, after he has once established a separate village. The Chief is supreme in his own village, but the people are very democratic, and have a very simple remedy if a Chief oppresses them, viz., to remove to another village. The Chief settles all disputes in the village, arranges where the *jhums* are to be, and when and where a village is to move. His house is the poorhouse of the village, and all orphans and others who have no means of support are received there, and get food in return for their labour. Formerly, a person who had committed some serious crime could enter the Chief's house and thus escape vengeance. When a child has been brought up in the Chief's house, it is in some respects a slave.

Girls are released on marriage, but the Chief receives the marriage price. Boys have to buy their release at the cost of a metna. A Chief sometimes buys a wife for a favourite slave, and sets him up in a separate house, and three years after the man will be considered free, but his children are sometimes considered slaves. The Chief's slaves are very well off, they wear the Chief's ornaments and eat the best food to be got, and do no more work than they would have to do if they were not slaves.

The Chief had several advisers, who are called '*Upa*'. They have the first choice of *jhums* land, and sometimes the Chief allows them to get a basket of rice from each house. The other village officials are the crier, who goes round the village after dark, shouting out the Chief's orders, the blacksmith, and the Pui-thiam or sorcerer, who performs sacrifices in case of illness. These persons generally receive a donation of rice from each house in return for their services.

The Chief receives from 1-5 baskets of rice according to the quality of the *jhums* land assigned to the cultivator; he also receives a hindquarter of every animal killed in the chase, besides some other small dues.

There is a regular code of punishments for different offences, the Chief of course receiving a share of every fine levied.

The only sort of cultivation known is *jhuming*. The chief crop is rice, which ripens in November and December, the other important crop is maize, which is reaped in August. Peas and beans of various kinds, and a certain amount of millet, are also grown. The same piece of land is seldom cultivated two years running, and this, of course, causes all the land within reach of the village to be quickly cleared, and then it becomes necessary for the village to be moved to some other site whence new land can be *jhumed*.

Villages and Houses

Villages are generally built on the top of a ridge or spur, and not on the slope of the hill, as is the custom among the Chins. The cause of this, I think, is that the hills are higher in the country inhabited by the Chins, and, therefore, they can get healthy sites without going to the top of the ridges. In former days, the choice of the village site was much influenced by its defensive capabilities, the migratory habits of the people precluding their constructing the elaborate defensive works found round the Chin villages. When we first occupied the hills every village was strongly stockaded, two and even three rows of stockades being found in some cases. The gateways were commanded by timber block houses, and at suitable points on the roads block houses were built, which were occupied whenever there was any fear of attack. The ground round the stockades and block houses was planted with sharpened bamboo spikes, which formed a very serious obstacle to a barefooted foe.

The villages are laid out in streets, all radiating from central open spot, facing which is the Chief's house, and the *zawlbuk* or guest-house. The houses are built on piles on the natural slope of the hill, and thus the floor of one house is often higher than the roof of the house below it. The houses are all constructed in the same manner and on the same plan. At the end nearest the road is a rough platform of logs, which is the place for cleaning the *dhanin*. On the front wall of the house over this platform are hung the horns of any animal the owner of the house may have killed, and among them are the basket in which the hens hatch out their broods. The doorway has a very high sill, and the door consist of a sliding panel of bamboo works. The fireplace consists of an earthen hearth, in which three upright stones are inserted to hold the cooking pot, above this are two bamboo shelves on which articles which require drying are kept. On each side of the fireplace are bamboo sleeping platforms, that farthest from the door being for the father and mother, the other for the daughters. Beyond the family sleeping platform is a partition, the space between which and the end wall of the house is used as a lumber room and closet, from this a back door opens out on to a small platform. The Chief's house only differs in size, generally having two rooms, the one nearest the entrance being for the use of the slaves. Windows in the sides of the house are considered unlucky, unless the right to make one has been purchased by killing two *metna* and feasting the village. The houses are built of timber uprights, but the walls, floor and roof frame are made of bamboo; the thatching material used is generally cane leaves, but occasionally grass is used. Over the cane leaves broad bands of split bamboo are tied down from eave to eave, giving the roof a rounded appearance from the outside. A long coop under the eaves is the sleeping place of the fowls, who gain access to it by a ladder made of a knotted stick.

The *zawlbuk* is a large hall, with a huge hearth in the centre and a sleeping platform at the far end. The front wall stops about three feet short of the ground, and to enter the building you have to stoop under this, and then climb over a barrier of equal height placed a few feet further in. This building is the sleeping place of the young men of the village, and of any strangers who stop there at the night. It is also a sort of general meeting house. The boys of the village have to keep up a sufficient supply of firewood for the *zawlbuk* fire.

In the centre of one of the streets will generally be found the blacksmith's forge, a small house, built on the ground level, but with a platform in front on which passers-by can sit, and lightens the labours of the smith by their conversation.The bellows consists of two hollow logs in which pistons are worked up and down, from the lower extremity of each log a tube runs to a hole in a stone placed immediately behind the stone on which the charcoal fire rests. A very moderate movement of the pistons gives an excellent draught. The blacksmith repairs all the tools of the village, but some of them are capable of a good deal more than this.

Marriage

Each clan has a regular fixed price for its girls, and anyone wishing to marry a girl must pay this price sooner or later. The price varies from three *metna* to ten according to the clan. The price is always stated in *metna*, but the actual articles given or the amount paid in cash is subject to arrangement. The father or the nearest male relative on his side receives this price, but the bridegroom has also to pay many other persons. The girl's aunt will get a sum varying from Rs. 40 to Rs. 5, the elder sister gets a small sum for having carried the bride about when she was young. The bride appoints a male and female friend or protector, and each has to be paid a small amount by the bridegroom. The bride takes with her certain cloths and ornaments, but these remain the property of the girl's male relatives unless she has a child to inherit them, in which case an extra payment, varying according to the quality of the dowry, has to be paid. The nearest male relative on the bride's mother's side has also to be paid a sum varying from Rs. 40 to Rs. 4. These sums are never paid at once,—in fact, many men never complete paying the price of their wives, and leave the debt to be cleared off by their children.

A young Lushai generally chooses his own wife, and sends a Palai, or ambassador, to her parents to arrange the details of the price to be paid. These settled, the bride is escorted to her future husband's parent's house, by a party of friends, being pelted with dirt by all the children of the village. The parents of the bridegroom receive the party with brimming cups of rice-beer, and when justice has been done to this, a fowl is produced by the bridegroom and slain by the *Pui-thiam*, or sorcerer, who mutters certain charms over it. Directly this is over, the bride and her girl friends retire, while the rest of the party indulge in a great feast, the bridegroom having to provide a fowl for each of those entitled to a share in the price of the bride. The following evening the bridegroom's mother goes and fetches the bride and hands her over to him at his house. The following morning, the bride returns to her parent's house and spends the day there, this she continues to do for some time. The bonds of matrimony are very loose. If a couple do not get on they can separate by mutual consent, or if the husband does not like the woman he can simply send her back to her parents. In both these cases, he does not recover any part of the price he may have paid, and the recipient of the price is bound to support the woman till she is married again. If the woman commits adultery, or leaves her husband without his consent, her relatives have to refund whatever they received on her account. A widow is at liberty either to return to her own people, in which case her late husband's relatives take all his property and his children; or she may continue to live in his house, in which case she retains his property in trust for his children, but should she indulge in an intrigue she is considered to be an adulteress, and her relatives have to pay back her price to her late husband's relations, who take all the property and also the children.

Until a girl is married, she may indulge in as many intrigues as she likes. But should she become pregnant her lover must pay a *metna* to her father; he will, however, be entitled to take the child when it is old enough to leave its mother. In case the child is a girl, the father of course gets the marriage price in due course. If a man is willing at once to marry a girl whom he has seduced he is not expected to pay more than the usual marriage price.

All clans interrmarry, the children taking the father's clan name. The marriage of first cousins is rare among the common people, chiefly because the parents of the girl prefer taking her price from some one outside their family circle. Among Chiefs, who are anxious to marry their children to the children of other Chiefs, the marriage of first cousins is more common. Except his mother, sisters, daughters and aunts, a man may marry many woman he likes.

Ceremonies connected with child-birth—After the birth of a child, the mother must not go down to the spring nor wash her child in cold water till two fowls have been sacrificed. Seven days after the birth of the child, the household spirit is appeased by the offering of small chicken and even packets of rice and vegetables, which are suspended under the eaves. During these seven days, the spirit of the child is supposed to spend some of its time perched like a bird on the clothes or bodies of the child's parents, who, for fear of injuring it, have to keep quiet during this period. Should they do any work, and the child get ill, the cure is to make a coil of a certain creeper, and at night, after the fire has been put out, to dip the child three times inside the coil. The parents give two feasts in honour of the birth of the child, the first two days and the second nine days after its birth. At one or the other of these feasts the nearest male relative on the mother's side gives the child its name. There are many other sacrifices connected with children, and they differ considerably in different clans.

Funerals

All the tribes in the hills bury their death eventually, though some of them take some time over it. After death, the corpse is dressed up in the best clothes available and fastened to a bamboo-frame in the sitting position. If the deceased is a man, his gun, *dao* and spear will be placed beside him. A pig, goat and dog are killed and their flesh cooked, and then all the friends and neighbours are asked to a great feast. Meat and drinks are offered to the corpse also. The spirits of the animals slain is supposed to accompany the deceased to '*Mi-thi-khua*', the dead men's village. Without this sacrifice the deceased's spirit cannot find rest. The dead are buried just outside the house in which they lived. The grave consists of a shaft about 4-5 feet deep, from which a tunnel is excavated long enough to receive the corpse. On the evening following the death, the corpse is placed in this grave, the nearest male relative making a short farewell speech and asking the spirit of the dead to prepare things for those who will shortly follow. Drinking is kept up throughout the funeral ceremonies. The bodies of members of the Chief's family and of well-to-do persons of more esteemed *Lushai* families are not buried more speedily. Instead of being placed in the grave, they are placed in the log of a tree which has been specially hollowed out, a lid is fitted on and the junction of the lid and the tree trunk is well plastered with mud. This coffin is placed on the floor of the house and an earthen hearth is made alongside on which a fire is kept burning day and night. A bamboo is passed through the bottom of the coffin and the floor into the ground; this conveys away all the liquid matter. The corpse is kept in this coffin for about three months, and all this time the nearest relatives sit beside it and feed the fire and drink rice-beer. At the end of this time little but bones is left. Some of these are buried, but the skull and certain of the larger bones are kept in a basket which occupies a shelf opposite the fireplace in the house of the nearest relatives, whence they are taken and dressed up at the feast of the dead. Should the first-born die within a year of its birth it will be buried without any ceremony under the house, subsequent children, however, early they may die, will, however, be honoured with a regular funeral. On a death, the maternal uncle of the deceased is entitled to a sum varying from rupees 2 to 20 from the heir.

Religion

The Lushais and all other tribes in the hills believe in a supreme being who made the world: He is known as Pathian, but is not thought to take much interest in the doings of people. Far more important to the average man are the numerous *Ram-huai*, or demons who are supposed to inhabit every hill and stream, and *Khuavang*, a spirit sometimes spoken of as the same as Pathian, but generally considered as less powerful, but more concerned with mankind. Every illness, every failure of crops is put down either to the influence of some demon or of *Khuavang*, and the whole of a hill man's existence is spent in propitiating these spirits. The *Pui-thiam*, or sorcerer, is supposed to know what particular spirit is the cause of the trouble, and what particular sacrifice will appease him. The number of these sacrifices, and the different ways in which they have to be performed, would fill a thick book. In all of them the flesh of the animal killed is eaten by the sorcerer and his assistants, the and some portions only being left for the demon. Small figures representing human being and animals are also offered to the demons. Besides these sacrifices, there is a special sacrifice to the patron spirit of the hearth. This can only be performed by a member of the clan, and the method of performing it varies in every clan.

The most generally accepted theory as to what happens after death, is that the spirits go to *Mit-thi-khua*; but those men who have slain men or animals in the chase or have feasted the village are able to cross the Pail river to an abode of great comfort, where there is plenty of food and drink to be got without any work. As women cannot go to war nor kill wild animals, and are not allowed to give feasts, they can only reach this happy land if their husbands take them. Existence in *Mit-thi-khua* is full of trouble and worry. After a certain period in one of these two abodes of departed spirits, the spirit is again born as a hornet, and after a time assumes the form of water, and if in the form of dew it falls on a man it is re-born as his child.

Feasts, etc.

In connection with the crops there are three feasts, called *Chap-char Kut*, *Mim Kut* and *Pawl Kut*. The first is the most important, and is thought to ensure a good harvest. It takes place about the time of sowing, and consists chiefly of drinking, the young men and girls dancing slowly round in circles, holding each other arms, while people inside the circle ply them with rice-beer. The Pawl Kut is held after the rice harvest has been reaped. It seems chiefly a festival for the children, who, dressed in their best, are fed with meat, rice and hard-boiled eggs. A good deal of rough play goes on the lads trying to force handfuls of food down the lasses' throats. *Mim Kut* is held when the maize harvest is reaped, and is of but little importance. *Mi-thi-rop lam*, or dance of the dead, is a feast held in honour of the deceased members of the clan. I think it is only held by true Lushai clans. Besides the usual eating and drinking, the special feature is the carrying round of effigies of the forefathers and the various persons giving the feast. In case the feast is given by a Chief, the bones of his ancestors will probably be dressed up. The effigies are all tied on to a square frame work, and this is carried about and danced up and dowr amid much shouting. In the centre of the frame is a large effigy, intendec to represent the first of the whole race, After this dancing of the effigies has gone on for some time, the eldest member of the clan present comes out of his house with a flag on of rice-beer and goes to each effigy in turn and whispers some words and pours a little of the beer into its mouth. He also arranges as to come to his own particular ancestor last, and, after having given the beer, he dashes the flag on the ground and, bursting into tears, runs into his own house. The effigies, after being danced about a little more, are taken away by respective descendants.

A Chief sometimes has to sacrifice a *metna* for the benefit of the village. After the Puithiam has muttered the proper charm over the animal and anointed it by blowing some rice-beer from his mouth over it, the Chief stabs it with a spear and then takes refuge in his house. He is not allowed to cross any running water for a month after this sacrifice, and should he do so dire disasters will certainly follow.

Besides this, semi-religious feasts, there are various others which are given by people who wish to be thought well of. These have to be given in a regular order and when a man has given a whole series he is entitled to wear a cloth of a certain pattern and to have a window in the side of his house.

Superstitions

Witchcraft: The Lushais are a very superstitious race. They will not kill certain animals, because it is unlucky, and yet I cannot find any trace of totemism in this superstition. The belief in witchcraft is universal, and people suspected of practising the black art were formerly killed, and portions of their lives given to their victims, with a view to affecting a cure. Wizards are said to make clay images of their victims, and to stick spikes into them to cause sickness to those whom the figures represent. To take up the impression of a person's foot in the mud and put it to dry over the fire is a sure way to cause sickness.

Besides the regular wizards, there are a number of people whose spirits are supposed to have the habit of leaving their bodies and entering into the bodies of others and causing them much trouble. It may here be noted that the common belief is that each person has three spirits. One of these is called *Khawhring*, and this is the one that sometimes wanders, the other two are spoken of as *Thlarao*, and one is supposed to be wise and one foolish, and the constant struggle between these two causes men's actions to be so unreliable.

Weapons and Warfare: Men of 60 and 70 years can remember the time when guns were hardly known, and fighting were carried on with spears and bows and arrows; but now-a-days the weapons of the people are flint-lock muskets, spears and *daos*, the last being evidently imitated from the Burmese *dah*, and called *kawlhnam*, which means Burmese knife. The spears are very inferior weapons, about 4 feet 6 inches long, with iron blades, and iron spikes at the other end of the shaft to allow of the weapons being stuck in the ground. The blades are attached to the shafts in a very inefficient manner. The essence of warfare is surprise. The greatest triumph that could be achieved was to surprise a village at day break, and dash in before the fighting men had time to make any resistance, then capture as many women and children as possible, load them up with their own property and get away before their relatives could organize a rescue party. The practice of waylaying people cultivating was considered unfair, and the Pois, by steadily practising it, drove the other clans out of any part of the country they coveted. Ambushing armed parties was regularly practised, but our experience has been that the ambusher was always so anxious to get off with a whole skin, that his fire was very apt to be ineffective. A raiding party, even after a march of several days, would retire without firing a shot if the enemy were found on the alert.

Hunting and Snaring: All the hill men are very fond of fresh meat, and are clever at trapping game. Long lines of rough fencing are run through the jungle, with small openings at intervals, in which snares are set. Pheasants, jungle, foul, etc., coming to one of these fences will always run along it till an opening is found, and thus get snared. Porcupines are killed by a bamboo spear fastened to a sapling bent back like a spring and so arranged that it shall be released just as the animal is opposite the spear point. Tigers are caught under a platform of heavy logs, which is supported in an inclined position by a strong cane passed over a cross piece held up by two uprights. In a hole under this platform is placed a pig in a basket; on the tiger pulling at the basket, the heavy platform falls and squashes him, while the pig, being in a hole, escapes. Deer, wild cats, etc., are caught in snares, a noose being arranged so that on the animals stepping in it a sapling to which the noose is attached, and which is held down in a bent position, is released, thus hoisting the animal up into the air. The method of releasing the trap or snare is in all cases is the same. Two uprights are driven into the ground, and a crossbar securely tied between them near the top. Near one end of a piece of string or rope is attached a piece of wood, one end of this is placed under the crossbar, and the other end is pressed down till it passes between the two uprights, then a loose piece of wood is passed across the upright under it. The other end of the string supports the weight which is to fall on the animal or is tied to the bent sapling. All the pressure is on the upper crosspiece, which is securely tied. The bait is tied to the lower crosspiece, or a piece of string tied to this crosspiece is fastened across the path. A very slight pressure will suffice to displace this lower crosspiece, and directly that happens the string is released and the weight falls or the sapling flies up.

Musical Instruments

Gongs and drums, the latter the common tom-tom, are the favourite instruments. A reed instrument is made by inserting reeds into a gourd. The reeds have finger holes, by crossing and opening of which while blowing into the gourd by another reed a regularly graded scale of notes can be produced.

Agricultural Implements

These are very simple and consist of a *dao*, an axe and a hoe. The *dao* is a knife with a triangular blade, about 3 inches wide at the end and half an inch at the handle. It is ground with a chisel edge, the broad end being also sharpened. This is used for clearing the jungle, and the broad end is used for grubbing the holes in which the seeds are placed. The axe heads are only about $1\frac{1}{2}$ inches wide at the edge, and taper almost to a point;

the handles are simply pieces of bamboo, the heads being thrust through the tough root portion. The hoes very closely resemble the axes, the heads being a little lighter and broader.

Arts and Trades

The women are very clever at weaving, and the cloths they make are strong and last a lifetime. The patterns they work are simple. The cotton used is grown in the *jhums*, and cleaned and spun by the women themselves. The men are expert basket-weavers. There are a very large number of different baskets, each with its proper name and use. Some very good moulding in brass is occasionally come across, and some of the blacksmith are very good workmen, being able to make gun-locks.

Inheritance

Among the Chiefs, the custom has been that as a son married he should be given a certain number of houses and started as an independent Chief. His father would also give him some of his possessions, such as guns, necklaces, etc., and send some of his most trusted slaves with him. The youngest son was an exception to this rule; he remained with his father till his death, and thus become his heir. Much the same custom is followed among the common people, each son as he marries setting up house for himself and receiving some of the family possessions, and it has thus become the custom for the youngest to take the father's property. The eldest son, however, sometimes asserts a claim to a share. Custom among the people of these hills is not very stable, and on a man's death practically any relative can take his goods if he will undertake to support the widow and the children, providing that the widow does not elect to continue to live in her husband's house, and that the children are not old enough to support themselves.

Tattooing

The only marks I have noticed are circles, which are said to be records of love affairs.

Circumcision

Is not practiced.

Snake Worship

I have found no special traces of any worship but *Rulpui* 'The big snake' figures frequently in the folklore of the people.

Deaths by Violence or Wild Animals

The victims are buried outside the village, but as far as I can gather, no disgrace is attached to such a death. In such cases no death duty can be claimed by the maternal uncle.

Origin

It is nearly universally believed that the ancestors of the present inhabitants came out from a cave in the earth. The position of this cave is variously described. Nearly every clan will tell you that its first villages were on the banks of the Manipur river, but they mean thereby the first communities of which they have any traditions.

Head-Hunting

It used to be considered that all inhabitants of these hills were head-hunters; in fact, so great an authority as Colonel Lewin derives the name Lushai from 'Lu', ahead, and 'shai' to cut. This is, of course, a mistake, as the name of the clan is not Lushai, but Lushei, and through 'shai' does mean to cut, it does not mean to cut off, and could not be used of cutting off a man's head; but that such a mistake should have been possible shows how firmly rooted was the belief that head-hunting was one of the peculiarities of the population of these hills. I believe that, as far as the Lushais and their kindred clans are concerned, head-hunting was not indulged in. By this I mean that parties did not go out simply to get heads. Of course a man who had killed his man was thought more highly of than one who had not and, therefore, when a man did kill a person, he brought the head home to show that he was speaking the truth; but the raids were made not to get heads but for loot and slaves, the killing and taking of heads were merely incidents in the raids, not the cause of it. I think that the Chins or Pois are in exception to this, and, as far as I can gather, the glory of bringing in a head was sufficient to send a young man and his friends off on the raid.

Clans which differ from the bulk of the population—I will now give briefly a few points in which certain clans differ considerably from those to whom the above description generally applies.

Ralte

This clan speaks a dialect which is very different from the Lushai or Dulian language, which may be considered the *lingua franca* of the hills. They keep very much together, and are now collecting in villages under headman of their own. In almost every customs they differ slightly from their neighbours. They bury their dead outside the village, and the chiefs bury their dead, not preserving the bones as the Lushai chiefs do. The Ralte are the most quarrelsome and talkative clan in the whole hills. Tradition says that when mankind was issuing from the earth the Raltes came out chattering so loudly that the stone was clapped down on them and, therefore, there are less Raltes than other clan.

In mode of dress, etc., they do not differ from other clans.

Ngente

The following information has been collected by Mr. Drake-Brockman:

Childbirth

Three months before her confinement a woman prepares rice-beer, which is kept and drunk inside the house after the birth of the child. The third day after the child's birth it is name by its maternal uncle, a red cock being killed, and some of the feathers tied around the child's neck, and also worn by the members of the family. In the autumn of each year, there is a feast which lasts three days in honour of the children born during the year. The first two nights, the adult population sits up all night drinking and eating yams. The third day men, dressed as women, and Pois, go from house to house, visiting all who have become mothers during the year, and being treated to drink and given some small present by each, in return for which they dance. Women are delivered at the head of the sleeping *machan*; the after-birth is placed in a gourd and hung up on the wall at the back of the house,

Death Ceremonies

The dead are buried at once, and anywhere the relatives choose.

Pois or Chins

There are many minor differences in feasts and customs.Mr. Drake-Brockman has supplied me with a good deal of information, but all the Pois in this direct are merely immigrants from the Chin Hills. I do not think it need be reproduced here, and will keep it for the ethnographical report.

Lakhers

These people are also immigrants from the Chin Hills, but they seem different in many respects from the Pois. Mr Drake-Brockman says that the name by which they call themselves is Tlongsai. The eldest son inherits the bulk of the property. Daughters only get what the brothers give them; younger brothers get a small share. If there are no sons, the nearest male relative inherits. The details of the price paid for brides differs somewhat from those given above. There are no guest houses. All members of the family sleep in the same house. The Chief's bodies are buried five days after death. People killed by animals or by accident, or women who die in child-birth, are buried outside the village, and ceremonies are abbreviated. Such a dead is an ill omen. Seven days after child-birth the mother washes at the spring, and then takes the child to her father's house, and gives some rice and a fowl in honour of the child. No particular sacrifices are connected with child-birth. Among the Lakhers there are no special sorcerers or priests, the head of the household is the priest, and does all necessary sacrifices. Lakher villages, like Chin villages, do not move and, therefore, more permanent. The dress of the people is the same as that of the Haka Chins.

Paithes

When we first occupied these hills, a very large number of this clan were living in different villages of Lushai chiefs, having being brought there and detained more or less forcibly. These have nearly all left now, and either returned to their own country, the Manipur Hills or settled in one or two villages under Paithe chiefs in the extreme north-east corner of the district.The Paithe dialect is quite unintelligible to a Lushai. Their marriage customs are very different. A young Paithe cohabits with his future wife for a period which may extend to three years if no child is born. During this time they sleep together, but otherwise live as if unmarried. If no child is born, or rather if the woman does not become pregnant, the couple separate. If the woman become pregnant the marriage is completed, and the price must be paid, and there can be no separation or divorce, as is so easily arranged among the Lushais. There is very little inter-marriage between the Paithe and the other clans; on account of the objection the Paithe women have to the casual way in which the males of other clans get rid of their wives. A Paithe chief's son is supposed to marry his first cousin. After death the corpse is rubbed with some greasy preparation, which preserves and hardens the skin. It is then dressed up in the best clothes obtainable, and a wonderful head-dress made of toucan tail feathers is placed on its head. During the daytime the corpse is kept in the house, but in the evening, when the people return from work, it is brought out and placed on the platform outside the house, and rice-beer is poured down its throat, and people sing and dance round it. This disgusting performance is kept up for periods, which varies from a month or two to a year, according to the wealth of dead's person family. The Paithes have many other peculiar customs, but I have had but little opportunity of studying them. They have no guest houses, the young man sleeping in the front verandahs of the Chief, and some wealthy men on special platforms. For this privilege, they each give a pig or a goat once a year.

Mr. Dundas notes that the women's petticoats overlap in front instead of at the side, that the unmarried girls wear their coats opening down the back, and that they do not wrap a cloth round them as the men do. The hair is dressed as follows: A lock is drawn down over the forehead, and then plaited and drawn back over the centre of the head, and tied into the knot in which the rest of the hair is tied over the nape of the neck. The women wear their hair in three plaits, one hanging over each ear and one down the back. The Paithe seem very closely allied to the Syins of the Northern Chin Hill.

The Hmar

Regarding these people, I have but little information. There are many different clans, who are all known to the Lushais under this name, and who speaks dialects very closely allied and unintelligible to the Lushais. They formerly had many wars with the Lushais, and lived north of Champhai; they now mostly live in the Manipur hills. The woman wear their hair in one long plait wrapped round the head, and instead of the blue petticoat worn by all other clans wear one with the blue stripe between two white ones, which overlap in front, and so, when seen from the front the petticoat appears white and, hence, the whole clan is often spoken of as Fen-ngo-white petticoats.

The Thado

There is only one village of these people in the district. They were driven out of the hills by the Lushais. They are said to be descendant of the same stock as the Chongthu. They say their ancestor found his way from some underground cavern. They placed their dead in logs as described above and dry them, but do it in a small house outside the village.

Conclusion

The above gives only a general idea of the customs of the inhabitants of the hills. Every clan has some particular custom of its own, especially as regards sacrifices; which form a very important feature in the people's existence. The customs as to punishments, paying of marriage price, etc., among people living under Lushais chiefs are practically the result of orders which the most powerful chiefs have given during their lives, and I find some differences between the customs of the northern and southern chiefs.

APPENDIX-II
The Making of Aijal
J. Shakespear

Aijal, or more correctly Aizawl had always been a very favourite village site, but was unoccupied when, in the spring of 1890 Mr. Dally of the Assam Police, arrived there with 400 men of the Silchar Military Police battalion, to co-operate with a column of troops under Col. Skinner, which was struggling down the valley of the Dhaleswari river to punish Lianphunga for raiding the Chittagong Hill Tracts.

It was on Mr. Dally's recommendation that Aijal was chosen as the site of the fortified post which Colonel Skinner had been ordered to construct before he left the country. The site, like all old village sites, was fairly clear of jungle. Lt. Patric of the Bengal Sappers and Miners, planned the post, which consisted of two stokades. These were composed to a great extent, of the trees which were common near the site.

The stockades and the buildings within them were constructed by Mr. Dally's men.

The smaller stockade was on the knoll on which the officers' mess and the club now stand. In it were the quarters of the officers and a small guard. The other stockade was on the next knoll northwards, on which now stand several masonry barracks, in this were the huts cf the rest of the garrison, which numbered 200 men in all, of the Silchar Military Police, under the command of Lieut. N.G. Cole of the 2nd Gurkhas.

At that time boats could not get higher up the Dhaleswari river than Changsil and here was established a post held by 100 men to guard the store houses. Changsil had long been a Bazar and there were good Lushai paths from it to Aijal and other villages also to Silchar. It was by this path that Mr. Dally's party came up in 1890 and it was along the line of this path that the first mule road was made by Mr. Sweet of the P.W.D. From Changsil the road ran more or less along the riverside to Sairang and thence to Aijal. The present Silchar road leading out from the northern end of Aijal was not made till shortly before I left the Hills. I had long meant to make it, but neither money nor labour was available earlier. The new road saved two marches and also avoided the unhealthy Dhaleswari valley,

The river between Changsil and Sairang was made passible for boats by Mr. Davies and Capt. Loch, who spent some time blasting away boulders. Directly the river was cleared, traders from Changsil transferred their ships to Sairang. It was not till the cart road from Sairang was opened that the Aijal Bazar became really important.

Lalmantu

The rising which began in September 1890, with the murder of Mr. Browne, the first *Political Officer* and attacks upon the Aijal and Changsil Posts, was put down by McCabe, who had made his name by subduing the Nagas. He earned the name of "Lalmantu", Lt Col. J. Shakespear was Superintendent of Lushai Hills 1897-1898, 1900-1903 and 1904-1905 so many rebel monarchs did he capture. Peace was restored by the spring of 1891 and from that date the expansion of Aijal began.

The remainder of the Silchar Police battalion was transferred to Aijal and Capt. Loch, 3rd Gurkhaŝ, arrived as commandant. The rising of the spring of 1892 was also quelled by Mr. McCabe, but having restored order his health gave way and he had to take sick leave and was succeeded at Aijal by Mr. G.W. Davies, also from the Naga Hills, where he had succeeded Mr. McCabe.

Davies and Loch worked well together and Aijal made a good start under them. Of the details of the changes which took place between 1891 and spring of 1897, when I arrived in Aijal and took over charge from Mr. A. Porteous, who had succeeded Davies as Political Officer in 1894, I can tell nothing.

House—Good and Fit for Issue

I found the Military Police in Aijal housed in good masonry barracks and the whole station a miracle of neatness, thanks to Loch, who though a good soldier, was by inclination an engineer and house builder. Having the roof of the two of his barracks blown clean off during a March storm he was determined to put an end to such disasters by building stone houses for himself and his men in place of wretched affairs of jungle timber and bamboo matting in which they were then living. He mentioned his intention to Davies who told him he did not think it worthwhile forwarding such a scheme to government for, he said, "We've been 10 years in Kohima and there's not one stone house there yet". "More shame to you" was Loch's reply and he set to work with his own men to build himself a house, at his own cost. When this had been achieved he asked permission to build barracks, etc. for the garrison of Aijal. His house having passed by the P.W.D. as "good and fit for issue", Loch was told to submit an estimate for all the buildings he considered necessary and this being sanctioned he went ahead. He engaged a Khasi contractor Sahon Roy and also employed many of his own men.

When I arrived early in 1897 he had built the assistant commandant's bungalow and all the Police barracks and hospital arid was building the Quarterguard and office building. With the completion of that the works estimated for would be completed except for the armourer's shop. Now Loch received a check. I told you that one estimate for all the buildings had been sanctioned. In framing that estimate, Loch had been guided by the cost of his house, but as the work went on new quarries had to be opened in more remote and less easily worked localities and so the cost of each building rose above the estimate and this excess increased steadily but the fact was not discovered by the P.W.D. until rhe Quarterguard building was finished when it could no longer escape notice.

Waterloo Gun at Aijal

The Qiuarterguard had, I believe, cost about double the estimated sum. The Chief Engineer rose in his wrath, and an order was issued that Loch should do no more building. This did not really much matter as the only Police building remaining was the armourer's shop, a small affair and even that was up to the plinth level when it was handed over to the Executive Engineer for completion. I had much pleasure in pointing out in my next annual report that though the building was a small one and was urgently required, the P.W.D. had not been able to complete it in a whole year and I suggested that Capt. Loch might be given a contract to complete it, which was approved of and the shop was finished within a few months. Before, leaving the Police buildings, I better mention the Queen Victoria Memorial parch added to the Quarterguard. The bust of the late Majesty, 1 think, was paid for by Loch. The two antique field pieces which flank the porch have a curious history. They were part of the armament of a ship-of-war, which was in the Chittagong river in 1857.

When the detachment of 34th Native Infantry stationed in Chittagong mutinied on 18th November, the guns were thrown overboard to prevent their falling into the hands of the mutineers. Later these were fished up and fitted with wheeled carriages and eventually found their way to Rangamati, whence they were sent to Lunglei during the trouble times in 1892. It struck me that these aged guns, one of which from its date might have been fired at Waterloo, would form a suitable addition to the memorial of the great Queen, so I had them brought over.

I. A.R. Ground Costed Rs. 1,200

The Parade Ground: When Loch took over command the married quarters were on a spur which ran out from the main range, where the Parade Ground now is, this spur ended in a knoll. The nearness of the ladies to the quarters at the gay bachelors, was a frequent source of trouble. Loch removed them to their present abodes, and the dovecotes were not so frequently disturbed. He then set to work to cut away the knoll throwing the spoil down on each side. When I arrived in 1897, the work was about half done, but a lump about 15 feet high still remained. At that time there was a road to the Post Office along the east face of the ridge as well as along the west. Loch asked me if he might cut the eastern road way, and I, of course, agreed as its removal greatly increased, the size of the parade ground. The cutting away of this road meant a lot of blasting. The labour for the parade ground was formed by the sepoys. Loch gave out contracts which were much sought after. To get the spoil away from the tract of the hill to the edge of the ground, the men worked in pairs, one wheeled the barrow, the other filled it, at the spot where the staff had to be tipped, a Gurkha Officer stood with a bag of paisa and paid for each barrow according to the length of the load. The money for all this was provided by the Canteen Fund, which was largely produced by the sums which the workers paid to satisfy the thirst produced by their labours. The only cost to government was Rs. 1,200. The range was also made by sepoy labour. Mostly on Saturdays when every man from the commandant to the last joined recruit put in about 8 hours Kamjarri, Loch's battalion was the only one in which there was never any trouble about Kamjarri, the reason being that there was very little except on Saturdays when every one worked. One day Loch said to me, "I think I must be a very good man". I did not dispute it but asked why he had come to that conclusion and he replied, "If you notice it very seldom rains on Saturdays, now there are about 800 men in barracks who pray for Saturdays and I also pray for fine ones, and my prayer is generally granted ergo I must be a good man." I agreed.

Now for the remainder of the Station:

Raj Niwas

The Superintendent's House (Now Raj Niwas): This was designed by my late wife. The first house was of the usual jungle timber type and stood at the south end of the present one. The house was just completed when I went home on leave in 1899. To keep the cost down I had put on a roof of bamboo shingles, which necessitated a plain roof with one slope from ridge to caves. This was not beautiful enough for Capt. Cole who acted for me. He put in the three gables which are of great improvement, but the roof leaked so wildly at the joints of gables and the main roof that after my return I had to put in an application for a corrugated iron roof and was wigged for my extravagance. Cole also made the pleasant terrace along the front of the house and handsome retaining wall and picturesque flight of steps in the corner. The lawn and garden south of the house I made and I also made the lower vegetable garden to the north. The garden immediately to the north of the house was made by Porteous, who preceded me as Superintendent. He built the wall along the western edge, to keep off the wind. He at a very great expense, had three feet of leaf mould carried from the jungle and deposited in the garden. The orange trees I brought from the Chin Hills.

Water for Aijal—First Efforts

In my days the road from Aijal southwards, passed along close under the Superintendent's house and on the opposite side of the "crater". This was the first effort made in the days of McCabe to solve the water supplying question. He had a big excavation made in a circular knoll that stood opposite the house, the spoils being thrown outwards. Then he cut a number of shallow drains on the face of the hill below the Assistant Commandant's house all joining into one channel from which by a corrugated iron aqueduct be carried through the drainage of that hill over the road, into his "Crater". The first burst the Civil Surgeon whose house stood on the north side of the "crater" complained of the dampness resulting from the experiment. So the aqueduct was removed and the "crater" remained till Cole succeeded me and the road round it was included in his gardens at least so I have been told. The next effort to improve the water supply was made by Loch and myself throwing a bund across the valley south of his house. This too was a failure for as in the first case the water would not stay, but run away under the embankment. Before I left finally a little water did remain as the silt filled up the leaks.

The Old Oak Trees

The Oak trees along the various roads were brought from Champhai, where Loch started a nursery. The fir below the Superintendent's house also came from Champhail. The Medical Officer's house and that of the Assistant Superintendent were also built under my orders. Mr. Cotton (later Sir Henry) had, as Chief Secretary in Bengal, seen how well the system of placing the public works under the Superintendent worked in the south Lushai Hills and when he became Chief Commissioner he introduced the system into the North Lushai Hills. The Superintendent was given a Chief Engineer and was granted the powers of a Superintending Engineer. He could sanction works upto Rs. 2,000. This enabled me and Loch to work together and I think we made good use of our powers. The Champhai road was traced by Loch, he supplied sepoys to oversee the labour I provided for its construction. So it was in everything we worked for the general good. When I went home on leave in 1899, Capt, Cole acted for me. He did much for Aijal. The Superintendent's office and the club were of jungle timber, built with primitive labour by McCabe, but the doors and windows came from Calcutta. I had plans for reconstructing them and told Cole about it. When I came back I found that Cole had removed the old buildings and started stone ones, which had got to plinth level. He had framed no estimate nor had got sanction for the money. We departed. I had to finish the buildings and got the wigging. Cole was a wonderful chap. He made such a name over the Assam camp at Delhi Durbar that he was entrusted with building temporary DELHI with four P.W.D. Executive Engineers under him. He made grand success of the job but he exceeded his estimates by some huge amount and instead of getting slayed, received the thanks of the Government of India. He told me how he achieved this. He used to take a plan up to the Head of Deprtment and say, "This is all I can do for you. It is not adequate I know, but I cannot do more for the money. If I had a little more, this is what I should like to do for you", showing another plan, "but it will cost a little rnore". The victims of course thought the second plan the best and ended by putting his initials to it. "So when the excess over the estimate came out 1 had their initialled plans to show", said the astute Cole.

Mualzavata Dawnkawn

The Little Tank just below the Superintendent's garden (now part of civil Secretariat) was made by Porteous, but did not hold water. Loch said If I would empty it, he'd get the leak stopped. I said it did not hold water but did hold a certain amount, and the leak could not be located till it was quite empty. We got some length of piping from the water works supply and made a gigantic "dawnkawn" with which he syphoned off the water. It was muddy and of much colour of zu and the Lushais crowded round calling our, "Muafza vata Dawnkawn". I suppose you know who Mualzavata is or was. The District Engineer's house, below the Lunglei road was only a kutcha erection and has probably disappeared. Hodgkins was the first District Engineer, a very competent man who did much good work. It was under him that the Melveng system of road maintenance was brought to perfection.

The Jail, Record Room and Civil Hospital were among the last buildings erected during my stay in Aijal.

Say it with a Photograph

The Post Office, when I arrived in Aijal was a most decrepit kutcha erection. The Department refused to find money for a stone building, till I sent a photograph of the office to Shillong that shamed the Department into sanctioning the stone building. There was fire in the building once and an energetic fool handed up a tin of kerosene, thinking it was water, to a fellow on the roof who threw it over the flames with no good results.

I think that is all I remember of the making of Aijal. If you care to ask me any question about other buildings, etc., it will be a pleasure to answer if I can.

Quarter-Guard
Built by Lt.Col.C.H.Loch, I.A.
around 1897

Lt.Col.C.H.LOCH, I.A.
(Imperial Army)
(Builder of Aizawl)

Silchar Military Police Battalion

Dr. J.V.Hluna and
Rini Tochhawng
in front of Waterloo Gun
on 12.05.2012 at Aizawl

Index